Samantha Joo
Provocation and Punishment

Beihefte zur Zeitschrift für die alttestamentliche Wissenschaft

Herausgegeben von
John Barton · Reinhard G. Kratz
Choon-Leong Seow · Markus Witte

Band 361

Walter de Gruyter · Berlin · New York

Samantha Joo

Provocation and Punishment

The Anger of God in the Book of Jeremiah
and Deuteronomistic Theology

W
DE
G

Walter de Gruyter · Berlin · New York

G

♾ Printed on acid-free paper which falls within the guidelines of the ANSI
to ensure permanence and durability.

ISBN-13: 978-3-11-018994-0
ISBN-10: 3-11-018994-1
ISSN 0934-2575

Library of Congress Cataloging-in-Publication Data

A CIP catalogue record for this book is available from the Library of Congress.

Bibliographic information published by Die Deutsche Bibliothek

Die Deutsche Bibliothek lists this publication in the Deutsche Nationalbibliografie;
detailed bibliographic data is available in the Internet at <http://dnb.ddb.de>.

Foreword

This book is a revised version of my dissertation completed at Brandeis University in 2003. It is a culmination and ultimately a reflection of my education under my teachers at University of Denver, Harvard University, Hebrew University in Jerusalem, and Brandeis University. They have imparted their wealth of knowledge, probing questions, and most importantly, love of Bible and Assyriology. I can never thank them enough for all I've learned inside and outside of the classroom.

Specific to the actual production of the dissertation, I would like to acknowledge and thank my committee members, Tzvi Abusch and Marc Zvi Brettler at Brandeis University, and Angela Bauer at Episcopal Divinity School. They have taken time to read and comment on the dissertation. I am particularly grateful to David P. Wright, my dissertation advisor, who has patiently and methodically critiqued and provided extremely helpful insights. His eye for detail and passion for scholarship pervades this work. The dissertation, thus this book, could not have been written without his guidance.

I would also like to express my gratitude to Monika C. Müller and the editorial board at Series BZAW for accepting this work for publication.

And, of course, I must thank my friends and family. They have given meaning, perspective, support, joy, and laughter. Life would definitely be dull and miserable without them.

For all of these people in my life, I thank God, who has and continues to bless me.

Finally, I dedicate this book to my parents: To my mother, Sarah Joo, for instilling my faith in God, the most prized possession and to my father, Bong Jong Joo, for always providing a secure and loving environment. I love you both.

Samantha Joo
June 2006

Table of Contents

Abbreviations

A. Abbreviations for the Hebrew Bible

Gen	Genesis	Nah	Nahum
Exod	Exodus	Hab	Habakkuk
Lev	Leviticus	Zeph	Zephaniah
Num	Numbers	Hag	Haggai
Deut	Deuteronomy	Zech	Zechariah
Josh	Joshua	Mal	Malachi
Judg	Judges	Ps/Pss	Psalms
1-2 Sam	1-2 Samuel	Job	Job
1-2 Kgs	1-2 Kings	Prov	Proverbs
Isa	Isaiah	Ruth	Ruth
Jer	Jeremiah	Song	Song of Songs
Ezek	Ezekiel	Eccl	Ecclesiastes
Hos	Hosea	Lam	Lamentations
Joel	Joel	Esth	Esther
Amos	Amos	Dan	Daniel
Obad	Obadiah	Ezra	Ezra
Jonah	Jonah	Neh	Nehemiah
Mic	Micah	1-2 Chr	1-2 Chronicles

B. Abbreviations for Secondary Sources

AB	Anchor Bible
AHw	*Akkadisches Handwörterbuch.* W. von Soden. 3 vols. Wiesbaden, 1965-1981
BASOR	*Bulletin of the American Schools of Oriental Research*
BDB	Brown, Francis, S.R. Driver, and Charles Briggs. *The New Brown-Driver-Briggs-Gesenius Hebrew and English Lexicon.* Peabody: Hendrickson, 1979
BEATAJ	Beiträge zur Erforschung des Alten Testaments und des antiken Judentum
BETL	Bibliotheca ephemeridum theologicarum lovaniensium

BHS	*Biblia Hebraica Stuttgartensia.* Edited by K. Elliger and W. Rudolph. Stuttgart, 1983
BibInt	Biblical Interpretation (Series)
BibInt	*Biblical Interpretation* (Journal)
BJS	Brown Judaic Studies
BKAT	Biblischer Kommentar. Altes Testament. Edited by M. Noth and H. W. Wolff
Bright	John Bright. *Jeremiah: A New Translation with Introduction and Commentary.* AB 21. Garden City, 1965
BZAW	Beihefte zur Zeitschrift für die alttestamentliche Wissenschaft
CAD	*The Assyrian Dictionary of the Oriental Institute of the University of Chicago.* Chicago, 1956-
Carroll	Robert Carroll. *Jeremiah: A Commentary.* OTL. London, 1986
CBC	Cambridge Bible Commentary
CBQ	*Catholic Biblical Quarterly*
CBQMS	Catholic Biblical Quarterly Monograph Series
CC	Continental Commentaries
ConBOT	Coniectanea bibilica: Old Testament Series
DDD	*Dictionary of Deities and Demons in the Bible.* Edited by K. van der Toorn, B. Becking, and P. W. van der Horst. Leiden, 1995
FOTL	Forms of the Old Testament Literature
GKC	*Gesenius' Hebrew Grammar.* Edited by E. Kautzsch. Translated by A. E. Cowley. 2d. ed. Oxford, 1910
HALOT	L. Koehler, W. Baumgartner, and J. J. Stamm. *The Hebrew and Aramaic Lexicon of the Old Testament.* Translated and edited under the supervision of M. E. J. Richardson. 4 vols. Leiden, 1994-1999
HAR	*Hebrew Annual Review*
HAT	Handbuch zum Alten Testament
Holladay	William Holladay. *Jeremiah: A Commentary on the Book of the Prophet Jeremiah.* 2 vols. Minneapolis, 1989
HSM	Harvard Semitic Monographs
HTR	*Harvard Theological Review*
HUCA	*Hebrew Union College Annual*
Hyatt	J. P. Hyatt. "The Book of Jeremiah." *IB* 5:777-1142
IB	*Interpreter's Bible.* Edited by G. A. Buttrick et al. 12 vols. New York, 1952-1957
IBHS	*An Introduction to Biblical Hebrew Syntax.* B. K. Waltke and M. O'Connor. Winona Lake, 1990

ICC	International Critical Commentary
IDB	*The Interpreter's Dictionary of the Bible*. Edited by G. A. Buttrick. 4 vols. Nashville, 1962
IRT	Issues in Religion and Theology
JBL	*Journal of Biblical Literature*
JHNES	Johns Hopkins Near Eastern Studies
Joüon	P. A. Joüon. *A Grammar of Biblical Hebrew*. Translated and revised by T. Muraoka. 2 vols. Subsidia biblica 14/1-2. Rome, 1991
JPS	Jewish Publication Society
JSOT	*Journal for the Study of the Old Testament*
JSOTSup	Journal for the Study of the Old Testament: Supplement Series
KAT	Kommentar zum Alten Testament
KHC	Kurzer Hand-Commentar zum Alten Testament
Lundbom	Jack Lundbom. *Jeremiah 1-20: A New Translation with Introduction and Commentary*. AB 21a. New York, 1999
McKane	William McKane. *A Critical and Exegetical Commentary on Jeremiah*. ICC 19. Edinburgh, 1986
NCB	New Century Bible
Nicholson	Ernest Nicholson. *The Book of the Prophet Jeremiah*. 2 vols. CBC. New York, 1973/1975
OBO	Orbis biblicus et orientalis
OTG	Old Testament Guides
OTL	Old Testament Library
OtSt	Oudtestamentische Studiën (Series)
OtSt	*Oudtestamentische Studiën* (Journal)
PTMS	Pittsburgh Theological Monograph Series
Rudolph	Wilhelm Rudolph. *Jeremia*. Tübingen: J. C. B. Mohr, 1958
SBLDS	Society of Biblical Literature Dissertation Series
SBLMS	Society of Biblical Literature Monograph Series
SBT	Studies in Biblical Theology
SJLA	Studies in Judaism in Late Antiquity
TDOT	*Theological Dictionary of the Old Testament*. Edited by G. J. Botterweck and H. Ringgren. Translated by J. T. Willis, G. W. Bromiley, and D. E. Green. 8 vols. Grand Rapids, 1977-
TLOT	*Theological Lexicon of the Old Testament*. Edited by E. Jenni, with assistance from C. Westermann. Translated by M. E. Biddle. 3 vols. Peabody, 1997
Volz	Paul Volz. *Der Prophet Jeremia*. KAT 10. Leipzig, 1928
VT	*Vetus Testamentum*
VTSup	Vetus Testamentum Supplements

WMANT   Wissenschaftliche Monographien zum Alten und Neuen
               Testament
ZAW   *Zeitschrift für die alttestamentliche Wissenschaft*
ZTK   *Zeitschrift für Theologie und Kirche*

Introduction

The central unifying issue in the book of Jeremiah is the problem of theodicy arising from the fall of Jerusalem.[1] The prophet[2] and later editors[3] of the book grapple with and attempt to respond to the questions that plagued their respective Judahite communities during and after the collapse of Jerusalem: Why is our city, the site of YHWH's dwelling, the temple, under the threat of annihilation and ultimately lying in ruins? How could we, who are in a covenantal relationship with YHWH, be under siege, face violence, and be exiled from our homeland? With such questions, the Judahites seem to search for answers to a timeless dilemma about the role of God in the face of a catastrophe. Yet how did the authors and editors of the book of Jeremiah try to explain and,

---

1   Most studies on the question of theodicy focus on the book of Job rather than prophetic books, except Thomas Raitt, *A Theology of Exile: Judgement/Deliverance in Jeremiah and Ezekiel* (Philadelphia: Fortress Press, 1977), 83-105, who mainly examines two prophetic books of the exilic period, Jeremiah and Ezekiel. Raitt, 85, defines theodicy as an effort to defend "God's justice and his control over history." Unfortunately the book is more descriptive than analytical. For discussion of other scholarship, see Raitt, 247-248, note 1, who considers many of the studies as too theological. For a more recent discussion, see John Kutsko, *Between Heaven and Earth: Divine Presence and Absence in the Book of Ezekiel* (Biblical and Judaic Studies 7; Winona Lake: Eisenbrauns, 2000), who discusses the question of theodicy in the book of Ezekiel by analyzing the role of idolatry.

2   It is the assumption of this study that the book grew out of the interpretations/additions to the sayings attributed to the prophet, Jeremiah, in response to the historical circumstances. Despite this assumption, I do not consider the portrayal of the prophet in the book to be accurate since the book constructs, rather than provide a historical account, of the figure of Jeremiah. One could describe this portrayal as a precursor to a hagiography.

3   By using the term, 'editor,' I do not intend to infer that the insertions/additions were mere glosses. In fact, these later 'editors' made significant contributions to the final composition and could be considered 'authors.' Throughout the study, numerous terms, such as 'author,' 'editor/redactor,' 'source,' 'level,' and so on, will be used to indicate later individuals responsible for the accretions. In the present state of biblical scholarship on the book of Jeremiah, we have limited understanding of the growth of the composition of the book, thus, making it impossible to definitively categorize the 'author' of the accretions. Therefore, there are no underlying reasons for the particular designations. Yet, despite the network of various hands, they appear to affiliate themselves with the prophet. Otherwise they would not have included their additions in the book attributed to Jeremiah. Thus they will be loosely considered his 'disciples.'

more importantly, to justify God? It is this very problem that the present study
will endeavor to illuminate.

In response to the disturbing questions stemming from a series of deportations and the desolation of Jerusalem, the oracles and sermons by and narratives concerning the prophet Jeremiah and his disciples were collected, expanded, and organized into the present book. Though scholarly discussions of
other prophetic books are complex, studies on the book of Jeremiah confront
additional hurdles in clarifying the history of its redaction. Beside debates over
the identification of and relationship between the *ipsissima verba* of the
prophet, to whom the book is named after, and later accretions, there are discussions concerning the two distinct literary media: poetry and prose; three
major genres:[4] oracles, sermons, and biography of the prophet; and the significantly different versions in the Greek and the Masoretic text (MT). Despite the
problems inherent in delineating the development of the book, the centripetal
theme of the book, as commentators would argue, is the question, "Why was
Judah captured and Jerusalem, with its temple and palace, destroyed?"[5] It
might have taken 52 chapters for the book of Jeremiah to expound on the reason, but the simple answer is because "you abandoned me and served foreign
gods in your land" (עזבתם אותי ותעבדו אלהי נכר בארצכם, 5:19b).

According to the authors of the book of Jeremiah, therefore, the blame for
the disaster would lie with the people and their sins. Why would God punish
unless he was initially provoked to anger? However, the people (the audience)
would not have necessarily agreed with the authors of the book of Jeremiah. If
they did, Jeremiah would not have needed to prophesy nor would the disciples
have felt the need to compose the book. After all, according to the authors of
the book of Jeremiah, these are the very people who, while worshipping other
gods, brought a lawsuit against God for not saving them (למה תריבו אלי,
"Why do you call me to account?" 2:29). From the perspective of the people,
thus, God is ultimately responsible for the catastrophe: "On account of what
did *YHWH, our God*, do all these things to us?" (תחת מה עשה יהוה אלהינו
לנו את־כל־אלה, 5:19a). What could the people have done so wrong to de-
serve such a calamity? They exclaim, "I am innocent; surely his anger has

---

4   This does not take into consideration the different types of oracles, i.e. judgment, hope,
     lament, *Aufforderungen zur Flucht* (Robert Bach, *Die Aufforderungen zur Flucht und zum
     Kampf im Alttestamentlichen Prophetenspruch* [WMANT 9; Neukirchen: Neukirchener Ver-
     lag, 1962]), and others, that are evident in the book of Jeremiah.
5   Martin Kessler, "Jeremiah 25:1-29: Text and Context. A Synchronic Study," *ZAW* 109
     (1997):68. See also Carroll, *Jeremiah*, 74, who has described the book of Jeremiah as a "*se-
     ries* of explanations of the fall of Judah and Jerusalem."

turned away from me" (נקיתי, אך שב אפו ממני, 2:35).[6] The onerous task that now lies before the authors of the book of Jeremiah is to convince the self-claimed innocent people of their responsibility in their own demise without undermining the idea of God's mastery over history.[7]

Methodology

In order to examine the ways in which the book of Jeremiah averted the responsibility for the fall of Jerusalem *away from* God and *to* the people, the present study will analyze the pericopes containing the term, הכעיס ("to provoke to anger"), in the Bible (Deut 4:25-28, 9:18-20, 31:27-29, 32:15-25, Judg 2:11-16, 1 Kgs 14:7-11, 14:15-16a, 15:29-30, 16:2-4, 16:7, 16:11-13, 16:25-26, 16:30-33, 21:20b-26, 22:53-54, 2 Kgs 17:7-23a, 21:2-15, 22:15-17, 23:19-20, 23:26-27, Hos 12:1-15, Ezek 8:1-18, 16:23-30, Isa 65:1-7, Pss 78:56-64, 106:28-31, 2 Chr 28:22-25) and trace its development in the book of Jeremiah (7:16-20, 8:18-23, 11:17, 25:1-14, 32:26-35, 44:1-14).

As this study will show, the hiphil conjugation of כעס, attested primarily in Deuteronomistic history (DtrH) and the book of Jeremiah, is the hinge upon which the catalog of sins is linked to the description of the punishment (sin-provocation-punishment).[8] Since הכעיס functions as the pivot, it demonstrates

---

6 The book of Jeremiah has sporadic references to the people's comments which exemplify their stubbornness. For example, the people say, "I will not serve" (לא אעבד, 2:20 - the Qere has לא אעבור, which translates to "I will not transgress," which does not fit the present situation and was probably a later addition to mitigate the people's defiance); "I am not defiled" (לא נטמאתי, 2:23); "it is no use for I love strangers, and after them I will go" (נואש כי־אהבתי זרים ואחריהם אלך, 2:25); etc.

7 Term, 'mastery', is borrowed from Jon Levenson, *Creation and Persistence of Evil: The Jewish Drama of Divine Omnipotence* (San Francisco: Harper and Row, 1988). In the face of a catastrophe in which a foreign nation, with its own panethon of gods, destroys Jerusalem, the monotheistic Yahwists of the book of Jeremiah needed to assert their God's mastery over the created world (10:12-16). Otherwise, the Yahwists would have had to concede to the Babylonian gods. This would have been inconceivable.

8 To link the sins to the punishment, DtrH also used other verbs of anger (see Appendices C and D): קצף ("be wroth;" Deut 1:34), התאנף/אנף ("be angry;"Deut 1:37, 4:21, 9:8, 20; 1 Kgs 8:46, 11:9; 2 Kgs 17:18), התעבר ("infuriate oneself;" Deut 3:26), and חרה אף ("burn with anger;" Deut 6:15, 7:4, 11:17, 29:26, 31:17, Josh 7:1, 23:16, Judg 2:14, 2:20, 3:8, 10:7; 2 Sam 6:7, 24:1; 2 Kgs 13:3). See Dennis McCarthy, "The Wrath of Yahweh and the Structural Unity of the Deuteronomistic History," in *Essays in Old Testament Ethics* (eds. James Crenshaw and John Willis; New York: Ktav Publishing House, 1974), 97-110, who argues that the expressions, חרה אף ב־ ("to be angry against") and התאנף ("to be angry"), are similar to הכעיס ("to provoke to anger") except that the "announcement of a penalty is not so close" with הכעיס (100). In other words, the punishment does not necessarily follow הכעיס.

the causal relationship between the sins of the people and their eventual pun-ishment. Why are the people punished? Because they have provoked God to anger. Therefore, הכעים becomes a central theological term in DtrH and the book of Jeremiah that justifies the consequent punishment. More importantly, though, הכעים being the harbinger of the punishment provides access to vari-ous formulations of the punishment.[9] The various formulations in turn provide distinct configurations of the role of God in history.

---

9   As will be demonstrated in the present study, his conclusion is incorrect. A significant differ-ence, however, lies between these verbs of anger and הכעים. While these verbs function as a prelude to the punishment, הכעים modifies the catalog of sins, like the 'straw that broke the camel's back.' As a result, the description of the punishment which ensues after הכעים can be formulated in various ways whereas the pericopes with קצף, אנף/התאנף, התעבר, and אף חרה *necessarily* involve some aspect of divine wrath (see Appendices C and D). Since nouns for 'anger' (אף, חרון אף, חרון, זעף, זעם, קצף, חמה) in DtrH and pre-exilic/exilic prophetic texts (including the book of Jeremiah) tend to function as either the instrument, motivation, or agency of destruction, not as a pivot to the punishment (see Appendices C, D, E, F), an examination of these terms would not have provided various formulations of the punishment. Any number of causal conjunctions like ב-, מ-, בגלל, יען/יען, על אשר, על אשר, מפני, כי, and על can function as a link between the sin and punishment in the book of Jeremiah (see Ap-pendix A). However, הכעים is a central term in DtrH whose development can then be traced in the book of Jeremiah. One significant disadvantage, however, lies in the fact that the bulk of the attestations occur in the prose sermons (7:18, 19, 11:17, 25:6, 7, 32:29, 30, 32, 44:3, 8) rather than in the poetic oracles (8:19) or in biographical-historical prose. In fact, הכעים oc-curs in many of the prose sermons, except for 18:1-12, 21:1-10, 34:1-7, 8-22, 35:1-9 (based on Mowinckel's delineation of the C source, see discussion below). Nevertheless, the differ-ent portrayals of YHWH's role in meting out the punishments in the prose sermons appear to reflect other parts of the book which do not use הכעים. Similar conceptualizations, especially in poetic oracles, will sometimes be highlighted either in the body or in the notes of the pre-sent study. See also Appendix A.

        A number of studies have examined the correspondence between sin and punish-ment. To list a few examples, H.W. Wolff, "Die Begrundung der prophetischen Heils und Unheilsspruche," *ZAW* 52 (1934):1-22 (Reprinted in *Gesammelte Studien zum Alten Testament* [Munchen: Kaiser, 1973], 9-35); Klaus Koch, "Gibt es ein Vergeltungsdogma im Alten Testament?" *ZTK* 52 (1955):1-42 (trans. Thomas Trapp, "Is There a Doctrine of Retri-bution in the Old Testament," in *Theodicy in the Old Testament* [ed. James Crenshaw; IRT 4; Philadelphia: Fortress Press, 1983], 57-87); Patrick D. Miller, Jr., *Sin and Judgment in the Prophets: A Stylistic and Theological Analysis* (SBLMS 27; Chico: Scholars Press, 1982); Joseph Blenkinsopp, "God and the Moral Order," in *Wisdom and Law in the Old Testament: The Ordering of Life in Israel and Early Judaism* (Oxford Bible; Oxford: Oxford University Press, 1995), 46-83; Lennart Bostrom, *The God of the Sages: The Portrayal of God in the Book of Proverbs* (ConBOT 29; Stockholm: Almqvist & Wiksell International, 1990), 134-140; and Gene M. Tucker, "Sin and 'Judgment' in the Prophets," in *Problems in Biblical Theology: Essays in Honor of Rolf Knierim* (eds. Henry Sun and Keith Eades; Grand Rapids: William B. Eerdmans Publishing Company, 1997), 373-388. Yet these studies tend to be general observations on the issue of the correspondence between sin-judgment in the Old Te-stament or Wisdom/Prophetic traditions rather than historical study on the development of changing depictions of the role of God in meting out punishments.

By examining the pericopes with the pivotal expression, הכעיס ("to provoke to anger"), the present study will distinguish five conceptual frameworks for understanding the varying roles of God in carrying out the punishment.[10]

First, human and natural catastrophes, without the explicit mention of God, execute the divine punishment against the people. God is implicitly behind the scenes controlling the outcome of historical events:

(God)
↓
Human/Natural Instruments
↓
People

Second, God is depicted as the primary active agent of the punishment working with human and natural instruments:[11]

God
↓
Human and Natural Instruments
↓
People

Third, God merely decrees/turns back on the people the evil or disaster which they have created.[12] I call this the "boomerang" effect or pattern:

God
↗ ↘
Evil (Catalog of Sins) Evil (Punishment)
↑ ↓
People People

---

10 An analysis of the pericopes with הכעיס yielded such an array. Since it is a limited corpus, the five conceptualizations may not be representative of the whole Bible.

11 To a certain extent, this conceptualization follows the principle of dual causality (Yairah Amit, "The Dual Causality Principle and its Effects on Biblical Literature," *VT* 37 (1987):385-400).

12 See Miller, Jr., *Sin and Judgment in the Prophets,* for various ways of establishing measure-for-measure punishment. Miller discusses the "device/pattern/motif of correspondence between sin and judgment, crime and punishment" (1). This correspondence between sin and punishment may fall under the category of K. Koch's idea of "synthetic view of life" ("Is There a Doctrine of Retribution in the Old Testament," 76, developed from Fahlgren's study of the word, *şedaqa*) or Tucker's "dynamistic perspectives" ("Sin and 'Judgment' in the Prophets," 374). However, as Miller has noted, descriptions of measure-for-measure punishment do not necessarily exclude God's agency.

Though God is the agent of the punishment, he is, to all intents and purposes, only the *Hermes* of the consequence of the people's self-destructive behavior; God does not act in response to their sinful activities but dispatches the results of their evil. Therefore, the people suffer their due punishment. Since the boomerang effect is sometimes evident in passages which emphasize God's decree in the book of Jeremiah (11:17, 25:13),[13] God is further distanced from the punishment than if he was to directly dispatch the evil/disaster:[14]

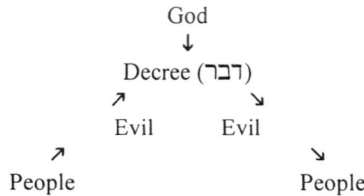

$$
\begin{array}{ccc}
 & \text{God} & \\
 & \downarrow & \\
 & \text{Decree (דבר)} & \\
 \nearrow & & \searrow \\
\text{Evil} & & \text{Evil} \\
\nearrow & & \searrow \\
\text{People} & & \text{People}
\end{array}
$$

Rather than God directly reprimanding the people, he decrees the punishment according to the magnitude of their sins. Nevertheless, God is still the agent, the one who delivers the punishment.

Fourth, God is replaced by a mental aspect of his agency, divine wrath. This divine wrath functions either as motivation, instrument, or sometimes its own agent:

People Sin → Provoke to Anger →
Divine Wrath (Motivation, Instrument, Agency) → People

---

13 In *Biblical Interpretation in Ancient Israel* (Oxford: Oxford University Press, 1985), 164, Michael Fishbane notes how the book of Deuteronomy refers to sources in the Tetrateuch with expressions like "which he commanded/swore/promised." See Jacob Milgrom, "Profane Slaughter and a Formulaic Key to the Composition of Deuteronomy," *HUCA* 47 (1976):4-13, for a more detailed discussion. Although such expressions do not seem to indicate a secondary hand in the book of Deuteronomy, it appears to be secondary in the book of Jeremiah. For a detailed discussion, see below in Part IV of this study.

14 The difference between the act of 'decreeing' and 'bringing' the disaster raises similar theological issues that are discussed in studies on the different creation accounts, where the Priestly source (Gen 1:1-2:4a), using word-creation, depicts a transcendent God as opposed to the more anthropomorphic deity in the Jahwist account (Gen 2:4b-3:24) which uses activity-creation. For a brief discussion of this, see Susan Niditch, *Chaos to Cosmos: Studies in Biblical Patterns of Creation* (Scholars Press Studies in the Humanities 6; Chico: Scholars Press, 1985), 20-21, esp. note 11. However, Claus Westermann, *Genesis 1-11, A Commentary* (trans. John Scullion; BKAT 1; Minneapolis: Augsburg Publishing House, 1984), 82-83, in his study of the Priestly account itself, does not really differentiate between "creation by word" from "creation by action." He quotes W. H. Schmidt, *Die Schöpfungsgeschichte der Priesterschrift* (WMANT 17; Neukirchen-Vluyn: Neukirchner Verlag, 1973), 19, who concludes, "would not the command-account follow the action-account by way of interpretation?" (translated by Scullion).

It may be a synecdochic or metonymic agent, where a part or aspect of the deity stands figuratively for God. Yet the focus of the agency is nonetheless, specifically, on the divine wrath caused by the people, not on the deity himself.[15]

Finally, in the fifth conceptualization, God is altogether absent. Though this idea is not as fully developed as the previous paradigms, there is a tendency to extricate the deity from executing the punishment:

People Sin → Shame/Hurt Themselves

Every sin they commit directly affects them without the mediation of God; they destroy themselves with their own sins (henceforth, designated as the self-destruction pattern).

What can be tentatively observed in this study is an evolving depiction of God's role in meting out punishments. This study will lay out the possible historical development in which the God of history (conceptualizations 1 and 2) also becomes the God who merely executes whatever disaster the people create (conceptualizations 3 and 4) and is sometimes, removed from history (conceptualization 5). In the early redaction of DtrH, God, like a movie director from behind the scenes, works through history with his temporal instruments. In the later redactions of DtrH, God's presence becomes more explicit, while at the same time, the sins determine the outcome of the punishment. As a result, the people experience the consequence of their actions. Like the later editors of DtrH, the book of Jeremiah tries to further exculpate God from the activities by 1) describing the punishment more in terms of the people's sins; 2) focusing on an aspect of God, divine wrath; and 3) absolving God altogether.[16]

Historically speaking, the Babylonians and the physical consequences of war, famine and disease, are responsible for what occurred in the events leading up to the fall of Jerusalem in 587 B.C.E. However, the authors/editors of

---

15 Though similar to the boomerang-pattern, the sins do not become the punishment but the consequence of the sins, the provocation, fuels the divine wrath that ultimately becomes the source for the punishment. Once the sins convert into kindling for divine wrath, the people only experience the combustion, the heat of the provocation, not the very sins.

16 It is an exercise in *zitathaftes Leben*, "the dependence of the great religious-cultural formations on authoritative views which are studied, reinterpreted, and adapted to ongoing life" (Michael Fishbane, *Biblical Interpretation in Ancient Israel*, 1, who borrows the term from Thomas Mann, "Freud und die Zukunft," in *Gesammelte Werke* [Frankfurt-am-Main: Fischer, 1960], ix. 497).

the book of Jeremiah wanted the people to conceptualize history that was consistent with their theo-political worldview. They wanted to convict the people of their fault while exonerating their God, the master of history.

Outline of the Present Study

In order to understand how the book of Jeremiah borrows and modifies the use of הכעים for the purpose of mapping out the role of YHWH, the function of הכעים in the Hebrew Bible needs to be examined. Therefore, the present study will be divided into five major Parts: I) discussion of הכעים in Deuteronomistic History (DtrH), redaction level one (DtrH1); II) discussion of הכעים in DtrH, redaction level two (DtrH2); III) discussion of הכעים in non-Deuteronomic attestations; IV) discussion of הכעים in the book of Jeremiah; and V) conclusion. The first four Parts are further subdivided into sections that will provide a detailed analysis of the pericopes containing הכעים.

Part I will first examine the definitions of the root in its varied use in the Hebrew Bible. It will outline the definition of the nominal form and the verbal conjugations, qal and piel, of כעס.

The rest of Part I and Part II will analyze pericopes containing the hiphil conjugation of כעס in DtrH. While analyzing the pericopes, this study will describe the pivot-function of הכעים which will become the basis for the present study. In order to observe its development, not so much in the actual function of הכעים but the purpose of the term in the overall structure of DtrH, the pericopes with the term in DtrH1 (Deut 32:15-25 [vv. 16, 21],[17] 1 Kgs 14:7-11 [v. 9], 15:29-30 [v. 30], 16:2-4 [v. 2], 16:11-13 [v. 13], 16:25-26 [v. 26], 16:30-33 [v. 33], 21:20b-26 [v. 22], 22:53-54 [v. 53]) will be studied separately from those in DtrH2 (Deut 4:25-28 [v. 25], 9:18-20 [v. 18], 31:27-29 [v. 29], Judg 2:11-16 [v. 12], 1 Kgs 14:15-16a [v. 15], 16:7, 2 Kgs 17:7-23a [vv. 11, 17], 21:2-15 [vv. 6, 15], 22:15-17 [v. 17], 23:19-20 [v. 19], 23:26-27 [v. 26]). The analysis of the passages along the divisions of DtrH will demonstrate how הכעים in DtrH1 occurs primarily in the context of oracles against the Northern dynasties that prophesy their utter decimation while the term is used to explain the fall of Samaria and then Jerusalem in DtrH2. Simultaneously, it will show how the description of the agency of destruction shifts from cases essentially centered on the God of history in DtrH1 to other fully developed

---

17   Though Deut 32:16 and 21 probably do not belong to DtrH1, it is nevertheless discussed under this section. Deut 32, the Song of Moses, may actually predate DtrH1 but there is no consensus. See discussion in Part I.

conceptualizations, that of boomerang (2 Kgs 22:16), synecdochic agency of divine wrath (2 Kgs 22:17), and self-destruction (Deut 31:29) in DtrH2.

Part III will then analyze the non-Deuteronomic pericopes containing הכעיס (Hos 12:1-15 [v. 15], Ezek 8:1-18 [v. 17], 16:23-30 [v. 26], Isa 65:1-7 [v. 3], Pss 78:56-64 [v. 58], 106:28-31 [v. 29], 2 Chr 28:22-25 [v. 25],[18] Neh 3:37) devoting a section to each pericope except Neh 3:37.[19] The analysis of these pericopes will show the continuity of the pivot-function of הכעיס in non-Deuteronomic texts (Hos 12:15, Ezek 16:26, Isa 65:3, Pss 78:58, 106:29, 2 Chr 28:25) and its varied use in Ezek 8:17. It will then outline the various concep-tualizations of the agency of punishment which includes God (Hos 12:15,[20] Ezek 8:18, 16:37-38, Isa 65:5b-7), his human instrument (Ezek 16:39-41, Ps 78:59-64), and unspecified agency (Ps 106:29, 2 Chr 28:27). Despite the mark-ed involvement of God in most instances, the punishment is described more in terms of the sins (Ps 78:56-64, Ezek 8:1-18, 16:23-30, Hos 12:1-15, Isa 65:1-7) so that people are held more responsible for their fate.

Part IV will then carefully study the passages in the book of Jeremiah (7:16-20 [vv. 18, 19], 8:18-23 [v. 19], 11:17, 25:1-14 [vv. 6, 7], 32:26-35 [v. 29], 44:1-14 [vv. 3, 8]). Since many of the pericopes are heavily redacted with interwoven formulations of the punishment, they will be analyzed individually in the order of their occurrences in the book, rather than by their different conceptualizations of God's activity.

Finally, Part V will conclude the present study by drawing upon the impli-cations of the development of הכעיס from its initial use in DtrH to its ex-panded use in the book of Jeremiah. It will show how the book of Jeremiah attempted to explain the realities of the fall of Jerusalem to its community.

Studies on the Book of Jeremiah

Up to recent times, scholarship on the book of Jeremiah has focused on sepa-rating the original words of Jeremiah, the *ipsissima verba*, from the secondary accumulations. Since the *ipsissima verba* of Jeremiah have been linked primar-ily to the poetic oracles and the secondary accretions to the prose, scholarly debates have raged over the relationship between poetry and prose. In essence,

---

18   Two other attestations of כעיס are present in 2 Chronicles (33:6, 34:25) but they parallel 2 Kgs 21:6 and 22:17, respectively.

19   Since Neh 3:37 does not follow nor elaborate upon the pattern, it will not be discussed in detail.

20   The description of the punishment is most likely a secondary insertion by a late redactor. See discussion in Part III.

scholars have proposed numerous theories on the growth of the book of Jeremiah which are usually either a rejection, slight modification, or development of the theories of Duhm and Mowinckel.[21] In his commentary published in 1903, Bernhard Duhm[22] separated three major strands which constituted the book: the poems of Jeremiah, the book of Baruch containing biographical material, and later supplements. On the basis of the division, Duhm focused on identifying the original words of Jeremiah, which comprised of approximately 280 verses (2:2b-3, 14-28; 2:29-37, 3:1-5, 3:12b, 13, 19, 20; 3:21-25; 4:1, 4; 4:5-8, 4:11b, 12a, 13, 15-17a; 4:19-21; 4:23-26; 4:29-31; 5:1-6a, 5:6b-9, 5:10-17; 6:1-5; 6:6b-8, 6:9-14; 6:16-17, 20; 6:22-26a; 6:27-30; 7:28-29; 8:4-7a; 8:8, 9, 13; 8:14-17; 8:18-23; 9:1-8; 9:9; 9:16-18; 9:19-21; 10:19, 20, 22; 11:15-16; 11:18-20; 12:7-12; 13:15, 16; 13:17, 13:18-19; 13:20, 21a, 22-25a, 26, 27; 14:2-10; 14:17, 18; 15:5-9; 15:10-12, 15-19a, 20, 21; 16:5-7; 17:1-4; 17:9, 10, 14, 16, 17; 18:13-17; 18:18-20; 20:7-11; 20:14-18; 22:6b-7, 10; 22:13-27; 22:18-19; 22:20-23; 22:24, 28; 23:9-12; 23:13-15; 30:12-15; 31:2-6; 31:15-16; 31:18-20; 31:21-22). The rest of the verses were distributed between the biography (220 verses; 26:1-3, 4, 6-24; 27:2, 3; 28:1a; 28:2-13, 15-17; 29:1, 3, 4a, 5-7, 11-15, 21-23, 24f, 26-29; 32:6-15; 34:1-7, 34:8-11; 35:1-11; 36:1-26, 32; 37:5, 12-18, 20, 21; 38:1, 3-22, 24-28a; 38:28b, 39:3, 14a, 40:6; 40:7, 42:9, 13a, 14, 19-21, 43:1-7; 44:15a, 16-19, 24f, 28b) and supplements which were influenced by the books of Deuteronomy, Ezekiel, and Second and Third Isaiah (850 verses; remainder).[23]

About a decade later, Sigmund Mowinckel[24] proposed a more elaborate explanation for the composition which has framed most of the discussions up to the present time. Mowinckel isolated four different sources in chs. 1-45: labelled A, B, C, and D. Source A consists of poetic oracles, primarily concentrated in chs. 1-25 (specifically, 1:4-10; 1:11f; 1:13-16; 2:2b-9; 2:10-13; 2:14-28a; 2:29-37; 3:1-5; 3:19-20; 3:21-4:4; 4:5-10; 4:11a -18; 4:19-22; 4:23-28;

21 Most commentaries and other scholarly treatment of the book of Jeremiah begin the discussion of the history of scholarship with Duhm and/or Mowinckel, Holladay, *Jeremiah*, 2:10-16; Carroll, *Jeremiah*, 38-50; Bright, *Jeremiah*, lx-lxxvii; Lundbom, *Jeremiah*, 63-67 (though he focused mostly on the differentiation between prose and poetry); McKane, *Jeremiah*, xli-l; Hyatt, "The Deuteronomic Edition of Jeremiah," in *A Prophet to the Nations: Essays in Jeremiah Studies* (eds. L. Perdue and B. Kovacs; Winona Lake: Eisenbrauns, 1984), 248-251; repr. from *Vanderbilt Studies in the Humanities* (ed. R. Beatty, et al; Nashville: Vanderbilt University Press, 1951), 71-95.
22 Bernhard Duhm, *Das Buch Jeremia, die poetischen und prophetischen Bücher des Alten Testaments* (KHC 11; Tübingen: Mohr, 1901).
23 Duhm, *Das Buch Jeremia*.
24 S. Mowinckel, *Zur Komposition des Buches Jeremia* (Videnskapsselskapets skrifter II. Hist.-filos.klasse; 1913, no. 5; Kristiania: Dybwad, 1914).

4:29-31; 5:1-9; 5:10-14; 5:15-17; 5:20-31; 6:1-6a; 6:6b-8; 6:9-15; 6:16-19; 6:20f; 6:22-26; 6:27-30; 8:4a -12; 8:13; 8:14-17; 8:18-23; 9:1-8; 9:9-11; 9:16-21; 9:22f; 9:24f; 10:17-22; 11:15f; 11:18-20, 22f; 12:1-6; 12:7-12; 13:12-14; 13:15-27; 14:2-10; 14:11-16; 14:17a -15:2; 15:5-9; 15:10-21; 16:1-13; 16:16-18, 21; 17:1-4; 17 9-10; 17:12-18; 18:13-17; 18:18-23; 20:7-13; 20:14-18; 21:11b-12; 21:13f; 22:6aβ-9; 22:10-12; 22:13-19; 22:20-23; 22:24-30; 23:5f; 23:9-15; 23:16-20; 23:21-24, 29; 24:1-10; 25:15f, 27-38). Source B consists of the historical narrative concentrated in chs. 26-44 (ch. 26; ch. 28; 29:24-32; ch. 36; 37:1-10; 37:11-16; 37:17-21; 38:1-13; 38:14-28a; 38:28b, 39:3, 14, 40:2-12; 40:13-43:7; 43:8-13, 44:15-19, 24-30), including 19:1-2, 10-11a, 14-20:6. Source C consists of sermons, which have been usually associated with the Deuteronomic school (7:1-8:3; 11:1-5, 9-14; 18:1-12; 21:1-10; 25:1-11a; 32:1-2, 6-16, 24-44; 34:1-7, 8-22; 35:1-19; 44:1-14). Source D consists of later additions, usually words of consolation, mainly in chs. 30-31. The remaining chapters, 46-52, are considered an appendix.[25]

The major point of contention among most scholars has been the relationship between the poetic oracles and prose sermons, namely sources A and C.[26] Basically, the scholarly opinion has divided into four camps: those who argue for Jeremianic influence in both sources (Bright,[27] Holladay,[28] Weippert[29]); those who attribute C source and the redaction to the Deuteronomic school

---

25   This does not, of course, encompass the successive levels of redactorial activity.

26   Many of the discussions concern the relationship between prose and poetry; see Lundbom, *Jeremiah*, 65-66. Despite some similar features, Lundbom, would still differentiate between the two literary types.

27   Holladay, *Jeremiah,* 2:12, categorizes Bright, *Jeremiah*, with Hyatt, *Jeremiah.* However, the significant difference between these two scholars is that Hyatt, *Jeremiah*, attributes the preservation of Jeremiah's words to Dtr while Bright, *Jeremiah*, would ascribe them to Jeremiah's followers. See Bright, *Jeremiah*, lxxi-ii, and "The Date of the Prose Sermons of Jeremiah," *JBL* 70 (1951):27 who argues that the prose tradition of Jeremiah "grew up on the basis of his words, partly no doubt preserving them exactly, partly giving the gist of them with verbal expansions, partly (e.g. 7:19-27) those words as understood or misunderstood in the circle of his disciples." He even admits, though, that the prose may be a "development and adaptation of his thought, the application of it to new situations, and ever on occasion some misunderstanding of it," lxxii.

28   The distinction by sources, according to Holladay, *Jeremiah*, 2:15-35, should be disregarded and the discussion should focus on the 'voice' of Jeremiah in both the poetic oracles and sermonic prose; see also William Holladay, "A Fresh Look at 'Source B' and 'Source C' in Jeremiah," *VT* 25 (1975):402-8.

29   Helga Weippert, *Die Prosareden des Jeremiabuches* (BZAW 132; Berlin: de Gruyter, 1973) does not distinguish between the poetic oracles and prose sermons since there is continuity of phrases/expressions between the two media. At the same time, she demonstrates how these phrases differ from those attested in DtrH.

(Hyatt,[30] Nicholson,[31] Thiel,[32] Stulman[33]); those who posit the exegetical expansion of the book, called the "rolling corpus" (McKane[34]); and those who assert the random nature of the collection (Carroll).[35] There are of course differences and debates between the scholars, even those in the same camp, about the specific dating, location, and nature of the relationship between the sources.[36] Nevertheless, the general classification of the theories seems to represent the main tendencies in most of the scholars' works. With the excep-

---

30   J. Philip Hyatt, "The Deuteronomic Edition of Jeremiah," 247-267. However, Hyatt, *Jeremiah*, 789, argues that DtrH preserved some of Jeremiah's prophecies.
31   Nicholson, *Jeremiah*, 10-16, and *Preaching to the Exiles: A Study of the Prose Tradition in the Book of Jeremiah* (New York: Schocken Books, 1970).
32   In contrast to Weippert, *Die Prosareden des Jeremiabuches*, Winfried Thiel, *Die deuteronomistische Redaktion von Jer 1-25* (WMANT 41; Neukirchen: Neukirchener, 1973), and *Die deuteronomistische Redaktion von Jer 26-45* (WMANT 52; Neukirchen: Neukirchener, 1981), demonstrates the continuity of the expressions in DtrH with those in the prose sermons and in some poetic oracles of the book of Jeremiah.
33   Louis Stulman, *The Prose Sermons of the Book of Jeremiah: A Redescription of the Correspondences with Deuteronomistic Literature in the Light of Recent Text-Critical Research* (SBLDS 83; Atlanta: Scholars Press, 1986).
34   In his very pedantic and dense style (see reviews of Walter Brueggemann, "Jeremiah: Intense Criticism/Thin Interpretation," *Interpretation* 42 [1988]:271-2, and Robert Carroll, "Radical Clashes of Will and Style: Recent Commentary Writing on the Book of Jeremiah," *JSOT* 45 [1989]:108-9), McKane, *Jeremiah*, lxxxiii, describes the whole process as the 'rolling corpus,' whereby kernels of Jeremiah's speech "triggers exegesis or commentary;" see also McKane, "Relations Between Poetry and Prose in the Book of Jeremiah with Special Reference to Jeremiah iii 6-11 and xii 14-17," in *A Prophet to the Nations* (eds. Leo Perdue and Brian Kovacs; Winona Lake: Eisenbrauns, 1984), 269-284; repr. from VTSup 32 (1980):220-237.
35   Carroll, *Jeremiah*, 65-82. One could easily understand Carroll's exasperation with the attempts to explain the *intentional* composition of the book of Jeremiah (see Carroll, "Halfway Through a Dark Wood," in *Troubling Jeremiah* [eds. A.R. Pete Diamond, Kathleen O'Connor, and Louis Stulman; JSOTSup 260; Sheffield: Sheffield Academic Press, 1999], 76-77, esp. notes 8 and 9). At the same time, though, his argument that "no consistent, coherent pattern can be established . . . [and that]. . . they must be seen as the product of different groups within the Judean territory," 70, does not explain why the traditions were collected under the figure of Jeremiah. Some editor(s) had a reason(s) for collecting the oracles, sermons, and narratives under the rubric of Jeremiah versus Ezekiel or any other prophet. Even if scholarly efforts have failed to provide a comprehensive picture of its composition, the book could not have mainly been a creation of a random selection of editors. Ultimately, the confusion concerning the history of the book of Jeremiah remains with the scholars, not with the book of Jeremiah.
36   Most would date the book of Jeremiah to the period after the destruction around 550 B.C.E., though Carroll, "Halfway Through a Dark Wood," 79-80, would argue for a much later date during the Persian rule. Also some have argued either for the Babylonian (Nicholson, *Jeremiah*, 116-135) or Palestinian (Carroll, *Jeremiah*, 69) setting for the final composition. As for the relationship between the Dtr circle-tradition-source-editor-school and the book of Jeremiah, it is nuanced for each proposal. These are just some of the disagreements.

tion of McKane and Carroll, these scholars have tried to clarify the link between poetry and prose to determine the 'original words' of the prophet.

Beside the countless debates about the relationship between poetry and prose, a number of studies have tried to shift away from the atomistic literary-critical study to approach the book as a literary whole.[37] Some have focused on the synchronic development of themes (Hill,[38] Unterman[39]); some on the coherent literary structure of the book (Rosenberg,[40] Kessler,[41] Hobbs[42]); and others on the distinct methods of reading (Brueggemann,[43] Lundbom,[44] Polk[45]). These studies have expanded our knowledge of the book beyond the separation of the original words of the prophet and later accretions, Deuteronomistic or not. Yet they do not adequately address the diachronic development of any theme, central or not, to the book.

Two works worthy of note have examined the effects of the historical circumstances on the development of an idea. Within the framework of the prose-poetry debate, Nicholson analyzes the literary aspects, theology, and historical background of the Deuteronomistic prose material[46] not only to elucidate the characteristics of prose sermons, but also to demonstrate how they have reapplied Jeremiah's oracles for the exilic community in Babylon. Similarly, Seitz attempts to distinguish two distinct recensions of the prose material in chs. 27-44, the Scribal Chronicle (post-597) and the Golah Redaction (post-

---

37 For a brief description of the types of scholarship on Jeremiah at the Composition of the Book of Jeremiah Consultation (SBL/AAR Annual Convention, 1992), see A.R. Pete Diamond, "Introduction," in *Troubling Jeremiah*, 15-32.

38 John Hill, *Friend or Foe? The Figure of Babylon in the Book of Jeremiah MT* (BibInt 40; Leiden: Brill, 1999), and "The Construction of Time in Jeremiah 25 (MT)," in *Troubling Jeremiah*, 146-160.

39 Jeremiah Unterman, *From Repentance to Redemption: Jeremiah's Thought in Transition* (JSOTSup 54; Sheffield: JSOT Press, 1987).

40 Joel Rosenberg, "Jeremiah and Ezekiel," in *The Literary Guide to the Bible* (eds. Robert Alter and Frank Kermode; Cambridge: Belknap Press of Harvard University Press, 1987), 184-194.

41 Martin Kessler, "The Function of Chapters 25 and 50-51 in the Book of Jeremiah," in *Troubling Jeremiah*, 64-72.

42 T.R. Hobbs, "Some Remarks on the Composition and Structure of the Book of Jeremiah," *CBQ* 34 (1972):257-275.

43 Walter Brueggemann's commentary, *Jeremiah*, discusses the literary-sociological-theological aspects.

44 Jack Lundbom, *Jeremiah: A Study in Ancient Hebrew Rhetoric* (SBLDS 18; 2d ed. Winona Lake: Eisenbrauns, 1975), xix-xlii, and more recently, his commentary, *Jeremiah*, 68-92, has discussed in detail, rhetorical criticism.

45 Timothy Polk, *The Prophetic Persona: Jeremiah and the Language of the Self* (JSOTSup 32; Sheffield: JSOT Press, 1984), examines the 'I' by focusing on the reading process.

46 Nicholson, *Preaching to the Exiles*.

587), by determining the likely response to the initial exile in 597 in contrast to the definitive exile in 587.[47] He constructs the shifting responses by analyzing the books of Kings' (2 Kgs 24-25) and Ezekiel's perspectives on the historical events prior to and surrounding the fall of Jerusalem.

Beside the last two works, studies on the book of Jeremiah have not examined the theological, socio-historical development of a theme; and none have discussed the topic of הכעיס. The oversight is apparent also in the studies on divine wrath, which have been too broad in scope, too synchronic, or too theological.

Previous Biblical Studies on Divine Wrath

Numerous studies on the wrath of God in the Bible have been published over the years. Most of the biblical encyclopedias, theological dictionaries, and theologies of the Old Testament have discussed the basic information on anger in the Bible. In addition, countless number of books and articles has mainly or cursorily examined biblical concepts of divine wrath. Due to the volume of secondary materials, the study will only provide a sampling of the types of scholarship.

There is a series of detailed philological studies on Hebrew terms for anger. Focusing on the eighth century prophets, William Simpson mainly examines the words for anger and describes their use in the various figures of speech.[48] Despite the comprehensive nature of his dissertation, it is basically a discussion of Hebrew terms for anger in a defined corpus. In a much more brief but informative article, J. Bergman and E. Johnson[49] also examine all the possible words for anger in the Hebrew Bible in addition to providing the ancient Near Eastern background and discussions of human and divine anger. Within the description of divine anger, Johnson has duly noted the various descriptions of God's wrath, usually portrayed in figurative language, ranging from the 'psychic' behavior to the concrete action.

Turning to a more topical study, Bruce E. Baloian[50] deals with the psychological and theological aspect of divine anger. Although the monograph exam-

---

47 Christopher Seitz, *Theology in Conflict: Reactions to the Exile in the Book of Jeremiah* (BZAW 176; Berlin: de Gruyter, 1989).
48 William Simpson, "Divine Wrath in the Eighth Century Prophets" (unpublished Ph.D. dissertation; Boston University, 1968).
49 J. Bergman and E. Johnson, *TDOT* 1:348-360.
50 Bruce Edward Baloian, *Anger in the Old Testament* (American University Studies; New York: Peter Lang, 1992).

ines both human and divine wrath, the former is studied primarily to elucidate the latter, which is understood in human terms. The monograph carefully accomplishes the author's object, which is to exemplify the interpersonal nature of divine wrath. However, the synchronic character of the research does not take into consideration the different historical backgrounds and theological conceptions and thus limits the relevance of the studies on specific passages.

There are studies on divine anger that are mainly theological. B.T. Dahlberg[51] provides an excellent study of the theological themes of divine wrath from the Hebrew Bible to the New Testament. Like Bergman and Johnson, Dahlberg also observed the natural and historical manifestations of divine wrath, and the concretization of the phenomenon.[52] Other theological discussions, unfortunately, do not follow Dahlberg. Most of them are infused with a modern Christian perspective. R.V.G. Tasker[53] looks at biblical doctrine of wrath in the Old and New Testament with Romans chapters 1-2 as the interpretive basis. In a similar but more analytical fashion, A. Hanson[54] traces the development of personal anger of the Old Testament to the impersonal wrath of the New Testament with the birth of Christ. On account of the very Christian outlook of both of the works, it is quite difficult to separate the exegesis of biblical texts from their modern Christian theological concepts.

The only book that has attempted to examine a defined corpus in its literary, historical, and ideological context is Latvus' *God, Anger and Ideology: The Anger of God in Joshua and Judges in Relation to Deuteronomy and the Priestly Writings*, an abridgement of his dissertation.[55] Latvus tries to analyze the theological themes within the various redaction levels of the books of Joshua and Judges but fails to justify his separation of the sources. A critical example is his pivotal argument that the literary strata emphasizing the theology of anger stemmed from the period of the exile. It is never proven nor discussed in detail.[56] Despite the failings, Latvus has turned the discussion of

---

51   B.T. Dahlberg, "Wrath of God," in *IDB* 4:903-908.

52   Dahlberg, "Wrath of God," 904.

53   R.V.G. Tasker, *The Biblical Doctrine of the Wrath of God* (Tyndale Biblical Theology Lecture; London: Tyndale Press, 1951).

54   Anthony Hanson, *Wrath of the Lamb* (London: S.P.C.K., 1957).

55   Kari Latvus, *God, Anger and Ideology: The Anger of God in Joshua and Judges in Relation to Deuteronomy and the Priestly Writings* (JSOTSup 279; Sheffield: Sheffield Academic Press, 1998).

56   Latvus, *God, Anger and Ideology*, 35. Perhaps the dissertation has a more detailed discussion but it was not available to the author of the present study. See Robert D. Miller II, "Review of *God, Anger and Ideology: The Anger of God in Joshua and Judges in Relation to Deuteronomy and the Priestly Writings*," n.p. [2000]. Online: http://www. bookreviews.org/Print/1850759227-P.html.

divine wrath in a historico-critical direction. Overall, though, none of the essays or books have examined הכעים in detail.

Assumptions of the Present Study

Rather than (re-)engage in the scholarly debate about the relationship between
prose and poetry, the present study will rely upon previous scholarly contributions[57] when relevant and modify them as the evidence presents itself. First,
the present study assumes that source C (prose sermons) is distinct from source
A (poetic oracles). However, it does not regard the literary growth of source A
to be completely independent and separate from the literary development of
source C. In fact, similar accretions occur across both sources.

Second, the present study assumes that the prose sermons are closely connected to the Deuteronomic school. Though the specific relationship between
the author/editor (or authors/editors) of the prose sermons and the Deuteronomic circle, or even between the prophet himself and the Deuteronomic
school, cannot be outlined due to the paucity of information, close affiliation is
clearly evident between them. Despite the link between the prose sermons in
the book of Jeremiah and DtrH, they are not one and the same. Some strands
within source C reflect a more elaborate development of God's role in meting
out punishments than DtrH. The development may be the contributions of
either a branch/outgrowth of DtrH or a distinct individual/group connected to
Jeremiah's 'disciples.'

Third, the present study assumes that the prose sermons are for the most
part later than the poetic oracles.[58] However, there are numerous exceptions
since some of the additions in the poetic units have been edited or composed
later by a redactor whose hand is also present in the prose sermons.

---

57   The following first three assumptions of the dissertation, without the nuances, correspond to
     those outlined in Louis Stulman, "The Prose Sermons as Hermeneutical Guide to Jeremiah 1-
     25: The Deconstruction of Judah's Symbolic World," in *Troubling Jeremiah*, 36-37, note 12.
58   Carroll, *Jeremiah*, 67-8, briefly discusses the "immediacy of the destructive consequences of
     the Babylonian invasion" in the poems (ex. 4:19-21, 29; 5:16-17; 6:22-26, 8:14, 16; 10:19-
     20; 12:10-13) which is absent in the Deuteronomistic elements in the book of Jeremiah, but
     also notes the difficulty in dating these elements. It may even have been written during the
     Persian period.

Fourth, it assumes that a later editor (or editors), who may or may not have been associated with the Deuteronomic school, collected, edited, and organized the material.[59]

These four assumptions do not explain the relationship between the prose sermons (source C) and the historical narrative (source B). Since there is no definitive evidence for or against the separation,[60] most commentators[61] tend to categorize both of them under the same author/editor but differentiate them based on literary types: sermon vs. narrative.[62] This will be the premise for the present study as well.

---

59   E. Tov, "The Literary History of the Book of Jeremiah in the Light of its Textual History," in *Empirical Models for Biblical Criticism* (ed. Jeffrey Tigay; Philadelphia: University of Pennsylvania, 1985), 211-237, has argued that the final redaction of MT is Deuteronomic, though Louis Stulman would argue to the contrary for a non-deuteronomic redaction of the final MT composition. For a discussion of the issue, see Raymond Person, "II Kings 24, 18-25, 30 and Jeremiah 52: A Text-Critical Case Study in the Redaction History of the Deuteronomistic History," *ZAW* 105 (1993):174-205, who agrees with Tov.

60   Michael Williams, "An Investigation of the Legitimacy of Source Distinctions for the Prose Material in Jeremiah," *JBL* 112 (1993):193-210.

61   See Nicholson, *Preaching to the Exiles*, 34-37.

62   The narrative cannot be categorically described as biographical or historical since it focuses on the suffering of Jeremiah. See Lundbom, *Jeremiah*, 68, contrary to J. Hyatt, "The Deuteronomic Edition of Jeremiah," who differentiates between Baruch's memoirs and Deuteronomistic additions.

Part I: Deuteronomistic History, Redaction Level One

1.1. Nominal and Verbal Use of כעס (Qal and Piel) in the Hebrew Bible[1]

The following brief discussion of the nominal and non-hiphil conjugations of כעס will demonstrate how the root, when used with the divine, functions as the motivation for God to mete out punishments. This will thus lay the groundwork for examining the pericopes containing the hiphil conjugations of the root in Parts I-IV, in which the pattern of sin-provocation-punishment is clearly set forth.

---

1   Since the root, כעס, has only a few cognates in the Northwest Semitic languages, its etymology and historical development need only be briefly treated in this note. The earliest non-biblical attestation occurs in Aramaic, in the proverbs of Ahiqar, the wise counselor of Assyria (according to N. Lohfink, *TDOT* 7:283). Given the complex history of their transmission, the story and wisdom sayings are difficult to date. However, the Aramaic manuscript can be dated paleographically to the late fifth century while the linguistic affinities with other Aramaic texts may suggest a date as early as the seventh century (for a more detailed discussion of the Aramaic Ahiqar, see James Lindenberger, *The Aramaic Proverbs of Ahiqar* [JHNES; Baltimore Johns Hopkins University Press, 1983], 19-20). Be that as it may, the only proverb with the attestation of כעס reads, [. . .] וְ[הִ]תהרוה [. . .] יִשְׂבַּע כעס מן לחם (Ahiqar, 187), which may be translated as "Let the angry man (?) satiate himself with bread, and let [. . .] get drunk [. . .]." Despite the proposed translation, כעס may not necessarily denote 'angry man' in the immediate context on account of the broken state of the text; in fact, כעס may refer to almost anything in the broad range of possible meanings. Without a larger context and comparisons from other occurrences of the root in the Aramaic proverbs, it would be difficult to determine what exactly the word denoted in the proverb. However, in later Aramaic texts, especially the Targum, which probably forms the basis for such a reading in the proverb, the word usually meant 'to vex' or 'to anger' (Ernest Klein, *A Comprehensive Etymological Dictionary of the Hebrew Language for Readers of English* [Jerusalem: Carta, 1987], 283, and Marcus Jastrow, *A Dictionary of the Targumim, the Talmud Babli and Yerushalmi, and the Midrashic Literature* [New York: Title Publishing Co., 1943], 1:656).

     Beside Aramaic, the word does not appear to have clear etymological counterparts. One may possibly relate the word etymologically to Punic *k's* or Arabic *kaši'a* ("was anxious") and *kaša'* ("anxiety") — see Klein, *A Comprehensive Etymological Dictionary*, 283, and *TLOT* 2:622, while *TDOT* 7:283, suggests Jakob Barth's reading, who etymologically connects the word to Arabic *kaša'a* (fear). On account of the limited cognates in the Semitic languages, comparative studies of the word do not aid in its clarification. For a better understanding of כעס and its development, one needs to primarily examine its attestations in the Bible.

1.1.1. Nominal Use

The nominal form of the root, כעש/כעס, appears 25 times in the Hebrew Bible. Its occurrences are concentrated in the wisdom literature (13 times)[2] although it is also attested in the book of Psalms (4 times),[3] DtrH (7 times),[4] and once in the book of Ezekiel (20:28). In these attestations, a distinct pattern emerges where כעס affecting humans, usually in the Writings,[5] tends to refer to internal vexation while divine כעס, mostly in the Prophets,[6] is accompanied by an externalized response.

When כעס is used of humans, it refers primarily to internal distress resulting from 'sadness' and/or 'annoyance.'[7] In fact, the term usually occurs in parallel construction or in conjunction with words denoting either physical or emotional pain: כעס is in parallel construction with "pain" (מכאוב, Eccl 1:18)[8] and "worry/anxiety" (שׂיח, 1 Sam 1:16),[9] while accompanied by sadness ("evil of face," רע פנים; Eccl 7:3) and weakening of the eyes ("wasting of my eyes," עששה עיני, Pss 6:8, 31:10; "dimming of my eyes," כהה עיני, Job 17:7). In these contexts, the term is rarely identified with the externalized manifestation of the vexation — i.e. angered response — justified or not.

---

2   Prov 12:16, 17:25, 21:19, 27:3, Eccl 1:18, 2:23, 7:3, 9, 11:10, Job 5:2, 6:2, 10:17, 17:7.
3   Pss 6:8, 10:14, 31:10, 85:5.
4   Deut 32:19, 27, 1 Sam 1:6, 16, 1 Kgs 15:30, 21:22, 2 Kgs 23:26.
5   With the exception of Job 10:17 and Ps 85:5 where the term refers to divine כעס/כעש.
6   With the exception of Deut 32:27 and 1 Sam 1:6, 16.
7   Both *BDB*, 495a, and *HALOT*, 491, provide two definitions — "grief" and "vexation." See *TLOT* 2:623, which defines כעס as the "emotional state directly, the bad mood, the agitation with a strong inclination to wrath, although it can also refer back to the cause of this mood, hostile intention, folly, or psychological pain, according to the context."
8   Also see Eccl 2:23.
9   See *BDB*, 967 and *HALOT*, 1320-1321. Another nominal form of כעס with human agency is attested in 1 Sam 1:6; however here, the noun should be emended to an infinitive absolute. On account of the emphatic גם (כעסה גם־כעס) צרתה before the internal object (*schema etymologicum* — *GKC* § 117p), which breaks the construction of the verb plus the cognate accusative, a grammatical problem arises. This may have been the reason why the Syriac, Targum, and Latin Vulgate reflect two verbal constructions rather than a verb plus a cognate accusative, leading P. K. McCarter, *1 Samuel* (AB 8; New York: Doubleday, 1980), 52, to emend the MT text to read a piel verbal form plus the infinitive absolute ("Yahweh had closed her womb, and, to make matters worse, her rival used to provoke her spitefully"). To support his reading, Driver cites similar examples in the Bible (Gen 31:15, 46:4, Num 16:13). *Notes on the Hebrew Text and the Topography of the Books of Samuel* (Oxford: Clarendon Press, 1913), 8-9, raises this possibility but does not take an absolute stand. If it is a infinitive absolute, it functions to highlight the piel verb form, in which Elkanah's rival-wife vexes the barren Hannah. On account of the contested form of the noun, it will not be included in the discussion above.

However, when the term is used of God (Deut 32:19, 1 Kgs 15:30, 21:22, 2 Kgs 23:26, Ezek 20:28, Ps 85:5), כעס triggers a divine reaction, namely the punishment of those who provoke him.[10] In Deut 32:19, the noun refers to the Israelites' provocation of God who is stirred to the point of rejecting them:

וירא יהוה וינאץ מכעס בניו ובנתיו

YHWH saw and he spurned (them) on account of his children's provocation

Similarly, in Ezek 20:28, the Israelites make an 'offensive offering' to God (כעס קרבנם, "their provocative offering"), whereupon they are to be punished (20:30-38). Finally in Ps 85, the punishment, described as the manifestation of כעס ("annul your anger against us," והפר כעסך עמנו, v. 5), provides the basis for the psalmist to plea for God's salvation. All in all, an externalized response — i.e. punishment — is expected when God is provoked to anger.

Other attestations of the nominal form of כעס with God as the recipient of the provocation are found in conjunction with either the piel or hiphil conjugations of the verb (1 Kgs 15:30, 21:22, 2 Kgs 23:26). Initially, these nouns may be thought to be cognate accusatives;[11] yet on closer observation, the nouns are not cognate accusatives for the purpose of emphasizing the verb but rather independent nouns which accentuate the evil deeds that provoke God to anger:

בכעסו אשר הכעיס את־יהוה אלהי ישראל

on account of his provocation with which he provoked YHWH, the God of Israel, to anger (1 Kgs 15:30b)

אל־הכעס אשר הכעסת ותחטא את־ישראל

on account of the provocation with which you provoked (me) to anger and caused Israel to sin (1 Kgs 21:22b)

על כל־הכעסים אשר הכעיסו מנשה

on account of all the provocations with which Manasseh provoked him to anger (2 Kgs 23:26)

---

10 According to Driver, *Notes on the Hebrew Text and the Topography of the Books of Samuel*, 8, the word only means "to vex," not to "provoke to anger." It is not clear from the context how he is differentiating these two definitions. From the perspective of this study, כעס can indicate both internal irritation (usually with humans as subject) and external/active anger (usually with God as subject). The word in of itself does not differentiate between human or divine use; rather the context determines which meaning is more relevant.

11 According to Lohfink, *TDOT* 7:283, who writes, "the noun functions as a cognate accusative with a piel (1 S. 1:6) or hiphil (1 K. 15:30; 21:22; 2 K. 23:26)."

In 1 and 2 Kings, the noun in its singular (1 Kgs 15:30, 1 Kgs 21:22) and its plural (2 Kgs 23:26)[12] forms emphasize the provocative deeds ("the provocation with which he provoked," הכעס אשר הכעים or variations thereof) that prompt God to punish Jeroboam, Ahab, and Judah, respectively. The declaration of punishment is connected to the phrase by the causal preposition בְּ (1 Kgs 15:30), אל (1 Kgs 21:22),[13] and על (2 Kgs 23:26). Thus the kings of Israel and Judah are punished because of the provocations that provoked God to anger. These כעס-deeds are evil, therefore angering enough, to prompt God to destroy.

1.1.2. Non-Hiphil Verbal Conjugations

Before a detailed analysis of the pericopes containing the hiphil conjugations of כעס, we will briefly discuss the qal and piel conjugations of the root. When the verb is conjugated in the qal, the subject is usually human (Eccl 5:16,[14] Ps 112:10, Neh 3:33, 2 Chr 16:10); it appears only once with God as the subject (Ezek 16:42). Among the qal attestations with human-subjects, כעס can be both internalized (Eccl 5:16) and externalized (Ps 112:10, Neh 3:33, 2 Chr 16:10), whereas the only occurrence with God as the subject (Ezek 16:42) refers to the externalized manifestation of the provocation:

והנחתי חמתי בך וסרה קנאתי[15] ממך ושקטתי ולא אכעס עוד

I will rest my anger against you and my jealousy will depart from you. I will be calm and no longer be angry.

God's pacification of his anger signified the end of the punishment.

When the verb is conjugated in the piel (Deut 32:21 and 1 Sam 1:6), it is either in parallel construction with (Deut 32:21b) or immediately followed by (1 Sam 1:7) the hiphil form of the same root. Since the piel conjugation is infrequently attested and always in conjunction with the hiphil, it may have

---

12   הכעסים may be an addition following some Greek recensions, Syriac, and Latin Vulgate, where it appears to be omitted.

13   Some Hebrew manuscripts have על instead of אל, which the BHS notes as the basis for LXX, Syriac, and Targum. However, this is not necessarily the case since the two prepositions interchange in the books of Samuel, Kings, Jeremiah, and Ezekiel. See *BDB*, 41, under note 2, and *HALOT* 1:50, which finds the phenomenon primarily in the books of Jeremiah and Ezekiel.

14   In Eccl 7:9, the word occurs as the infinitive construct of כעס in the qal.

15   קנאה connotes the "ardour of anger" (*BDB*, 888) or the "punitive sense" of wrath (*HALOT* 3:1111).

developed by analogy to the hiphil form.[16] This is supported by the fact that no significant difference exists between the piel and the hiphil conjugation of כעס; both have the causative sense. In fact, the connotation derived from the piel is compatible with the meanings of the hiphil in their immediate context. In 1 Sam 1:6, the rival-wife would vex (piel) Hannah, provoking her on a annual basis (hiphil, v.7) while in Deut 32:21, the Israelites provoke God (piel) so that God is motivated to provoke (hiphil) them to anger by rejecting them:[17]

1 Sam 1:6-7

וכעסתה צרתה גם־כעס בעבור הרעמה כי־סגר יהוה בעד רחמה
וכן יעשׂה שׁנה בשׁנה מדי עלתה בבית יהוה כן תכעסמה ותבכה ולא תאכל

Because YHWH had closed up her womb, her rival would provoke her until she was annoyed. Thus it happened year after year. As often as she went up to the temple of YHWH, she would provoke her and she would weep and not eat.

Deut 32:21

הם קנאוני בלא־אל כעסוני בהבליהם
אני אקניאם בלא־עם בגוי נבל אכעיסם

They make me jealous with no-god,
they provoke me to anger with their delusions.[18]
I will make them jealous with no-people,
with foolish-nation I will provoke them to anger

On account of the close link between כעס and קנא, their relationship will be briefly discussed here. In Deut 32:21, Ps 78:58, and Job 5:2, all poetic verses, either the verbal conjugation of קנא or the noun (קנאה) are in parallel construction with כעס. In Deut 32:21 and Job 5:2, the bicolon corresponds in morphology and syntax, thus forming a grammatically equivalent parallel structure. Ps 78:58 also corresponds but in a chiastic structure (abba).

---

16 *TDOT* 7:283.

17 This sense of the verse derives from the clever use of לא־עם ("no people"), people with which God does not have a covenantal relationship (see Hos 1:9 where God severs his covenant with the Israelites in response to their rejection of him). God will establish a relationship with these people (who are furthermore "foolish" [נבל]) inciting their jealousy (קנא, hiphil) and anger. For a similar understanding, see A. D. H. Mayes, *Deuteronomy* (NCB; London: Oliphants, 1979), 388-389.

18 This revealing expression refers to other gods, 1 Kgs 16:13, 26; Jer 8:19, 10:8, 14:22; Ps 31:7 (Eng. 31:6), and Jon 2:9 (Eng. 2:8).

Deut 32:21

הם קִנְאוּנִי בלא־אל כִעֲסוּנִי בהבליהם
אני אַקְנִיאֵם בלא־עם בגוי נבל אַכְעִיסֵם

They make me jealous with no-god,
they provoke me to anger with their delusions.
I *will make them jealous* with no-people,
with foolish-nation *I will provoke them to anger*

Job 5:2

כי לאויל יהרג־כַּעַשׂ
ופתה תמית קִנְאָה

For *provocation* will kill a fool
jealousy will slay the simple.

Ps 78:58

וַיַּכְעִיסוּהוּ בבמותם ובפסיליהם קִנְיאוּהוּ

They provoked him to anger with their high places,
with their idolatrous images, *they made him jealous.*

Given the synonymous parallel structure of these passages, כעס/שׂ and קנאה can be similar word pairs.[19] In fact, they are lexical and semantic equivalents. Since the order of the two terms is not circumscribed so that both sequences, כעס/קנא and קנא/כעס, do occur,[20] the two words can be interchanged. Therefore, the two terms are an example of paradigmatic synonyms.

Yet what aspect of קנא characterizes כעס? According to BDB,[21] the noun, קנאה, can be categorized under three meanings: 1) "ardour of jealousy;" 2) "ardour of zeal;" and 3) "ardour of anger," while the piel of קנא is to "be jealous, zealous" and the hiphil is to "provoke to jealous anger."[22] Based on these

---

19   Though these two words form a pair, it probably does not fit in the category of 'stock of fixed pairs.' The pair does not occur frequently enough to constitute a fixed pair; however, there is a close correspondence between the words.

20   It is not a fixed order whereby it is "always A and then B; never B and then A;" see Adele Berlin, *The Dynamics of Biblical Parallelism* (Bloomington: Indiana University Press, 1985), 68-72, esp. 72. She discusses the psycholinguistic approach to the study of word pairs in which she provides an example from the English language: "*frigid* elicits *cold*, but *cold* does not elicit *frigid*." This does not apply to the word pair, כעס/קנא.

21   888.

22   *BDB*, 888.

definitions, כעס may then connote jealousy. If so, what may be the significance of this meaning for כעס? Well, the importance may not be so much in
the definition but the contexts in which the jealousy is aroused. When קנא is
used of God against Israel, the nouns as well as the verbal forms occur in contexts involving other gods: God is stirred to jealousy because of Israel's idolatry.[23] If one looks at the contexts of Deut 32:21 and Ps 78:58, the passages
under discussion, this is also evident;[24] both passages refer to foreign dei-
ties/practices: "no-god" (לא־אל), "their vanities" (הבליהם), "their high-
places" (במותם),[25] and "their images' (פסיליהם). The idolatrous context of
קנא/קנאה is crucial in understanding the hiphil attestations of כעס, which also
occurs primarily in indictments of Israel for their idolatry. And it is to this very
topic that we will now turn.

---

23   In examples of God's jealousy against Israel, the noun is usually attested in the context of
     idolatry. In the book of Ezekiel, where it is most frequently attested (5:13, 16:38, 42, 23:25),
     קנאה usually reflect God's response to the Israelites' act of idolatry (for 5:13, "on account of
     all your fetishes and all your abominations," בכל־שקוציך ובכל־תועבתיך, 5:11; for 16:38,
     42, Jerusalem's harlotry; for 23:25, Oholibah's [Jerusalem] harlotry). This is most explicitly
     laid out in Ezek 8:3 (and v. 5, without המקנה), where the term is used to describe an idola-
     trous image, (סמל הקנאה המקנה: "infuriating image that provokes fury," according to JPS;
     "statue of outrage that outrages," according to Greenberg, *Ezekiel 1-20* [AB 22; Garden City:
     Doubleday & Co., 1983], 164. Deut 29:19 also refers to the jealousy-anger aroused from
     idolatry (v. 17, ללכת לעבד את אלהי הגרים ההם, "going to serve the gods of those na-
     tions"). The only other occurrence of קנאה where God's jealousy against Israel does not oc-
     cur explicitly in the context of idolatry is in Ps 79:5. Here, the devastation of Jerusalem is de-
     scribed as the concrete manifestation of divine jealousy. Most of the verbal constructions of
     קנא, primarily in the Piel, refer to human zeal, jealousy or envy of other humans: Num 5:14,
     30, 11:29, 25:11, 2 Sam 21:2, 1 Kgs 19:19, 14, Isa 11:13 (jealous); Gen 26:14, 30:1, 37:11,
     Ezek 31:9, Pss 37:1, 73:3, 106:16, Prov 3:31, 23:17, 24:1, 19 (envy). When it is used of God,
     it indicates God's 'zealous vigilance' to maintain Israel's faithfulness, Ezek 39:25, Joel 2:18,
     Zech 1:14, 8:2. When describing God's jealous anger against Israel, the verbal constructions
     are used in idolatrous contexts; see 1 Kgs 14:22, where Judah provokes God to jealousy with
     "the abhorrent practices of nations" (התועבת הגרים, v. 24); and Deut 32:21and Ps 78:58,
     both of which are discussed above.
24   Since Job 5:2 refers to human jealousy/provocation, it is not relevant.
25   Given the context, the 'high places' here do not refer to those constructed for the legitimate
     (1 Sam 9:12, 13, 14, 19, 25, 10:5, 13, 1 Kgs 3:2, 3, 4, 1 Chr 16:39, 21:29, 2 Chr 1:3, 13) or il-
     legitimate worship of YHWH (1 Kgs 14:23, 22:44, 2 Kgs 12:4, 14:4, 15:4, 14, 35, 16:4, 18:4,
     22, 21:3, 23:5, 8, 9, 2 Chr 14:2, 4, 15:17, 20:33, 21:11, 28:4, 25, 31:1, 32:12, 33:3, 17, 19, Isa
     36:7, Jer 7:31, 17:3, Ezek 20:29), or those in the North (1 Kgs 12:31, 32, 13:2, 32, 38, 2 Kgs
     17:9, 11, 29, 32, 23:5, 8, 9, 15, 19, 20, 2 Chr 11:15, Hos 10:8, Amos 7:9), but the ones dedi-
     cated to other deities (Ba'al, Num 22:41, Jer 19:5, 32:35; Moab, Isa 15:2, 16:12, Jer 48:35;
     Chemosh and Milkom, 1 Kgs 11:7; general, Lev 26:30, Num 33:52, Ezek 6:3, 6). For a much
     fuller discussion, see *BDB*, 119

1.2. Introduction to the Redaction of DtrH

Before analyzing the pericopes containing the pivotal-term, הכעיס, in DtrH, a brief discussion of the redaction of DtrH is necessary. This section will lay the groundwork for the division of the passages into DtrH1 and DtrH2.

Several authors/redactors are responsible for composing DtrH, a unified, coherent work.[26] In fact, at least two layers of editorial work can be detected, though other additions are definitely evident.[27] Since it would be too difficult to trace and account for all other additions (secondary, tertiary, and beyond), the present study has adopted the most common demarcation of DtrH, that of the two level theory, which will be modified as the evidence presents itself in the individual analysis of the texts.

In its simplest formulation, the first redactor of DtrH (DtrH1) compiled a continuous narrative from a pool of stories (pre-Dtr) or an earlier prophetic source (pre-DtrP)[28] during the period of Josiah, which the second redactor (DtrH2) modified to explain the fall of Jerusalem and by extension, the fall of Samaria, which functioned as a warning for its southern neighbor. It is not completely clear as to whether the first redactor collected and pieced together stories that were circulating in ancient Israel or made a few additions and adjustments to an already well-developed narrative. Nevertheless, it would be

---

26   Though Mark O'Brien, *The Deuteronomistic History Hypothesis: A Reassessment* (OBO 92; Freiberg, Schweiz: Universitätsverlag; Göttingen: Vandenhoeck u. Ruprecht, 1989), questions the extent of the pre-Dtr sources, he does not go as far as deny the existence of DtrH.

27   Frank Moore Cross, *Canaanite Myth and Hebrew Epic: Essays in the History of the Religion of Israel* (Cambridge: Harvard University Press, 1973), 274-289, Richard Nelson, *The Double Redaction of the Deuteronomistic History* (JSOTSup 18; Sheffield: JSOT Press, 1981), and Iain Provan, *Hezekiah and the Books of Kings: A Contribution to the Debate about the Composition of the Deuteronomistic History* (BZAW 172; Berlin: Walter de Gruyter: 1988). For discussions of alternative hypothesis, see Provan, *Hezekiah and the Books of Kings*, 4-31, O'Brien, *The Deuteronomistic History Hypothesis*, 3-12, Erik Eynikel, *The Reform of King Josiah and the Composition of the Deuteronomistic History* (OtSt 33; Leiden: E.J. Brill, 1996), 7-31, and Gary Knoppers and J. Gordon McConville, eds., *Reconsidering Israel and Judah: Recent Studies on the Deuteronomistic History* (Sources for Biblical and Theological Study 8; Winona Lake: Eisenbrauns, 2000). O'Brien, *The Deuteronomistic History Hypothesis*, 272-287, himself divides the redaction into three main levels with further redaction. For additional studies arguing for three levels of redaction, see Baruch Halpern and David Vanderhooft, "The Editions of Kings in the 7th-6th Centuries B.C.E.," *HUCA* 62 (1991):179-244, and William Schniedewind, "History and Interpretation: The Religion of Ahab and Manasseh in the Book of Kings," *CBQ* 55 (1993):650, note 4, where he finds traces of three stages of development but not throughout DtrH. Since the present study is not necessarily a thorough discussion of DtrH, it does not pretend to provide an exhaustive bibliography.

28   As outlined by Antony Campbell, *Of Prophets and Kings: A Late Ninth-Century Document (1 Samuel 1-2 Kings 10)* (CBQMS 17; Washington D.C.: Catholic Biblical Association of America, 1986), and advanced by O'Brien, *The Deuteronomistic History Hypothesis*.

safe to say that the editor was aware of and used well-established traditions, which he framed and molded according to his ideological and theological agenda. As a matter of fact, the obvious endorsement of the Davidic dynasty and its center of royal power, Jerusalem, in the first redaction would most likely reflect the period of King Josiah,[29] in whose reign the southern kingdom needed to mass support for its politically motivated religious reforms. Since the optimistic tone of the first redaction could not address and explain the reality of the despoliation and the destruction of the Temple, another editor in the post-exilic community inserted incriminations against Judah and additional indictments against Israel. In the end, the catastrophes of 722 B.C.E. and 587 B.C.E. would fall neatly into the framework of DtrH2's retributive schematization of history.

This brief introduction to the redaction of DtrH provides the context for the following discussion of the hiphil conjugation of כעס in the books of Deuteronomy to 2 Kings. In both levels of redaction, the term has a tendency to link the catalog of sins to the description of the punishment (sin-provocation-punishment).[30] As a pivot, though, the term has distinct roles, more or less along the two literary strands of DtrH. The ones attested in the first level of redaction[31] (1 Kgs 14:9, 15:30, 16:2, 13, 26, 33, 21:22, 22:53) are directed to the first three dynasties of the northern kingdom, Israel, while the attestations in the second level of redaction (Deut 4:25,[32] Deut 9:18,[33] 31:29,[34] Judg 2:12,[35]

---

29   Some scholars would date the first redaction to the period of Hezekiah (Provan, *Hezekiah and the Books of Kings*), when a mass of dissidents and refugees migrated from the north to the south. Though this is a possibility, especially with the positive and extensive portrayal of Hezekiah in the book of Kings (2 Kgs 18-20), the imminent threat of Assyrian aggression and the reparations after the siege during Hezekiah's reign would have preoccupied the king and the people. Although Jerusalem was still standing, supposedly a sign for the people of God's election of the city and its king, the rest of the kingdom was lying in utter ruins, "like a hut in a vineyard; like a cucumber in a field" (Isa 1:8; כסכה בכרם כמלונה במקשה). On the other hand, the power vacuum during the period of Josiah, resulting from the waning power of the Assyrian and Aramean forces, would have provided ample opportunity for the ambitious king, with an ideological program, to build and to consolidate his control over Judah and beyond. Thus, the first redaction probably dated to the period of Josiah's reign (with Erik Eynikel, *The Reform of King Josiah*). At the same time, though, an initial, limited redaction at the time of Hezekiah cannot be completely ruled out.

30   Exceptions and variations of this pattern (Deut 32:16, 21, 1 Kgs 14:9, 15, 16:26, 2 Kgs 17:11, 21:6) do arise in DtrH, but most of them are either additions or part of the larger framework of the pattern. These passages will be discussed in detail in the analysis of the pericopes.

31   The division of the references follow Nelson, *The Double Redaction*, 68, unless otherwise noted.

32   With Mayes, *Deuteronomy*, 148-149, and Jon Levenson, "Who Inserted the Book of the Torah?," *HTR* 68 (1975):203-233, contrary to Nelson, *The Double Redaction*, 68.

1 Kgs 14:15,[36] 16:7,[37] 2 Kgs 17:11, 17, 21:6,[38] 21:15, 22:17, 23:19, 26) are primarily concerned with explaining the demise of Samaria and Jerusalem. Within the two levels, a pattern emerges whereby the "God of history" works through his temporal instruments in DtrH1 while a variety of explanations — boomerang, divine wrath, and God with his instruments — appear in DtrH2.

Before analyzing the DtrH references, a short discussion of הכעיס in v. 16 and v. 21 of Deut 32, the Song of Moses, will be laid out separately since the Song stands apart from the two levels of redaction.

1.3. Deuteronomy 32:15-25 (vv. 16, 21)

Since the Song in Deut 32 is considered one of the earliest examples of biblical poetry, it is neither linked to DtrH1 nor DtrH2. However, the use of הכעיס in the Song, to a certain extent, lays the foundation for the way it functions in DtrH and also the book of Jeremiah. Though הכעיס in v. 16 and v. 21 does not function as a pivot, the fulcrum that balances the sin and the punishment, the term and its nominal form of the root (v. 19) does become the thematic word that links the indictment to the judgment. In fact, the punishment, in which

---

33   With Anthony Campbell and Mark O'Brien, *Unfolding the Deuteronomistic History: Origins, Upgrading, Present Text* (Minneapolis: Fortress Press, 2000), 61, contrary to Mayes, *Deuteronomy*, 194-196.

34   With Mayes, *Deuteronomy*, 379, and Levenson, "Who Inserted the Book of the Torah?," contrary to Nelson, *The Double Redaction*, 68.

35   Nelson, *The Double Redaction*, 68, attributes Judg 2:12 to DtrH1, but Cross, *Canaanite Myth and Hebrew Epic*, 275, correctly, attributes Judg 2:12 to the exilic editor (his DtrH2).

36   Though Eynikel, *The Reform of King Josiah*, 70, 72 (esp. note 115), and Nelson, *The Double Redaction*, 68, argue that the verse is DtrH1, it appears to be an exilic insertion. Eynikel, note 115, acknowledges the problem that "nowhere the Asherahs are mentioned in the description of Jeroboam's cult," but at the same time, he argues that "here Israel is condemned and this accusation is typical of DtrH1." This observation is not entirely true. DtrH1 is interested in the condemnation of Israelite kings, not the totality of Israel. Its people are only condemned in DtrH2 as it appears in 2 Kgs 17. Therefore, it should be attributed to DtrH2 (with O'Brien, *The Deuteronomistic Hypothesis*, 191, and Gary Knoppers, *Two Nations Under God: The Deuteronomistic History of Solomon and the Dual Monarchies* [HSM 52-53; Atlanta: Scholars Press, 1993-1994], 2:99-100, who would only attribute v. 15b to DtrH2).

37   Nelson, *The Double Redaction*, 68, attributes 1 Kgs 16:7 to DtrH1, which is inaccurate as will be discussed in the analysis of the passage. Eynikel, *The Reform of King Josiah*, 74, correctly attributes 1 Kgs 16:7 to the post-exilic editor. The inclusion of מעשׂה ידיו ("work of his hands") makes it a later insertion; see discussion below.

38   With Eynikel, *The Reform of King Josiah*, 70, 112-114, contrary to Nelson, *The Double Redaction*, 68. He argues that the vague reference to the sins is a sign of the post-exilic editor.

both YHWH and his divine wrath are the agents, is formulated to parallel the description of the sin, creating a measure-for-measure punishment.

Deut 32:1-44, originally independent of the book of Deuteronomy,[39] consists of a Song purported to have been taught by Moses to the Israelites before his death. The poem in the expanded lawsuit (ריב) form[40] reflects on God's salvific deeds, Israelites' violations, the consequent punishment consisting of

---

39　According to Gerhard von Rad *Deuteronomy: A Commentary* (OTL; Philadelphia: Westminster Press, 1966), 195. Since the Song seems to recognize and legitimate other minor deities (vv. 8-9), many have considered the Song to be quite distinct from the book of Deuteronomy. The Song recites how God allotted the foreign nations to the 'sons of god' (v. 8; based on LXX, Qumran scrolls, Symmachus, and Latin fragment, in contrast to the MT which has בני ישראל ["the sons of Israel"] which is probably an editorial modification to 'tone down' the allowance of other deities). If this is the case, then the Song presumes that there are other deities (contrary to Patrick Skehan, "The Structure of the Song of Moses in Deuteronomy (32:1-43)," reprinted in *A Song of Power and the Power of Song: Essays on the Book of Deuteronomy* [ed. Duane Christensen; Sources for Biblical and Theological Study 3; Winona Lake: Eisenbrauns, 1993], 156-159), which, according to some scholars, would contradict the book of Deuteronomy since it emphasizes the sole existence of YHWH (see 4:35, 39, 6:4, 7:9, 32:39, and J.T.A.G.M. van Ruiten, "The Use of Deuteronomy 32:39 in Monotheistic Controversies in Rabbinic Literature" in *Studies in Deuteronomy: In Honour of C.J. Labuschagne on the Occasion of his 65ᵗʰ Birthday* [VTSup 53; eds. F. Garcia, et al; Leiden: E.J. Brill, 1994], 223-241). However, this does not necessarily contradict vv. 8-9 but represent the tension between the two notions in the Song as well as in the book of Deuteronomy which also recognizes other heavenly beings; see Deut 4:19, where "YHWH, your God allotted them (the heavenly bodies) to other people everywhere under the heavens" (חלק יהוה אלהיך אתם לכל העמים תחת כל־השמים), 29:25, and Yair Hoffman, "The Conception of 'Other Gods' in Deuteronomistic Literature," *Israel Oriental Studies* 14 (1994):103-118. A more convincing argument for the separation between the Song and the rest of the book is the failure of the poem to mention the covenant which plays a significant role in the book of Deuteronomy.

40　As briefly discussed by Mayes, *Deuteronomy*, 380-381, and in detail, G. Wright, "The Lawsuit of God: A Form-Critical Study of Deuteronomy 32," in *Israel's Prophetic Heritage: Essays in Honor of James Muilenburg* (eds. Bernhard Anderson and Walter Harrelson; New York: Harper & Brothers, 1962), 26-67; contrary to George Mendenhall, "Samuel's 'Broken Rib': Deuteronomy 32," in *A Song of Power and the Power of Song: Essays on the Book of Deuteronomy* (ed. Duane Christensen; Sources for Biblical and Theological Study 3; Winona Lake: Eisenbrauns, 1993), 178-179, who considers the Song to be a "prophetic oracle essentially concerned with the interpretation of history past, and appealing for public opinion that would make the future more palatable." For rejection of the whole genre, see Michael de Roche, "Yahweh's *rib* Against Israel: A Reassessment of the So-Called 'Prophetic Lawsuit' in the Preexilic Prophets," *JBL* 102 (1983):563-574, and Dwight Daniels, "Is There a 'Prophetic Lawsuit' Genre?," *ZAW* 99 (1987):339-360, who both argue against the existence of the 'prophetic lawsuit' genre.

　　Since it contains both legal indictments as well as wisdom instructions, scholars have categorized the Song under the covenant lawsuit, wisdom instruction, or instructions of the dying sage (for this genre, see Steven Weitzman, "Lessons from the Dying: The Role of Deuteronomy 32 in its Narrative Setting," *HTR* 87 [1994]:377-393; the article also discusses the present state of scholarship on the topic).

war and natural disasters, and their restoration. Given the vague and general allusions to the destructive elements, for example, references to natural calamities (v.24)[41] and violence (v. 25),[42] it is difficult to date the Song. Therefore scholars have dated the Song anywhere from the period of the judges (ca. 1200-1000 B.C.E.) to the post-exilic period (post-586 B.C.E.).[43] Yet the majority of the proposals place the Song in the pre-exilic period since many of its themes reverberate in the Bible, in particular, DtrH[44] and the book of Jeremiah.[45] One of these themes is the use of הכעיס in v. 16 and v. 21.

To understand the placement of the terms (vv. 16, 21), we will briefly discuss the overall structure of the poem, before focusing on the immediate contexts of הכעיס. The chapter opens with a summon to the heavenly and earthly witnesses (v. 1). Then it contrasts the 'corruption' of Israel with the faithfulness of God forming a type of a historical prologue (vv. 2-14). The formal segment of the indictment does not appear until vv. 15-18 which is then followed by the verdict (punishment) in vv. 19-25.[46] Thereafter vv. 26-43 con-

---

41   For example, "wasting famine" (מזי רעב), "consuming pestilence" (לחמי רשף), "deadly plague" (קטב מרירי), "fangs of beasts" (שן־בהמות), and "venom of vipers" (חמת זחלי עפר).

42   For instance, "sword" (חרב) and "terror" (אימה).

43   Many scholars would date the text to the pre-exilic period. Moshe Weinfeld, *Deuteronomy 1-11: A New Translation with Introduction and Commentary* (AB 5; New York: Doubleday, 1991), 9, states that it is an old poem; Jeffrey Tigay, *Deuteronomy: The Traditional Hebrew Text with the New JPS Translation* (JPS Torah Commentary; Philadelphia: Jewish Publication Society, 1996), Excursus 30, 508-513 (see Mayes', *Deuteronomy*, discussion, 381), prefers to date the poem to the period of the judges, while Paul Sanders, *The Provenance of Deuteronomy 32* (OtSt 37; Leiden: E.J. Brill, 1996), dates most of the poem to the period of Hezekiah. S.R. Driver, *A Critical and Exegetical Commentary on Deuteronomy* (ICC 3; Edinburgh: T. & T. Clark, 1902), 346, would however date it to the period of Jehoash or Jeroboam. On the other hand, Mayes, *Deuteronomy*, 382, dates the poem to the exilic or post-exilic period on account of the lawsuit form and wisdom elements.

44   According to Jon Levenson, "Who Inserted," 217, "the Song of Moses exerted not only an influence of a literary nature on the exilic hand, but also a profound theological influence over the entirety of his bracket. The exilic frame to Dtn is the sermon for which the Song of Moses is the text." This is further discussed in Sanders, *Provenance*, 333-352. Moreover, the poem seems to reverberate in other parts of the Bible. There are many parallels between the poem and the book of Hosea as well as Isaiah and Jeremiah and parts of the poem spring up in Pss 78 and 106. As a result, it seems more likely that the poem was earlier than all of these writings. See also Driver, *A Critical and Exegetical Commentary on Deuteronomy*, 347.

45   See George Mendenhall, "Samuel's 'Broken Rîb,'"169-180.

46   According to Sanders, *The Provenance of Deuteronomy 32*, 264, as opposed to Wright, "The Lawsuit of God," 35, who would extend the section only to v. 29. Yet Wright also acknowledges that vv. 26-29 shifts to the enemy nation.

tinue to elaborate on the true God's beneficence upon the faltering Israelites and vengeance on their enemies.[47]

With the broad structure of the Song outlined, the two occurrences of הכעיס can now be discussed in their contexts. The first attestation (v. 16) occurs in the indictment (vv. 15-18) while the other (v. 21) appears in the judgment section of the Song (vv. 19-25), both of which are then connected by the nominal form of the root, כעס, in v. 19:

Catalog of Sins (vv. 15-18):
    Rejection of God

(15 וישמן ישרון ויבעט שמנת עבית כשית
ויטש אלוה עשהו וינבל צור ישעתו

    Worship of Other Deities — Provocation (Hiphil)

(16 יקנאהו בזרים בתועבת <u>יכעיסהו</u>

    Additional Description of Idolatry

(17 יזבחו לשדים לא אלה אלהים לא ידעום

---

47   As partially outlined by Herbert Huffmon, "The Covenant Lawsuit in the Prophets," *JBL* 78 (1959):289. He would begin the accusation section with vv. 5-6a, interrupted by God's mighty deeds (vv. 6b-14), which then resumes in v. 15. Sanders, *Provenance*, 264, provides a more detailed outline of the structure as follows:

    Vv. 1-2:   Exhortation to listen

    Vv. 3-4:   Introduction to the song's theme, the laudability of YHWH because of his character

    Vv. 5-6:   Accusation of Israel because of its disloyalty

    V. 7:   Admonition to remember the past

    Vv. 8-14:   Description of YHWH's election of Israel and of his care for Israel in the past

    Vv. 15-18:   Description of Israel's apostasy and its veneration of foreign gods

    Vv. 19-25:   Description of YHWH's reaction: He decides to punish Israel with all kinds of disasters

    Vv. 26-31:   YHWH's change of opinion because of lack of insight on the part of Israel's enemy

    Vv. 32-35:   Israel's adversaries are cruel towards Israel but YHWH stresses that he remains in control of his wrath and that his wrath is going to strike the enemies too

    V. 36:   YHWH will have compassion on Israel

    Vv. 37-38:   YHWH tries to demonstrate that the veneration of foreign gods is useless as these gods are unable to interfere in human affairs

    V. 39:   YHWH says he is the only real god and claims sovereignty over both life and death

    Vv. 40-42:   YHWH promises to take vengeance on Israel's enemies

    V. 43:   The poet summons the celestials to honour YHWH for his vengeance on Israel's enemies and his restoration of Israel

The outline does not exactly resemble the two basic outlines of a lawsuit as presented in Herbert Huffmon, "The Covenant Lawsuit in the Prophets," 285-286 nor are the accusations primarily in second person. Nevertheless, it does contain elements of a lawsuit, namely the appeal to the natural elements.

חדשים מקרב באו לא שערום אבתיכם

18) צור ילדך תשי ותשכח אל מחללך

Verdict (vv. 19-25) — Provocation (Noun)

19) וירא יהוה וינאץ מכעס בניו ובנתיו

20) ויאמר אסתירה פני מהם אראה מה אחריתם

כי דור תהפכת המה בנים לא־אמן בם

Reason — Provocation (Piel)

21) הם קנאוני בלא־אל כעסוני בהבליהם

Punishment — Provocation (Hiphil)

ואני אקניאם בלא־עם בגוי נבל אכעיסם

22) כי־אש קדחה באפי ותיקד עד־שאול תחתית

ותאכל ארץ ויבלה ותלהט מוסדי הרים

23) אספה עלימו רעות חצי אכלה־בם

24) מזי רעב ולחמי רשף וקטב מרירי

ושן־בהמות אשלח־בם עם־חמת זחלי עפר

25) מחוץ תשכל־חרב ומחדרים אימה

גם־בחור גם־בתולה יונק עם־איש שיבה

15) When Jeshurun grew fat, he kicked; you grew fat, thick, and sated.[48]
He forsook God, who made him, and he scoffed at the rock of his salvation.

16) They stirred him to jealousy with foreign gods; with abominations, they provoked him to anger.[49]

17) They sacrificed to demons which are not gods, to gods they had not known; To new gods who came recently, whom your[50] fathers had not revered.

18) You neglected the rock which bore you; you forgot the God who gave you birth.

---

48   The Greek has third masculine singular form for the three verbs (כשה — "to be sated," עבה — "to be thick," שמן — "to be fat") instead of second masculine singular in the MT.

49   V. 16 has textual variants for all its words: Samaritan manuscript has ויקניאהו ("and they stirred him to jealousy") and the Greek, except Ambrosianus, has first person common singular suffix ("they stirred me to jealousy") instead of the third masculine singular suffix ("they stirred him to jealousy," יקנאהו); the Vulgate may possibly reflect an Urtext of באלהים זרים ("with foreign deities") for בזרים ("with foreigners"); Samaritan manuscript, Latin, Syriac, and Vulgate reflect ובתועבת ("and with abominations") for בתועבת ("with abominations"); and G, except Vaticanus, reflect first person common singular suffix ('they provoked me to anger') instead of the third masculine singular suffix for יכעיסהו ("they provoked him to anger"). The variants may represent the more correct reading but they are not significant except the different pronominal suffixes on the verbs, יקנאהו and יכעיסהו. However, with the shifting of persons in the poem, it is difficult to decide the original reading.

50   As opposed to Greek, minus the Origen recension, Targum, and Vulgate have third masculine plural suffix ('their') instead of the MT second masculine plural form ('your').

19) YHWH saw and he spurned on account of the <u>provocation</u> of his sons and his daughters.

20) He said, "I will hide my face from them. I will see what will be their end, for they are a perverse generation, children in whom there is no faithfulness.

21) They have stirred me to jealousy with no-god; <u>they have provoked me to anger</u> with their vanities. Therefore, I will stir them to jealousy with no-people; with a foolish nation, <u>I will provoke them to anger</u>.

22) For a fire is kindled in my nose, and it burns to the depths of Sheol; It devours the earth and its increase, and it sets aflame the foundations of the mountains.

23) I will gather[51] calamities upon them; I will spend my arrows against them.

24) Emptiness from hunger, consumption by pestilence, bitter destruction, and fangs of beasts, I will send against them, along with the venom of vipers.

25) Outside, the sword will bereave, from inner-chambers, terror, the young man and young woman, the infant with the gray-haired man.

The catalog of sins (vv.15-18) elaborates on the sins of Israel, namely their complacency and apostasy, which comprises of two parts — rejection of God and worship of other deities. To emphasize the gravity of the misdeeds, synonyms for verbs referring to the opulence, rejection of God, and worship of other gods, as well as various terms for these deities, are concentrated in the four verses. When Jeshurun (יְשֻׁרוּן),[52] another name for Israel, grew fat (וַיִּשְׁמַן, "he grew fat;" עָבִיתָ, "you grew thick;" and כָּשִׂיתָ, "you were sated," v. 15a), they spurned their God (וַיִּטֹּשׁ, "he forsook;" וַיְנַבֵּל, "he scoffed," v. 15b; וַתִּשְׁכַּח, "you forgot;" and חָשׁ, "you neglected," v. 18) and stirred God's angering jealousy (יַקְנִאֻהוּ, "they stirred him to jealousy;" יַכְעִסֻהוּ, "they provoked him to anger," v. 16) with other deities (בְּזָרִים, "with foreign gods;" בְּתוֹעֵבֹת, "with abominations," v. 16) and sacrificed to them (שֵׁדִים, "demons who are not gods;" לֹא אֱלֹהַּ, "gods they had not known," v. 17a).

It is within the context of clarifying the apostasy, where הַכְעִיס first appears in the Song. The perfectly chiastic, parallel bicolon introduces the Israelites' idolatry:

They stirred him to jealousy *with foreign gods*;	A B	יַקְנִאֻהוּ בְּזָרִים
With abominations they provoked him to anger.	B'A'	בְּתוֹעֵבֹת יַכְעִיסֻהוּ

---

51   Since the hiphil of סָפָה does not make sense, *BDB*, 705 and BHS note vocalize the verbal form to a qal of אָסַף ('gather') which may reflect the Greek and Vulgate.

52   Deut 33:5, 26 and Isa 44:2; see also Sander's, *Provenance*, 179-180, for a brief discussion of the word.

At this point, one might expect the punishment according to the pivot pattern, but instead, the following verses (vv. 17-18) specify the means by which the Israelites were worshipping other deities. As a result, הכעיס may not function as a pivot, pointing directly to the punishment; nevertheless, it is ultimately linked to the verdict through the use of its root in the nominal form in v. 19[53] and its recurrence in v. 21.

In the opening verse of the verdict (v. 19), God is said to "take notice" (וירא) and "reject" (וינאץ) because of the "provocation" (כעס) of his children. This "provocation" (כעס) most likely refers back to the הכעיס of v. 16 so that God's response, i.e. rejection, could only have been evoked by God's anger aroused by the idolatry:

$$\text{Sin (Apostasy-יכעיסהו, v. 16)} = \text{Provocation (כעס, v. 19)} \rightarrow$$
$$\text{Punishment (Rejection, v. 19)}$$

Thus, while the generally pivotal term, הכעיס, did not directly introduce the punishment in the Song, it signaled the coming of the punishment. In other words, it sparked the flames that developed into the fire of the punishment.

Here, the initial part of the punishment, as laid out in v. 19, does not completely correspond to the description of the sin. However, later on in v. 21, the punishment corresponds measure-for-measure.

The first half of v. 21, the reason for the punishment, contains a variation of v. 16, which is then followed by an elaboration of the punishment in the second half of v. 21:

They stirred him to jealousy with foreign gods,	יקנאהו בזרים
with abominations they provoked him to anger.	בתועבת יכעיסהו (v.16)
They have stirred me to jealousy with no-god;	הם קנאוני בלא־אל
they have provoked me to anger with their vanities.	כעסוני בהבליהם (v. 21a)
Therefore, I will stir them to jealousy with no-people;	ואני אקניאם בלא־עם
with a foolish nation I will provoke them to anger.	בגוי־נבל אכעיסם (v. 21b)

Though v. 21a neither follows the chiastic structure nor the verbal conjugation (hiphil) of v. 16, it nevertheless uses the same verbal roots, albeit in the piel, and develops the theme of idolatry. In order to establish the cause-effect relationship between the catalog of sins and the punishment that appears in the

---

53 Notice the recurrence of the noun (v. 27) in reference to the "provocation of the enemy" (כעס). In this instance, the enemy's provocation prevents God from completely destroying the Israelites whereas in v. 19, it provides the motivation for God to act in wrath.

following bicolon (v. 21b), the explicit parallels were made to echo the sins of v. 16. Since the people stirred God's jealousy and anger with useless gods, God, in return, will "stir them to jealousy" (אקניאם) with "no people" (לא־ עם) and to "provoke them to anger" (אכעיסם) with a "foolish nation" (גוי נבל).[54] Therefore, apostasy leads directly to a measure-for-measure punishment:

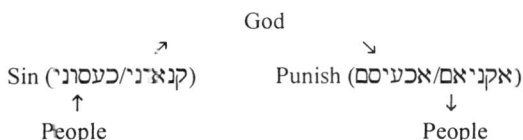

What goes around comes around, completing a whole circle.

Yet the full elaboration of the punishment (vv. 22-25) is more varied in describing the agency of the destruction. First of all, in v. 22, a concretized manifestation of divine wrath ("fire sparked in my nose," אש קדחה באפי) becomes the means of destruction. This "fire" acts independently; it "burns" (ותיקד), "consumes" (ותאכל), and "ignites" (ותלהט)[55] the earthly realm to the very depths. Second, in v. 23, God actively punishes with his instrument — the deity "gathers" (אכפה) his calamities, "consumes" (אכלה) with his arrows, and "sends" (אשלח) natural disasters. Third and finally, the "sword/terror" (חרב/אימה, v. 25), perhaps metaphors for war, are active in executing the punishment by "bereaving" (תשכל) the general populace.

Why would the Song list the various agents from the fire of God's wrath (v. 22) to God and his weapons (vv. 23-24), and then to the weapon itself (v. 25)? Most likely, the Song wanted to provide a thorough description of the punishment. That way, every catastrophic event would fall under God's control.

All in all, Deut 32 provides various formulations of the punishment which appear in DtrH and the book of Jeremiah with God and his instruments occur-

---

54   As evident in the derogatory designation of the foreign nations, the Song did not favor them more than the Israelites. After all, the "no people" (לא־עם) and "foolish nation" (גוי־נבל) worshiped "no god" (לא־אל) and "vanities" (הבלים). It would not make sense for a 'superior' people to follow such useless deities. Compare with the esteemed portrayal of Nebuchadnezzar in the book of Jeremiah, which is discussed in Part III.

55   There are variant readings of these verbs: Greek, minus some minor manuscripts, omit the copula before ותיקד ("and it burned") while the Samaritan Pentateuch and a Hebrew manuscript has תוקד ("it was burned"); the Samaritan Pentateuch, Greek, Syriac, and Targum does not have a copula before תאכל ("it will consume"); and the Samaritan Pentateuch, Greek, and Targum does not have a copula before תלהט ("it will ignite"). These variants seem to accentuate the imperfect aspect of the verbs.

ring more frequently in the earlier levels of DtrH1 and the book of Jeremiah
and other formulations — boomerang, divine wrath, and self-destruction — in
later levels (DtrH2 and later additions of Jeremiah).

1.4. Redaction Level One – Dynastic Curse Formulae

In the first level of redaction, הכעיס is used only against the northern kingdom, not to forebode the fall of Samaria, but to augur the destruction of the
initial dynasties. The term appears most prominently in the curse formulae
against the first three dynasties — the houses of Jeroboam (1 Kgs 14:9, 15:30),
Baasha (1 Kgs 16:2, 13), and Omri (1 Kgs 16:26, 33, 21:22, 22:54). Therefore,
הכעיס is primarily evident in indictments of the northern dynasties that rule
the rebellious kingdom of Israel.

1.4.1. Introduction to Dynastic Curse Formulae

In DtrH1, the term, הכעיס, figures primarily in the curse formulae prophesying
the decimation of the first three dynasties. Usually the curse formulae against
the individual dynasties consist of two components: 1) the prophetic pronouncement of the dynastic founder's utter cessation; and 2) an account of its
fulfillment in the postlude of the last king of the dynasty. Whereas the pattern
is consistent in the narrative of the first two dynasties (Jeroboam and
Baashide), it begins to disintegrate in the account of the third dynasty (Omride) and disappears altogether in the accounts of the subsequent rulers. Before
a detailed analysis of the individual dynastic curse formulae, an overview of
the general pattern will be initially laid out.

1.4.1.1. Prophetic Pronouncements

The founders of the first two houses — Jeroboam and Baasha — and Ahab,
the *de facto* head of the Omride dynasty,[56] receive the prophetic pronouncement of dynastic destruction that is introduced by הכעיס:

---

56 The *de jure* founder of the third dynasty, Omri, is also attributed with provoking God (1 Kgs
    16:26); however the accusation of sins occurs without an elaboration of the punishment:

    וילך בכל־דרך ירבעם בן־נבט ובחטאתיו אשר החטיא את־ישראל
    להכעיס את־יהוה אלהי ישראל בהבליהם

    He walked in all the ways of Jeroboam, son of Nebat, and in all his sins which he made Israel
    commit, provoking YHWH, God of Israel, with their delusions.

A) Jeroboam (1 Kgs 14:9-11):

9) ‏... להכעיסני ...‏
10) ‏לכן הנני מביא רעה אל־בית ירבעם‏
‏והכרתי לירבעם משתין בקיר עצור ועזוב בישראל‏
‏*ובערתי אחרי בית־ירבעם* כאשר יבער הגלל עד־תמו‏
11) ‏<u>המת לירבעם בעיר יאכלו הכלבים</u>‏
‏<u>והמת בשדה יאכלו עוף השמים</u> כי יהוה דבר‏

9) ... to provoke me ...
10) Therefore I am about to bring evil against the house of Jeroboam. I will cut off from Jeroboam, every male, both bond and free in Israel; *I will exterminate the house of Jeroboam* as one burns up dung until it is completely consumed.
11) <u>The dogs will consume the dead belonging to Jeroboam in the city; the birds of the heavens will consume the dead in the field.</u> For YHWH has spoken.

B) Baasha (1 Kgs 16:2-4):

2) ‏... להכעיסני בחטאתם‏
3) ‏*הנני מבעיר אחרי בעשא ואחרי ביתו*‏
‏ונתתי את־ביתך כבית ירבעם בן־נבט‏
4) ‏<u>המת לבעשא בעיר יאכלו הכלבים</u>‏
‏<u>והמת לו בשדה יאכלו עוף השמים</u>‏

2) ... to provoke me with their sin
3) *I am about to exterminate Baasha and his house.* I will make your house like the house of Jeroboam, the son of Nebat.
4) <u>The dogs will consume the dead belonging to Baasha in the city; the birds of the heavens will consume his dead in the field.</u>

C) Ahab (1 Kgs 21:21-24):[57]

21) ‏הנני מבי אליך רעה *ובערתי אחריך*‏
‏והכרתי לאדאב משתין בקיר ועצור ועזוב בישראל‏
22) ‏ונתתי את־ב־תך כבית ירבעם בן־נבט וכבית בעשא בן־אחיה‏
‏אל־הכעס אשר הכעסת ותחטא את־ישראל‏
23) ‏וגם־לאיזבל דבר יהוה לאמר‏
‏הכלבים יאכלו את־איזבל בחל יזרעאל‏
24) ‏<u>המת לאחאב בעיר יאכלו הכלבים</u>‏
‏<u>והמת בשדה יאכלו עוף השמים</u>‏

21) I am about to bring evil against you and *exterminate you.* I will cut off from Ahab, every male, both bond and free, in Israel.

---

57 As will be discussed in section 1.4.4.3., vv. 21-22a, 24 may have been originally intended for Omri but was later transposed to Ahab.

22) I will make your house like the house of Jeroboam, son of Nebat, and like
the house of Baasha, son of Ahijah, on account of the provocation with
which you provoked (me) to anger and caused Israel to sin.

23) And also for Jezebel, YHWH said, "The dogs will consume Jezebel in the
fortress of Jezreel.

24) <u>The dogs will consume the dead belonging to Ahab in the city; the birds of
the heavens will consume the dead in the field.</u>

Despite the variation in the prophetic pronouncements, the promise to "exterminate" (בער אחרי) the dynasty (in italics above), and consumption by the
dogs[58] and birds (underlined above) are consistent. This would indicate a pur-
poseful link between these three dynasties.[59]

1.4.1.2. Fulfillments with the Last King of the Dynasty

After the prophetic pronouncements against the dynastic founders (as listed
above), DtrH1 then documents its fulfillment in the postludes of the last kings
of each dynasty, except the Omride dynasty where the fulfillment is dispersed
throughout the accounts of Ahab's death (1 Kgs 22:37-38) and Jehu's rise (2
Kgs 9-10). Within the extrapolation of the prophetic fulfillment, הכעיס provides the justification for the punishment, again except for the Omride dynasty:

A) House of Jeroboam — Last Ruler, Nadab (1 Kgs 15:30):

30) *על־חטאות ירבעם אשר חטא ואשר החטיא את־ישראל*
בכעסו אשר הכעיס את־יהוה אלהי ישראל

30)   *... on account of the sins of Jeroboam which he committed and had made
Israel commit,* (namely) the provocation with which he provoked YHWH,
the God of Israel, to anger.

---

58 The dogs' consumption of Jezebel (1 Kgs 21:23), most likely an addition (see below for
discussion), is echoed in 2 Kgs 9:10, 36 when the judgment is fulfilled.

59 What is unique to the curse formula against Ahab is the phraseology (v. 22b) that appears in
the fulfillment oracle that is outlined below. The willing partner in crime, Ahab, and his des-
potic wife, Jezebel, receive considerable negative attention and much disapproval. This may
explain the additional accusation with הכעיס against Ahab (1 Kgs 16:33) which does not follow any of the formulaic pronouncement:

33) ויעש אחאב את־האשרה
ויוסף אחאב לעשות להכעיס את־יהוה אלהי ישראל
מכל מלכי ישראל אשר היו לפניו

33) Ahab made the Asherah and he did more to provoke YHWH, the God of Israel, to anger
more than all the kings of Israel who were before him.

B) House of Baasha — Last Ruler, Elah (1 Kgs 16:13):

13) *אל כל־חטאות בעשא וחטאות אלה בנו*
אשר חטאו ואשר החטיאו את־ישראל
להכעיס את־יהוה אלהי ישראל בהבליהם

13)   *... on account of all the sins of Baasha and the sins of Elah, his son, which they committed and had made Israel commit,* <u>provoking YHWH, the God of Israel, to anger with their delusions.</u>

However, הכעיס appears in the account of Ahaziah, the second to the last ruler of the Omride dynasty, in the form of another indictment:

House of Omri (Ahab) — Second to Last Ruler, Ahaziah (1 Kgs 22:53-54):[60]

53) ויעש הרע בעיני יהוה וילך בדרך אביו ובדרך *אמו*
ובדרך ירבעם בן־נבט אשר החטיא את־ישראל
54) ויעבד את־דבעל וישתחוה לו
<u>ויכעס את־יהוה אלהי ישראל ככל אשר־עשה אביו</u>

53)   He did evil in the eyes of YHWH and he walked in the ways of his father and his mother and Jeroboam, son of Nebat, *who made Israel sin.*

54)   He served Ba'al and worshipped him and <u>provoked YHWH, the God of Israel, to anger like all that his father had done.</u>

The three kings (Nadab, Elah, and Ahaziah) are thus accused of sins with which they provoke YHWH to anger. Yet how is their punishment executed?

---

60   Ultimately, Jehoram is the last and only Omride ruler, unlike Omri, Ahab, and Ahaziah, who avoids the prophetic pronouncement and its accompanying fulfillment oracle. Most likely, the curse formulae against the dynastic rulers was extended to Ahab for his supposed introduction of Ba'alism (1 Kgs 16:33), and Ahaziah, who continued to worship Ba'al (1 Kgs 22:53), as opposed to Jehoram, the final Omride, who removed the pillars of Ba'al (2 Kgs 3:2). Jehoram may have followed the sins of Jeroboam but he did not follow in his fathers' footsteps; therefore, he is not attributed with having provoked God to anger. Thus in DtrH1, הכעיס functions primarily as a pivot to signal the end of a dynasty with a special link to the Omride dynasty for its royal endorsement of Ba'alism. Thus, הכעיס is not specifically linked to the sin of Jeroboam. In fact, הכעיס occurs primarily in the context of apostasy with the mention of particular deities (1 Kgs 16:33 — Asherah; 22:54 — Ba'al); in general (1 Kgs 14:9 — אלהים אחרים ומסכות, "other gods and molten images"); 16:13 and 26 — בהבליהם, "with their delusions"); or without specific mention (1 Kgs 15:30, 21:22, 2 Kgs 23:19). Beside an indirect reference (1 Kgs 14:9) and circuitous link (1 Kgs 15:30, 15:26, and 21:22) to the 'sin of Jeroboam,' the expression is not exclusively related to the sin that is connected to the demise of Samaria (2 Kgs 17:21). Had הכעיס been connected to the 'sins of Jeroboam,' the expression would then have been attributed to all the kings of Israel. However, this is not the case. See next note.

In general, the prophetic pronouncements attribute the role of punishing the culprits to God; however, when it comes to the actual act in the account of the fulfillment, human instruments take center stage as executors of the destruction. While God may be the one who promises to annihilate the dynasties (1 Kgs 14:9, 16:2, 21:22), it is actually the human pawn, the illegitimate rulers-to-be, who carry out the oracles (1 Kgs 15:30, 16:13, 1 Kgs 22:37-38, 2 Kgs 9-10). Even in the indictment of Ahaziah where the punishment is only implied within the literary context, a human instrument executes the prophetic oracle. In 1 Kgs 22:54, the description of the sin of apostasy is not directly followed by an outline of the consequent punishment. Rather the catalog of sins is juxtaposed to a historical footnote (2 Kgs 1:1), which functions as the description of the punishment itself. Therefore, the editor who organized the stories intended Moab's rebellion in 2 Kgs 1:1 to be read as a punishment for Ahaziah (1 Kgs 22:54).

Given the prophetic curse-fulfillment pattern against the dynasties, in which the agency of destruction is primarily divine-human, there is some correspondence between the sin and the punishment. For the Israelite kings' act of apostasy (Jeroboam, Baasha, and Ahab), the punishment consisting of the dynasties' utter decimation does not necessarily seem to fit their sins. Could the rulers' rejection of God earmark the cessation of a dynasty? However, since the people of Israel do not usually suffer the consequences of the kings' wrongdoings, the punishment seems just: The kings reject God and God, in return, reject the king and his family. At the same time, though, this simple equation does not span out in situations where the mass population is affected (2 Kgs 1:1).

For full elaboration of the pattern, the accounts of each dynasty will be discussed in detail below.

Chart A: Pericopes with הכעיס in DtrH1

Passage	Type of Sin	Form of הכעיס	Culprit	Pivot	Type of Punishment	Agency
Deut 32:15-25						
v. 16	Idolatry	לכעסהו	Israel	No. But מכעס (v. 19) = pivot	See below	See below
v. 21	Idolatry	כעסוני (Piel) // אכעיסם (Hiphil)	Israel	No	V. 21: Boomerang	V. 21: God / V. 22: Divine wrath / Vv. 23-25: Instruments
1 Kgs 14:7-11 [9] (Jeroboam)	Idolatry + ("molten images")	להכעיסני	Jeroboam	No. But motivate punishment	Evil and decimation of dynasty	God
1 Kgs 15:29-30 [30] (Baasha)	Sin of Jeroboam	בכעסו אשר הכעיס	Jeroboam	Yes – Reverse	Fulfillment of prophecy Decimation of dynasty	Baasha – According to God's word
1 Kgs 16:2-4 [2] (Baasha)	Sin of Jeroboam	להכעיסני	Baasha	Yes	Decimation of dynasty	God
1 Kgs 16:11-13 [13] (Zimri)	Sin of Baasha and Elah	הכעיסו	Baasha	Yes – Reverse	Fulfillment of prophecy Decimation of dynasty	Zimri – According to God's word
1 Kgs 16:25-26 [26] (Omri)	Sin of Jeroboam	הכעיסו	Omri	No	No punishment	NA
1 Kgs 16:30-33 [33] (Ahab)	Sin of Jeroboam + Baal + Asherah	להכעיס	Ahab	Yes	Drought (1 Kgs 17:1)	Implied – God
1 Kgs 21:20b-26 [22] (Ahab)	"Sold" (התמכר) to do evil	הכעסת אשר הכעסת	Ahaziah	Yes	Rebellion of Moab (2 Kgs 1:1)	Moab

1.4.2. The Dynasty of Jeroboam
1 Kings 14:7-11 (v. 9) and 15:29-30 (v. 30)

In the DtrH worldview, YHWH could only be worshipped in the Temple of Jerusalem. As a result, any and all alternative sanctuaries were perceived as a serious affront to the DtrH God. Therefore, the establishment of separate centers of worship in Bethel and Dan with the formation of the northern kingdom sealed the fate of the founding Israelite king, Jeroboam I, and the consequent rulers of Israel.[61] With this sacrilege, Jeroboam provokes God and his dynasty receives its due punishment from a usurper, Baasha.

1.4.2.1. 1 Kings 14:7-11

The term, הכעיס, occurs twice in the narrative concerning Jeroboam, to first provide the justification for the prophetic pronouncement against his dynasty (1 Kgs 14:9) and second to explain the relationship between the sin and the punishment in its fulfillment.[62] On account of the emphasis on the prophetic word in DtrH, the message of Jeroboam's demise is mediated through Ahijah,

---

61   The list of northern kings who followed the sins of Jeroboam and provoked God (see Appendix B which has a chart of הכעיס as it occurs among the kings of Israel and Judah): 1 Kgs 14:9 (Jeroboam — do evil and make other gods and images, מסכות); 1 Kgs 14:15 (recounting the sins of Jeroboam); 1 Kgs 15:30 (Nadab — misled Israel with the sin of Jeroboam); 1 Kgs 16:2 (Baasha — followed the way of Jeroboam and caused people to sin); 1 Kgs 16:7 (Baasha — with מעשׂה ידיו ["work of his hands"] and being like the house of Jeroboam); 1 Kgs 16:26 (Omri — following the ways of Jeroboam); 1 Kgs 21:22 (Ahab — like the house of Jeroboam); and 1 Kgs 22:54 (Ahaziah, son of Ahab — in the ways of Jeroboam); and fall of Samaria (2 Kgs 17:21).
      Even those who did not receive a 'rating' in the form of an accusation of provoking God are accused of following Jeroboam: Jehoram (no incriminating comments on this king perhaps on account of the confusion between him and Joram of Judah - perhaps the same person, see J. Maxwell Miller and John Hayes, *A History of Ancient Israel and Judah* [Philadelphia: Westminster Press, 1986], 223); Jehu (rid the land of Ba'al worship but still followed the sins of Jeroboam, 2 Kgs 10:28-31), Jehoahaz (followed sins of Jeroboam, 2 Kgs 13:11), Joash (no incriminating comments), Jeroboam II (followed sins of Jeroboam, 2 Kgs 14:24), Zechariah (followed sins of Jeroboam, 2 Kgs 15:9), Shallum (no incriminating comments), Menahem (followed sins of Jeroboam, 2 Kgs 15:17), Pekahiah (followed sins of Jeroboam, 2 Kgs 15:24), and Pekah (followed sins of Jeroboam, 2 Kgs 15:28).
      Jeroboam was the archetypal *Unheilsherrscher*, Carl Evans, "Naram-Sin and Jeroboam: The Archetypal *Unheilsherrscher* in Mesopotamian and Biblical Historiography," in *Scripture in Context II: More Essays on the Comparative Method* (eds. William Hallo, James Moyer, and Leo Perdue; Winona Lake: Eisenbrauns, 1983), 97-125. In the article, he compares Jeroboam with Naram-Sin, both principal founding 'anti-hero' figures whom the ancient authors tend to base their assessment of the consequent history.
62   The word also appears in 14:15 but this is a later addition to include all of Israel; see next section on DtrH2.

the prophet (14:7-11), whose word is then fulfilled in 15:28-30. In the context of the historical account of Jeroboam,[63] Jeroboam's child, Abijah, becomes sick, whereupon the king sends his wife to the prophet, Ahijah. Upon her arrival, Ahijah delivers the prophecy declaring the utter decimation of the dynasty. It is within this prophetic oracle where Ahijah elaborates on Jeroboam's sins that הכעיס appears (1 Kgs 14:7-11):

Special Status — Jeroboam (vv. 7-8)

7) לכי אמרי לירבעם כה־אמר יהוה אלהי ישׂראל
יען אשׁר הרימתיך מתוך העם ואתנך נגיד על עמי ישׂראל
8) ואקרע את־הממלכה מבית דוד ואתנה לך
ולא־היית כעבדי דוד אשׁר שׁמר מצותי
ואשׁר־הלך אחרי בכל־לבבו לעשׂות רק הישׁר בעיני

Catalog of Sins (v. 9)

9) ותרע לעשׂות מכל אשׁר־היו לפניך
ותלך ותעשׂה־לך אלהים אחרים ומסכות

Provocation

להכעיסני ואתי השׁלכת אחרי גוך

Punishment (vv. 10-11)

10) לכן הנני מביא רעה אל־בית
ירבעם והכרתי לירבעם משׁתין בקיר עצור ועזוב בישׂראל
ובערתי אחרי בית־ירבעם כאשׁר יבער הגלל עד־תמו
11) המת לירבעם בעיר יאכלו הכלבים והמת בשׂדה יאכלו עוף השׁמים
כי יהוה דבר

7)   Go, tell Jeroboam, "Thus says YHWH, God of Israel: 'Since I raised you from among the people and made you ruler over my people, Israel,

8)   and tore the kingdom from the house of David and gave it to you, but you were not like my servant, David, who kept my commandments and who followed me with all his heart, doing only what was right in my eyes,

9)   and you had done more evil than all your predecessors and you went and you made for yourself other gods and molten images, _provoking me to anger_, and casting me behind your back;

---

63   1 Kgs 14:1-18 represent several levels of redaction where it "incorporates legendary motifs, recounts a prophetic consultation, involves succession, and addresses the fate of dynasty and nation" (Gary Knoppers, _Two Nations Under God_ 2:74). Since the prophetic message has very little correspondence to the beginning (vv. 1-6) and to the closing of the narrative (17-18) about the ailing son, many scholars have attributed only vv. 7-16 to the Dtr editors (see H.N. Wallace, "The Oracles Against the Israelite Dynasties in 1 and 2 Kings," _Biblica_ 67 [1986]:21-40; Steven McKenzie, "The Prophetic History and the Redaction of Kings," _HAR_ 9 [1985]:203-220; and general discussion of the scholarship on this pericope, Burke O. Long, _1 Kings with an Introduction to Historical Literature_ [FOTL 9; Grand Rapids: William B. Eerdmans, 1984], 154) and the storyline to the prophetic historian (see McKenzie, "The Prophetic History," 203-204).

10) Therefore I am about to bring evil against the house of Jeroboam. I will cut off from Jeroboam, every male, both bond and free in Israel; I will consume the house of Jeroboam as one burns up dung until it is completely consumed.

11) The dogs will consume the dead belonging to Jeroboam in the city; the birds of the heavens will consume the dead in the field. For YHWH has spoken.'"

Since judgment oracles are juridical in nature,[64] they consist of two parts: the description of the offense and the consequent punishment. Before listing the offenses, though, the prophet at first elucidates on Jeroboam's election: God had raised Jeroboam to bestow upon him a substantial share of David's kingdom (v. 8).[65] Only after establishing God's kind gesture does the oracle list Jeroboam's various sins: He had failed to maintain the standards of David who "only" (רק, v. 8) did what was right;[66] he did more evil than his "predecessors" (לפניו);[67] and he had made "other gods" (אלהים אחרים)[68] and "molten images" (מסכות),[69] provoking God. These offenses are summed up in a metaphor

---

64 See Claus Westermann, *Basic Forms of Prophetic Speech* (trans. H. White; Philadelphia: Westminster, 1967), 157, and Knoppers, *Two Nations Under God,* 2:103.

65 Interestingly, the message is careful not to include the original reason, namely the sins of Solomon (1 Kgs 11:11, 33), that had initially led God to offer Jeroboam the northern kingdom instead of bestowing the entire territory to Rehoboam.

66 Contrast with 1 Kgs 15:5 where the formulaic expression reflects on the sin "in the matter of Uriah, the Hittite," בדבר אוריה החתי, where the sin of David is explicitly mentioned. Interestingly, the expression is absent in the Greek.

67 The Hebrew expression for the "predecessors," לפנים, parallels the Akkadian word, *mahru,* frequently attested in the royal inscriptions to refer to the kings of the past (*šarru pani mahri*). This reflects the different orientation of time in the ancient Near East. The past was considered to be 'before' the people while the future was 'behind' them.

68 The reference to "other gods" (אלהים אחרים) is typical Deuteronomistic phraseology. Yet the specific verb, עשה ("make"), is never used with the expression, like other verbs, such as הלך אחרי ("follow," Deut 6:14, 8:19, 11:28, 13:3, 17:3, 29:25, 28:14, Judg 2:12, 2:19; Jer 7:9, 11:10, 13:10, 16:11, 25:6, 35:15); עבד ("serve," Deut 7:4, 11:16, 13:7, 14, 17:3, 28:36, 64, 29:25; Josh 23:16; 1 Sam 8:8; 1 Kgs 9:6; 2 Kgs 21:21; Jer 16:13, 44:3; according to Weinfeld, *Deuteronomy and the Deuteronomic School* [Oxford: Oxford University Press, 1972], 320, the expression was pre-Dtr and present in the Elohistic source); לקטר ("burn incense," 2 Kgs 22:17; Jer 1:16, 19:4, 44:5, 8, 15); להשתחוה ("worship," variations of expressions accompany this verb, see Weinfeld, *Deuteronomy and the Deuteronomic School,* 321); and להחזיק ("embrace," 1 Kgs 9:9, repeated in 2 Chr 7:22). However, given the context, the phrase is appropriate for the situation. The prophet is chastising Jeroboam for having created new deities in the image of a calf — two golden calves — one for Bethel and the other for Dan, which causes the northern kingdom to sin, resulting in their downfall. DtrH wants to create an illusion that the calves were idolatrous deities, rather than an adoption of an old iconography for YHWH.

69 The plural form of מסכה ("molten image") only occurs in four places beside this attestation: 2 Chr 28:2 which describes how king Ahaz "made the molten images for Ba'alim" (עשה

of utter rejection; Jeroboam cast God behind his back.[70] The stark contrast between God's beneficence, on the one hand, and Jeroboam's sins, on the other hand, heightens the sinfulness of his activities.[71]

In the catalog of sins, the act of making other gods and molten images is accompanied by a modifier, namely that it had "provoked [God] to anger" (להכעיסני).[72] Based on the grammatical structure, the sin of idolatry provides fodder for the provocation. With the provocation, one would then expect a description of the punishment; however, it does not immediately follow. Instead a general remark of Jeroboam's rejection of God ("did you cast me be-

---

מסכות לבעלים; absent in 2 Kgs 16:3); 2 Chr 34:3, 4 which narrates the reform of Josiah (again absent in 2 Kgs); and Num 33:52, in which God commands the people to drive out the previous inhabitants and to destroy the carved figures, "their molten images" (צלמי מסכתם), and high places. Here, the nominal form of מסכת ("their molten images") may have been chosen because of its near homonym to משכיתם ("their carved figures") which occurs in the same verse; see Jacob Milgrom, *Numbers: The Traditional Hebrew Text with the New JPS Translation* (JPS Torah Commentary; Philadelphia: The Jewish Publication Society, 1990), 330, note 33. Everywhere else, the term occurs in the singular, especially in reference to either Aaron's golden calf (Exod 32:4, 8; Deut 9:12, 16; Neh 9:18; Ps 106:19) or Jeroboam's golden calves (2 Kgs 17:16). The book of Kings does not refer to Jeroboam's golden calves as מסכה ("molten image") but just שני עגלי זהב ("two calves of gold," 1 Kgs 12:28; 2 Kgs 10:29; 2 Chr 13:8) or just עגלים ("calves," 1 Kgs 12:32; 2 Chr 11:15). Only in the diatribe against the northern kingdom in 2 Kgs 17:16, is מסכה ever used of Jeroboam's images. Therefore, the use of מסכות ("molten images") demonstrates the author's concerted effort to present the calves as a form of idolatry, not just a substitution for the "ark of the covenant" in Jerusalem.

70 It is a way to express neglect of God (Ezek 23:35) who is substituted with תורה ("teaching") in Neh 9:26 (see Ps 50:17 for a similar formulation — אחר ["behind"] instead of אחרי גוה ["behind the back of'] — and Isa 38:17, where God is the subject in regards to the people's sins). The 'front' was the position of attentiveness while the 'back' reflected lack of attention.

71 Compare the series of first person verbs (הרימתיך, "I raised you;" ואתנך, "I made you;" and ואקרע, "I tore;" ואתנה, "I gave it") with the second person verbs (לא היית כעבדי, "you were not like my servant;" תרע, "you did evil;" and ותלך ותעשה, "you went and made") in vv. 7-9.

72 The construction of the infinitive with the ־ל can function similarly to למען, either as purpose (*modal-epexegetische*) or as a consequence (*konsekutiv*) to the previous clause (see Joüon §124 l and o, which, according to Joüon §124 l and §169 g, is similar to למען; H.A. Brongers, "Die Partikel למען in der biblisch-hebräischen Sprache," *OtSt* 18 [1973]:84; and Ilmari Soisalon-Soininen, "Der Infinitivus Constructus mit ל im Hebräischen," *VT* 22 (1972):82-90). In this case, it is not for the purpose of vexing God that Jeroboam commits the sin but the provocation is a consequence of the sin of idolatry. The infinitive construct, in this specific instance, reflects the consequence of the main verb — 'so that' — *IBHS* 36.2.3d. Nonetheless, Soisalon-Soininen would argue that there is a larger number of the *modal-epexegetische* where even להכעיסו (from Deut 4:25) should be understood as a purpose clause. The problem with his argument is that it focuses primarily on other scholars' translation of the expressions rather than a thorough discussion of the occurrences in the Hebrew text. One should give priority to the context.

hind your back," גוך אחרי השלכת אתי) follows the הכעיס-modifier so that the clause, not the term (הכעיס), functions as a literary pivot[73] between the sin and the punishment. At the same time, though, הכעיס triggers the judgment since the manufacture of the molten images, which causes the provocation, is tantamount to rejecting God, the final clause before an elaboration of the punishment.

The way in which the punishment is worded, God is portrayed as the executor. In v. 10, the judgment section opens with the typical introductory word, "therefore" (לכן). Here, God is the subject of the verb of destruction; God is the one who is "about to bring evil" (הנני מביא רעה)[74] against Jeroboam's house. The evil specifically refers to the annihilation of his male descendants,[75] not the destruction of Samaria. Just as God had established Jeroboam's dynasty, he will decimate his seed on account of his sins: God will "cut off" (הכרתי) from Jeroboam every male descendant[76] and God will "exterminate" (בערתי אחרי) his household.[77] Ultimately, however, the oracle is fulfilled, not by God, but by Baasha (1 Kgs 15:27-30), who kills Nadab, Jeroboam's son, and Jeroboam's whole household.

---

73   The literary pivot of the oracle is the final accusation in which Jeroboam is censured for having "cast [God] behind his back" (גוך אחרי השלכת אתי). The succession of converted imperfects, listing the sins of Jeroboam, is disrupted by ואתי ("and me"). While the disjunctive construction emphasizes the recipient of the "casting away" (שלך, hiphil), God, it essentializes the sin of idolatry. In essence, idolatry is the rejection of God; one cannot worship both other deities and God. This climatic statement is what augurs the punishment.

74   This particular expression occurs frequently in the books of Kings and Jeremiah. It is first attested in 2 Sam 17:14 in reference to Absalom upon whom God wanted to bring disaster (לבעבור הביא יהוה אל־אבשלום את־הרעה, "so that YHWH may bring evil upon Absalom"). This reference has an accusative and definite article marker on רעה which does not occur except in Solomon's prayer (1 Kgs 9:9). Usually, the word is indefinite, 1 Kgs 21:21, 2 Kgs 21:12, 22:16 (//2 Chr 34:24 — with some variations), Jer 4:6, 6:19, 11:11, 11:23, 19:3, 23:12, 45:5, 49:37, and Dan 9:12, 13. In cases where רעה is definite, it is not accompanied by an accusative marker (1 Kgs 21:29 - twice, Jer 42:17). הנה ("here") plus the participle usually expresses the future with "immanency — the so-called *futurum instans* participle" (*IBHS* §37.6f).

75   The expression for annihilation, אחרי plus the piel of בער, occurs in one other place, 1 Kgs 21:21, and partly in 1 Kgs 16:3, where it appears to be a hiphil of בער. All three attestations, in reference to Jeroboam, Ahab, and Baasha, respectively occur in prophetic pronouncements against dynasties. See section 1.4.1.

76   The phrase, משתין בקיר ("those who piss against the wall"), is used in 1 Sam 25:22, 34 (in regard to Nabal), 1 Kgs 16:11 (Baasha), 1 Kgs 21:21, and 2 Kgs 9:8 (both in regard to the house of Ahab) to refer to the male gender.

77   Though God promises to execute the punishment, the formulaic curse assigns natural elements to consume what had been destroyed: Dogs will devour the dead in the city and the birds of the heavens in the field (1 Kgs 14:11). However, this is more of an expression to indicate the totality of the annihilation rather than the actual attribution of agency. It also appears in 1 Kgs 16:4 (against Baasha's dynasty) and 1 Kgs 21:24 (against Omride dynasty).

1.4.2.2. 1 Kings 15:29-30

In order to establish a correlation between the judgment oracle and the actual fulfillment of the punishment, DtrH1 recalls the prophecy of Ahijah in which the sin-provocation-punishment pattern is delineated (1 Kgs 15:29-30):

Punishment

29) ויהי כמלכו הכה את־כל־בית ירבעם
לא־השאיר כל־נשמה לירבעם עד־השמדו

כדבר יהוה אשר דבר ביד־עבדו אחיה השילני

Reason

30) על־חטאות ירבעם אשר חטא ואשר החטיא את־ישראל

Provocation

בכעסו אשר הכעיס את־יהוה אלהי ישראל

29) When he became king, he struck down the whole house of Jeroboam;[78] he did not leave anyone with breath in the house of Jeroboam until he destroyed it according to the word of YHWH which he spoke through his servant, Ahijah, the Shilonite,

30) on account of the sins of Jeroboam which he committed and had made Israel commit, (namely) the <u>provocation with which he provoked</u> YHWH, the God of Israel, <u>to anger.</u>[79]

Although the punishment is described as the fulfillment of God's word as relayed through Ahijah, Baasha, a temporal executor, "strikes" (הכה) down the house of Jeroboam. It is this very human agent, not God, who fulfills the prophecy.

Once the passage narrates how Baasha decimates Jeroboam's family, it justifies his violent activities by extrapolating on the reason, the sins of Jeroboam. This particular sin is further described as a provocation (יהוה בכעסו אשר הכעיס את, "the provocation with which he had provoked God"). Since the punishment, outlined in v. 29, is followed by the reason which is explained as having provoked God, הכעים then functions as a pivot between the punishment and sin but in the reverse-order:

---

78 The Greek does appear to reflect בית ("house").

79 The clause, בכעסו אשר הכעיס את יהוה, is made difficult with the ב-preposition before כעסו. The Hebrew Vorlage of the Greek, minus the Lucian recension, and Targum seem to have a waw-ו ("and") before the expression. This reading may be an improvement since כעס could then be in parallel construction with חטאות so that the two offenses, sin and provocation, combined may have resulted in the annihilation. The ב-preposition, having a causal force, then would be parallel to על. However, this translation is not without difficulties since the sin of Jeroboam is the reason for the provocation in 1 Kgs14:9, not an additional sin. See section 1.1.1.

Punishment Because of Sin ← Provocation

As a result, הכעים provides the justification for the punishment which a human agent carries out. It is a paradigmatic example of God acting through his historical instruments.

1.4.3. The Dynasty of Baasha
1 Kings 16:2-4 (v. 2) and 16:11-13 (v. 13)

1.4.3.1. 1 Kings 16:2-4

Though Baasha fulfilled God's word, albeit without his knowledge, he too receives the prophetic pronouncement against his household. Baasha was God's instrument in fulfilling the judgment against the dynasty of Jeroboam. Nevertheless, DtrH1 attributes to him the sin that plagued the northern kingdom, the sin of Jeroboam (1 Kgs 15:34). Thus, through Jehu, the prophet, DtrH1 denounces the dynasty of Baasha (1 Kgs 16:2-4):

Special Status — Baasha (v. 2a)

2) יען אשר הרימתיך מן־העפר ואתנך נגיד על עמי ישראל

Catalog of Sins (v. 2b)

ותלך בדרך ירבעם ותחטא את־עמי ישראל

Provocation

להכעיסני בחטאתם

Punishment (vv. 3-4)

3) הנני מבעיר אחרי בעשא ואחרי ביתו
ונתתי את־ביתך כבית ירבעם בן־נבט
4) המת בעשא בעיר יאכלו הכלבים
והמת לו בשדה יאכלו עוף השמים

2)   Since I exalted you from out of the dust and made you ruler over my people, Israel, but you walked in the way of Jeroboam and caused my people, Israel, to sin, <u>provoking me to anger</u> with their sins,[80]

3)   I am about to exterminate Baasha and his house. I will make your house like the house of Jeroboam, son of Nebat.

4)   The dogs will consume the dead belonging to Baasha in the city; the birds of the heavens will consume his dead in the field.

---

80   The Greek appears to reflect the Hebrew Vorlage of בהבליהם ("with their vanities") instead of בחטאתם ("with their sins"), see 16:13, 26. If the indictment is directed to the individual king, then one would expect a third, masculine singular pronominal suffix (ו) rather than the third, masculine plural (ם/הם). It would appear that the king's 'causing Israel to sin' made the endeavor a corporate effort.

Worded and structured similarly to Ahijah's oracle against Jeroboam (14:7-11), DtrH1 justifies the message of doom. Both the judgment oracles against Jeroboam and Baasha contain the same causal conjunction (in italics) and succession of verbs (underlined):

Jeroboam (1 Kgs 14:7-9)

יַעַן אֲשֶׁר הֲרִימֹתִיךָ מִתּוֹךְ הָעָם וָאֶתֶּנְךָ נָגִיד עַל עַמִּי יִשְׂרָאֵל ...
וַתֵּלֶךְ וַתַּעֲשֶׂה לְךָ אֱלֹהִים אֲחֵרִים וּמַסֵּכוֹת לְהַכְעִיסֵנִי ...

on account that I raised you from among the people and made you ruler over my people, Israel ... (but) you made for yourself other gods and molten images, provoking me to anger ...

Baasha (1 Kgs 16:2)

יַעַן אֲשֶׁר הֲרִימֹתִיךָ מִן־הֶעָפָר וָאֶתֶּנְךָ נָגִיד עַל עַמִּי יִשְׂרָאֵל וַתֵּלֶךְ
בְּדֶרֶךְ יָרָבְעָם וַתַּחֲטִא אֶת־עַמִּי יִשְׂרָאֵל לְהַכְעִיסֵנִי בְּחַטֹּאתָם ...

on account that I raised you from out of the dust and made you ruler over my people, Israel but you walked in the way of Jeroboam and caused my people, Israel, to sin, provoking me to anger with their sins ...

Like the oracle against Jeroboam, the pronouncement against Baasha juxtaposes God's benevolence with the king's rejection of YHWH. By means of the contrast, DtrH1 indicts Baasha for sinning against YHWH in spite of his divine promotion to kingship. As a result, God is provoked to anger, which then supplies the fuel for the consequent punishment. Baasha will experience the very fate which befell Jeroboam: God, the agent, will utterly destroy his whole family.

Despite the similarities between the oracles against Jeroboam and Baasha, there is one significant difference in the overall structure.[81] The difference lies in the position of הכעיס; rather than just signaling the punishment as in the pronouncement against Jeroboam, the term functions as the pivot in the account of Baasha. In the account of Jeroboam, the final clause, וְאֹתִי הִשְׁלַכְתָּ אַחֲרֵי גֶוְךָ ("casting me behind your back"), linked the catalog of sins to the description of the punishment. However, here, the provocation is the literary hinge between the sin and the consequent punishment (vv. 3-4):

---

81   There are other minor differences in the wording of the oracles. For example, Ahijah's oracle is more elaborate and unlike the oracle of Ahijah, in which Jeroboam is accused of provoking God to anger by making other gods, here Baasha provokes God by following in the footsteps of Jeroboam. Nevertheless, these differences will not be discussed here.

Sin (of Jeroboam, v. 2b) → Provocation (הכעיס, v. 2b) → Punishment (vv. 3-4)

Thus, the punishment is the direct result of the provocation.

1.4.3.2. 1 Kings 16:11-13

To demonstrate the efficacy of Jehu's oracle, DtrH1 describes its fulfillment in 1 Kgs 16:11-13, recalling the words of the pronouncement (1 Kgs 16:2-4):

Punishment (v. 12)

11) ויהי במלכו כשבתו על־כסאו הכה את־כל־בית בעשא
לא־השאיר לו משתין בקיר וגאליו ורעהו
12) וישמד זמרי את־כל־בית בעשא
כדבר יהוה אשר דבר אל־בעשא ביד יהוא הנביא

Reason (v. 13a)

13) אל כל־חטאות בעשא וחטאות אלה בנו אשר חטאו
ואשר החטיאו את־ישראל

Provocation (v. 13b)

להכעיס את־יהוה אלהי ישראל והבליהם

11) When he became king and seated himself upon his throne, he struck down the whole house of Baasha; he did not leave him a single male among his kinsmen or his friends.

12) Zimri destroyed the whole house of Baasha according to the word of YHWH which he spoke to Baasha through Jehu, the prophet,

13) on account of all the sins of Baasha and the sins of Elah, his son, which they committed and made Israel commit, provoking YHWH, the God of Israel, to anger with their delusions.[82]

During the reign of Elah (1 Kgs 16:8-14), the son of Baasha, Zimri, the "commander of half the chariotry" (שׂר מחזית הרכב), usurped the throne. Though Zimri was probably motivated by political reasons to destroy his enemies, DtrH1 interprets the historical event as the fulfillment of God's word spoken through Jehu, the prophet (v. 12). Therefore, Zimri becomes God's instrument. As such, for DtrH1, God acts through history so that humans are merely chess pieces in God's game.

Again similar to the account of the fulfillment of Ahijah's oracle (1 Kgs 15:30), DtrH1 elucidates the reason for the punishment, establishing the sin-provocation-punishment pattern. DtrH1 attributes the punishment to the sins of Baasha and Elah, which provoked God:

---

82   Deut 32:21, Jer 8:19, 10:8, 14:22, Ps 31:7, and Jon 2:9.

Punishment Because of (אל) Sin ← Provocation (הכעיס)

Since the provocation resulting from the sins motivated the punishment, it functions as a reverse-pivot. All in all, הכעיס is the pivot-term in both the prophetic pronouncement against the dynasty of Baasha and its fulfillment, in which God is portrayed as controlling history.

1.4.4. The Dynasty of Omri
1 Kings 16:25-26 (v. 26), 16:30-33 (v. 33), 21:20b-26 (v. 22); 22:53-54 (v. 54)

As the narrative turns to the Omride dynasty, the pronouncement-fulfillment pattern is somewhat haphazard. Instead of directing the prophetic pronouncement to Omri, the *de jure* founder of the dynasty, DtrH denounces Ahab, the *de facto* head[83] (1 Kgs 21:22). Moreover, its fulfillment is dispersed throughout the account of Ahab's death (1 Kgs 22:37-38) and rise of Jehu (2 Kgs 9-10). Furthermore, DtrH1 accuses the Omride dynasty of additional provocations against Omri (1 Kgs 16:26), Ahab (1 Kgs 16:33), and Ahaziah (1 Kgs 22:54). Except for Jehoram (2 Kgs 3:1-3, 9:14-26), the last king, all the Omride kings provoke God, who, in turn, uses temporal instruments to punish them. Rather than outline the pronouncement-fulfillment pattern, this section will discuss the occurrences of הכעיס as it appears in the historical narrative of the Omride dynasty.

1.4.4.1. 1 Kings 16:25-26

During the turbulent period of regional factionalism, Omri, a military commander, usurped the throne (16:23-27). Though the shortlived king (885-873 B.C.E.) gets a brief report, DtrH1 manages to include a catalog of sins indicting the founding ruler (1 Kgs 16:25-26):

Catalog of Sins (vv. 25-26)

(25) ויעשה עמרי הרע בעיני יהוה וירע מכל אשר לפניו

(26) וילך בכל־דרך ירבעם בן־נבט ובחטאתיו אשר החטיא את־ישראל

Provocation

להכעיס את־יהוה אלהי ישראל בהבליהם

---

83 Compared to other Israelite kings, Ahab receives much attention in the books of Kings. It is not insignificant that Manasseh, the scapegoat for the destruction of Jerusalem, is compared to Ahab (2 Kgs 21:3). In describing the punishment, the future destruction of Jerusalem is compared to the "measuring line of Samaria and the weights of the House of Ahab" (קו שמרון ואת־משקלת בית אחאב 2 Kgs 21:13). It is not the weights of the House of Jeroboam, the father of Israel, nor the House of Omri, the founder of Samaria, but Ahab.

25)   Omri did evil in the eyes of YHWH and he did more evil than all his predecessors.

26)   He walked in all the ways of Jeroboam, son of Nebat, and in all his sins which he made Israel commit, <u>provoking</u> YHWH, God of Israel, <u>to anger</u> with their delusions.

Significant differences lie between the prophetic pronouncements against the founding rulers of the first two dynasties (Jeroboam and Baasha) and the brief indictment of Omri. First of all, no prophet relays the indictment. Second, the outline of the punishment is absent; it neither precedes nor ensues the catalog of sins.[84] Therefore, the pattern is incomplete in its final form; nevertheless the punishment may have been transposed to Ahab for whom DtrH holds the full pattern.[85]

1.4.4.2. 1 Kings 16:30-33

Accompanying the politically motivated marriage between Ahab and Jezebel, the daughter of Ethbaal, king of the Sidonians, the Omri dynasty spirals to ignominy as reported in the books of Kings. Consequently, DtrH1 begins its introduction of Ahab by listing his sins which lead to the provocation of God (1 Kgs 16:30-33). However, this text is not the formulaic pronouncement against the dynasty (1 Kgs 21:20b-26) which will be discussed below:

Catalog of Sins (vv. 30-33)

30) ויעש אחאב בן־עמרי הרע בעיני יהוה
מכל אשר לפניו

31) ויהי הנקל לכתו בחטאות ירבעם בן־נבט
ויקח אשה את־איזבל בת־אתבעל מלך צידנים
וילך ויעבד את־הבעל וישתחו לו

32) ויקם מזבח לבעל
בית הבעל אשר בנה בשמרון

33) ויעש אחאב את־האשרה

Provocation

ויוסף אחאב לעשות <u>להכעיס</u>[86] את־יהוה אלהי ישראל
מכל מלכי ישראל אשר היו לפניו

---

84   Perhaps the absence of the silluq (:) at the end of the verse (בהבליהם) in the MT demonstrate an awareness of the lack of a punishment formula. However, many of the other Hebrew manuscripts have it.

85   See section 1.4.4.3.

86   The LXX seems to reflect a noun, כעסים ("provocations"), after לעשות to probably clarify what he was doing.

30) Ahab, son of Omri, did more evil in the eyes of YHWH, than his predecessors.

31) As if it was trivial for him to walk in the sins of Jeroboam, son of Nebat,
he took for a wife, Jezebel, the daughter of Ethbaal, king of the Sidonians,
and he went and served Ba'al and worshipped him.

32) He set up an altar to Ba'al in the temple of Ba'al[87] which he had built in
Samaria.

33) Ahab made an asherah and Ahab continued to do more to provoke
YHWH, the God of Israel, to anger than all the kings of Israel who were
before him.

Beside following in the footsteps of Jeroboam, Ahab had compounded his sins
by marrying Jezebel, worshipping Ba'al, establishing an altar dedicated to
Ba'al in Samaria, and finally, constructing the sacred pole.[88] These sins inevitably provoke God to anger, thus forming the pattern:

Catalog of Sins (vv. 30-33a) → Provocation (v. 33b)

According to the sin-provocation-punishment pattern, though, one would then
expect a description of the punishment; however, like 1 Kgs 16:26, the punishment is absent. Yet unlike 1 Kgs 16:26, where the punishment is altogether
absent, the pattern eventually unfolds with the circuitous introduction of the
punishment in 1 Kgs 17:1.

Even though the punishment section does not follow right after הכעיס, the
assessment of Ahab's deeds seems to set the stage for the upcoming drought (1
Kgs 17:1) at the beginning of the prophetic cycles of Elijah and Elisha (1 Kgs
17:1-2 Kgs 9:37).[89] Before outlining the punishment, however, DtrH1 inserts a

---

87 The LXX has a different reading (προσόχθισμα, "house of God") which has led some
scholars to think that ב"ת הבעל ("the sanctuary of Ba'al") was secondary for which בית
אלהים ("house of God") was the original reading. However, the mention of בית הבעל ("the
sanctuary of Ba'al") in 2 Kgs 10:21, 23, and 25-27 would indicate that someone had built the
temple previous to Jehu. So why not Ahab? Though not conclusive, J.A. Emerton, "The
House of Ba'al in 1 Kings XVI 32," VT 47 (1997):293-300, prefers the MT.

88 According to William Schniedewind, "History and Interpretation," 651-652, building upon
the observations of Saul Olyan, Asherah and the Cult of Yahweh in Israel (SBLMS 34; Atlanta: Scholars Press, 1986), 652, who considers v. 33 to be an addition, "suggesting that the
worship of Ba'al and Asherah are related."

89 Scholarly opinion is divided over the exact order of the collection of the book. Some have
attributed the Elijah-Elisha cycles to a later redactor which would then make DtrH2 (or some
late redactor) responsible for establishing the sin-anger-punishment pattern. However, Nadav
Na'aman, "Prophetic Stories as Sources for the Histories of Jehoshaphat and Omrides," Biblica 78 (1997):153-173, considers the Elijah-Elisha cycles to be prior to the historical reports
and were included by the first redactor. Therefore DtrH1 would have been re

mysterious, brief interlude on Hiel, the Bethelite (1 Kgs 16:34),[90] who is punished for fortifying Jericho as spoken by God through Joshua (Josh 6:26):[91]

Foreshadowing Comment (v. 34)

16:34) בימיו בנה חיאל בית האלי את־יריחה
באבירם בכרו יסדה
ובשׂגיב צעירו הציב דלתיה
כדבר יהוה אשר דבר ביד יהושע בן־נון

Punishment (17:1)

17:1) ויאמר אליהו התשבי מתשבי גלעד אל־אחאב
חי־יהוה אלהי ישׂראל אשר עמדתי לפניו
אם־יהיה השׁנים האלה טל ומטר כי אם־לפי דברי

16:34) In his days, Hiel, the Bethelite, built Jericho. He laid its foundation at the cost of Abiram, his first-born, and its gates at the cost of Segub, his youngest son, according to the word of YHWH who spoke through Joshua, son of Nun.

17:1) Elijah, the Tishbite, from Tishbe of Gilead, said to Ahab, "As YHWH, the God of Israel, before whom I stand, lives, there will be neither dew nor rain these years except by my word."

Although v. 34 appears intrusive, it prepares the reader for the consequent punishment (17:1) by exemplifying the sin-punishment pattern.[92]

---

sponsible for establishing the pattern. Either way, a conscious effort to present history in a mechanical fashion is evident.

90   In the Lucian recension of the Greek, 1 Kgs 16:34 is omitted.
91   Joshua declares (Josh 6:26):

ארור האישׁ לפני יהוה אשר יקום ובנה את־העיר הזאת את־יריחו
בבכרו ייסדנה ובצעירו יציב דלתיה

Cursed is the man before YHWH who undertakes to build this city, Jericho:
With his firstborn, he will lay its foundations; with his youngest, he will set up its gates.

The curse is invoked "before YHWH" (לפני יהוה) so that God is called upon to punish the offender. Most likely, the phrase, "before YHWH," which is omitted in several Hebrew and Greek versions, was added later to correspond to the DtrH1 formulation of the curse in 1 Kgs 16:34.

92   According to Charles Conroy, "Hiel Between Ahab and Elijah-Elisha: 1 Kgs 16,34 in Its Immediate Literary Context," *Biblica* 77 (1996):210-218, who notes the parallel description of the sins between Ahab and Hiel in the grammatical, structural, thematic, and lexical levels. Just as Hiel's two sons died, so do the two sons, Ahaziah (2 Kgs 1) and Jehoram (2 Kgs 9) die prematurely. Thus, it is a fitting "transition between the introduction of Ahab and the start of the Elijah narratives in chapter 17" (215).

The drought of 1 Kgs 17:1 does not necessarily seem to result from Ahab's sins. Yet, in order to demonstrate the deterministic principle of his understanding of history, DtrH1 uses the short lesson on Hiel to show how the drought could only have been the outcome of Ahab's sins. Just as Hiel was punished for fortifying (בנה, "he built") Jericho against "the word of God," Ahab will also be punished for building (בנה, "he built") the "temple of Ba'al" (בית לבעל) in Samaria. Since no sin goes unpunished, even the fortification of a town, v. 34 clearly links Ahab's sins to the drought in 1 Kgs 17:1. Therefore, the pattern of sin-provocation-punishment is ultimately established.

Whereas the punishment of drought results from Ahab's endorsement of Ba'al, it is not completely measure-for-measure. On the one hand, the drought corresponds to the sin in that Ba'al, the central object of Ahab's foreign worship, fails to carry out his duty. Though Ba'al is the god of storm, Israel suffers from drought, which is the absence of rain.[93] By divesting Ba'al of his powers at a time when Ahab was building an altar and a sanctuary for the deity, DtrH1 simultaneously diminishes the power of Ba'al and punishes the culprit. Ultimately, DtrH1 promotes YHWH, who *is* in control over nature.[94] On the other hand, the punishment extends beyond Ahab to the people, the innocent bystanders.

All in all, the pattern of prophetic pronouncement-fulfillment is not developed in the accounts of Omri (1 Kgs 16:25-26) and Ahab (1 Kgs 16:30-33) as it was in the first two dynasties. Rather the pattern is expanded later in the

---

93 See "Ba'al" in *DDD*, 132-140.

94 While the punishment undermines Ba'al's power over the storm, it implicitly asserts YHWH's power over the storms through his servant, Elijah. The passage does not state outright that God had stopped the dew and the rain; rather in a curse-formula, Elijah declares that "As YHWH, the God of Israel whom I serve, lives there will be no dew or rain except at my bidding" (חי יהוה אלהי יש־אל אשר עמדתי לפניו אם־יהיה השנים האלה טל ומטר כי אם־לפי דברי). Now, the expression, חי יהוה (Judg 8:19, Ruth 3:13, 1 Sam 14:39, 45, 19:6, 20:21, 25:34, 26:10, 16, 23:10, 29:6, 2 Sam 4:9, 12:5, 14:11, 15:21, 1 Kgs 1:29, 2:24, 17:1, 12, 18:10, 22:14 [// 2 Chr 18:13], 2 Kgs 5:16, 20, Hos 4:15, Jer 4:2, 5:2, 12:16, 16:14, 15, 23:7, 8, 38:16; variations: חי אל [Job 27:2], חי האלהים [2 Sam 2:27], חי אדני יהוה [Jer 44:26], and חי יהוה צבאות [1 Kgs 18:15, 2 Kgs 3:14]; and with God, Num 14:21, 28, Deut 32:40, Isa 49:18, Jer 22:24, 46:18, Ezek 5:11, 14:16, 18, 20, 16:48, 17:16, 19, 18:3, 20:3, 31, 33, 33:11, 27, 34:8, 35:6, 11, Zeph 2:9), is an oath-formula which is not necessarily used as an assertion of God's power. However, Elijah's claim that God is "before whom he stands" (אשר עמדתי לפניו) would point to God's power over the natural forces. The phrase, עמד לפני ("to stand before"), clearly establishes the hierarchal relationship between God, the superior, and his servant, Elijah. Elijah stands before God until he receives a message to relay to the recipients. Therefore, if the "dew and rain" will not come except at Elijah's bidding, then the storms will not come without God's command. While God is the implied agent, he uses Elijah, his prophet, to navigate the storm.

report concerning Ahab (1 Kgs 21:20b-26) and in the account of his death and rise of Jehu (1 Kgs 22:37-38, 2 Kgs 9-10).

1.4.4.3. 1 Kings 21:20b-26

The prophetic pronouncement against the Omride dynasty appears in 1 Kgs 21:20b-26. While Ahab is enjoying Naboth's vineyard, acquired through questionable methods, Elijah makes his appearance. Disappointed with Ahab's passive participation in the death of Naboth, Elijah, the prophet, relays a message of doom (1 Kgs 21:20b-26):

Reason (v. 20b)

20b) יען התמכרך לעשׂות הרע בעיני יהוה

Punishment (vv. 21-22a)

21) הנני מבי אליך רעה ובערתי אחריך
והכרתי לאחאב משׁתין בקיר ועצור ועזוב בישׂראל
22) ונתתי את־ביתך כבית ירבעם בן־נבט וכבית בעשׁא בן־אחיה

Reason — Provocation (v. 22b)

אל־<u>הכעס אשׁר הכעסת</u> ותחטא את־ישׂראל

Punishment — Jezebel (v. 23)

23) וגם־לאיזבל דבר יהוה לאמר
הכלבים יאכלו את־איזבל בחל יזרעאל

Punishment — Formulaic Curse (v. 24)

24) המת לאחאב בעיר יאכלו הכלבים
המת בשׂדה יאכלו עוף השׁמים

Catalog of Sins — Addition (vv. 25-26)

25) רק לא־היה כאחאב אשׁר התמכר לעשׂות הרע בעיני יהוה
אשׁר־הסתה אתו איזבל אשׁתו
26) ויתעב מאד ללכת אחרי הגללים
ככל אשׁר עשׂו האמרי אשׁר הוריש יהוה מפני בני ישׂראל

20b)   Since you sold yourself to do evil in the eyes of YHWH,

21)   I am about to bring evil against you. I will exterminate you and cut off from Ahab, every male, both bond and free, in Israel.

22)   I will make your house like the house of Jeroboam, son of Nebat, and like the house of Baasha, son of Ahijah, on account of <u>the provocation with which you provoked (me) to anger</u> and caused Israel to sin.

23)   And also for Jezebel, YHWH said, "The dogs will consume Jezebel in the fortress of Jezreel.

24)   The dogs will consume the dead belonging to Ahab in the city; the birds of the heavens will consume the dead in the field.

25)   (There was no one like Ahab who sold himself to do evil in the eyes of YHWH, as urged by Jezebel, his wife.

26)   He acted abominably, going after the idols, like all that the Amorites, whom YHWH drove out before the Israelites, committed).

The overall structure of the oracle (reason-punishment-reason-provocation-punishment-catalog of sins) shows no clear pattern. Most likely, the account underwent much redaction.

Schniedewind[95] has convincingly demonstrated the secondary nature of vv. 23, 25-26,[96] which were added to emphasize the role of Jezebel in encouraging Ahab to sin against God. If one excises vv. 23, 25-26, then the structure of the oracle would be as follows:

Reason (v. 20b) → Punishment (vv. 21-22a) →
Provocation (v.22b) → Punishment (v. 24)

Even with the extraction of Schniedewind's suggested additions, the structure of the passage is still problematic since v. 22b is intrusive; one would expect reference to the provocation — the consequence of the offense — after v. 20b, not in the middle of the judgment. If we compare the structure of vv. 20b-22b, 24 to other dynastic curse formulae, this is apparent:[97]

1 Kgs 14:7-11 (Dynastic Curse Formula Against Jeroboam):
Special Status (vv. 7-8) → Catalog of Sins (v. 9a) →
Provocation (v. 9b) → Punishment (vv. 10-11)

---

95 Schniedewind, "The Religion of Ahab and Manasseh," 653-655. Since the language of the insertion is similar to that of the description of sins attributed to Manasseh (2 Kgs 21), he dates the addition to the second level of redaction. According to James Montgomery, *A Critical and Exegetical Commentary on the Books of Kings* (ICC 6; Edinburgh: T. & T. Clark, 1951), 332, the curse formula, vv. 20b-26, appears to be an editorial supplement to the story of Naboth's vineyard, whereas John Gray, *1 & 2 Kings: A Commentary* (OTL; London: S.C.M., 1970), 442-443, only considers vv. 25-26 to be a deuteronomistic addendum. Gray explains how v. 21 is probably the *ipsissima dicta* of the pre-Deuteronomistic prophetic compiler.

The expression "to sell oneself" (התמכר), interestingly, occurs in two other places: once in Deut 28:68 and the other in 2 Kgs 17:17. The attestation in the book of Deuteronomy helps determine the background of the expression — one sells oneself to slavery — so that the people enslave themselves to the bondage of evil. The reference in 2 Kgs 17:17 is significant in demonstrating how the later editor of DtrH used this expression to reflect on the utter depravity of the Israelites.

96 Marsha White, "Naboth's Vineyard and Jehu's Coup: The Legitimation of a Dynasty Extermination," *VT* 44 (1994):66-76, offers an alternative division of the sources. She considers vv. 20b, 22, 24-26 as Dtr while vv. 21, 27-29 are original to the story. Vv. 21 and 27-29 then set up the story for fulfillment in the account of Jehu's assasinations (2 Kgs 9:36, 10:10, and 10:17).

97 Invariably יען ("on account of") is followed by the reason for and the description of the punishment/reward in DtrH (1 Kgs 20:42, 2 Kgs 22:19 // 2 Chr 34:27) or the punishment/reward precedes יען which is then followed by the reason (1 Kgs 14:13). This may be the reason why Burke Long, *1 Kings*, 223-230, outlines the structure of the oracle as such: Reason (20bβ) and Announcement of Punishment (21-22, 24) so that v. 22b is considered part of the punishment.

1 Kgs 16:2-4 (Dynastic Curse Formula Against Baasha):
Special Status (v. 2a) → Catalog of Sins (v. 2b) →
Provocation (v. 2c) → Punishment (vv. 3-4)

Though Schniedewind would not excise v. 22b, אל־הכעס אשר הכעסה
ישראל את ותחטא ("on account of the provocation with which he provoked
to anger and caused Israel to sin"), it too may be secondary in that the wording
of the provocation is not similar to the pronouncement of the curse but its
fulfillment. Typically, one would expect an infinitive construct of הכעיס with
a ל-prefix after a catalog of the sins in the pronouncement formulae, which is
not characteristic of v. 22b:

Pronouncement Form of הכעיס:
    1 Kgs 14:9 (Jeroboam) – להכעיסני
    1 Kgs 16:2 (Baasha) – להכסעיסני בחטאתם
    1 Kgs 21:22b (Ahab) – אל־הכעס אשר הכעסת

Nevertheless, the reference to the provocation in v. 22b actually resembles the
wording of the curse fulfillment in 1 Kgs 15:30 (Jeroboam dynasty):[98]

Fulfillment Wording:
1 Kgs 15:30 (Nadab – last ruler of Jeroboam dynasty):
        על־חטאות ירבעם אשר חטא ואשר החטיא את־ישראל
        בכעסו אשר הכעיס את־יהוה אלהי ישראל

1 Kgs 21:22b (Ahab):

        אל־הכעס אשר הכעסת ותחטא את־ישראל

Here I would argue that a later editor moved the curse pronouncement (minus
v. 22b) against Omri to indict Ahab, who has come to represent the Omride
dynasty. In other words, vv. 21-22a, 24 were originally the closing judgment
against Omri, which would then explain the absence of a punishment formula
after 1 Kgs 16:26:

---

98   However, 1 Kgs 21:22b does not resemble the other fulfillment formula against the Baasha
      dynasty:
      1 Kgs 16:13 (Elah – last ruler of Baasha dynasty):

                          אל כל־חטאות בעשא וחטאות אלה בנו
                          אשר חטאו ואשר החטיאו את־ישראל
                          להכעיס את־יהוה אלהי ישראל בהבליהם
      Despite the difference, there are similarities in the way 1 Kgs 16:13 mentions how the kings
      caused the people to sin.

1 Kgs 16:25-26

(25) ויעשה עמרי הרע בעיני יהוה וירע מכל אשר לפניו
(26) וילך בכל־דרך ירבעם בן־נבט ובחטאתיו אשר ־חטיא את־ישראל
להכעיס את־יהוה אלהי ישראל בהבליהם

1 Kgs 21:21-22a, 24

(21) הנני מבי אליך רעה ובערתי אחריך
והכרתי [לאחאב] משתין בקיר ועצור ועזוב בישראל
(22) ונתתי את־ביתך כבית ירבעם בן־נבט וכבית בעשא בן־אחיה
(24) המת לאחאב בעיר יאכלו הכלבים
המת בשדה יאכלו עוף השמים

25) Omri did evil in the eyes of YHWH and he did more evil than all his predecessors.
26) He walked in all the ways of Jeroboam, son of Nebat, and in all his sins which he made Israel commit, provoking YHWH, God of Israel, to anger with their delusions.

21) I am about to bring evil against you. I will exterminate you and cut off from [Ahab,] every male, both bond and free, in Israel.
22) I will make your house like the house of Jeroboam, son of Nebat, and like the house of Baasha, son of Ahijah,
23) The dogs will consume the dead belonging to Ahab in the city; the birds of the heavens will consume the dead in the field.

This would fit nicely into the curse pronouncement formulae present in the oracles against Jeroboam and Baasha (see section 1.4.1). However, in the transmission of the text, a later editor moved the curse pronouncement to the narrative concerning Ahab and Jezebel. As the wording of the final form demonstrates, Ahab was like no other king, even in the northern kingdom.

Rather than beginning the oracle with God's selection of the king as it does with Jeroboam (1 Kgs 14:7) and Baasha (1 Kgs 16:2), the account of Ahab begins with an indictment of his evil (1 Kgs 21:20):

יען אשר הרימתיך מתוך העם ואתנך נגיד על עמי ישראל (1 Kgs 14:7)
יען־אשר הרימתיך מן־העפר ואתנך נגיד על עמי ישראל (1 Kgs 16:2)
יען   התמכרך לעשות הרע בעיני יהוה (1 Kgs 21:20)

Since I raised you from among the people and made you ruler over my people, Israel (1 Kgs 14:7)

Since I raised you from out of the dust and made you ruler over my people, Israel (1 Kgs 16:2)

Since you sold yourself to do evil in the eyes of YHWH (1 Kgs 21:20)

Instead of the expected acknowledgement of the ruler's chosen status after the יען-conjunction, Ahab is accused of "selling himself to do evil in the eyes of YHWH."

Not only does a later editor attribute the curse pronouncement to Ahab and Jezebel, the editor also may have moved the fulfillment oracle (v. 22b) from Jehoram, the last Omride, to the present place. This, however, is not clear since the fulfillment of the pronouncement is far from formulaic.

Just as the pronouncement against Ahab is unusual, the fulfillment does not follow the paradigm outlined in the accounts of Jeroboam (1 Kgs 15:30) and Baasha (1 Kgs 16:13). The fulfillment appears partially in the postlude of Ahab's account and in the account of Jehu, the king selected to decimate the dynasty of Ahab; however, neither accounts refer to the provocation of God. As mentioned above, 1 Kgs 21:22b was probably part of the fulfillment formula which was attributed to Ahab. It is unclear where it might originally have been placed. Nevertheless, a human instrument is depicted as the primary executor of the punishment.

An account of Ahab's death in a battle against Aram is provided in 1 Kgs 22:29-38.[99] According to the report, a certain man strikes Israel's king in the chariot with his bow and arrow (v. 34). Afterwards, the blood on the chariot is washed which is then interpreted as a fulfillment of God's word (v. 38b):[100]

וישטף את־הרכב על ברכת שמרון
וילקו הכלבים את־דמו והזנות רחצו
בדבר יהוה אשר דבר

He washed the chariot in the pool of Samaria
and the dogs licked up his blood (where the prostitutes washed),
according to the word of YHWH which he spoke.

This most likely refers to 1 Kgs 21:19b where Elijah speaks of dogs licking up Ahab's blood.

Later on in the account of Jehu's prophetic legitimization and actual rise to power, the final fulfillment of God's promise to destroy Ahab's household is

---

99   The account of the battle of Israel and Judah against Aram (1 Kgs 22:29-38) never explicitly mentions Ahab. Instead the battle report refers to the king of North ("king of Israel," מלך ישראל, vv. 29, 30 - twice, 31, 32, 33, 34; or just "the king," מלך, vv. 34, 35, 37 - twice) which is unusual since Jehoshaphat is mentioned explicitly (vv. 29, 30, 32 - twice). Only from the surrounding context could the reader associate this king with Ahab.

100 Few Hebrew manuscripts and Targum has an added phrase, "through the hands of Elijah" (ביד אליהו).

outlined. A servant of Elisha prophesies to Jehu that he will become the head
of a new dynasty and kill off Ahab's household (2 Kgs 9:7-10):[101]

7) והכיתה את־בית אחאב אדניך ונקמתי דמי עבדי הנביאים
ודמי כל־עבדי יהוה מיד איזבל

8) ואבד כל־בית אחאב והכרתי לאחאב משתין בקיר ועצור ועזוב בישראל

9) ונתתי את־בית אחאב כבית ירבעם בן־נבט וכבית בעשא בן־אחיה

10)ואת־איזבל יאכלו הכלבים בחלק יזרעאל ואין קבר ויפתח הדלת וינס

7) You will strike the house of Ahab, your master, and I[102] will avenge the
blood of my servants, the prophets, the blood of all the servants of YHWH
from the hand of Jezebel.

8) The whole house of Ahab will be destroyed. I[103] will cut off from Ahab
every male, slave or free, in Israel.

9) I will make the house of Ahab like the house of Jeroboam, son of Nebat,
like the house of Baasha, son of Ahijah.

10) As for Jezebel, the dogs will consume on the ground of Jezreel, and no one
will bury her. He opened the door and ran.

Though Jehu will execute the punishment (v. 7), it is God who declares to
destroy Ahab (vv. 7, 8, 9).[104] Yet in the extended fulfillment account, the executor of the punishment, like the previous oracles against the dynasties, is a
human instrument who acts according to God's word. Jehu kills Jehoram (2
Kgs 9:25), Jezebel (2 Kgs 9:36-37), the princes (2 Kgs 10:10-11), and the

---

101 The wording of the punishment resembles Elijah's oracle against Ahab (1 Kgs 21:21-23):
"cutting off every male, slave or free, in Israel," "making Ahab's house like that of Jeroboam, son of Nebat, and Baasha, son of Ahijah," and "dogs consuming Jezebel." However,
rather than listing off the catalog of sins in 1 Kgs 21:20b, 25-26 ("selling oneself to do evil"
and "behaving in the vilest manner by going after idols"), the servant explains that the punishment had resulted from the blood of the prophets in the hands of Jezebel (2 Kgs 9:7):

ונקמתי דמי עבדי הנביאים ודמי כל־עבדי יהוה מיד איזבל

I will avenge the blood of my servants, the prophets, and the blood of the servants of YHWH
from the hand of Jezebel.

No mention is made of the provocation.

102 The Greek has "You" instead of "I."

103 The Greek has "You" instead of "I."

104 The difference between the "I" (YHWH) of the MT and "You" (Jehu) of the Greek reflect the
tension in attributing the activities to the temporal or divine agency at some point in the textual transmission.

remaining members of Ahab's household (2 Kgs 10:17).[105] In sum, the whole
house of Ahab dies in the hand of a human instrument.

1.4.4.4. 1 Kings 22:53-54

The final הכעיס against the Omride dynasty appears in the account of Ahaziah
(1 Kgs 22:53-54), not so much as a fulfillment of the oracle, but as an indictment of the king:

Catalog of Sins (vv. 53-54)

53) ויעש הרע בעיני יהוה
וילך בדרך אביו ובדרך אמו
ובדרך ירבעם בן־נבט אשר החטיא את־ישראל
54) ויעבד את־הבעל וישתחוה לו

Provocation

ויכעס את־יהוה אלהי ישראל ככל אשר עשה אביו

53) He did evil in the eyes of YHWH and he walked in the ways of his father
     and his mother and Jeroboam, son of Nebat, who made Israel sin.
54) He served Ba'al[106] and worshipped him and <u>provoked</u> YHWH, the God of
     Israel, <u>to anger</u> like all that his father had done.

By virtue of his kingship over Israel and filial relationship to Ahab, Ahaziah
was doomed from the beginning. He was not only blamed for doing evil and
following in the sins of Jeroboam, but also imitating his parents by "serving"
(ויעבד) and "worshipping" (וישתחוה) Ba'al. These sins, listed in a succession
of converted imperfects (וישתחוה ויעש . . . וילך . . . ויעבד . . .), syntactically
leads to the final verb (ויכעס, "and he provoked to anger").[107] As a consequence, the pattern of sin-provocation is apparent in the narrative. Yet the
following verse does not detail any harm against his family or his own self, but
is actually a historical note.

---

105 Even when the prophecies are completely fulfilled, the specific accusations against Ahab are
    not mentioned even though the messenger, Elijah, is. When Jehu kills Jehoram (2 Kgs 9:25),
    he mentions only the "blood of Naboth and his sons" (את־דמי נבות ואת־דמי בניו, v. 26); in
    the execution of Jezebel, Elijah's judgment of dogs (2 Kgs 9:36-37); in the mass murder of
    the princes, according to Elijah's word (2 Kgs 10:10-11); and killing of Ahab's family (אב־
    הנשארים לאח, "the remnant of Ahab") in Samaria, according to Elijah's word (2 Kgs
    10:17). Thus, הכעיס is not mentioned as a justification for the punishment of Ahab and his
    household.
106 The LXX has the plural form of בעל.
107 The succession of *wyqtl* is "mostly temporally or logically succeeding," so that a "logical
    entailment from preceding situation(s) . . . is expressed" (*IBHS* §33.2.1).

In 2 Kgs 1:1, the narrative shifts away from Ahaziah and reports on the rebellion of Moab against Israel, only then to return to the subject of Ahaziah's accident in 2 Kgs 1:2:

1) ויפשע מואב בישראל אחרי מות אחאב
2) ויפל אחזיה ...

1) Moab rebelled against Israel after the death of Ahab.
2) Ahaziah fell ...

The brief historical interlude is unexpected and somewhat unnecessary[108] since the rebellion is fully outlined later in the account of Jehoram (2 Kgs. 3:4-27), the brother of Ahaziah, who tries to quell the rebellion. In fact, the wording of 2 Kgs 3:5 is similar to that of 2 Kgs 1:1:

(2 Kgs 3:5) ויהי כמות אחאב ויפשע מלך־מואב במלך ישראל
(2 Kgs 1:1) ויפשע מואב בישראל אחרי מות אחאב

When *Ahab died*, the king of Moab rebelled against the king of Israel (2 Kgs 3:5)
Moab rebelled against Israel after *the death of Ahab* (2 Kgs 1:1)

Beside the difference in some of the words (underlined) and the reversal of the order (death-rebellion vs. rebellion-death), the two verses are similar. If 2 Kgs 1:1 is a repetitive, extraneous interlude,[109] then why was the verse included in the present pericope? Given the common pattern of sin-provocation-punishment, the report of the rebellion was probably intended to function as the description of the punishment for Ahaziah's sin.[110] Though the rebellion is

---

108 Contrary to Cogan and Tadmor, *2 Kings*, 22, who argues that the verse is in the right place as it is "based on the Israelite annals." If that were the case, then wouldn't one expect the note on Mesha's rebellion after a record of Ahab's death (1 Kgs 22:40) rather than in the middle of Ahaziah's account? DtrH is not mainly interested in presenting the information in the royal annals but demonstrating how history unravels itself according to certain theological principles, namely of determinism. Ahaziah has sinned, thus he must be punished.

109 One could argue that 2 Kgs 3:5 is a repetition of 1:1, not vice-versa. However, 3:5 is essential to the report in 2 Kgs 3:4-27 since it presents the background for the war between Israel/Judah and Moab, whereas 1:1 is peripheral to the narrative. One may perhaps argue that 1:1 was a *Wiederaufnahme* of 3:5 so as to include the prophetic narrative of Elijah and Elisha (2 Kgs 1:2-2:25). However, this literary feature does not take into consideration the historical note on Joram, son of Ahab (2 Kgs 3:1-3).

110 Even without 2 Kgs 1:1, the following pericope (2 Kgs 1:2-17) concerning the accident of Ahaziah may suffice as the punishment for Ahaziah's act of idolatry. Since he sinned against God by following the sins of Jeroboam and worshipping Ba'al, he fell through the windows resulting in his death. Yet this punishment must have not been completely sufficient since DtrH needed to mention Mesha's rebellion here.

recorded to have ensued "after Ahab's death" (אחרי מות אחאב), that is prior to Ahaziah's enthronement, not after the fact, it is positioned after the statement of the provocation. This could only point to its function as the punishment. If the rebellion literarily acts as the punishment, then here, the agency of God is nowhere apparent; it is a human army which is set against Israel, not just the king as in 2 Kgs 3:5 (במלך ישראל, "against the king of Israel"). The implied human instrument is thus the executor of the punishment.

1.5. Conclusion

In sum, הכעיס in DtrH1 usually functioned as a pivot, heralding the punishment in the curse formulae against the first three dynasties — Jeroboam, Baasha, and Omri — and in the narrative recounting their fulfillment. The pattern is fully established against the houses of Jeroboam (1 Kgs 14:9-11) and Baasha (1 Kgs 16:2-4) whose sons, Nadab (1 Kgs 15:30) and Elah (1 Kgs 16:13), respectively faced the consequences of the family's sins, death in the hands of God's temporal instruments. However, the pattern begins to disintegrate with the Omride dynasty whose founder, Omri, only gets a partial mark of disapproval (1 Kgs 16:26) while Ahab is accredited with not one but two references for having provoked God to anger (1 Kgs 16:33, 21:24) among which 1 Kgs 21:24 functions as the prophetic pronouncement against the dynasty. Its fulfillment is dispersed throughout the accounts of Ahab and Jehoram/Jehu, with the final mention of הכעיס found in the account of Ahaziah (1 Kgs 22:53-54), the second to the last Omride ruler. In all instances, it is ultimately God working through history — human and natural instruments (see Chart A for a summary).

Part II: Deuteronomistic History, Redaction Level Two

2.1. Introduction

From the oracles against individual kings and their dynasties in DtrH1, הכעים in DtrH2 occurs primarily in explanations of the destructions of Samaria (722 B.C.E.) and Jerusalem (587 B.C.E.).[1] As argued in the previous section (Part I), DtrH1 used the term, הכעיס, to indict Israel's first three dynasties (Jeroboam, Baasha, Omri/Ahab).[2] Only in DtrH2 does הכעיס appear in the ac-

---

1   Contrast H. N. Wallace, "The Oracles Against the Israelite Dynasties in 1 and 2 Kings," 21-40, who attributes the present shape of the oracles against the Israelite dynasties to the Dtr editor, who constructs a framework leading to the downfall of Israel (2 Kgs 17). He argues that the oracles are not without older material but is primarily a composition of the Dtr editor.

2   After the elimination of the Omride dynasty, only one other significant dynasty survived in the North, that of Jehu's. Since Jehu eradicated the house of Ahab and Ba'alism in Israel but failed to discontinue the sin of Jeroboam (2 Kgs 10:29, 31), he is ensured of a dynasty only up to the fourth generation (2 Kgs 10:39). In other words, the survival of his dynasty is portrayed as a blessing. If one looks at v. 30, it provides a positive reason for Jehu's dynasty: It is "on account" (יען אשר) of Jehu's good deeds (הטיבה לעשות הישר בעיני ככל אשר בלבבי עשית לבית אחאב, "you have done well in doing what is right in my eyes; according to all that was in my heart you did to the house of Ahab"). Therefore, even though he persists in following the ways of Jeroboam, DtrH1 does not indict him of provoking God. He is promised a dynasty whereas the only other dynasties of Jeroboam I, Baasha, and Omri are cursed with the cessation of their descendants. They receive the prophetic oracle of doom which followed the pattern of sin-provocation-punishment. Since no stable dynasty forms thereafter, the consequent kings of Israel are not recorded to have 'provoked God to anger.' Even though, Jehu's descendants, Jehoahaz (2 Kgs 13:1-8), Joash (2 Kgs 13:10-13), Jeroboam II (2 Kgs 14:23-29), and Zechariah (2 Kgs 15:8-12), continued to follow the sins of Jeroboam (13:2, 14:24, 15:9) respectively, they did not warrant a commentary that they had provoked God to anger. However, in the account of Jehoahaz, the kingdom of Israel, not the king himself, elicits a statement that God was angry with them (ויחר־אף ישראל, "he was angry with Israel," 2 Kgs 13:3). In a style very imitative of the book of Judges, in which the pattern — people sin, God gets angry, God gives/sells them to the oppressors, people plead/cry, God hears, and sends them a deliverer — is established (Judg 2:11-19, 3:7-11, 3:12-30, etc.), God gave Israel over to the powers of Aram, who then afflicted them, impelling Jehoahaz to beseech God for help. Thereupon, God sends a anonymous "deliverer" (מושיע; see Judg 2:18, 3:9, 15) and saves Israel. This brief account (13:3-5) is most likely an addition (v. 6a is a repetitive resumption of v. 2, in which v. 6a lays the blame on all of Israel rather than Jehoahaz: אך לא־סרו מחטאות בית־ירבעם אשר החטי את ישראל בה הלך,

counts of the destruction of the religio-political centers of the two kingdoms so that the 'provocation' that led to the decimation of the dynasties is now extended to the destruction of Samaria and Jerusalem.

Except for 1 Kgs 16:7 and 2 Kgs 23:19, הכעים in DtrH2 either forebode (Deut 4:25, 9:18,[3] 31:29, Judg 2:12, 1 Kgs 14:15) or explicitly explain the fall of Samaria (2 Kgs 17:11, 17) and Jerusalem (2 Kgs 21:6, 15, 22:17, 23:26). Before the historical narratives recount the reasons for the fall of Samaria and Jerusalem, DtrH2 outlines the pattern of sin-provocation-punishment in which Israel will eventually face disaster (Deut 4:25-28, 9:18-20, 31:27-29, Judg 2:11-16, 1 Kgs 14:15-16a). In these outlines, DtrH2, who writes *after the fact*, warns the people of the consequences of their sins in an attempt to hold the people (and their sins) responsible for the destructions. Had they obeyed the commandments, relayed through Moses, Jerusalem with its Temple would have been standing.

To link these warnings to the destructions of the religio-political centers, the definitive consequence of their disobedience, DtrH2 develops the pattern of sin-provocation-punishment in the accounts of the fall of the North and

---

"Nevertheless, they did not turn aside from the sins of the house of Jeroboam who caused Israel to sin but he walked in it [other ancient translations have the plural form, "they walked in them"]; וילך אחר חטאת ירבעם בן־נבט אשר־החטיא את־ישראל, "he went after the sin of Jeroboam, son of Nebat, who caused Israel to sin") in which הכעים is not used.

After the Jehu dynasty, a sequence of usurpers come to power. A succession of shortlived kings, Shallum (745; interestingly, Shallum is not attributed with the sin of Jeroboam [2 Kgs 15:13-15]), Menahem (745-736), Pekahiah (736-735), Pekah (735-732), and Hosea (732-723) ruled the Northern kingdom, among whom only Menahem was able to bestow the kingdom to his offspring. Though Menahem, Pekahiah, and Pekah, according to DtrH, followed the ways of Jeroboam (2 Kgs 15:18, 24, 28, respectively), they supposedly did not provoke God to anger (see Appendix B for a summary).

The "sin of Jeroboam" more than the reference to the 'provocation' may have been the linchpin that explained the fall of Samaria in DtrH1. See F.M. Cross, *Canaanite Myth and Hebrew Epic*, 279-281, who argues that the climax of Jeroboam's sins is the fall of Samaria in 2 Kgs 17; E. Theodore Mullen, "The Sins of Jeroboam: A Redactional Assessment," *CBQ* 49 (1987):212-232 (it should however be noted that Mullen does not take into considertation the several levels of redaction but posits "one author or edition of the history" so that the "theme is not completely resolved ... until the destruction of Jerusalem (2 Kings 24-25)" [215, note 11]); and John Holder, "The Presuppositions, Accusations, and Threats of 1 K. 14:1-18," *JBL* 107 (1988):27-38, who argues that the sin of Jeroboam is the reason for the fall of the northern kingdom: "exile becomes the ultimate consequence of the illegitimate cult of the North" (37). This does not exclude an a-priori disapproval of the Jeroboam dynasty which is later subsumed in the overarching framework.

3   According to Weinfeld, *Deuteronomy 1-11*, 423, the golden calf episode "reflects here the historical sin of the northern Israelites, who were worshipping the golden calves (cf. 1 Kgs 12:28-29 and especially Hos 8:5-6; 10:5, 13:2)." For general discussion, see Gary Knoppers, "Aaron's Calf and Jeroboam's Calves," in *Fortunate the Eyes That See: Essays in Honor of David Noel Freedman in Celebration of His Seventieth Birthday* (eds Astrid Beck, et al; Grand Rapids: Eerdmans, 1995), 92-104.

South. Samaria (2 Kgs 17:7-23a) and Jerusalem, specifically Manasseh (2 Kgs 21:2-15), both commit an extensive list of sins which inevitably provoke God to anger. This provocation then stirs God to action. Even with all the religio-political reforms of Josiah, God is still provoked (2 Kgs 22:15-17, 23:26-27) and will eventually destroy Jerusalem.

Yet there are exceptions in DtrH2, where הכעיס does not address the destructions of Samaria and Jerusalem (1 Kgs 16:7 and 2 Kgs 23:19-20). The former provides an additional justification for the death of Baasha and the latter, Josiah's despoliation of the sanctuaries in Samaria. Nevertheless, both will be discussed to illuminate the use of הכעיס and the role of God in carrying out punishments.

Whereas in these attestations, God is portrayed as the main executor, sometimes with his human instruments, there is a tendency either to make the punishment correspond more with the sin or to extricate God from the destructive activities. Without doubt, God is depicted in meting out punishments, whether by himself (Deut 4:26-27, 1 Kgs 14:15-16a, 16:7, 2 Kgs 22:16, 23:26-27) or with an instrument (Judg 2:14-15, 2 Kgs 17:19-20, 21:15). However, DtrH2 and what appears to be later additions to DtrH2 attempt to exonerate God from the punishment in three different approaches. First, the punishment corresponds more with the sins (Deut 4:25-28, Judg 2:11-16, 1 Kgs 14:15-16a, 16:7, 2 Kgs 17:19-20, 21:12-14, 22:16) so that the people are depicted as deserving their due; second, God either responds in anger (Deut 9:20, Judg 2:14, 2 Kgs 17:18, 21-22, 23:26-27), uses anger (Deut 9:19) or his divine wrath acts on his behalf (2 Kgs 22:17) which the people had initially caused; and third, the people's evil function as their very punishment (Deut 31:27-29). These attempts, as will be demonstrated in Part IV, reflect the general tendency in the book of Jeremiah.

Chart B: Pericopes with הכעיס in DtrH2 and Additional Levels

Passage	Type of Sin	Form of הכעיס	Culprit	Pivot	Type of Punishment	Agency
Deut 4:25-28 [25]	Idolatry and evil	להכעיסו	Future Israel	Yes	Destruction, dispersal; Partial measure-for-measure	God
Deut 9:18-20 [18]	Golden calves	להכעיסו	Israel	Yes	Potential destruction	V. 19: God, with divine wrath; V. 20: God, motivated by divine wrath
Deut 31:27-29 [29]	Idolatry and evil	להכעיסו	Future Israel	Yes	Evil – self-destruction	Evil of people
Judg 2:11-16 [12]	Idolatry	ויכעסו	Israel	Yes, minus v. 13	Angry, deliver to enemy; Partial measure-for-measure	God (motivated by divine wrath) → human
1 Kgs 14:15-16a [15]	Idolatry	בכעסיהם	Israel (North)	Yes	V. 15: Strike Israel, dispersal; V. 16a: Deliver to enemy (?)	V. 15: God; V. 16a: Human (?)
1 Kgs 16:7 [7]	Evil = Idolatry	להכעיסו	Baasha and dynasty	Yes	Strike Baasha; Partial measure-for-measure	God
2 Kgs 17:7-23a	Vv. 7-11a: Idolatry; Vv. 12, 15-17: Disobey God; Vv. 13-14: Disobey prophets		Israel (North)			
V. 11		הכעיסו		No; Middle of catalog	See below	See below

V. 17	See above	להכעיסו	See above	Yes	Vv. 18, 21-22: Angry, God removed Israel; Vv. 19-20: God rejected and deliver to enemy; Partial measure-for-measure	Vv. 18-21-22: God, motivated by divine wrath; Vv. 19-20: God → human
2 Kgs 21:2-15	Vv. 2-7: Idolatry; Vv. 8-9a: People Disobey God; V. 10: Disobey prophets		Vv. 2-7: Manasseh; Vv. 8-10: People			
V. 6		להכעים		No; Middle of catalog	See below	See below
V. 15	See above	מכעים	Judah	Yes; Reverse	Evil, measure of Samaria, deliver to enemy; Partial measure-for-measure	God → human
2 Kgs 22:16-17 [17]	Idolatry	להכעיס למעני	Judah	Yes	V. 16: Evil; Boomerang V. 17: Divine wrath	V. 16: God; V. 17: Divine wrath
2 Kgs 23:19-20 [19]	Sanctuaries	להכעיס	Kings of Israel	Yes	Removal of sanctuaries	Human (Josiah)
2 Kgs 23:26-27 [26]	Provocations	אשר הכעים הכעיס למעני הכעם	Manasseh	Yes	Angry, God removed and rejected	God, motivated by divine wrath

2.2. Deuteronomy 4:25-28 (v. 25)

As the Israelites are about to enter the Promised Land, Moses outlines their future disobedience and punishment (Deut 4). In this outline, הכעים functions as the pivot for the potential punishment in which God is the primary executor.

Unlike the first three chapters of the book of Deuteronomy, which recount the events leading up to the crossing over the Jordan, 4:1-40 is the first hortatory sermon[4] dated to the post-exilic period (4:25-31).[5] The central concern of this sermon is the worship of images (vv. 16-25); it contrasts YHWH who is without form (v. 15) with the various physical images of foreign nations (v. 28). This warning against all graven images (כל תמונת פסל, "image in the form of anything," v. 23) is undergided (כי, "because") with the statement, "YHWH, your God, is a consuming fire, a jealous God" (שׁ אשׁ יהוה אלהיך אכלה הוא אל קנא, v. 24). It contains within itself the possibility of a punishment if the people fail to keep God's covenant since fire represents judgment. After the declaratory warning, the sermon turns to the ramifications for the possible neglect of the commandment in the future.

Thus, vv. 25-28 describe a scenario in which the Israelites might come to disobey God and receive their due punishment:

Future Catalog of Sins (v. 25)

25) כי־תוליד בנים בני בנים ונושנתם בארץ
והשחתם ועשיתם פסל תמונת כל ועשיתם הרע בעיני יהוה אלהיך
Future Provocation

להכעיסו

Future Punishment (vv. 26-28)

26) העידתי בכם היום את־השמים ואת־הארץ
כי־אבד תאבדון מהר מעל הארץ
אשר אתם עברים את־הירדן שמה לרשתה
לא־תאריכן ימים עליה כי השמד תשמדון
27) והפיץ יהוה אתכם בעמים
ונשארתם מתי מספר בגוים אשר ינהג יהוה אתכם שמה
28) ועבדתם־שם אלחים מעשה ידי אדם
עץ ואבן אשר לא־יראון ולא ישמעון ולא יאכלון ולא יריחן

25)   When you have children and grandchildren and have grown complacent in the land, and you act corruptly and make an image in the form of anything and do evil in the eyes of YHWH, your God, <u>provoking him to anger</u>,

---

4   It is the beginning of Moses' farewell address which is the first sermon characteristic of DtrH (Weinfeld, *Deuteronomy 1-11*, 214-215).
5   According to Moshe Weinfeld, *Deuteronomy 1-11*, 230.

26)   I call upon the heavens and earth as witnesses against you for you will
       surely, quickly perish from the land where you are crossing over Jordan to
       inherit and your days will not be long upon it for you will surely be de-
       stroyed.
27)   YHWH will disperse you among the peoples and only a few will survive
       among the nations to where YHWH will drive you.
28)   There you will serve gods, the work of human hands, made of wood and
       stone which neither see, hear, eat, nor smell.

When Israel is established in the land, according to Moses, they will break the
covenant which is primarily based on the ban against graven images. At the
point in which the people make "sculptured images" (פסל תמונת כל), they
provoke God to anger.[6] This provocation consequently leads to the punishment
(vv. 26-28), forming the sin-provocation-punishment pattern.

In the description of the punishment, God is depicted as the agent. The
punishment opens by invoking the heavens and earth as witnesses to the divine
warning.[7] However, God, not the natural elements, is the agent who will punish Israel. Although the initial verbs of destruction (v. 26) do not indicate the
agent of the punishment, clearly God is the one who punishes: The first two
verbal clause, אבד תאבדון ("be utterly destroyed") and השמד תשמדון ("be
completely destroyed") are without active subjects since the former verb is a
stative while the latter is conjugated in the niphal stem. However, YHWH is

---

6   Though there is a succession of verbs, והשחתם ועשיתם ... ועשיתם ("you have acted cor-
     ruptly, you have made, ... you have done"), the accusation is focused on making of graven
     images. The first two verbs are coordinated in a hendiadys structure (co-ordination of com-
     plementary verbal ideas; see GKC §120d) where the first verb describes the manner in which
     the primary action is expressed in the second verb so that both verbs characterize the means
     by which an idol is constructed. As for the final verb, nothing within the structure of the sen-
     tence indicates that the clause is subordinate to the central verbal idea. Therefore, given its
     form, the sentence could be formulated as two sins: making of images and doing evil. How-
     ever, within the context of the sermon, 'making images' is the only 'evil' one could do in the
     eyes of YHWH. Thus, 'doing evil' modifies 'making images.'
         Weinfeld, *Deuteronomy 1-11*, 194, translates the verse, "act destructively and make for
     yourselves a sculpted image in any likeness, causing YHWH your God displeasure and vexa-
     tion," while Tigay, *Deuteronomy*, 51-52, translates "should you act wickedly and make for
     yourselves a sculptured image in any likeness, causing the LORD your God displeasure and
     vexation." Both make the first two verbs into two distinct verbal ideas while subordinating
     the third verb. Yet it proscribes the 'act of image-making' as destructive/wicked act. The de-
     fault of their translation is placing 'displeasure' on the same level as 'vexation.' 'Image-
     making' is 'doing evil' against God; it does not 'cause displeasure' but only provokes God to
     anger.
7   On a literary level, the invocation hints at a treaty where the natural forces are called upon as
     witnesses in case of a violation. For a short discussion on this, see Tigay, *Deuteronomy*, 52.

the subject of the following two active verbs: YHWH "will scatter" (והפיץ)
them among peoples to whom he "had driven" (וינהג) them.

Since destruction and dispersal do not correspond to the sin of idolatry, the
punishment is not measure-for-measure. Yet in v. 28, the people will be forced
to worship idols which they had made in the Promised Land in foreign lands:

Sin [Construct Images (in own land)] → Punishment
[Destruction and Dispersal + Worship Works of Their Hand (in foreign land)]

Therefore, there is partial measure-for-measure correspondence between the
sin and the punishment which God will mete out.

2.3. Deuteronomy 9:18-20 (v. 18)

In the Deuteronomic retelling of the Golden Calf episode, הכעים links the
catalog of sins to a potential, but not realized, punishment, where God, motivated by his anger would have been the executor.

Deuteronomy 9:1-10:11 recalls the people's past sins to prevent them from
transgressing against God, eventually undermining the covenantal relationship.
Within this larger framework, 9:7-24[8] recounts the Golden Calf incident which
initially appears in Exod 32.[9] Yet the account in Deuteronomy is quite distinct

---

8   Actually the Golden Calf episode includes only vv. 8a-21. However, the literary unit
     encompasses a larger section from vv. 7-24 based upon the inclusio structure, Moshe A.
     Zipor, "The Deuteronomic Account of the Golden Calf and its Reverberation in Other Parts
     of the Book of Deuteronomy," *ZAW* 108 (1996): 24. The section opens and closes with the
     expression, "you have been rebellious against the YHWH" (ממרים הייתם עם־יהוה, vv. 7,
     24). Also, the unity is reflected in the three occurrences of the hiphil of קצף in vv. 7, 8 and
     22, the only times it appears in the Pentateuch.

9   Though scholars generally agree that Exod 32 is the final product of different sources, they
     disagree on the actual delineation of the sources in the chapter. Brevard Childs, *Exodus: A
     Commentary* (OTL; London: S.C.M., 1974), 558-562, attributes most of the chapter to J with
     deuteronomistic additions in vv. 7-14 (similar to Martin Noth, *Exodus: A Commentary* [OTL;
     London: S.C.M., 1962], 242, though he would only attribute vv. 9-14 to DtrH) and a later,
     independent expansion in vv. 25-29. Though vv. 7-14 may be deuteronomistic, they were
     probably not added at the same time that Deut 9:7-24 was composed since significant
     difference occurs between them. See below, where the Exodus account seems to precede the
     one in Deuteronomy.
         Since Deut 9:12-14 (similar to Exod 32:7-10) falls outside the scope of this study, it
     will not be discussed above. At the same time, though, a interesting observation should be
     noted. In place of the expression for God's anger ("to be angry," חרה אף) in Exod 32:10,
     Deut 9:14 instead elaborates upon the destruction. Deut 9:12-13 resembles the wording of
     Exod 32:7-9 which reflects on the people's quick tendency to rebel:
     Exod 32:

7) וידבר יהוה אל־משה לך־רד כי שחת עמך אשר העלית מארץ מצרים
8) סרו מהר מן־הדרך אשר צויתם עשו להם עגל מסכה וישתחוו־לו יזבחו־לו
ויאמרו אלה אלהיך ישראל אשר העלוך מארץ מצרים
9) ויאמר יהוה אל־משה ראיתי את־העם הזה והנה עם־קשה־ערף הוא

7) YHWH spoke to Moses, "Go down, for your people, whom you brought up from Egypt, have corrupted themselves.

8) They have quickly turned aside from the path which I have commanded them; they have made for themselves a molten calf and worshipped it and sacrificed to it. They have said, 'These are your gods, O Israel, who brought you out from the land of Egypt.'"

9) YHWH said to Moses, "I have seen these people and they are a stiff-necked people."

Deut 9:

12) ויאמר יהוה אלי קום רד מהר מזה כי שחת עמך אשר הוצאת ממצרים
סרו מהר מן־הדרך אשר צויתם עשו להם מסכה
13) ויאמר יהוה אלי לאמר ראיתי את־העם הזה והנה עם־קשה־ערף הוא

12) YHWH said to me, "Get up, go down quickly from here, for your people, whom you brought out from Egypt have corrupted themselves. They have quickly turned aside from the path which I have commanded them; they have made for themselves a molten image."

13) YHWH said to me, "I have seen this people and they are stiff-necked people."

Then there is a significant difference in the parallel accounts:

(Exod 32:10)

10) ועתה הניחה לי *ויחר־אפי* בהם ואכלם
ואעשה אותך לגוי גדול

Now, leave me alone so that *my anger may burn* against them and I will consume them. Then I will make you into a great nation.

(Deut 9:14)

14) הרף ממני *ואשמידם ואמחה* את־שמם מתחת השמים
ואעשה אותך לגוי־עצום ורב ממנו

Leave me alone so that *I may destroy them and blot* their name from under the heavens. Then I will make you into a mightier and greater nation than them.

Exod 32:10a makes a general statement of God's anger and plan to consume the Israelites which is paralleled in Deut 9:14a with a description of God's destruction: God will "destroy" (hiphil of שמד) and "erase" (Qa of מחה) their names. The stories converge once again in v. 14b and v. 10b, where God promises to make Moses into a great nation. The difference in the accounts is crucial. Whereas God's anger is used in Exod 32 to describe God's readiness to punish, the actual description of the punishment is laid out in Deut 9. For the author of Deut 9, divine wrath signified divine punishment. See also Deut 9:25b where God is said "to destroy" (להשמיד) and 9:26 where Moses implores God "not to destroy" (אל־השחת) whereas Exod 32:11 has Moses ask YHWH why his anger burns ("Why, YHWH, does your anger burn against your people," למה יהוה יחרה אפך בעמך).

from[10] while at the same time, dependent upon the composite version in Exod 32.[11] Interestingly, the subunit containing הכעים (Deut 9:18-20) is without an explicit parallel in Exod 32, unlike the surrounding verses which have parallels in the Exodus account. For example, there is basic correspondence between Deut 9:12-14 and Exod 32:7-10,[12] Deut 9:15-17, 21 and Exod 32:15-20,[13] and

---

10 See Weinfeld's, *Deuteronomy 1-11*, 428, brief comparison of the two accounts in Exodus and Deuteronomy.

11 Though Christopher Begg, "The Destruction of the Golden Calf Revisited (Exod 32,20/Deut 9,21)," in *Deuteronomy and Deuteronomic Literature: Festschrift C.H.W. Brekelmans* (eds. M. Vervenne and J. Lust; BETL 133; Leuven: Leuven University Press, 1997), 469-479, focuses on one particular verse, his findings have larger implications. He concludes that "the author of Deut 9, 7b-10, 11 presumes throughout his version reader familiarity with the story of Exodus 32-34 to which he then gives his own emphases" (478), in response to John van Seters,' *The Life of Moses: The Yahwist as Historian in Exodus-Numbers* (Kampen, Netherlands: Kok Pharos Publishing House, 1994), 306-307, opposite conclusion that Exodus is dependent upon the account in Deuteronomy.

12 See note 9.

13 Though the parallels are not exact, there are significant similarities. Moses 'turns and goes down' with the two stone tablets:

Deut 9

15) ואפן וארד מן־ההר וההר בער באש ושני לחת הברית על שתי ידי

I turned and went down from the mountain (the mountain was ablaze with fire). The two tablets of the covenant were in my two hands.

Exod 32

15) ויפן וירד משה מן־ההר שני לחת העדת בידו
לחת כתבים משני עבריהם מזה ומזה הם כתבים

Moses turned and went down the mountain with the two tablets of the testimony in his hand. The tablets were inscribed on both sides, front and back.

The Exodus account further elaborates on the tablets and emphasizes the servant role of Joshua (Exod 32:16-18), which is absent in the Deuteronomy account. Afterwards the similar storyline continues. Moses sees the calf, triggering his anger, whereupon he casts the tablets to the ground:

Deut 9

16) וארא והנה חטאתם ליהוה אלהיכם עשיתם לכם
עגל מסכה סרתם מהר מן־דרך אשר־צוה יהוה אכחם
17) ואתפש בשני הלחת ואשלכם מעל שתי ידי ואשברם לעיניכם

16) I looked and here, you had sinned against YHWH, your God. You had made for yourselves a molten calf. You had turned quickly away from the path which YHWH had commanded you.

17) I took the two tablets and cast them out of my two hands and broke them before your eyes.

Exod 32

Deut 9:25-29 and Exod 32:11-14,[14] while Deut 9:22-24 recalls other episodes of rebellion.

As a result, vv. 18-20 appear to have been a Dtr addition to the story borrowed from Exod 32. This is crucial since the first verse (v. 18) functions as the pivot in the overall structure of the pericope (Deut 9:7-24).[15] In Deut 9:7-24, הקציף ("to provoke to wrath") appears in three key locations, at the beginning (vv. 7-8), middle (v. 18). and end of the pericope (vv. 22-24). Vv. 7-8 and vv. 22-24 form the outer framework of the pericope in which the people are said to have provoked God to wrath during the period of the wilderness (v. 7), Horeb (v.8), and Taberah, Massah, and Kibroth-hattavah (v. 22). They form a inclusio structure which is made all the more evident with the wording of the rebellion motif in vv. 7 and 24:

---

(19) ויהי כאשר קרב אל־המחנה וירא את־העגל ומחלת
ויחר־אף משה וישלך מידו את־הלחת וישבר אתם תחת ההר

When he drew near the camp and saw the calf and the dancing, Moses was angry. He cast the tablets from his hand and broke them at the foot of the mountain.

Thereafter, Deut 9 adds vv. 18-20, which are discussed above, and closes the parallel account in v. 21:

Deut 9

(21) את־חטאתכם אשר־עשיתם את־העגל לקחתי
ואשרף אתו באש ואכת אתו טחון היטב עד
אשר־דק לעפר ואשלך את־עפרו אל־הנחל הירד מן־ההר

Your sin, the calf, which you have made, I took and burned it in fire. Then I crushed it, grinding (it) into powder as fine as dust. I cast its dust to the stream that flowed down from the mountain.

Exod 32

(20)ויקח את־העגל אשר עשו וישרף באש
ויטחן עד אשר־דק ויזר על־פני המים וישק את־בני ישראל

He took the calf which they had made and burned it in fire. He ground (it) until it was fine and he sprinkled (it) on the water and made the Israelites drink (it).

14 The correspondence is not verbatim but similarities are apparent: 'to bring out from Egypt with a strong hand' (הוצאת ממצרים יד חזקה, "you brought out from Egypt with a mighty hand" [Deut 9:26b]; הוצאת מארץ מצרים בכח גדול וביד חזקה, "you brought out from the land of Egypt with great strength and a mighty hand" [Exod 32:11b]), 'remember Abraham, Issac, Jacob/Israel' (Deut 9:27a, Exod 32:13), and variation of 'what will Egypt say' (Deut 9:28; Exod 32:12).

15 Despite the apparent parallels between certain sections within Exod 32 and Deut 9, references to divine wrath are numerous in Exod 32:7-14, the section containing God's response to the debacle, whereas they are confined to key places in Deut 9:7-24. In Exod 32:7-14, God's anger (אף דרה/ון - vv. 10, 11, 12) characterizes the divine response to the Golden Calf incident which is then assumed by Moses in the following section (vv. 19, 22). Moses, the intermediary, reflects the divine wrath before the people.

A   *למן־היום אשר־יצאת מארץ מצרים*

B   עד באכם עד המקום הזה <u>ממרים הייתם עם יהוה</u> (v. 7)

B   <u>ממרים הייתם עם־יהוה</u>

A   *מיום דעתי אתכם* (v. 24)

7) *From the day that you came out from the land of Egypt* until you came to this place, you have been rebelling against YHWH.

24) You have been rebelling against YHWH *from the day I knew you.*

Not only is the phrase for the rebellion similar (underlined) but the time frame of their rebellion (in italics) is the same; they have rebelled from the beginning of the covenantal relationship.

While not literally in the center of the subunit, the critical verse, 9:18, describes the turning point in which Moses finds himself interceding on behalf of the Israelites who had infuriated the deity (vv. 19-20):[16]

Description of Moses' Experience at Horeb and Sin of the Molten Calf (vv. 7-17)

Moses' Response (v. 18a)

18) ואתנפל לפני יהוה כראשנה ארבעים יום וארבעים לילה
לחם לא אכלתי ומים לא שתיתי

Description of Sin (v. 18b)

על כל־חטאתכם אשר חטאתם לעשות הרע בעיני יהוה

Provocation

להכעיסו

Potential Punishment (v. 19)

19) כי יגרתי מפני האף והחמה אשר קצף יהוה עליכם להשמיד אתכם
וישמע יהוה אלי גם בפעם ההוה

God's Anger Against Aaron (v. 20)

20) ובאהרן התאנף יהוה מאד[17] להשמידו ואתפלל גם־בעד אהרן בעת ההוא

18) I prostrated myself before YHWH[18] again, forty days and forty nights. I did not eat bread and I did not drink water because of all your sin[19] which

---

16 Given the concentric structure of vv. 8b-21, v. 18 was meant to be the structural center of the chapter. Robert H. O'Connell, "Deuteronomy IX 7-X 7, 10-11: Panelled Structure, Double Rehearsal and the Rhetoric of Covenant Rebuke," *VT* 42 (1992):492-509, calls this B-section and sets out to show the "concentric compound inverse frame" (495).

17 Codex Vaticanus does not appear to have the phrase, יהוה מאד. Since YHWH is clearly indicated as the subject of the verb, the variant is not significant except that it does not modify the anger as extreme (מאד, "very").

18 Notice how this verse is repeated in 9:25.

you had committed. doing evil in the eyes of YHWH,[20] <u>provoking him to anger</u>.[21]

19)   For I was afraid because of the fiery wrath which YHWH had kindled against you to destroy you. But YHWH listened to me also that time.

20)   And YHWH was greatly angry with Aaron to the point of destroying him but I also prayed for Aaron at that time.

According to v. 18, Moses pleads for the people on account of their sin which is defined as their "doing evil" (לעשות הרע), resulting in the provocation of God. Since God's anger is provoked, Moses is "afraid" (root יגר, v. 19)[22] in anticipation of a punishment, which had materialized into "the fiery anger" (האף והחמה) which God had "kindled" (קצף) against them:

Sin (v. 18כ) → Provocation (v. 18b) →
Fear (v. 19) — Potential Punishment (האף והחמה)

This fiery anger, the potential punishment, could only have been the result of the provocation that the Israelites caused with their sins (v. 18). As a result, הכעיס is the trigger for what would have been the Israelites' punishment.

Yet the punishment is formulated in a manner that obfuscates what would have been the agent of the disaster. Clearly, Moses was afraid "because of" (מפני) the fiery wrath rather than God. At the same time, though, God is the one who "kindled" (קצף) this fiery wrath which is an instrument set "to destroy" (להשמיד) the people (v 19b):

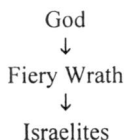

God
↓
Fiery Wrath
↓
Israelites

---

19   Samaritan text, LXX, Vulgate, Peshitta, and Targum Pseudo-Jonathan read חטאתיכם, plural form as opposed to the singular in the MT. This variant reading may reflect the overall structure of multiple sins versus the MT which focuses specifically on the molten calf.

20   Several ancient versions appear to have an addition, אלהיך.

21   The first infinitive with - ל (לעשות, "doing") functions as a complementary infinitive, which is "very frequently used in a much looser connexion to state motives, attendant circumstances, or otherwise to define more exactly" (*GKC* §114o). Also the second infinitive construct, להכעיסו, functions as the result clause that "express a consequence of the main verb" (*IBHS* §36.2.3d, example #16).

22   This episode reflects the differences between Exodus and Deuteronomy in the portrayal of Moses. First, Moses is not as forthcoming in the book of Deuteronomy. Whereas Moses prostrates himself (hithpael of נפל) before the LORD in Deuteronomy (v. 18), Moses appeases (piel of חלה) the LORD in Exodus. It reflects the transcendence of God in Deuteronomy, rather than the decreased status of Moses. God is more inaccessible to humans, even to the super-prophet like Moses.

Despite the central role of the fiery wrath, it is nevertheless YHWH who is ultimately depicted as the agent of the potential destruction. This formulation differs slightly in v. 20 where God is motivated by anger to destroy Aaron: "YHWH was extremely angry to the point of destroying him" (התאנף יהוה מאד להשמידו). The anger is not so much an instrument but a stimulus to God's design to wipe out the instigator of the idolatrous misdeed. Though the role of anger varies between v. 19 and v. 20, God is still portrayed as the primary executor of a punishment which had been deterred. Had the punishment been carried out, it would not have corresponded at all to the people's sin of worshipping the calf constructed by Aaron.

In sum, the pivotal term, הכעיס, signaled the averted destructive wrath which functioned as a instrument to (v. 19) and motivation (v. 20) for God to act.

2.4. Deuteronomy 31:27-29 (v. 29)

Part of the epilogue to the book of Deuteronomy, 31:29 succinctly establishes the sin-provocation-punishment pattern in which people bring about their own demise. Chapter 31 is a repetitive and problematic introduction to the epilogue of the book of Deuteronomy (chs. 31-34) which may reflect different literary sources.[23] In general, the chapter prepares for the appointment of Joshua and sets up for the public reading of the law and song in chapter 32.[24] At the same time, God (vv. 16-19) and Moses (vv. 27-29) reflect upon the inevitable misfortune that will befall the people on account of their wickedness (ערפך הקשה, "your stiff neck," and מריך, "your rebellion," v. 27). Within the context of Moses' speech, the prophet meditates on Israelites' sin and the consequent punishment which would have resulted from the provocation in the future (אחרית הימים, "the end of days"):[25]

---

23 Tigay, *Deuteronomy*, Excursus 29, 502-507.

24 There appears to be two introductions to the Song in chapter 32. In vv. 16-21, God introduces the Song to Moses whereas in vv. 28-30, Moses summons the people to recite the words of the Song. Moreover, the first introduction focuses on God's realization that the people will sin while the second introduction reflects on Moses' frustration with the people's stubborn ways. Given the characteristic Deuteronomic phraseology of vv. 28-30, these verses probably represent the Deuteronomic hand whereas God's introduction has expressions reflective of other sources, in particular, JE (Tigay, *Deuteronomy*, 503). However, the final unit, vv. 28-30, is not coherent. Vv. 28-29 do not allude to the poem but the phraseology has been used of the Teaching. Thus, some have argued that vv. 28-29 and 32:45-47 actually frame a different text other than the present Song.

25 In the Pentateuch, except for the book of Deuteronomy, the expression designates the projected future of the United Monarchy (Gen 49:1 and Num 24:14). In the prophetic texts, it

Moses' Accusation of Israel's Rebellious Nature (v. 27)

(27) כי אנכי ידעתי את־מריך ואת־ערפך הקשה
הן בעודני חי עמכם היום ממרים היתם
עם־יהוה ואף כי־אחרי מותי

Summon (v. 28)

(28) הקהילו אלי את־כל־זקני שבטיכם ושטריכם
ואדברה באזניהם את הדברים האלה
והאעידה בם את־השמים ואת־הארץ

Future "Turning Away" (v 29a)

(29) כי ידעתי אחרי מותי כי־השחת תשחתון
וסרתם מן־הדרך אשר צויתי אתכם

Future Punishment (v. 29b)

וקראת אתכם הרעה באחרית הימים

Reason for Future Punishment (v. 29c)

כי־תעשׂו את־הרע בעיני יהוה

Provocation (v. 29d)

להכעיסו במעשה ידיכם

27) For I know how rebellious and stubborn you are. While I am still alive
with you today, you have been rebelling against YHWH, how much more
so after my death?

28) Assemble before me all the elders of your tribes and your officials so that I
may speak these words in their hearing and call upon the heavens and
earth as witnesses against them,

29) for I know that after my death, you will definitely act corruptly and turn
from the road which I commanded you. Evil will befall[26] you in the future
for you have done evil in the eyes of YHWH, provoking him to anger with
the work of your hands.

Moses is certain that the people will falter after his death, which is the reason
why he summoned the people. Thereupon, Moses lays out the simple pattern
of sin-provocation-punishment but in reverse order.

---

includes a variety of scenarios. It refers to a period of punishment (Jer 23:20 = Jer 30:24,
Ezek 38:16 — attack of Gog, Dan 10:14 — period of Antiochus Epiphanes), an idyllic period
after the punishment (Isa 2:2 = Mic 4:1, Hos 3:5), and restoration of foreign nations (Jer
48:47 — Moab; 49:39 — Elam). The only other occurrence of the phrase in Deuteronomy is
4:30. It denotes the period where the people will seek God and obey his voice. For further
discussion, see *BDB*, 31. Here, it refers to the period when the Israelites will experience
adversity for the evil they have committed. In general, the phrase refers to some future time.

26 Given the succession of verbs, וקראת ... וסרתם תשחתון השחת ("you will definitely act
corruptly, turn ... will befall"), the punishment — "evil" — seems to follow as a consequence
of the sin of "turning away." However, v. 29a provides the justification for the warning in v.
28. In other words, Moses gathers the people and speaks to them "because" (כי) they will
quickly turn away. V. 29b then begins a new clause.

According to Moses, "evil" (הרעה) will befall the people "because" (כי) they did "evil" (הרע), "provoking [God] with the work of [their] hands" (להכעיסו במעשה ידיכם):

> Punishment ("Evil," הרעה, v. 29b) Because of Sin ("Evil," הרע, v. 29c)
> ← Provocation (v. 29d)

In this schema, the provocation triggers the "evil"- punishment which resulted from the "evil"- sin they commit against God. Therefore, Israel receives her exact due; the very "evil" they commit fuels the "evil"-disaster they experience.

What makes the formulation of the pattern more exacting is the absence of an agent. This "evil"- punishment "happens" (קראת) to the people:

> "Evil"- Sin = "Evil"- Punishment

For every sin the people commit, they provide fodder for their own punishment without any mediating agent;[27] they are basically flagellating themselves with each act of idolatry. All in all, Deut 31:29 lays out a measure-for-measure punishment where God is altogether absent as an agent of destruction; thus, people ultimately bring upon their own demise.

---

27   In the parallel account where God, not Moses, reflects on the future sin of Israel (vv. 16-19), God's agency is absent. YHWH lays out what will happen to Israel upon Moses' death. The people will surely worship foreign deities and break the covenant. As a result of this idolatry, God will "become angry" (וחרה אפי) impelling him to abandon them (פני מהם והסתרתי, "I will hide my face from them;" עזבתים, "I will abandon them") altogether. This divine abandonment, like its development in the neighboring Mesopotamian literature, makes the people susceptible to all sorts of disaster. Whereas in Mesopotamian, other gods conquer and destroy the cities, here in Deut 31:17, "numerous evils will come upon them" (רבות ומצאהו רעות). Without an explicit agent, bad things happen to the people whose God has left them for good reasons — the abrogation of the covenant. As v. 18 further elaborates, these "evil" - disasters are the result of "all the evil" (כל־הרעה) which they committed.

2.5. Judges 2:11-16 (v.12[28])

Whereas the pattern of sin-provocation-punishment is clearly outlined in Judg 2:11-16, God, more in conformity with DtrH1 than DtrH2, partially uses human instruments to carry out the punishment. Nevertheless, the punishment is described more in terms of their sin so that the sinners appear more culpable, demonstrating the tendency to exonerate God.

Chapter 2:11-23[29] lays out the Deuteronomic template (sin-anger-punishment-deliverance) for the book of Judges.[30] However, the elaboration of

---

28   הכעיס occurs only once in the book of Judges (2:12) laying out the pattern of sin-provocation-punishment-deliverance. Since this pattern does not occur in the book of Judges, but only its shortened version, sin-punishment-deliverance, the term seems to signal events beyond the book of Judges. Given the centrality of the destructions of Samaria and Jerusalem for DtrH2, the pattern with הכעיס most likely foreshadows them. Two significant phrases in Judg 2:14aβ and 17 demonstrate this connection. First, the phrase, שסים יתנם ביד ("he delivered them into the hand of the plunderers," v. 14a) occurs in one other place in 2 Kgs 17:20. According to 2 Kgs 17 20, Samaria, on account of their sins, is "delivered into the hands of the plunderers" (ויתנם ביד שסים), which in this context refer to the Assyrians. It is as if the ultimate demonstration of the pattern plays itself out in the conquest of Samaria and the dispersal of its inhabitants.

Second, סרו מהר מן־הדרך ("to quickly turn aside from the path," Judg 2:17), appears in the Golden Calf episode (Exod 32:8 and Deut 9:12, 16). Though the connection to the fall of Samaria is not explicit, the Golden Calf episode looks forward to the sin of Jeroboam, which is one of the reasons for the fall of Samaria. According to the Deuteronomist, Israel's dalliance with other gods begins with the molding of the golden calf, which resembles Jeroboam's golden calves in Bethel and Dan (1 Kgs 12:28-29). Such acts of idolatry pervaded during the period of the judges and climaxed with the northern kingdom, resulting in their destruction under the oppressors. Thus, the overall framework exemplified the sin-provocation-punishment cycle. This pattern then becomes the paradigm for the destruction of Jerusalem.

29   The larger context, ch. 2:11-3:6. provides the framework for the book of Judges which had been heavily edited.

30   Frederick Greenspahn, "The Theology of the Framework of Judges," 385, sums up the pattern as "Israelite idolatry angers God who therefore allows his people to be oppressed; when their suffering leads to repentance, God provides a leader to bring deliverance." However, the template, the skeletal pattern of the cycle in Judg 2:11-16, is not replicated in any of the individual accounts (see F. Greenspahn, "The Theology of the Framework of Judges," 385-396), not even the heavily edited sections, specifically 2:17-3:6 and 10:6-16, in the book of Judges. Since the individual stories of the different judges/saviors constitute a collection of traditions, except for the story of Othniel (3:7-11) which provides a paradigmatic storyline, the pattern of sin-provocation-punishment-deliverance is external to the stories. Moreover, in the Dtr sections, the introduction (2:17-3:6) and the prologue to Jephthah's account (10:6-16), הכעיס does not describe the result of the people's sin. The people sin: Israelites do evil in the eyes of YHWH (3:7, 12, 4:1, 6:1, 10:6, 13:1); they "forget" (שכח, 3:7) or "abandon" (עזב, 10:6, 10, 13) their God and "follow" (הלך אחרי, 2:19), "serve" (עבד, 2:19, 3:7, 10:6, 10, 13), and "worship" (השתחוה, 2:19) "other gods" (אלהים אחרים, 2:19, 10:13), Baalim (3:7, 8:33, 10:6, 10), "Ashtaroth" (עשתרות, 10:6 —

the pattern is somewhat repetitive and unorderly, which has led numerous scholars to conjecture the existence of different levels of redaction.[31] Suffice it to say that very little consensus has been reached as to the exact nature of the development of the final composition. Therefore, for the purpose of this study, we will focus only on the immediate context of הכעיס (vv. 11-16):

Catalog of Sins (vv. 11-12a)

11) ויעשׂו בני־ישׂראל את־הרע בעיני יהוה ויעבדו את־הבעלים

12) ויעזבו את־יהוה אלהי אבותם המוציא אותם מארץ מצרים וילכו אחרי אלהים אחרים מאלהי העמים אשר סביבותיהם וישׁתחוו להם

Provocation (v. 12b)

<u>ויכעסו</u> את־יהוה

Additional Sin (v. 13)

13) ויעזבו את־יהוה ויעבדו לבעל ולעשׁתרות

Punishment (vv. 14-15)

14) ויחר־אף יהוה בישׂראל ויתנם ביד־שׁסים וישׁסו אותם וימכרם ביד אויביהם מסביב ולא־יכלו עוד לעמד לפני אויביהם

15) בכל אשׁר יצאו יד־יהוה היתה־בם לרעה כאשׁר דבר יהוה וכאשׁר נשׁבע יהוה להם ויצר להם מאד

Deliverance (v. 16)

16) ויקם יהוה שׁפטים ויושׁיעום מיד שׁסיהם

11)   The Israelites did evil in the eyes of YHWH and served the Baʻalim.
12)   They rejected YHWH, the God of their fathers, the one who brought them out from the land of Egypt; and they went after other gods from among the gods of the people who surrounded them and worshipped them; and <u>they provoked</u> YHWH <u>to anger</u>.
13)   They rejected YHWH and served Baʻal and Astharoth.
14)   YHWH was angry with Israel and he gave them into the hand of the plunderers who plundered them. He sold them to their enemies from the surrounding area before whom they were no longer able to withstand.
15)   Wherever they went, the hand of YHWH was against them for evil as YHWH had spoken and as YHWH had sworn to them. It was very distressing for them.

---

list is extended to include the gods of Aram, Sidon, Moab, Ammonites, and Philistines) or "Asheroth" (אשׁרות, 3:7 — few Hebrew manuscripts, Syriac, and Targum have עשׁתרות). A description of their sin is immediately followed by the expression, "to become angry" (חרה אף, 3:8, 10:7), rather than הכעיס.

31 For brief discussion, see A. D. H. Mayes, *Judges* (OTG; Sheffield: JSOT Press, 1985), 31-32, who separates the "basic narrative" (Judg 2:11, 12a, 13b, 14-16, 18-19) from the additions. Also, Barnabas Lindars, *Judges 1-5: A New Translation and Commentary* (Edinburgh: T&T Clark, 1995), 98-112, A. Soggin, *Judges* (OTL; London: S.C.M., 1987), 41-44, George Moore, *A Critical and Exegetical Commentary on the Book of Judges* (ICC 4; New York: Charles Scribner's Sons, 1895), 68-75, and Charles Burney, *The Book of Judges* (Library of Biblical Studies; New York: Ktav Publishing House, 1970), 52, note the problems in the text, though they provide different explanations.

16)   YHWH raised judges and they delivered them from the hand of their plun-
        derers.

In vv. 11-16, the pattern of apostasy-provocation-punishment is outlined.
Beside v. 13, which is probably an addition,[32] the pattern is clear: The Israelites sin against God with their idolatry (vv. 11-12a), provoking God to anger
(v. 12b), which then triggers the punishment (vv. 14-15):

Sin (Idolatry, vv. 11-12a) → Provocation (הכעיס, v. 12b) →
Punishment (חרה אף, vv. 14-15)

The succession of converted *yqtl* verbs laying out the people's idolatry (ויעשו
וישתחוו ... וילכו אחרי ... ויעזבו ... ויעבדו ... , "they did ... and they served ...
and they abandoned ... and they followed ... and they worshipped") consequently leads to the provocation. This in turn feeds the anger (אף ויחר, "he
was angry"), the first stage of divine punishment. Thus, the provocation fuels
the anger which motivates God to punish.

Though God is the executor of the punishment, a human instrument still
plays a participatory role. God "delivers them" (ויתנם)[33] into the hands of the
oppressors who are the ones to "subjugate them" (אותם וישסו). It is to these
very enemies whom God "sells them" (וימכרם, v.14b), so that they will not be
able to withstand. Thus, God takes the initiative but it is the human instrument
which carry out the actual act of oppression.

How then does this differ from the DtrH1 formulations of the punishment
where human instruments execute God's prophesy against the dynasties? Well,
in this passage, it is not so much the issue of "Who" but the way in which the
punishment is worded to correspond to the sin. First, the people worship the
gods of the surrounding nations who come to oppress them: The Israelites
followed gods from among "the nations *around* them" (אשר העמים

---

32   Since v. 13 repeats parts of v. 11 and v. 12, it is most likely an addition. It is unclear as to
     why the verse was inserted here or by whom. A redactor may perhaps have wanted to add the
     worship of עשתרות to the list. It should be noted that בעל occurs in the singular which is
     unusual since it appears mostly in the plural form, בעלים, in the book of Judges (2:11, 3:7,
     8:33, 10:6, 10; others, 1 Sam 7:4, 12:10, 1 Kgs 18:18, 2 Chr 17:3, 24:7, 28:2, 33:3, 34:4, Jer
     2:23, 9:13, Hos 2:15, 19, 11:2). When the singular form does occur in the book of Judges, it
     is attested in the heavily edited chapter (6:25, 28, 30, 31, 32; others,1 Kgs 16:31, 32, 18:19,
     21, 22, 25, 26, 40, 19:18, 22:54, 2 Kgs 3:2, 10:18, 19, 20, 21, 22, 23, 25, 26, 27, 28, 11:18,
     17:16, 21:3, 23:4, 5, 2 Chr 23:17, Jer 2:8, 7:9, 11:13, 17, 12:16, 19:5, 28:13, 27, 32:29, 35,
     Hos 2:10, 13:1, Zeph 1:4).
33   V. 14aβ, וישסו שסים ביד ויתנם is probably an addition with v. 13. V. 14b is probably the
     continuation of v. 14aα since וימכרם occurs frequently in the book of Judges (2:14, 3:8, 4:2,
     10:9).

סביבותיהם) to whom (נמכרו אויביהם ביד, "in the hands of their enemies all *around*) they were sold. One would expect the gods of these foreign nations to help the Israelites for worshipping them; instead, God uses the foreign nations to punish them. Second, "the hand of YHWH was against them for *evil*" (לרעה יהוה היתה בם יד, v. 15a) since they did "*evil*" (הרע, v. 11). As a result, DtrH2 coordinated the punishment to correspond to Israel's sins.

2.6. Brief Additions to the Accounts of Jeroboam and Baasha

2.6.1. Introduction

In the accounts of Jeroboam (1 Kgs 14:15) and Baasha (1 Kgs 16:7), two additional attestations of הכעיס are found. Though 1 Kgs 14:15 can be attributed to DtrH2, it is not so clear as to whether or not 1 Kgs 16:7 can be assigned to the same redactor. However, 1 Kgs 16:7 is definitely secondary to the dynastic oracle that was initially aimed at Baasha (1 Kgs 16:2-4). Within these two additions, the redactor(s) tend to attribute the destructive activities to God, rather than human instruments. Moreover, in 1 Kgs 14:15, the blame for the destruction is shifted to corporate Israel rather than the individual kings. As a result, the additions put God more in control over the punishments for which the people, not the king, are responsible.

2.6.2. 1 Kings 14:15-16a (v.15)

Whereas the formulaic oracle against Jeroboam and his household occurs in 1 Kgs 14:7b-11, an unusual elaboration on the eventual demise of the whole northern kingdom appears in 1 Kgs 14:15-16a. The former prophetic oracle, containing DtrH1's indictment of Jeroboam's dynasty (1 Kgs 14:7-11), describes the punishment, which is then fulfilled by a temporal instrument, Baasha (1 Kgs 15:29-30). However, another curse formula (1 Kgs 14:15-16a), contextually intrusive, occurs a few verses later incriminating all of Israel, not just Jeroboam, for the punishment resulting in the downfall of Israel. Here, unlike the dynastic oracle, God himself will strike down the culprit.

The story of desperate parents, Jeroboam and his wife, seeking the welfare of their ill son forms the background of the oracles against the dynasty and Israel. To these anxious parents, Ahijah the prophet first delivers God's judgment against Jeroboam and his dynasty (1 Kgs 14:7b-11) and secondly attends to the immediate concern in the pericope, the fate of Abijah, the son of Jeroboam (vv. 12-14). Then unexpectedly, vv. 15-16a turn the reader's attention away from Jeroboam and his son and forecasts the punishment of all of Israel:

Punishment (v. 15a)

15) והכה יהוה את־ישראל כאשר ינוד הקנה במים
ונתש את־ישראל מעל האדמה הטובה הזאת אשר נתן לאבותיהם

Reason (v. 15b)

וזרם מעבר לנהר יען אשר עשו את־אשריהם

Provocation

מכעיסים את־יהוה

Punishment (v. 16a)

16a) ויתן את־ישראל

15) YHWH will strike down Israel as the reed shakes in water and he will up-root Israel from this good land which he gave to their ancestors and dis-perse them beyond the River on account that they made their asherah poles, <u>provoking YHWH to anger</u>.

16) He will deliver Israel.

By itself, v. 15 follows the reverse pattern of sin-provocation-punishment, with an incomplete note on the deliverance of Israel, presumably to an enemy (v. 16a). The first half of the verse (v. 15a) elaborates upon the punishment, namely the smiting and dispersal of Israel, which is motivated by the provoca-tion (v. 15bβ) resulting from their sin of idolatry (v. 15bα):

Punishment (v. 15a) Because of Sin (v. 15bα) ← Provocation (v. 15bβ)

This common pattern is then disrupted by v. 16a, which further describes the punishment:

Punishment (Striking and Dispersal)
← Reason →
Punishment (Deliverance 'to enemy')

However, v. 16a is incomplete; God plans to "give Israel" (ויתן את ישראל), but to whom or to what? The indirect object is altogether absent. As a result, v.16a was probably inserted to link the addition, v. 15, to v. 16b, which pro-vides the reason for the judgment outlined in v. 14a. In other words, the text would have originally read:

14a) והקים יהוה לו מלך על־ישראל אשר יכרית את־בית ירבעם
16b) בגלל חטאות ירבעם אשר חטא ואשר החטיא את ישראל

16b) YHWH will establish for himself a king over Israel who will cut off the house of Jeroboam

16b) because the sins of Jeroboam which he committed and made Israel com-mit.

With the addition of v. 15, v. 16b could not have logically developed what now preceded:

14a) והקים יהוה לו מלך על־ישׂראל אשר יכרית את־בית ירבעם
15) והכה יהוה את־ישׂראל כאשר ינוד הקנה במים
ונתשׁ את־ישׂראל מעל האדמה הטובה הזאת אשר נתן לאבותיהם
וזרם מעבר לנהר יען אשׁר עשׂו את־אשׁריהם מכעיסים את־יהוה
16b) בגלל חטאות ירבעם אשׁר חטא ואשׁר החטיא את ישׂראל

14a) YHWH will establish for himself a king over Israel who will cut off the house of Jeroboam.
15) YHWH will strike down Israel as the reed shakes in water and he will uproot Israel from this good land which he gave to their ancestors and disperse them beyond the River on account that they made their asherah poles, provoking YHWH to anger.
16b) Because of the sins of Jeroboam which he committed and made Israel commit.

Since the narrative does not flow, the editor placed transitional phrases to 'smooth-out' the rough spots; the editor inserted v. 14b to join v. 14a to v. 15 and v. 16a to tie v. 15 to v. 16b:

14a) והקים יהוה לו מלך על־ישׂראל אשר יכרית את־בית ירבעם
14b) *זה היום ומה גם־עתה*
15) והכה יהוה את־ישׂראל כאשר ינוד הקנה במים
ונתשׁ את־ישׂראל מעל האדמה הטובה הזאת אשר נתן לאבותיהם
וזרם מעבר לנהר יען אשׁר עשׂו את־אשׁריהם מכעיסים את־יהוה
16a) *ויתן את־ישׂראל*
16b) בגלל חטאות ירבעם אשׁר חטא ואשׁר החטיא את ישׂראל

14a) YHWH will establish for himself a king over Israel who will cut off the house of Jeroboam.
14b) *This is today and even now,*
15) YHWH will strike down Israel as the reed shakes in water and he will uproot Israel from this good land which he gave to their ancestors and disperse them beyond the River on account that they made their asherah poles, provoking YHWH to anger. *He will deliver Israel*
16) because of the sins of Jeroboam which he committed and made Israel commit.

As a result, v. 14b and v. 16a are primarily linking clauses, not integral to the pattern set up in v. 15.

Be that as it may, why did a later redactor feel the need to add v. 15 in the first place? Were the oracles against Jeroboam's dynasty (vv. 7-11 and vv. 14a, 16b) not adequate? The oracles were definitely sufficient for DtrH1, who used them to explain the annihilation of the dynasty. However, for DtrH2,[34] the oracles had failed to account for the ultimate demise of Samaria.[35] And since the fall of Samaria prefigured the fall of Jerusalem in the conceptual framework of DtrH2, v. 15 was crucial in laying out the course of history for both Israel and Judah. Both Israel and Judah will be uprooted and dispersed.

Besides elaborating on the fall of Samaria, the addition of v. 15 reconfigures the source of the sin and the role of God in executing the punishment. Unlike the oracles where Jeroboam is primarily responsible for sinning against God, here Israel makes the asherah poles and provoke God.[36] Since Israel sins against their God, they are the ones who receive the punishment. Moreover, God, not a human instrument, exacts this punishment. Though the earlier dynastic oracle (vv. 7-11) formulated the punishment with God as the executor, it is realized through a human instrument, Baasha (1 Kgs 15:28). This is made more emphatic in v. 14a where YHWH promises to "raise" (הקים) a king who will then destroy the house of Jeroboam. This is contrary to v. 15, where God

---

34   The wording of the addition is not typical of Dtr. For example, נתש ("to uproot") and זרה ("to scatter") are uncommon words for dispersal which appear mostly in prophetic books (נתש— Deut 29:27, Jer 1:10, 12:14, 15, 17, 18:7, 14, 24:6, 31:28, 40, 42:10, 45:4, Amos 9:15, 2 Chr 7:20; זרה — Lev 26:33, Jer 31:10, Ezek 5:2 [symbolic], 10, 12, 6:8, 12:14, 15, 20:23, 22:15, 36:19, Pss 44:12, 106:27). As a result, someone other than DtrH2 may possibly have made the addit on. Nevertheless, the addition appears to be late.

35   The punishment could only refer to the destruction of Samaria in 722 B.C.E. Though the phrase, מעבר לנהר ("beyond the river"), does not occur anywhere else (except in a variant form, with the river in plural occur in Isa 18:1 and Zeph 3:10 in reference to the rivers of Nubia), it could only refer to the region beyond the Euphrates river. The מן ... ל־ construction indicates "on the other side of" or "beyond" (BDB, 578b, 1c). This alludes to the dispersal of Israel in the Mesopotamian region; it cannot refer to any events prior to the fall of Samaria.

36   This is not a complete shift from DtrH1 since throughout DtrH1, Israel, the corporate entity, is not completely blameless for the prevalence of sins in the North. If one looks carefully at the wording of Jeroboam's sin in the accounts of the Israelite kings, the rulers are not the only ones who sin; they also "make Israel sin" as well (החטיא את־ישראל; 1 Kgs 14:16, 15:26, 30, 34, 16:2, 13, 26, 21:22, 22:53, 2 Kgs 3:3, 10:29, 31, 13:2, 6, 11, 14:24, 15:9, 18, 24, 28, 17:21, 23:15 and in reference to Judah, see 2 Kgs 21:11, 16). Even though people sin, it is the kings who cause (hiphil of חטא) the people to sin which would then make the leaders responsible, not the people. The people are innocent pawns of the devious kings. Therefore, the first three dynasties of kings were punished. However, this outlook could not cohere with the destruction of Israel and then Judah, where the people suffered just as much. Thus, in DtrH2, the explanation for the fall of Samaria, the corporate entity, the people of Israel, are held more accountable for the sins.

intends to deal the final blow: YHWH will "strike" (והכה), "uproot" (ונתש),
"disperse them" (וזרם), and "deliver" (ויתן).

In sum, הכעיס functions as the literary pivot in v. 15 which was added to
explain the fall of Samaria by laying the blame on Israel who will then be
punished by God.

2.6.3. 1 Kings 16:7

In the account of Baasha, the founder of the second dynasty, an additional note
on his provocation appears in an unexpected place (1 Kgs 16:7).[37] Though the
verse seems superfluous, it provides a simple but complete formulation of sin-
provocation-punishment, in which God is the executor of the punishment.

After the formulaic statement of Baasha's death (1 Kgs 16:5-6), where one
would then expect the end of his account, an additional comment on Baasha
(v. 7) is provided:

Closing Formula (v. 5)

5) ויתר דברי בעשא ואשר עשה וגבורתו
הלא־הם כתובים על־ספר דברי הימים למלכי ישראל

Death and Burial (v. 6)

6) וישכב בעשא עם־אבתיו ויקבר בתרצה וימלך אלה בנו תחתיו

Prophetic Oracle (v. 7)

7) וגם ביד־יהוא בן־חנני הנביא דבר־יהוה היה אל־בעשא ואל־ביתו

Sin

ועל[38] כל־הרעה אשר־עשה בעיני יהוה

Provocation

להכעיסו במעשה ידיו[39] להיות כבית ירבעם

Punishment

---

37 This is a problematic passage which many scholars have understood as secondary; see James
    Montgomery, *Books of Kings*, 282, for various proposals. Montgomery, *Books of Kings*, and
    John Gray, *I & II Kings*, 361, do not consider the passage to be secondary by translating ועל
    אשר הכה אתו as 'despite that' rather than 'because that' "he struck him." However, they do
    not provide examples for such an understanding of ועל אשר. According to *BDB*, 754, 758,
    על אשר usually denote the reason or cause, 'on account of, because of;' see also *HALOT*
    2:827. Given this definition, the passage does not fit in the context and is probably an
    addition.

38 The MT has ועל ("and because of") while few Hebrew manuscripts, Syriac, and Targum
    (codex Reuchlinianus) do not reflect a ־ו ("and"). Here, the other textual variants seem to
    have the better reading.

39 It is a late Deuteronomic phrase which refers to idols, craftsman's handiwork: Deut 4:28,
    27:15, 31:29; 2 Kgs 19:18 (Isa 37:19), 22:17; Jer 1:16, 25:6, 7, 32:30, 44:8; Isa 2:8, Hos
    14:4; Mic 5:12.

ועל אשר־הכה אתו

5) The rest of Baasha's deeds, what he did and his might, are they not written in the annals of the kings of Israel?

6) Baasha laid down with his fathers and was buried in Tirzah and Elah, his son, ruled in his place.

7) And also the word of YHWH came to Baasha through Jehu, the son of Hanani, the prophet: "On account of all the evil which he committed in the eyes of YHWH, provoking him with the deeds of his hands, being like the house of Jeroboam; on account of which he struck him."

Vv. 5-6 closes Baasha's account with the typical reference to the "Annals of the Kings of Israel:"

ויתר דברי X ואשר עשה וגבורתו
הלא הם כתובים על ספר דברי הימים למלכי ישׂראל[40]

And the rest of the deeds of X, what he did and his might, are they not written in the annals of the kings of Israel.

and the place of his burial:

וישׁכב X עם אבתיו ויקבר ב-Y וימלך Z בנו תחתיו[41]

And X laid down with this fathers and was buried in Y and his son, Z, ruled in his place.

These verses would normally conclude the accounts of the kings. However, DtrH2 adds v. 7,[42] an abridgement of Jehu's message mentioned in 1 Kgs 16:1-4 (prophetic pronouncment). Like the prophetic pronouncement, v. 7 lays out

---

40   For both the kings of Israel and Judah, 1 Kgs 11:41, 14:29, 15:7, 23, 31, 16:5, 14, 20, 27, 22:39, 46, 2 Kgs 1:18, 8:23, 10:34, 12:20, 13:8, 12, 14:15, 18, 28, 15:6, 11, 15, 21, 26, 31, 36, 16:19, 20:20, 21:17, 25, 23 28, 24:5; and its parallel accounts in Chronicles, 2 Chr 13:22, 20:34, 25:26, 26:22, 27:7, 32:32, 33:18, 35:26, 36:8.

41   This formula with or without ויקבר ("and he was buried") usually concludes most of the Judahite and Israelite kings' reign. See 1 Kgs 2:10, 11:43, 14:20, 31, 15:8, 24, 16:6, 28, 22:40, 51, 2 Kgs 8:24, 10:35, 13:9, 13, 14:16, 29, 15:7, 22, 38, 16:20, 20:21, 21:18, 24:6; and its parallels in Chronicles, 2 Chr 9:31, 12:16, 13:23, 16:13, 21:1, 25:23, 26:9, 28:27, 32:33, 33:20. See also the judgment formula for the kings, Iain Provan, *Hezekiah and the Books of Kings*, 33, where the "notice about the succession" may follow the "information about the king's death and burial." The 'judgment formulae' would usually precede both sections.

42   M. Cogan and H. Tadmor, *II Kings: A New Translation with Introduction* (AB 11; Garden City: Doubleday, 1988), 269, states that וגם ("and also"), which opens the verse, usually indicates an addition.

the pattern of sin-provocation-punishment, in which the evil of Jeroboam's sins provokes God to anger, leading to the punishment:

Sin (of Jeroboam) → Provocation → Punishment

Moreover, the addition is worded similarly to the account of the prophetic fulfillment (1 Kgs 16:11-13):

1 Kgs 16:7

7) וגם ביד־יהוא בן־חנני הנביא דברי־הוה היה אל־בעשא ואל־ביתו
ועל כל־הרעה אשר־עשה בעיני יהוהלהכעיסו במעשה ידיו
להיות כבית ירבעם ועל אשר־הכה אתו

7)   And also the <u>word of YHWH</u> came to Baasha <u>through Jehu, the son of Hanani, the prophet</u>: "On account of all the evil which he committed in the eyes of YHWH, *provoking him* with the deeds of his hands, being like the house of Jeroboam; on account of which *he struck* him."

1 Kgs 16:11-13

11) ויהי במלכו ... הכה את־כל־בית בעשא
12) וישמד זמרי את כל־בית בעשא
כדבר יהוה אשר דבר אל־בעשא ביד יהוא הנביא
13) אל כל־חטאות בעשא ... להכעיס ... בהבליהם

11)   When he began to rule ... *he struck* the whole house of Baasha.
12)   Zimri destroyed the whole house of Baasha <u>according to the word of YHWH</u> which he spoke <u>through Jehu, the prophet</u>,
13)   on account of the sins of Baasha ... *provoking to anger* ... with their delusions.

Like 1 Kgs 16:7, the house of Baasha is struck according to the word of YHWH which he spoke through Jehu. If v. 7 is repetitious, why did DtrH2 add the note after the postlude of Baasha's account? What would have been its function?

Though not consistent throughout DtrH, the addition (v. 7) may reflect two tendencies in DtrH2. One is to penalize the culprit rather than his descendants; the other is to attribute the execution of the punishment to God. First, v. 7 transfers the punishment to Baasha, who is primarily responsible for bringing the curse against his family. He is the one who provokes God with his sin of following Jeroboam (1 Kgs 16:2); therefore, Baasha, not Elah (his son), must be punished. Elah, under whom the judgment is carried out in DtrH1, does nothing except come to inherit his father's throne whereupon Zimri conspires against him (1 Kgs 16:8-9).[43] Beside the generic note about "sins of Elah" (וחטאות אלה), in addition to the "sins of Baasha" (1 Kgs 16:13), DtrH1 does not attribute other misdeeds to Elah. As a result, DtrH2 may perhaps have added v. 7 in the account of Baasha to explain his death, a form of punishment, *as the result* of his sins. Thus, Baasha, the sinner, dies as a consequence of his evil so that he receives his due punishment.

In addition to directly linking the sinner with his punishment, v. 7 secondly shifts the act of punishing from a human executor to God. Whereas Zimri (1 Kgs 16:11), a human instrument, executes the punishment in DtrH1, here, God is the agent of the punishment. Zimri undertakes what God had ordained by striking (הכה, v. 11) and destroying (וישמד, v. 12) Baasha's house. However, in v. 7, though God is not explicitly named, it would appear that YHWH is the intended subject of the verb, הכה ("to strike"). Since God is the provoked party and no other individuals are mentioned, beside Jehu who prophesied in the past, the offended deity is probably the intended agent of the "striking." Thus, God repays Baasha with his death for his sin of "evil." Yet the punishment is not worded to correspond to Baasha'a catalog of sins.

In conclusion, הכעיס is a pivotal term that leads to a description of a deity who directly executes the transgressor.

2.7. Destruction of Samaria

2.7.1. 2 Kings 17:7-23a (vv. 11, 17)

DtrH2 uses the term, הכעיס, twice, first to mark the midsection of the catalog of sins (v. 11) and second to function as the pivot to the punishment (v. 17) in the heavily redacted pericope explaining the destruction of Samaria (2 Kgs 17:7-23a).[44] Though heavily redacted, the multi-descriptions of the punishment depict God as the primary agent of destruction.

---

43   Even Nadab, Jeroboam's son, receives an assessment for having "done evil in the eyes of YHWH," "following in the ways of his father," and "causing Israel to sin with his sins" (1 Kgs 15:26). To a certain extent, according to DtrH2, Nadab, unlike Elah, deserves the punishment directed to the dynasty which may have been the reason why no addition was made in Nadab's account.

44   For a clear and brief discussion of the history of scholarship on this chapter, see Provan, *Hezekiah and the Books of Kings*, 70-71, and Eynikel, *The Reform of King Josiah*, 87-94.

In the diatribe against the North (2 Kgs 17:7-23a),[45] a list of all possible sins, actual and/or fabricated, justifies the historical reality, the eventual demise of the capital city, Samaria, under Assyrian domination. Though the overall structure of the pericope, sin (vv. 7-17)-provocation (v. 17b)-punishment (vv. 18-23a), seems coherent and thus unified, it is actually the product of several redactors.[46] In fact, the pericope has two distinct levels, DtrH1 and DtrH2, with further additions emphasizing the role of God's decree and prophets:

Reason — Catalog of Sins (vv. 7-17a):
List A (vv. 7-11a) — Local Foreign (Israelite) Practices

7) ויהי כי־חטאו בני ישראל ליהוה אלהיהם
המעלה אתם מארץ מצרים מתחת יד פרעה מלך־מצרים
וייראו אלהים אחרים

8) וילכו בחקות הגוים אשר הוריש יהוה מפני בני ישראל
ומלכי ישראל אשר עשו

9) ויחפאו בני־ישראל דברים אשר לא־כן על־יהוה אלהיהם
ויבנו להם במות בכל־עריהם ממגדל נוצרים עד־עיר מבצר

10) ויצבו להם מצבות ואשרים
על כל־גבעה גבהה ותחת כל־עץ רענן

11) ויקטרו־שם בכל־במות כגוים אשר־הגלה יהוה מפניהם

Provocation (v. 11b)

ויעשו דברים רעים <u>להכעיס</u> את־יהוה

List B (Decree; vv. 12, 15-17)

---

45 The *Wiederaufnahme* in v. 23b of v. 6b, אשורה ... ויגל ישראל ("and he exiled Israel ... to Assur," demarcates the Dtr insertion, which is a commentary on the historical account. See Burke Long, "Framing Repetitions in Biblical Historiography," *JBL* 106 (1987):397. The general division follows Shemaryahu Talmon, "Polemics and Apology in Biblical Historiography — 2 Kings 17:24-41," in *The Creation of Sacred Literature: Composition and Redaction of the Biblical Text* (ed. Richard Elliott Friedman; University of California Publications, Near Eastern Studies 22; Berkeley: University of California Press, 1981), 57-68, although the specific division of the sources follow Cogan and Tadmor, *II Kings*, 206-207, who view vv. 19-20 to be secondary. On the contrary, Pauline Viviano, "2 Kings 17: A Rhetorical and Form-Critical Analysis," *CBQ* 49 (1987):552, does not consider these verses (vv. 19-20) to be intrusive. According to Viviano, the catalog of sins are directed more to Judah rather than Israel; therefore, the whole section "highlights Judah's failings" (552). If this is the case, then v. 19 is essential to the section while v. 20bβ, השליכם מפניו ("he cast them from his presence") is the resumptive repetition of v. 18aβ, ויסרם מעל פניו ("he removed them from his presence"). This is quite a stretch. See Marc Brettler, "Ideology, History and Theology in 2 Kings XVII 7-23," *VT* 39 (1989):270 who observes a *Wiederaufnahme* of v.18 in v. 23a, הסיר יהוה את ישראל מעל פניו ("YHWH removed Israel from his presence"), which would make more sense.

46 Despite the several levels of redaction, Brettler, "Ideology, History and Theology," 282, states that the question, "Why was the north exiled," and I would add, "What are the ramifications of the destruction of Samaria for Judah?," unite the pericope.

12) ויעבדו הגללים אשר אמר יהוה להם אל תעשו את־הדבר הזה

List C (Prophet; v. 13-14)

13) ויעד יהוה בישראל וביהודה ביד כל־נביאו כל־חזה
לאמר שבו מדרכיכם הרעים
ושמרו מצותי חקותי ככל־התורה אשר צויתי את־אבתיכם
ואשר שלחתי אליכם ביד עבדי הנביאים

14) ולא שמעו
ויקשו את־ערפם כערף אבוחם אשר לא האמינו ביהוה אלהיהם

15) וימאסו את־חקיו ואת־בריתו אשר כרת את־אבותם
ואת עדותיו אשר העיד בם
וילכו אחרי ההבל ויהבלו ואחרי הגוים אשר סב־בתם
אשר צוה יהוה אתם לבלתי עשות כהם

16) ויעזבו את־כל־מצות יהוה אלהיהם ויעשו להם מסכה שנים עגלים
ויעשו אשירד וישתחוו לכל־צבא השמים ויעבדו את־הבעל

17) ויעבירו את־בניהם ואת־בנותיהם באש ויקסמו קסמים וינחשו

Provocation (v. 17b)

ויתמכרו לעשות הרע בעיני יהוה להכעיסו

Punishment:

Punishment X (v. 18)

18) ויתאנף יהוד מאד בישראל ויסרם מעל פניו
לא נשאר רק שבט יהודה לבדו

Punishment Y (vv. 19-20)

19) גם־יהודה לא שמר את־מצות יהוה אלהיהם
וילכו בחקות ישראל אשר עשו

20) וימאס יהוה בכל־זרע ישראל וענם ויתנם ביד־שסים
עד אשר השליכם מפניו

Punishment X (vv. 21-22)

21) כי־קרע ישראל מעל בית דוד וימליכו את־ירבעם בן־נבנ
וידא ירבעם את־ישראל מאחרי יהוה והחטיאם חטאה גדולה

22) ויכלו בני ישראל בכל־חטאות ירבעם אשר עשה לא־סרו ממנה

Punishment Z (v. 23)

23) עד אשר־הסיר יחוה את־ישראל מעל פניו
כאשר דבר ביד כל־עבדיו הנביאים

7)   It was thus because the Israelites sinned against YHWH, their God, who brought them out from the land of Egypt from under Pharaoh, the king of Egypt. They revered other gods.

8)   They followed the practices of (other) nations which YHWH drove out before the Israelites and what the kings of Israel had done.

9)   The Israelites secretly did deeds which were not right against YHWH, their God, and they built for themselves high places in all their cities from watchtower to fortified city.

10)   They set up sacred stones for themselves and asherah poles on every high hill and under every spreading tree.

11)   There they burned incense on all the high places like nations which YHWH exiled before them and they committed evil deeds to provoke YHWH to anger.

12) They served the idols which YHWH said to them, "You will not do this deed."

13) YHWH warned Israel and Judah through all his prophets and seers, saying, "Turn from your evil ways and observe my commandments, my statutes, according to all the Teaching which I commanded your fathers and which I sent to you through my servants, the prophets."

14) But they did not listen and they hardened their necks like their fathers who did not trust YHWH, their God.

15) They rejected his statutes and his covenant which he made with their fathers and his warnings with which he warned them. They went after worthless idols — becoming worthless — and after the nations around them which YHWH commanded them not to do like them.

16) They abandoned all the commandments of YHWH, their God; they made for themselves images of two calves and they made Asherah and they worshipped all the host of heaven and they served Ba'al.

17) They sacrificed their sons and their daughters in fire and they practiced divination and sorcery. They sold themselves to do evil in the eyes of YHWH, provoking him to anger.

18) YHWH became very angry at Israel and he removed them from his face. Only the tribe of Judah was left.

19) But also Judah did not keep the commandment of YHWH, their God, and they walked in the practices of Israel which they had committed.

20) YHWH rejected the whole seed of Israel and he afflicted them and gave them into the hands of oppressors until he cast them from his presence.

21) For Israel tore away[47] from the house of David and made Jeroboam, son of Nebat, king. Jeroboam enticed Israel away from YHWH and caused them to commit a great sin.

22) The Israelites walked in all the sins of Jeroboam which he committed. They did not turn aside from it,

23) until YHWH removed Israel from his presence as he spoke through all his servants, the prophets.

In the overall structure of vv. 7-23a, vv. 7-17 makes up the protasis while vv. 18-23a forms the apodosis of the judgment oracle. The protasis, opening with the expression, ויהי כי ("because," v. 7),[48] outlines an extensive catalog of the people's sins (vv. 7-17)[49] in which הכעיס occurs thematically and structurally

---

47 According to Brettler, "Ideology, History and Theology in 2 Kings XVII 7-23," 278, who quotes the new JPS translation, "For Israel broke away from the house of David." Though I adopt his translation, I do not agree with his overall conclusion that vv. 21-22 (his C source) are later than vv. 13-18a +23 (his B source).

48 It is the formulaic phrase which begins the protasis section; see Gen 26:8, 27:1, 43:21, 44:24, Exod 1:21, 13:15, Josh 17:13, Judg 1:28, 6:7-8, 16:16, 2 Sam 6:13, 7:1-2, 19:26, Job 1:5. See Provan, *Hezekiah and the Books of Kings*, fnt 40, 71.

49 Pauline Viviano, "2 Kings 17," 550-551, tries to find some pattern in the catalog. She argues that the "author starts by focusing on each sin, qualifying and explaining it; but as he builds

at the middle (v. 11b) and end of the list (v. 17b). Though the הכעים of v. 11b[50] is not followed by an elaboration of the punishment, it looks ahead to the הכעים of v. 17b,[51] which then leads to the punishment (vv. 18-23a):

Catalog of Sins (Sins - Provocation - Sins, vv. 7-17a) →
Provocation (v. 17b) → Punishment (vv.18-23a)

As a result, הכעים foreshadows as well as links the catalog of sins to the punishment in the pericope.

---

to his climax as he uses as few words as possible, piling one sin atop another, overwhelming his audience not simply with the fact of Israel's idolatrous practices but also with their variety and quantity. Only in the conclusion does the author break from the list-form." However, this is more descriptive than analytical and does not provide the pattern to the inexplicable list of sins. The guiding principle for the specific order is not apparent but a larger structure is evident; see discussion above.

50   V. 11 begins with an accusation against the burning of incense (ויקטרו, "they will burn incense") "on the high places" (במות). The accusation closes with a foreshadowing comment, "like the nations which God had exiled before them" (מפניהם כגוים אשר הגלה יהוה). Since the term, הגלה ("to exile"), is never used with other nations, beside Israel and Judah (2 Kgs 15:29, 16:9, 17:6, 26, 27, 28, 33, 18:11, 24:14, 15, 25:11, Jer 13:19, 20:4, 22:12, 24:1, 27:20, 29:1, 4, 7, 14, 39:9, 40:1, 7, 43:3, 52:15, 28, 29, Ezek 39:28, Amos 1:6, 5:27, Lam 4:22, Esth 2:1, 6, Neh 7:6, 1 Chr 5:26, 41, 5:6, 8:6, 7, 9:1, 2 Chr 36:20), it may have foreshadowed the end of Israel. Therefore the word connects the people's sin to those of the nations around them in order to predict a similar end for Israel.
      This pivotal verse is the midpoint of the catalog since it is flanked on both sides of the list with reference to the nations in v. 8 (וילכו בחקות הגוים אשר הוריש יהוה מפני בני ישראל, "they followed the practices of (other) nations which YHWH drove out before the Israelites") and v. 15 (אחרי הגוים אשר סביבתם אשר צוה יהוה אתם לבלתי עשות כהם, "after the nations around them which YHWH commanded them not to do like them"). It is at this juncture that the phrase הכעים appears: The people have committed evil deeds to provoke God (ויעשו דברים רעים להכעיס את יהוה, "they committed evil deeds to provoke YHWH to anger," v. 11b). This phrase does not document an additional sin but sums the previous list as evil deeds that provoke God. In the early stages of the development of list, the verse concluded the catalog of sins with the consequent punishment appearing in v. 18. When the additional sins were added to the list, v. 11 formed a brief pause as if to briefly remind the reader of the consequence of the list of sins.

51   The second half of the catalog closes with the remark that the people have "sold themselves to do evil in the eyes of YHWH, provoking him" (ויתמכרו לעשות הרע בעיני יהוה להכעיסו, v. 17b). Like v. 11b, the closing phrase is a summary of the catalog of sins, not a description of another sin. The resemblance between the two clauses is not without merit. Besides הכעים, they both share variations of עשה ("to do"), רעה ("evil"), and יהוה ("YHWH"). Whereas v. 11b marks the middle, v. 17b closes the whole catalog of sins. As a consequence of all the sins, the people have provoked God, building up on the previous הכעים, which ultimately would result in a punishment.
      The phrase, ויתמכרו לעשות הרע בעיני יהוה ("they sold themselves to do evil in the eyes of YHWH"), is used only in Elijah's oracle against Ahab (1 Kgs 21:20, 25) which may be the editor's way of linking Israel's sins to those of Ahab. This oracle against Ahab consists of DtrH2 additions, especially vv. 23, 25-26 (see Schniedewind, "History and Interpretation," 653-654).

Despite the organized structure, the unit betrays the work of several redactors. The catalog of sins reflects three distinct levels: 1) emphasis on foreign practices (vv. 7-11a); 2) emphasis on God's decree (vv. 12, 15-17); and 3) emphasis on the mediation of prophets (vv. 13-14). These levels most likely correspond to the division of DtrH in which the first level may be attributed to DtrH2 while the second and third belong to redactors later than DtrH2.

As for the description of the punishment, it too can be divided into several levels. Here, three different formulations of the punishment can be distinguished: 1) punishment X (vv. 18, 21-22) which attributes the sins to Jeroboam;[52] 2) punishment Y (vv. 19-20) which includes the destruction of Judah who disobeyed God's commands; and 3) punishment Z (v. 23) which emphasizes the role of prophets. These are linked to the different levels in the catalog of sins: punishment X is probably linked to DtrH1; Y and Z to later redactors where Y belongs to level 2 of the catalog of sins and Z to the third level. Therefore, a list of sins is not attached to punishment X while the first subunit of sins (vv. 7-11a) is added without a formulation of the punishment. To clearly set forth the development of the pericope, we will first discuss DtrH1 and then move to DtrH2 and finally, the later redactors.

In DtrH1 of 2 Kgs 17:7-23a, the pattern of punishment-sin is laid out:

Punishment (v. 18) ← Sin of Jeroboam (vv. 21-22)

Despite the emphasis on the sin of Jeroboam in the accounts of Israel's kings from Jeroboam to Hosea,[53] it does not figure prominently in the catalog of sins[54] but appears only indirectly in v. 16a[55] and explicitly in the description of

---

52 Compare with Provan, *Hezekiah and the Books of Kings*, 71-73 who attributes 17:7a , 18a, 21-23 to the first level of redaction where the pattern of sin - anger (התאנף) - punishment is present; then the second level of redaction consist primarily of 17:7aβ-17, 19-20 — the catalog of sins and the punishment against Judah and all of Israel.

53 See note 2.

54 None of the sins in the catalog (vv. 7-17) seem to correspond to DtrH1. Most of the sins resemble those listed against Manasseh (2 Kgs 21:2-15; 23:4-14; see Nelson, *The Double Redaction*, 57-60, and Brettler, "Ideology, History and Theology in 2 Kings XVII 7-23"). Therefore, the redactor who is responsible for the catalog of sins against Manasseh is also responsible for much of 2 Kgs 17:7-23a (one could argue that the redactor of Manasseh's sins actually borrowed from the list of sins attributed to the North, but this would not be as viable; DtrH was not as concerned with the fall of Samaria, except for how it foreshadowed the fall of Jerusalem). Since most scholars would agree that the list of Manasseh's sins are post-exilic (look at the most recent and definitive work supporting this argument, Percy Keulen, *Manasseh Through the Eyes of the Deuteronomists: The Manasseh Account (2 Kings 21:1-18) and the Final Chapters of the Deuteronomistic History* [OtSt 38; Leiden: E.J. Brill, 1996]), then much of 2 Kgs 17:7-23a, with the exception of vv. 21-23a, should also be attributed to DtrH2 (see Nelson, *The Double Redaction*, 55-63, Provan, *Hezekiah and the*

the punishment, specifically vv. 21-22.[56] Thus, vv. 21-22, which open with the causal conjunction כִּ ("because"), provide the reason for the punishment. Israel sins by anointing Jeroboam to the throne whereupon he causes Israel to sin. This particular sin finds its corresponding punishment in v. 18. Since v. 18b acknowledges the existence of Judah (לֹא נִשְׁאַר רַק שֵׁבֶט יְהוּדָה לְבַדּוֹ; "none was left but the tribe of Judah only"), the whole verse is probably linked to DtrH1 who writes before the fall of Jerusalem. According to this verse, God, motivated by anger (וַיִּתְאַנַּף יְהוָה מְאֹד, "YHWH became very angry")[57] exiles them. Here, consistent with the DtrH1 who uses הַכְעִים primarily in pronouncement-fulfillment oracles against the dynasties, the provocation of God is not mentioned.

In this level, God is the agent of destruction. He is the one who "became angry" (וַיִּתְאַנַּף) and "removed them" (וַיְסִרֵם). Moreover, the punishment corresponds only in its wording. Israel sins by not "turning aside" (qal of סוּר)

Books of Kings, 71-73, Cogan and Tadmor, *II Kings*, 206-207; contrary to Eynikel, *The Reform of King Josiah*, 86-94, who attributes most of the text to DtrH1). It may account for the generic reference to "the seed of Israel" (זֶרַע יִשְׂרָאֵל, v. 20), which may actually reflect accusations implicitly set against both Israel *and* Judah, and explicit mention of Judah (v. 19; but not v. 18b in which Judah is portrayed positively, perhaps reflecting the period before the fall of Judah).

55   One could also perhaps include v. 8b, אֲשֶׁר עָשׂוּ וּמַלְכֵי יִשְׂרָאֵל, as reference to the Israelite kings, which would include Jeroboam. However, the whole phrase if not part of the phrase, וּמַלְכֵי יִשְׂרָאֵל, appears to be secondary. The whole phrase is omitted in the Syriac whereas part of the phrase is missing in several Hebrew manuscripts and few Greek manuscripts. Perhaps it was added by a later hand to make the catalog of sins more in line with the previous parts of the books of Kings where the Israelite kings were usually under judgment.
     The reference to the golden calves (מַסֵּכָה שְׁנֵי עֲגָלִים, "image of two calves") in v.16 is unusual compared to 1 Kgs 12:28, 32, 2 Kgs 10:29, which refers to them as either זָהָב עֶגְלֵי (with or without ה; "calves of gold," 1 Kgs 12:28, 2 Kgs 10:29) or עֲגָלִים ("calves," 1 Kgs 12:32). However, 1 Kgs 14:9 seems to refer to them as מַסֵּכוֹת ("images"). Even the references in Exod 32: 4, 8 and Deut 9:16 are distinct (עֵגֶל מַסֵּכָה, "calf image"). Perhaps both forms are conflated to emphasize the idolatrous nature of the sin, i.e. the two calves are images; or the "two calves" is in apposition to "image" to clarify what the author intended with מַסֵּכָה ("image") — see BHS notes which considers שְׁנֵי עֲגָלִים to be an addition. In either situation, it would point to a later redactor like v. 8b.

56   Bob Becking, "A Josianic View on the Fall of Samaria," in *Deuteronomy and Deuteronomic Literature: Festschrift C.H.W. Brekelmans* (eds. M. Vervenne and J. Lust; BETL 133; Leuven: Leuven University Press, 1997), 279-297, considers this section to be independent from the rest of the Dtr homily. It was probably an older textual unit, perhaps Weippert's, *Die Prosareden des Jeremiabuches*, Josianic RII or Cross's, *Canaanite Myth and Hebrew Epic*, DtrH1.

57   The hithpalel of אנף is an expression of anger justifying punishment that is about to, does, or prevented from happening. Since God was angry, Moses could not enter the promised land (Deut 1:37, 4:21); Israel would have been destroyed at Horeb (Deut 9:8); Aaron would have been destroyed for the Golden Calf incident (Deut 9:20); and Solomon lost his 10 tribes (1 Kgs 11:9). In the present case, God removed the Israelites, namely dispersed them beyond the Euphrates.

from Jeroboam's sin so that God "removed" (hiphil of סור) them from his presence. Yet in essence, the punishment of removal does not measure up to the sin of following Jeroboam.

Then DtrH2 inserts the first subunit of sins (vv. 7-11a) without its own formulation of the punishment. Vv. 7-11a focus on Israel's imitation of other nations' religious practices,[58] including the establishment of high places (vv. 9, 11), sacred stones, and asherah poles (v. 10). It is concerned with their *act* of committing these sins. At the end of the list (v. 11b), DtrH2 refers to the provocation of God to establish the pattern of sin-provocation-punishment:

Sin (vv. 7-11a) → Provocation (v. 11b) →
Punishment (v. 18) + Reason (vv. 21-22)

Therefore, the fall of Samaria is integrally linked to the provocation of God in DtrH2.

In the decree-redaction (level 2 of the catalog of sins and punishment Y), the redactor is concerned with the people's failure to adhere to God's word. Beginning with v. 12, the accusations are directed not so much against the act but the *abrogation* of what God had commanded: The people worship other deities "which YHWH told" (אשר אמר יהוה, v. 12), "had warned" (העיד, v. 15), and "commanded" (צוה, v. 15) them not to do. They "rejected" (וימאסו, 15) and "abandoned" (ויעזבו) God's law. This emphasis on divine commandment is found in the formulation of the punishment in vv. 19-20, which is preceded by reference to a provocation:

Catalog of Sin (List A [vv. 7-11a] + List B [vv. 12, 15-17a]) →
Provocation (v. 17b) → Punishment (X [Israel; vv. 18, 21-22] + Y [Judah; vv. 19-20])

Rather than indicting just Israel, the redactor includes a punishment of Judah, which failed to keep God's "commandment" (מצות).

According to vv. 19-20, God is again the ultimate agent: He "rejected" (וימאס) the seed of Israel (זרע ישראל),[59] "afflicted them" (ויענם), and "gave

---

58   Though these practices are emphasized as being foreign, i.e. "practices of the nations" (הגוים בחקות, v. 8) and "like the nations" (כגוים, v. 11), they are actually indigenous practices which DtrH tries to root out from Israel. Such practices undermine DtrH's policy of centralization.

59   This expression, occurring limited times (Isa 45:25, Jer 23:8 [זרע בית ישראל, "the seed of the house of Israel," also Ezek 44:22], 31:36, 37, 33:26, Ps 22:24, Neh 9:2, 1 Chr 16:13; compare with זרע אפרים ["the seed of Ephraim"], Jer 7:15; זרע יעקב ["the seed of Jacob"], Jer 33:26, Ps 22:24; with בית ["house"], Ezek 20:5; זרע אברהם ["the seed of Abraham"], Isa 41:8, Jer 33:26, Ps 105:6) refers to the exilic community (see *TDOT*, 4:155-156, 160-161). It usually occurs in the context of restoration where God will renew the

them over to oppressors" (ויתנם ביד שסים) until God "cast them from his presence" (השליכם מפניו).[60] God is the primary agent while the human instrument merely receives what God delivers to them; they do not actively participate at all in the actual execution of the punishment. This punishment partially corresponds to the list of sins.[61] Just as the people are continuously accused of following the customs and gods of "foreign nations" (הגוים, vv. 8, 11, 15), they will then be delivered to them (שסים, "oppressors," v. 20):

Israel Follow Foreign Nations → Israel Delivered to "Oppressors"

Though the same word is not used to indicate the "nations," the foreigners appear to have been the intended oppressors. Moreover, just as the people "rejected" (וימאסו, v. 15) God's commands, God had "rejected" (וימאס, v. 20) them.

In the final level of redaction (vv. 13-14, 23), the focus is on the "prophets" ([62]נביא, הנביאים, v. 13) who transmit the divine word. God warned "by every prophet [and] every seer" (ביד כל־נביאו כל־חזה) and sent "through my servants the prophets" (ביד עבדי הנביאים). Yet the people refused to listen (לא ישמעו, "they did not listen"). To further emphasize the centrality of the prophets, this redactor includes its own formulation of the punishment in v. 23. The wording of the punishment does not differ significantly from v. 18, both of which have God, the agent, remove Israel, but v. 23 adds, "as he spoke through all his servants, the prophets" (ביד כל־עבדיו הנביאים כאשר דבר).

---

covenant that was promised to the fathers, namely Jacob, through whom the blessing was bestowed. One should note the similarities between 2 Kgs 17:20 and Jer 31:37 where God declares that he will reject the seed of Israel (גם אבי אמאס בכל זרע ישראל, "Also I will reject all the seed of Israel").

60 There is a concentration of specific rejection language. God "removed" (hiphil of סור), "rejected" (מאס), and "cast" them (hiphil of שלך) from his presence. Although the significance of each expression is unclear, the general sense of all the terms is the distance from God and the people. God withdraws his protective shield over the people, making them vulnerable to the vicissitudes of external machinations and divine punishment. It marks the dissolution of the covenant between the Israelites and their God. In sum, divine displeasure results in the quasi-physical removal of divine protection from the Israelites, whether God removes himself or the Israelites/Judahites from his presence. Note the absence of the following rejection terms: הסתיר פנים ("to hide face"), עזב ("to abandon"), and נתש ("to uproot"). No comprehensive study has been done for all the terms. The main sources on the topic are Samuel Balentine, The Hidden God: The Hiding of the Face of God in the Old Testament (Oxford Theological Monographs; Oxford: Oxford University Press, 1983); Thomas Raitt, A Theology of Exile: Judgment/Deliverance in Jeremiah and Ezekiel (Philadelphia: Fortress Press, 1977); and Richard Elliott Friedman, "The Biblical Expression: Mastîr Panîm," HAR 1 (1977):139-148.

61 The punishment of v. 20 corresponds more with the catalog of sins than the punishment outlined in v. 18.

62 The Qere reading is נביאי which is supported by few other Hebrew manuscripts.

Since the prophets had warned them, they are without excuse, thus deserving of their punishment. Here, the redactor makes minor additions to the previous text with the established pattern of sin-provocation-punishment.

Despite the multiple levels of redaction, with הכעיס ultimately functioning as the pivot in the final composition, God is portrayed throughout the account as the main executor of the punishment, with some movement to make the punishment correspond more to the description of the sin.

2.7.2. 2 Kings 23:19-20 (v. 19)

After the extensive account of Samaria's fall (2 Kgs 17), הכעיס is attested one other time in regards to Samaria. In the context of reporting Josiah's reforms *(Reformsbericht)* in the North (2 Kgs 23:15-20), the term, הכעיס, provides the justification for the destruction of the sanctuaries in Samaria. Here, unlike other descriptions of the punishment in DtrH2, a human instrument, Josiah, takes the forefront in executing God's plan.

The *Reformsbericht* lists three different reasons for Josiah's reforms in the North which have led scholars to posit distinct levels of redaction. According to the report, Josiah carried out the reforms, first to destroy the cult at Bethel (1 Kgs 12:28-33; 2 Kgs 23:15), second to fulfill the prophetic oracle given at the time of Jeroboam I (1 Kgs 13:1-2; 2 Kgs 23:16-18)[63] — an example of *vaticinium ex eventu* — and third to remove and to defile the sanctuaries in Samaria (2 Kgs 23:19-20).[64] These distinct reasons — v. 15, vv. 16-18, and vv.

---

[63] For a more detailed separation of the two legends, see Eynikel, *The Reform of King Josiah,* 274, and his article, "Prophecy and Fulfillment in the Deuteronomistic History: 1 Kgs 13; 2 Kgs 23, 16-18," in *Pentateuchal and Deuteronomistic Studies* (eds. C. Brekelmans and J. Lust; BETL 94; Leuven: Leuven Univ. Press, 1990), 227-237, where he isolates vv. 1a, 3, 4, 8a, 9aαβ, 10 of 1 Kgs 13 as the first legend. The redactor (probably DtrH1) who inserted 2 Kgs 23:16-18 is responsible for the pivotal additions to the first legend, vv. 1b, 2, 8b, 9aβ, 11-32, 33-34.

[64] It is ambiguous as to which cultic sins these verses were referring. There are no other references to בתי במות ("houses of high places") except in 1 Kgs 13:32, which resembles the wording of 2 Kgs 23:19a, and in the singular form (בית, "houses"), 1 Kgs 12:31, 2 Kgs 17:29, 32. As for the phrase, ערי שמרון ("the cities of Samaria"), it appears in 1 Kgs 13:32 and 2 Kgs 17:26. The wording of 2 Kgs 17:24-33 (as distinct from 2 Kgs 17:34-40) is very similar to parts of 1 Kgs 12:31-13:34 (the demarcation of 12:31-13:34 rather than 12:25-13:34 follows Provan, *Hezekiah and the Books of Kings,* 78-81, who correctly notes the *Wiederaufnahme,* ויהי הדבר הזה לחטאת ("this thing became a sin"), in 12:30a and 13:34a; this is contrary to D. W. van Winkle, "1 Kings XII 25 - XIII 34: Jeroboam's Cultic Innovations and the Man of God From Judah," *VT* 46 [1996]:101-114). The similarities between these two texts (1 Kgs 12:31-13:34; 2 Kgs 17:24-33) and 2 Kgs 23:16-20 are evident. Dating any one of these passages would shed light on all three texts. As Provan

19-20 — can be attributed to two different redactors. Since there is continuity between 1 Kgs 12:31-13:34 and 2 Kgs 23:15-18,[65] reasons one and two (vv. 15-18) seem to legitimate Josiah's actions in the North. Therefore, they were most likely the product of DtrH1, which is dated to the period of Josiah. Later, DtrH2[66] added vv. 19-20[67] to indict Samaria, the kingdom, as opposed to just the cult at Bethel.[68] Since vv. 15-18[69] are not the primary concern of this study, focus will be on vv. 19-20:

Sin ("houses of the high places")

19) וגם את־כל־בתי הבמות אשר בערי שמרון אשר עשו מלכי ישראל

Provocation

להכעיס

Punishment

הסיר יאשיהו ויעש להם ככל־המעשים אשר עשה בבית־אל
20) ויזבח את־כל־כהני הבמות אשר־שם על־המזבחות
וישרף את־עצמות אדם עליהם וישב ירושלם

---

argues, the addition of 1 Kgs 12:30-13:34 shifts the interest away from the Golden Calves at Bethel and Dan to the high places of Bethel alone. Therefore, he dates the insertion to DtrH2. This would correspond well with the late dating of 2 Kgs 17:25-28, 29b, 32-41, 18:12 (see Shemaryahu Talmon, "Polemics and Apology in Biblical Historiography — 2 Kings 17:24-41," 57-68).

65 D.W. Winkle, "1 Kings XII 25-XIII 34," 101-114, considers 1 Kgs 12:25-13:34 to be a single literary unit so that vv. 15-18 could not be divided into two separate units (v. 15; vv. 16-18).

66 This is not without some disagreements among commentators. For a summary of the discussion, see Gary Knoppers, *Two Nations Under God*, 197-215, and Eynikel, *The Reform of King Josiah*, 272-287. Knoppers considers vv. 16-18 to be an earlier composition upon which the DtrH1 editor added vv. 15, 19-20. Also see Cogan and Tadmor, *II Kings*, 299-300, who think that vv. 15-18 are part of the Josianic propaganda, thus part of DtrH1. Contrary to Provan, *Hezekiah and the Books of Kings*, 147-148, who asserts that the "present form of 2 Kgs 22:1-23:30 is accepted by all as dating from no earlier than the exile." Therefore, the so-called *Reformsbericat* cannot have a pre-exilic context (150-151).

67 V. 19 opens with a waw ("and") + גם ("also") particle, which either indicates an insertion or a subordinate clause (see Eynikel, *The Reform of King Josiah*, 272-273, for a brief analysis of the phrase in DtrH). In some ways, v. 19 can be a modified *Wiederaufnahme* of v. 15. They both share the same beginning, וגם את ("and also"), and then they turn to their respective interests: v. 15 focuses on "the altar in Bethel" (המזבח אשר בבית־אל) while v. 19 turns to "all the sanctuaries of the high places in the cities of Samaria" (כל־בתי במות אשר בערי שמרון). The close integration of vv. 15-20 can be seen in the attestation of the phrase, אשר עשה בבית־אל ("which he did at Bethel"), in v. 19b which connects vv. 19-20 to v. 15 and also vv. 16-18.

68 Interestingly, בערי שמרון ("in the cities of Samaria;" the LXX omits ערי ["the cities of"]) is mentioned in 1 Kgs 13:32. Given the complete absence of שמרון ("Samaria") in the narrative of the Golden Calves, it would appear to be secondary. As a matter of fact, שמרון ערי ("the cities of Samaria") only occurs in 2 Kgs 17:24, 28 which are usually attributed to DtrH2.

69 The reason why v. 15 is differentiated from vv. 19-20 is the singular form of במה ("high place") in contrast to the plural form (במות, "high places") in vv. 19-20.

19)   And also all the houses of the high places which are in the cities of
      Samaria which the kings of Israel made <u>to provoke (God)</u>[70] <u>to anger,</u>
      Josiah removed. He did to them according to all that he did at Bethel.
20)   He sacrificed all the priests of the high places who were there, on the al-
      tars, and he burned human bones on them. Thereupon, he returned to Jeru-
      salem.

In the succinct addition (vv. 19-20), the pattern of sin-provocation-punishment
is developed. To outline the sin, the idolatrous objects, the "sanctuaries of the
high places" (בתי הבמות), are grammatically forefronted. The direct-object
marker (את) and the subordinate clause (אשר עשו מלכי ישראל[71] להכעיס,
"which the kings of Israel made to provoke [God] to anger") precede the verb
and the subject (הסיר יאשיהו, "Josiah removed") of the sentence (v. 19). It
was as if the redactor wanted to outline the sin and the resulting provocation to
explain the following destructive activities of Josiah:

Sin ("houses of the high places") → Provocation →
Punishment (Removal and Defilement)

However, here, the punishment is not retributive, disciplining the culprits for
their misdeeds, but corrective. In other words, Josiah is *undoing*, whether by
"removing" (הסיר) or defiling, what Israel had *done* against God. He does not
punish Samaria, the *doers* of the sin. Therefore, a human instrument, motivated by the provocation against God, corrects Samaria's misdeeds.

2.8. Fall of Jerusalem

2.8.1. Introduction

The pivotal term, הכעיס, is altogether absent in the accounts of Judah's kings
until DtrH2 explains the fall of Jerusalem (see Appendix B). Since the kings of
Judah claim their ancestry to David, the founder of the dynasty, the curse formula to terminate the dynasty does not appear in DtrH1's account of Judahite
kings.[72] Even when Athaliah temporarily seizes control (2 Kgs 11:1-16), the

---

70   Although the object is not indicated in the clause (הכעיס), it probably refers to God. The
     Greek, Syriac, and Targum seems to suggest this.
71   The ambiguous reference to the Israelite kings would incriminate the whole kingdom, not
     just Jeroboam.
72   As a result, when the Judahite kings do evil in the eyes of the Lord, הכעיס is never used:
     Rehoboam (though the text has Judah, 1 Kgs 14:22), Abijam (1 Kgs 15:3) and Amon (2 Kgs

rightful Davidic king, Jehoash, is ultimately put back on the throne (vv. 9-12), making it unnecessary to terminate her 'dynasty.' With the destruction of Jerusalem and cessation of the Davidic dynasty, however, a theological explanation was expedient. What were the reasons that could have possibly caused the demise of the center of DtrH's world? Who or what was responsible? For DtrH2, the agonizing questioning led him to scapegoat Manasseh for the downfall of Jerusalem. Manasseh committed a list of evil deeds[73] which had stirred God to destroy the Judahites, albeit somewhat delayed.[74] He is the progenitor of the evil that marked the end of the dynasty; the idolater, *par excellence*, whose deeds 'desacralized' the city. He is thus the Jeroboam[75] and Ahab[76] of Judah, who provokes God to anger.

21:20), kings before Josiah, supposedly committed sins against God but neither they nor their actions are recorded to have provoked God. Even when some kings, Jehoram (2 Kgs 8:18), Ahaziah (2 Kgs 8:27), and Ahaz (2 Kgs 16:3), followed the ways of Israel and/or the house of Ahab, they did not provoke God. No matter how grave the sin, the Davidic dynasty held sway over Judah in Jerusalem and never warranted the curse. For instance when king Solomon displeases God with foreign deities, he does not provoke God to anger (הכעיס), rather God responds with anger (ויתאנף, 1 Kgs 11:9) against Solomon to warrant a punishment. The closest that a southern king comes to provoking God is when Judah makes God "jealous" (piel, ויקנאו, 1 Kgs 14:22) with all their fathers' sins during the reign of Rehoboam. However, even this is a secondary insertion by DtrH2. Though the account concerns Rehoboam (1 Kgs 14:21), v. 22 shifts the focus to corporate Judah, a rare occurrence in the earlier accounts of the kings where the individual kings are held accountable. Moreover, the elaborate list of sins in vv. 23-24 resembles those of 2 Kgs 17 and those against Manasseh (2 Kgs 21). Therefore, it was probably a later addition. See Provan, *Hezekiah and the Books of Kings*, 74-77. Contrary to Eynikel, *The Reform of King Josiah*, 95-99, who separates the pericope into smaller units but attribute most of them to DtrH1.

73 See Eynikel, "The Portrait of Manasseh and the Deuteronomistic History," in *Deuteronomy and Deuteronomic Literature* (eds. M. Vervenne and J. Lust; BETL 133; Leuven: Leuven University Press, 1997), 233-261, for a detailed discussion of Manasseh.

74 It should be noted that Jeroboam, Baasha, and Ahab did not suffer dire consequences but their descendants. It was Nadav, Elah, and Joram who met violent deaths at the hands of usurpers.

75 S. Lasine, "Manasseh as Villain and Scapegoat," in *The New Literary Criticism and the Hebrew Bible* (eds. J. C. Exum and D. Clines; JSOTSup 143; Sheffield: JSOT, 1993), 163-183, acknowledges the comparison made to Ahab. However, he sees more continuity between Manasseh and Jeroboam.

76 2 Kgs 21:3. It is true that Ahab was portrayed in view of Manasseh's sins (William Schniedewind, "History and Interpretation," 649-661). Nevertheless, the reason why Ahab was selected to resemble Manasseh was on account of his reputation as an 'evil' king. Ahab's evil may have been enhanced with his association with Manasseh but he and Jeroboam provided a model for Manasseh as the reason for the termination of the Davidic dynasty and destruction of Jerusalem, the sacred site.

2.8.2. Manasseh: 2 Kings 21:2-15 (vv. 6, 15)

In the accounts of Judah, הכעים appears four times all in connection to Manasseh (2 Kgs 21:6, 15, 22:17, 23:26). Since the latter two attestations (22:17, 23:26) occur in the account of Josiah, they will be considered separately from the former two (21:6, 15).

Given his place as the scapegoat for Jerusalem's destruction, DtrH2 attributes to Manasseh a wide-array of sins (2 Kgs 21:1-9, 16), which resembles the list of accusations against Samaria (2 Kgs 17:7-17) and the very sins which Josiah tries to overturn (2 Kgs 23:4-14).[77] On account of the sins, punishment inevitably follows (vv. 12-15). Unfortunately, this simple delineation of sin-punishment is not without problems since Manasseh's account (21:1-18), like 2 Kgs 17:7-20, betrays multiple levels of redaction.[78] However, in the final form, הכעים does function as the pivot to the punishment in which God is the primary executor.

Though the structure of vv. 2-15[79] is more complex than 2 Kgs 17:7-23a, the unit forms a pattern of sin-provocation-punishment and reflects similar levels of redaction:

Catalog of Sins (vv. 2-11)
List A (vv. 2-7, v. 9b) — Manasseh

2) ויעש הרע בעיני יהוה
כתועבת הגוים אשר הוריש יהוה מפני בני ישראל[80]

---

77   Ehud Zvi, "The Account of the Reign of Manasseh in II Reg 21,1-18 and the Redactional History of the Book of Kings," *ZAW* 103 (1991):363.

78   See Nelson, *The Double Redaction*, 65-69; Cogan and Tadmor, *II Kings*, 270-273; Eynikel, "The Portrait of Manasseh," in *Deuteronomy and Deuteronomic Literature*, 233-261; Ehud Zvi, "The Account of the Reign of Manasseh," 355-374; and Percy Keulen, *Manasseh Through the Eyes of the Deuteronomists*, 161-203.

79   V. 1, report of the king's accession (1 Kgs 22:42, 2 Kgs 8:26, 14:2, 15:2, 9-10, 33, 18:1, 21:19, 22:1, 23:31, 36, 24:18), and vv. 17-18, the death formula, provide the skeleton in which the catalog of sins and punishment were incorporated. As for v. 16, since it opens with וגם ("and") and lists an additional sin outside of the catalog of sins, it is most likely an insertion. If that is the case then v. 15 originally closed the unit rather than v. 16.

80   Though v. 2 begins with a typical assessment of the kings (2 Kgs 8:18, 23:32, 37, 24:8, 19), the following accusation, כתועבת הגוים אשר הוריש יהוה מפני בני ישראל ("like the abominations of the nations which YHWH drove out before the Israelites"), is not common. Similar clause appears in 1 Kgs 14:24 (Rehoboam; the construction is awkward since תועבת ["abominations"] is preceded by a definite marker ה-; it is not in construct with הגוים ["the nations"]), which is a secondary insertion, and 2 Kgs 16:3 (Ahaz). A variation of this theme appears in 2 Kgs 17:8 ("they followed the practices of the nations which YHWH drove out before the Israelites," וילכו בחקות הגוים אשר הוריש יהוה מפני בני ישראל). Though 1 Kgs 14:24 and 2 Kgs 17:8 both have the people as subject of the sins, 2 Kgs 16:3 and 21:2 hold the two kings accountable.

‫3) וישב ויבן את־הבמות אשר אבד חזקיהו אביו‬
‫ויקם מזבחת לבעל ויעש אשרה כאשר עשה אחאב מלך ישראל‬
‫וישתחו לכל־צבא השמים ויעבד אתם‬
‫4) ובנה מזבחת בבית יהוה‬
‫אשר אמר יהוה בירושלם אשים את־שמי‬
‫5) ויבן מזבחות לכל־צבא השמים בשתי חצרות בית־יהוה‬
‫6) והעביר את־בנו באש ועונן ונחש ועשה אוב וידענים‬

Provocation (v. 6b)

‫הרבה לעשות הרע בעיני יהוה להכעיס‬[81]

‫7) וישם את־פסל האשרה אשר עשה‬
‫בבית אשר אמר יהוה אל־דוד ואל־שלמה בנו בבית הזה‬
‫ובירושלם אשר בחרתי מכל שבטי ישראל אשים את־שמי לעולם‬

List B (vv. 8-9a) — People

‫8) ולא אסיף להניד רגל ישראל מן־האדמה אשר נתתי לאבותם‬
‫רק אם־ישמרו לעשות ככל אשר צויתים ולכל־התורה‬
‫אשר־צוה אתם עבדי משה‬
‫9) ולא שמעו‬
‫ויתעם מנשה לעשות את־הרע‬
‫מן־הגוים אשר השמיד יהוה מפני בני ישראל‬

List C (v. 10; perhaps v. 8b) — Prophets

‫10) וידבר יהוה ביד־עבדיו הנביאים לאמר‬

Explicit Reason X (v. 11)

‫11) יען אשר עשה מנשה מלך־יהודה התעבות האלה‬
‫הרע מכל אשר־עשו האמרי אשר לפניו‬
‫ויחטא גם־את־יהודה בגלוליו‬

Punishment (vv. 12-14)

‫12) לכן כה־אמר יהוה אלהי ישראל הנני מביא רעה על ירושלם ויהודה‬
‫אשר כל־שמעיו תצלנה שתי אזניו‬
‫13) ונטיתי על־ירושלם את קו שמרון ואת־משקלת בית אחאב‬
‫ומחיתי את־ירושלם כאשר־ימחה את־הצלחת מחה והפך על־פניה‬
‫14) ונטשתי את שארית נחלתי‬[82] ‫ונתתים ביד איביהם‬
‫והיו לבז ולמשסה לכל־איביהם‬

Explicit Reason Y (v. 15) — Provocation (v. 15a)

‫15) יען אשר עשו את־הרע בעיני ויהיו מכעסים אתי‬
‫מן־היום אשר יצאו אבותם ממצרים ועד היום הזה‬

2) He did evil in the eyes of YHWH, according to the abominations of the nations which YHWH drove out before the Israelites.

3) He rebuilt the high places which Hezekiah, his father, destroyed. He set up altars[83] to Ba'al and made an Asherah[84] as Ahab, the king of Israel, did. He worshipped all the host of heaven and he served them.

---

81 Several Hebrew manuscripts, LXX, Syriac, Targum (codex Reuchlinianus), and Vulgate have a third masculine pronominal suffix to ‫להכעיס‬.

82 This expression occurs in Mic 7:18. Both appear to refer to the remnant that remains after the destruction of Samaria.

4) He built altars in the temple of YHWH of which YHWH said, 'In Jerusalem I will set my name.'

5) He built altars to all the host of heaven in two courts of the temple of YHWH.

6) He devoted his son by fire, practiced sorcery and divination, and consulted mediums and spiritists. He did much evil in the eyes of YHWH, <u>provoking him to anger.</u>

7) He set up the image of Asherah which he made in the temple, of which YHWH said to David and to Solomon, his son, 'In this house and in Jerusalem which I have chosen from among all the tribes of Israel I will set my name forever.

8) I will not cause the feet of Israel to wander from the land which I gave to their fathers, if only they are careful to do according to all that I commanded them and according to all the Teaching which my servant, Moses, commanded them.'

9) But they did not obey. Manasseh led them astray, doing more evil than the nations which YHWH destroyed before the Israelites.

10) YHWH spoke through his servants, the prophets, saying,

11) 'On account that Manasseh, the king of Judah, committed these abominations, doing more evil than the Amorites who were before him, and causing also Judah to sin with his detestable idols,'

12) therefore, says YHWH, God of Israel: 'I am about to bring evil against Jerusalem and Judah that the ears of those who hear will tingle.

13) I will stretch the measuring line of Samaria and the plumb line of the house of Ahab over Jerusalem. I will wipe out Jerusalem as one wipes a dish, wiping it and turning it upside down.

14) I will cast off the remnant of my inheritance and I will set it in the hands of their enemies. They will become an object of spoil and plunder for all their enemies.

15) On account that they did evil in my eyes and were <u>provoking me</u> from the day their fathers set out from Egypt until today.'

The multi-leveled catalog of sins (vv. 2-11) is linked to the punishment (vv. 12-14):

Catalog of Sins (vv. 2-11) → Punishment (vv. 12-14)

However, this pattern omits the pivotal term, הכעיס, which instead appears in v. 6b,[85] the middle of the catalog of sins, and at the end of the pericope (v. 15).

---

83 The LXX has a singular form rather than the plural of MT.

84 The LXX, Syriac, and Targum has the plural form of אשרה over against the singular form in MT.

85 After הכעיס in v. 6b, more sins are listed:

Sin (Idolatry) + Provocation (להכעיס) + More Sins (Idolatry & Disobedience) → Punishment

If one then follows the overall structure, then the pattern of sin-provocation-punishment is established but as an afterthought:

Catalog of Sins (vv. 2-11) → Punishment (vv. 12-14) Because of Provocation (v. 15)

The punishment results from the sins because of the provocation that had been caused by the list of sins.

The catalog of sins can be divided into three distinct levels based on the different foci: 1) Manasseh's sins (vv. 2-7, 9b);[86] 2) abrogation of God's decree (vv. 8-9a); 3) prophetic mediation (v. 10). In the earliest level, most likely DtrH2,[87] Manasseh is the primary *provocateur*: He "committed evil" (ויעש הרע, v. 2), "built" (ויבן, v. 3) high places, "set up" (ויקם, v. 3) altars to Ba‘al, "constructed" (ויעש, v. 3) Asherah, "worshipped" (וישתחו, v. 3) the starry host, "served" (ויעבד, v. 3) them, "built" (ובנה, v. 4) altars in the Temple, "built" (ויבן, v. 5) altars for the starry host, "consigned" (העביר, v. 6) children in fire, "practice soothsaying" (עונן, v. 6), "divined" (נחש, v. 6), "consulted ghosts" (ועשה, v. 6), "established" (וישם, v. 7) the image of Asherah, and "made them wander" (ויתעם, v. 9b). Without doubt, Manasseh is the subject of the succession of these third masculine singular verbs.

However, a shift in person and description of sins occur in vv. 8-9a,[88] where they, corporate Israel (v. 8a), disobey God. God will not make the feet of Israel wander if "they are careful to do all that I (God) commanded them" (ישמרו לעשות ככל אשר צויתים) and "all the Teaching" (כל־התורה); however "they did not obey" (ולא שמעו).

An additional change occurs in v. 10 in which the message is mediated through the prophets.[89] Thus three distinct levels, like the division of sources in 2 Kgs 7-17a, are evident in the catalog of sins against Manasseh.

With addition of sins after the comment on the provocation, it amplifies Manasseh's and the people's culpability and abets the divine anger. See 2 Kgs 17:11b where הכעים functions similarly.

86 Though v. 8 forms part of the quotation which begins in v. 7 ("in this house ... I will set my name forever ... I will not cause the feet of Israel to wander"), it is an addition. A later decree-editor adds to the quote to emphasize the corporate Israel's failure to obey God's word, not the kings of Judah (specifically David and Solomon), to whom v. 7 was addressed.

87 Though the final form of vv. 2-7, 9b is a product of DtrH2, there may have been a list of sins which DtrH1 may have included in Manasseh's account. Yet, given the limitations of our knowledge of DtrH1, I have not separated the catalog into two different levels.

88 The shift is further supported by the disjunctive syntactical structure; both clauses begin with a waw + negation (ולא).

89 Though in v. 8a, Moses, prophet *par excellence*, plays a pivotal role in DtrH, the plural form of נביא ("prophet") occur mostly in later editorial additions of the books of Kings (2 Kgs 17:13, 23, 24:2; it also occurs in 2 Kgs 9:7, but differs in context, since it refers to all the

The first two levels of redaction, DtrH2 (Manasseh) and decree source, correspond to the two reasons for the punishment in v. 11 and v. 15. The first explicit justification (v. 11) attributes the punishment to Manasseh: He had committed "these abominations' (התעבות האלה) and "caused Judah to sin with his idols" (ויחטא גם־את־יהודה בגלוליו[90]). Since Manasseh is at fault, v. 11 is probably linked to the list of sins ascribed to the king (vv. 2-7, 9b). However, v. 15 blames the people for the punishment: "They have done evil" (עשׂו את הרע), "provoking" (ויהיו מכעיסים) God ever since they left Egypt.[91] Since corporate Israel is held responsible for the fall, v. 15 is probably connected to the sins outlined in vv. 8-9a. As for the prophetic addition (v. 10), the redactor does not provide his own formulation of the reason.

The first justification for the punishment (v. 11) does not follow the pattern characteristic of הכעיס while a later decree-redactor provides the motivation, namely the provocation, for the punishment. In DtrH2, הכעיס occurs within the catalog of sins and does not signal the punishment. However, in the decree redaction, הכעיס does function as the link between the catalog of sins which provokes God and the deserved judgment (see discussion above on the overall structure of the pericope).

Despite the multi-levels of redaction in the catalog of sins and reasons, there is one description of the punishment (vv. 12-14). Since DtrH2 would not have outlined a catalog of sins without its consequent punishment, this redactor is most likely the author of vv. 12-14. DtrH2 depicts a deity who executes the punishment and attempts to make the punishment correspond to the catalog of sins.

In the description, God is the primary agent of destruction with a minor role for the instrumental human oppressor. God is the subject of a series of verbs: "I am about to bring up evil" (הנני מביא רעה, v. 12)[92] against Jerusa-

---

blood of the prophets that Jezebel sheds) and in Jeremiah (7:25, 25:4, 26:5, 29:19, 35:15, 44:4, though it occurs less frequently in Amos 3:7, Ezek 38:17, Zech 1:6, Ezra 9:11, and Dan 9:6, 10). Since God has spoken through the prophets, the people are without excuse.

90 It is interesting that this word for idolatry is attested throughout the book of Ezekiel, 6:4, 5, 6, 9, 13, 8:10, 14:3, 4, 5, 6, 7, 16:36, 18:6, 12, 15, 20:7, 8, 16, 18, 24, 31, 39, 22:3, 4, 23:17, 25, 30, 37, 39, 49, 30:13, 36:18, 25, 37:23, 44:10, 12, while occurring only once in the book of Jeremiah (50:2) in an oracle against Babylon. As for the book of Kings, it appears in reference to Asa, who removes the "fetishes" (1 Kgs 15:12); Ahab, who strays after them (1 Kgs 21:26); Samaria (2 Kgs 17:12); and Josiah, who removes them (2 Kgs 23:24). Beside these books, it is attested in Lev 26:30 and Deut 29:16.

91 From the beginning of their identity as Israel, the people have sinned. This idea is integrally connected to some of the later additions in the book of Jeremiah as will be discussed in Part IV.

92 The phrase, הנה אנכי מביא רעה על ("I am about to bring evil against," v.12), introduces the punishment, playing on רעה. It is present in the curse formula against the dynasties (1

lem, "I will stretch out" (ונסיתי, v. 13) the measuring line, "I will wipe out" (ומחיתי, v. 13) Jerusalem, "I will uproot" (נטשתי, v. 14) the remnant, and "I will deliver them" (ונתתים, v. 14) to the enemies. Only after God carries out the punishment, the people will become "loot and plunder" (לבז ולמשסה) to "all their foes" (לכל־איביהם). Thus God delivers Judah to the foes who pillage them.

Simultaneously, the punishment is worded to correspond to the catalog of sins and reason outlined in vv. 2-7, 9a, 11. Two specific accusations against Manasseh, his "evil" (הרע, vv. 2, 6, 9, 11; also in v. 15) and adherence to sins of Ahab (v. 3), are the basis for the judgment in vv. 12-14. Since Manasseh repeatedly committed "evil," God will bring "evil" (רעה) upon Jerusalem (v. 12):

"Evil" Sin (vv. 2, 6, 9, 11, 15) → "Evil" Punishment (v. 12)

Also, since Manasseh followed the sins of Ahab (v. 3), God will prescribe a fate similar to that of Ahab (v. 13):

Sin of Ahab (v. 3) → Punishment Equal to Ahab (v. 13; Annihilation of Dynasty)

Moreover, the tools, משקלת ("plumb line") and קו ("measuring line"),[93] that may have been used for the construction of the various structures dedicated to other deities (במות, "high places," v. 3; מזבחת, "altars," vv. 3, 4, 5), are used for destruction.

Yet a major kink in seeing a measure-for-measure punishment here, is that Jerusalem, not the guilty party, Manasseh, will inevitably suffer the consequences. Such inequity is rectified with the addition of vv. 8-9a and v. 15, where Judah is now accused of committing sins, namely "evil" (הרע, v. 15). Therefore, the later additions not only establish the pattern of sin-provocation-punishment but they make the culprit responsible for his/her own demise. All in all, God, the primary agent of the promised punishment, becomes more justified in implementing the judgment with the inclusion of the people's sins.

Kgs 14:10 [Jeroboam] and 1 Kgs 21:21, partially in 1 Kgs 21: 29 [Ahab]), judgment against Judah (2 Kgs 22:16 and partially in 2 Kgs 22:20) and in the poetry and prose of Jeremiah (Jer 4:6, 6:19, 11:11, 19:3, 15, 35:17, and 45:5; also, for its variant forms, see 11:23, 23:12, 32:42, 39:16, 49:37, and 51:64).

93   See Isa 34:11 and Lam 2:8 and the brief discussion in Cogan and Tadmor and Tadmor, *II Kings*, 269.

2.8.3. 2 Kings 22:15-17 (v. 17)

In the account of Josiah's 'discovery' of the scroll of Teachings, explanations for the destruction of Jerusalem are provided. Upon the accidental recovery of the scroll, Josiah is horror-stricken with the judgment set against Judah which Huldah, the prophetess, essentially confirms. While explaining God's word in the scroll, she outlines two distinct formulations of the destruction of Judah. In the first (v. 16), God becomes the messenger of the disaster which the people create while in the second (v. 17), his divine wrath, provoked by the people, burn against the Temple. Both formulations distance God from the active role of meting out the punishment.

When the king's officials discover a scroll in the Temple, they, commanded by Josiah, seek out God's word through Huldah, the prophetess. She provides an oracle (vv. 15-20) which has two purposes: On the one hand, it prophesizes evil for Jerusalem (vv. 16-17, 20b)[94] while on the other hand, it proclaims the peaceful burial of the king (vv. 18, 20a). Though these messages do not contradict each other, they do provide two distinct outlooks on the larger ramification of Josiah's reforms. Therefore, many commentators have divided the oracle into two sources: the positive oracle to DtrH1 and the judgment of doom to DtrH2. However, the two perspectives are so intricately interwoven that it is quite difficult to unravel the different sources. One cannot understand the prediction of Josiah's peaceful death without comparing his good luck to the fate of the inhabitants of Judah. Rather than separating the sources based on the two distinct judgments, one for the nation (vv. 15-17) and another for Josiah (vv. 18-20), one should look within the specific wording of the judgments. Since הכעים appears only in the doom oracle against Jerusalem, focus will mainly be on vv. 15-17:

Introduction (v. 15)

15) ותאמר אליהם כה־אמר יהוה אלהי ישראל
אמרו לאיש אשר־שלח אתכם אלי

Punishment (v. 16)

16) כה אמר יהוה הנני מביא רעה אל־המקום הזה ועל־ישביו
את כל־דברי הספר אשר קרא מלך יהודה

Reason (v. 17a)

---

94 Tadmor and Cogan, *II Kings*, 295, consider v. 19 to be part of the judgment, most probably from the presence of *Wiederaufnahme* in v. 18 (אל מלך יהודה השלח אתכם, "to the king of Judah, the one who sent you") of v. 15 (לאיש אשר שלח אתכם אלי, "to the man who sent you to me"). However, rather than picking up a different theme, v. 19 incorporates the doom-oracle while contrasting it with Josiah's contrition. If one is to argue for dual redaction based on the content of the oracle, one cannot consider v. 19 a significant part of DtrH1. The language resembles too much of other prophetic texts that prophesy destruction for Jerusalem.

Provocation

17) תחת אשר עזבוני ויקטרו לאלהים אחרים

למען הכעיסני בכל מעשה ידיהם

Punishment (v. 17b)

ונצתה חמתי במקום הזה לא תכבה[95]

15) She said to them, "Thus says YHWH, God of Israel: Speak to the man who sent you to me.

16) Thus says YHWH: I am about to bring evil upon this place and upon its inhabitants, all the stipulations of the book which the king of Judah read.

17) Since they abandoned me and burned incense to other gods so as to provoke me to anger with all the work of their hands, my wrath is kindled against this place; it will not be extinguished."

In the oracle against Jerusalem (vv. 15-17), two distinct formulations of the punishment (v. 16 and v. 17b) surround the pivotal term, הכעיס (v. 17a). These two formulations of the punishment, representing two different sources whose identities are unknown but are definitely post-exilic, reflect distinct conceptualizations of the role of God in executing the punishment. In v. 16, God "is about to bring evil" (הנני מביא רעה) to the people and the Temple in Jerusalem. This evil is the realization of God's word which had been spoken against the people in the Scroll. Though grammatically separated from the noun it complements, the phrase, "stipulations of the book which the king of Judah read" is in apposition to "evil:"

הנני מביא רעה אל־המקום הזה ועל־ישביו
את כל־דברי הספר אשר קרא מלך יהודה

I am about to bring evil upon this place and upon its inhabitants,
all the stipulations of the book which the king of Judah read.

---

95 The expression, לא תכבה ("it will not be extinguished"), is a common expression. In the book of Leviticus (6:5, 6), it refers to the fire of the altar which should never be extinguished. Isaiah appears to play with this in 34:10, where the abundance of slaughter at Edom will not extinguish the fire, and 66:24, where all the corpse of rebellious people will burn without extinguishing. At the same time, the expression refers to inextinguishable fire (Isa 1:31 – note its use in Isa 42:3 where it refers to the servant, a dim wick, which will not be extinguished) which is developed from Ezekiel (21:3, 4) and perhaps Amos (5:6). This is also reflected in the book of Jeremiah (17:27) where the fire spreads from the gates to the palaces of Jerusalem. At the same time, the book of Jeremiah has a molten imagery attached to the expression (Jer 7:20; see also 2 Chr 34:25) which appears to be secondary. 2 Kgs 22:17 actually uses יצת for the very expression which is connected to fire. This may be what is behind the metaphors in Jer 4:4 and 21:12.

Since the "stipulations of the book" are the "evil," the very words which the ancestors had failed to keep (לא־שמעו אבתינו על־דברי הספר הזה, "our fathers have not obeyed the stipulations of this book"), the punishment is measure-for-measure:

> People Disobey "Stipulations of the Book" (v. 13) →
> People Suffer "Stipulations of the Book" (v. 16)

Judah receives her exact due from God, the agent of the evil.

This formulation of the punishment (v. 16) is distinct from the one in v. 17 in which the pattern of sin-provocation-punishment is established. Verse 17 opens with the conjunction, תחת אשר ("on account of"),[96] where God accuses the people of the two-tiers of apostasy, the rejection of God (עזבוני, "they rejected me") and the worship of other deities (ויקטרו לאלהים אחרים, "they burned incense to other gods"). This leads to the provocation of God, igniting his wrath (ונצתה חמתי, "my wrath is ignited"):

> Apostasy → Provocation → Divine Wrath is Ignited

Since the people provoke the deity to wrath, they, not God, are responsible for the ignition. This very wrath, a synecdochic metaphor of the destructive power, burns against the place in which the people reside. Therefore, in both formulations of the punishment, there is measure-for-measure punishment; however God executes the punishment in the first (v. 16) while in the second (v. 17b), his divine wrath acts on his behalf.

2.8.4. 2 Kings 23:26-27 (v. 26)

Despite all of Josiah's efforts to reestablish Yahwistic practices in Jerusalem, the judgment against Judah is sealed. Judah will suffer God's divine wrath (2 Kgs 23:26-27) which had been fueled by Manasseh's provocations. Nevertheless, this divine wrath does not function apart from God but is actually prompted by the deity. As such, God is still the executor.

After carrying out reforms in the North (2 Kgs 23:15-20), Josiah returns to Jerusalem to fully promulgate the worship of YHWH. He re-instates the Pass-

---

96 *BDB*,1066, provides two definitions for the conjunction, תחת אשר, "instead of that" and "in return for (the fact) that, because that." In this context, the latter meaning would make most sense. The effect/outcome could either precede (Num 25:13, Deut 21:14, 22:29, 1 Sam 26:21, Isa 53:12, Jer 29:19, 50:7) or follow the reason (Deut 28:47, 2 Chr 21:12).

over (vv. 21-23) while continuing to stamp out "mediums and spiritists" (האבות ואת הידענים), "household images" (התרפים), "fetishes" (הגללים), and "detestable things" (השקצים, v. 24). This unit closes on a high note, with an assessment of Josiah as the king *par excellence* who followed the Teachings of Moses (v. 25).[97] Despite his efforts, Jerusalem will be punished.

Therefore, in the following verses (vv. 26-27), DtrH2 inserts a judgment oracle against Judah:

Punishment of Great Wrath (v. 26a)

26) אך לא־שב יהוה מחרון אפו הגדול אשר־חרה אפו ביהודה

Reason (v. 26b) — Provocation

על כל־הכעסים אשר הכעיסו מנשה

Punishment (v. 27)

27) ויאמר יהוה גם את־יהודה אסיר מעל פני כאשר הסרתי את ישראל
ומאסתי את־העיר הזאת אשר־בחרתי את־ירושלם ואת־הבית
אשר אמרתי יהיה שמי שם

26) Nevertheless, YHWH did not turn away from his great anger which burned against Judah on account of all the provocations with which Manasseh provoked him to anger.

27) YHWH said, "I too will remove Judah from my presence as I removed Israel. I will reject this city, Jerusalem, which I had chosen, the house concerning which I said, 'My name will be there.'"

In v. 26, the pivotal function of הכעיס is succinctly formulated where YHWH's great wrath results "on account" (על) of the provocatives deeds with which Manasseh provoked God:

Punishment Because of Sins (Provocative Deeds) ← Provocation

---

97 This assessment:

וכמהו לא־היה לפניו מלך אשר־שב אל־יהוה
בכל־לבבו ובכל־נפשו ובכל־מאדו ככל תורת משה ואחריו לא־קם כמהו

Neither before nor after him was there a king like him who turned to YHWH with all his heart and with all his being and with all his might according to all the Teaching of Moses

is partially paralleled with the one for Hezekiah (2 Kgs 18:5):

ביהוה אלהי־ישראל בטח ואחריו לא־היה כמהו בכל מלכי יהודה ואשר היו לפניו

He trusted in YHWH, the God of Israel. There was no one like him among all the kings of Judah, either before him or after him.

Since, according to the DtrH framework, "the Teachings" had not yet been discovered, Hezekiah was only attributed with having trusted God.

In this reverse pattern of sin-provocation-punishment, the "great wrath"[98] is explicitly linked to the provocations of Manasseh:

Great Wrath Against Judah ← Provocative Deeds of Manasseh

The very divine anger that Manasseh aroused becomes the very punishment that the people must suffer. Yet God, not the "great wrath," is the subject of the verb (לֹא־שָׁב יהוה, "YHWH did not turn away").[99] Therefore, God is the executing agent of the destruction. As the following verse (v. 27) elaborates, God "will remove Judah from before [his] face" (גַּם אֶת־יְהוּדָה אָסִיר מֵעַל פָּנַי)[100] and God "will reject" (וּמָאַסְתִּי) Jerusalem, reversing the initial election. Though Manasseh is mainly at fault, the people are the ones who ultimately experience God's wrath. As a result, the punishment partially corresponds to the sin.

---

98 V. 26a asserts that "YHWH had not turned away from his great anger that burned against Judah" (לֹא־שָׁב יהוה מֵחֲרוֹן אַפּוֹ הַגָּדוֹל אֲשֶׁר חָרָה אַפּוֹ בִּיהוּדָה). No mention had been made of God's "anger" (אַף חָרוֹן) nor of his coming into anger (חָרָה אַף, "he became angry") against Judah in the chapter. Then to what divine anger is the verse referring? Although the exact phraseology does not appear, one could argue that God's anger is present in 2 Kgs 22:13 when Josiah 'discovers' the scroll of the Teaching. Josiah exclaims, "for great is the wrath of God that has been kindled against us" (בָּנוּ כִּי גְדוֹלָה חֲמַת יהוה אֲשֶׁר־הִיא נִצְּתָה). However, what is distinct about this passage is the responsibility attributed to the ancestors (אֲבֹתֵינוּ לֹא שָׁמְעוּ, "our fathers did not obey"), not just Manasseh. Perhaps חֲרוֹן אַף ("anger") of 23:26 was alluding to חֲמַת יהוה ("the wrath of YHWH") of 22:13 indirectly.
       The only other reference to חָרָה אַף ("he became angry") in the books of Kings is 2 Kgs 13:3, where the anger accompanies the punishment against Israel. God became angry so that the Israelites were delivered to the Arameans. The absence of חֲרוֹן אַף in the books of Kings is even more unusual when compared with the books of Chronicles where it occurs four times in non-parallel texts (2 Chr 28:11, 13, 29:10, 30:8). In the books of Kings, a different word for 'anger' is used in Solomon's prayer (אָנַף, 1 Kgs 8:46) or in the account concerning God's anger with Solomon (הִתְאַנַּף, 1 Kgs 11:9; used in connection with fall of Samaria, 2 Kgs 17:18). In another context (2 Kgs 3:27), a different term for wrath is used (קֶצֶף גָּדוֹל, "great wrath"). However, here, it is unclear whether God or the Moabite god, Chemosh, was angry.

99 See Exod 32:12, Deut 13:18, Josh 7:26, Jonah 3:9, and Ps 85:4, where God is also the subject of the verbal clause, contrary to Num 25:4, 2 Chr 29:10, 30:8, Ezra 10:14, Jer 4:8, 30:23, where divine wrath is the subject.

100 This judgment resembles Israel's punishment as outlined in 2 Kgs 17:18, 23. It is repeated against Judah in the account of Jehoiakim (2 Kgs 24:3).

2.9. Conclusion

Overall, הכעים in DtrH2 and later additions functions as the pivot leading to various formulations of the punishment. In the post-exilic levels of DtrH, הכעים usually links the catalog of sins to the punishment (Deut 4:25, 9:18, 31:29, Judg 2:12, 1 Kgs 14:15, 16:7, 2 Kgs 17:17, 2 Kgs 21:15, 22:17, 23:19, 23:26), except for 2 Kgs 17:11 and 21:6, in which הכעים occurs in the middle of the catalog. Within the pericopes containing these attestations of הכעים, God is usually the agent of the punishment (Deut 4:27-28, Judg 2:14-15, 1 Kgs 14:15, 16:7, 2 Kgs 17:18-23, 21:12-15, 22:16, 23:26), sometimes leaving a minor role for human instruments (Judg 2:14, 1 Kgs 14:16a, 2 Kgs 17:19-20, 21:12-15). Only in 2 Kgs 23:19 does Josiah, a human instrument, carry out the destruction; but here, Josiah *undoes* the cultic abuses of Samaria rather than punish its inhabitants.[101] Thus, God in the role of meting out punishments is central to the theology of DtrH2 and later redactors.

At the same time, though, these redactors were concerned in exonerating their God of the destructive activities. But how does one put God in control while exonerating him? This is no easy task. Nevertheless, the late redactors mitigate God's involvement by 1) making the punishment correspond more to the sin (Deut 4:25-28, Judg 2:11-16, 1 Kgs 14:15-16a, 16:7, 2 Kgs 17:7-23a, 21:2-15, 22:16); 2) using divine anger either as motivation (Deut 9:20, Judg 2:14-15, 2 Kgs 17:18, 21-22, 23:26-27), instrument (Deut 9:19), or the agent of the destruction (2 Kgs 22:17); and 3) constructing the punishment out of the people's own "evil" (self-destruction; Deut 31:27-29). All in all, post-exilic editors attempt to ascribe to the culprits the consequences of their actions.

---

101 Compare this with DtrH1, in which human instruments play a vital role in fulfilling the prophetic pronouncements against the individual dynasties (see Part I).

Part III: Non-Deuteronomic Attestations of הכעים

3.1. Introduction

Among the non-Dtr references, the term, הכעים, usually functions as the pivotal link between the catalog of sins and the description of the punishment. The sins of the people provoke God to anger, which then becomes the stimulus for the consequent punishment. This pattern is explicitly evident in Hos 12:15, Ezek 16:26, and Pss 78:58 and 106:29, but is less clearly formulated in Isa 65:3, Ezek 8:17, and 2 Chr 28:25. In Isa 65:3, הכעים introduces rather than closes the list of sins that leads to the punishment; in Ezek 8:17, הכעים occurs before the final sin to heighten the misdeeds; and in 2 Chr 28:25, the seeming hidden punishment is found in the death formula. As a result, the non-Dtr attestations generally follow the pattern established in DtrH.

In the non-Dtr attestations, several conceptualizations of God's role in carrying out the destruction are evident. Except for Ps 106:29 (plague) and 2 Chr 28:25 (v. 27, improper burial) where God is perhaps the implied agent of the punishment, God is the primary agent (Hos 12:15, Ezek 8:18, 16:17 [also vv. 36-38, 41b-43], Isa 65:5-7) who sometimes uses human instruments (Ezek 16:39-41a, Ps 78:61). Though not always consistent, there is a tendency to make the punishment more (Ps 78:56-64, Hos 12:15, Isa 65:6-7) or less (Ezek 8:1-18, Ezek 16:23-30 [overall structure vv. 1-43]) correspond to the sins. To demonstrate this, we will analyze each of the pericopes with the exception of Neh 3:37, which does not expand on the function of הכעים.[1] It beseeches God to punish rather than outline the actual description of the punishment.

---

1   According to Neh 3:37:

ואל־תכס על־עונם וחטאתם מלפניך אל־תמחה כי הכעיסו לנגד הבונים

which NRSV (4:5) translates as:

Do not cover their guilt, and let not their sin be blotted out from thy sight; for they have provoked thee to anger before the builders.

In the Hebrew, it is ambiguous as to whether God is the patient of the provocation or the builders (see JPS which translates, "they hurled provocations at the builders") since הכעים does not indicate the direct object. On account of the ambiguity and lack of any description of the punishment, it will not be discussed. The term also occurs in Ezek 32:9 but God is the provoker while the people are the patient of the provocation: God "will trouble the hearts of many peoples when (the Egyptians) are brought to destruction" (והכעסתי לב עמים רבים בהביאי שברך). As a result, it too will not be discussed in this Part.

Chart C: Pericopes with הכעיס in Non-Deuteronomistic Books

Passage	Type of Sin	Form of הכעס	Culprit	Pivot	Type of Punishment	Agency
Hos 12:1-15 [15]	Catalog – Variety	הכעיס	Ephraim	Yes	Boomerang – Secondary	God → Sin
Ezek 8:1-18 [17]	Idolatry + Violence	להכעיסני	Judah	No – הכעס + Additional Sin	Respond in anger	God, motivated by divine anger
Ezek 16:23-30 [26]; (vv. 35-43)	Alliance with Egypt + previous list of idolatry and child sacrifice	להכעיסני	Jerusalem	Yes	V. 27: God cut ration and deliver to enemy; Vv. 36-38: God punishes; Vv. 39-41a: Lovers punish	God → Human
Isa 65:1-7 [3]	Idolatrous practices	המכעיסים	Post-exilic community	Yes – Introduction	Boomerang – secondary	God → Human
Ps 78:56-64 [58]	Idolatry	ויכעיסוהו	Israel	Yes	God rejects and delivers to enemy; Measure-for-measure	God → Human
Ps 106:28-31 [29]	Ba'al Peor	ויכעיסו	Israel	Yes	Outbreak of plague	Plague: God – implied
2 Chr 28:22-25 [25]	Catalog – Variety	ויכעס	Ahaz	Yes – Indirectly	Improper burial	Human: God – implied
(Neh 3:37)	Obstacle of rebuilding of wall	הכעיסו	Sanballat and company	No	NA	NA

3.2. Hosea 12:1-15 (v.15)

Influenced by DtrH the book of Hosea uses הכעיס to link the catalog of sins to the description of the punishment. According to many commentators, Hosea, the prophet, may actually be a precursor or, at least, affiliated with the pre-Dtr circle.[2] In fact, some have argued for the Dtr redaction of the final collection.[3] Whether or not the whole composition can be attributed to the Dtr circle, it is clearly evident that the sin-provocation-punishment structure in the final form of Hosea 12:1-15 resembles that of DtrH.

Hosea 12:1-15,[4] in its final form, constitutes a poetic unit that may have been either a compilation of several independent units[5] or the result of a succession of redactions or a combination of both.[6] On account of the lack of

---

2　Wolff, *Hosea* (Hermeneia; Philadelphia: Fortress Press, 1974), xxxi and 40, goes as far as to remark that Hosea was "one of the fathers of the early Deuteronomic movement" and further notes, 226, how the "(Judean) redaction of Hosea's prophecies may be more or less contemporary and parallel with the redaction of (Ur) Deuteronomy or Josiah's book of the Law, promulated in 621 BC." See also A. A. Macintosh, *Hosea* (ICC; Edinburgh: T. & T. Clark, 1997), lxxii, and William Moran, "The Ancient Near Eastern Background of the Love of God in Deuteronomy," in *Essential Papers on Israel and the Ancient Near East* (ed. Frederick Greenspahn; Essential Papers on Jewish Studies; New York: New York University Press, 1991), 103-115, who agrees generally but then argues for "deuteronomic originality" in regards to covenantal love.

3　See James Mays, *Hosea: A Commentary* (OTL; Philadelphia: Westminster Press, 1969), 17, and Gale Yee, *Composition and Tradition in the Book of Hosea: A Redaction Critical Investigation* (SBLDS 102; Atlanta: Georgia, 1987), 229-248. Though the 'heart' of Hosea's sayings may be as early as the period of Jeroboam, the final redaction of the book may have occurred as late as the 6th century in response to the Babylonian threat (Francis and D. Noel Freedman, *Hosea* [AB 24; Garden City: Doubleday, 1980], 52-57; and Macintosh, *Hosea*, lxxxii). According to Hans Wolff, *Hosea*, xxi, chs. 1-8 should be dated to the last years of Jeroboam II (747-746 B.C.E.) while chs. 9-12 seem to correspond with the events of Shalmaneser V (727) and chs. 13-14 to the period before or beginning of the siege of Samaria (725-724). See also James Mays, *Hosea*, 3-5.

4　Some have argued that 13:1-3 is a continuation of 12:15 (see Holt, *Prophesying the Past: The Use of Israel's History in the Book of Hosea* [JSOTSup 194; Sheffield: Sheffield Academic Press, 1995], 30, note 1). Though there is mention of idolatry in 13:1-3, which may correlate well with הכעיס in 12:15, there is a decisive break at the end of 12:15.

5　So Holt, *Prophesying the Past*, 30; Macintosh, *Hosea*, 473-517; Andersen and Freedman, *Hosea*, 593-623, esp. 597-598; and Wolff, *Hosea*, 208, who breaks the chapter into "five loosely connected rhetorical units."

6　See Gale Yee, *Composition and Tradition*, 229-48, who basically divides the unit into two redactions: earliest Hosean tradition (vv. 1a, 2-4, 8-9, 13, 15) and R2, the exilic-Deuteronomistic redactor (vv. 1b, 5-7, 12, 14). Since the unit is heavily redacted according to many commentators, they have suggested various rearrangements of the verses to get to the original form of the units; see Macintosh, *Hosea*, 517.

continuity, constant shift in time frame (present – past), and intermittent references to Judah (vv. 1, 3), the pericope could not have been originally a unified unit:[7]

Sin 1 (Ephraim and Judah[8] are Deceitful; vv. 1-2)

1) סבבני בכחש אפרים ובמרמה בית ישראל
ויהודה עד רד עם־אל ועם־קדושים נאמן

2) אפרים רעה רוח ורדף קדים כל־יום כזב ושד ירבה
וברית עם־אשור ישמן למצרים יובל יכרתו

Past Judgment and Accusation Against Israel[9] (vv. 3-7)

3) וריב ליהוה עם־יהודה
ולפקד על־יעקב כדרכיו כמעלליו ישיב לו

4) בבטן עקב את־אחיו ובאונו שרה את־אלהים

5) וישר אל־מלאך ויכל בכה ויתחנן־לו
בית־אל ימצאנו ושם ידבר עמנו

6) ויהוה אלהי הצבאות יהוה זכרו

7) ואתה באלהיך תשוב
חסד ומשפט שמר וקוה אל־אלהיך תמיד

Sin 2 (Ephraim is Dishonest; vv. 8-9)

8) כנען בידו מאזני מרמה לעשק אהב

9) ויאמר אפרים אך עשרתי מצאתי און לי
כל־יגיעי לא ימצאו־לי עון אשר־חטא

Proclamation of God's Past - Future Act of Redemption (vv. 10-11)

10) ואנכי יהוה אלהך מארץ מצרים
עד אושיבך באהלים כימי מועד

11) ודברתי על־הנביאים ואנכי חזון הרביתי

---

7   Holt, *Prophesying the Past*, 30, provides a topical outline which is somewhat reflected in the outline above:
    vv. 1-2 Ephraim and Judah are faithless
    vv. 3-7 The Jacob traditions
    vv. 8-9 Canaan and Ephraim are faithless
    vv. 10-11 The Exodus will be repeated
    v. 12   The worship of idols in Gilead and Gilgal
    vv. 13-14 The Jacob tradition and the Exodus tradition
    v. 15   The bloodguilt of Ephraim must be punished
8   It is unclear whether Judah (v. 1b), most likely a later insertion, is faithful or faithless since v. 1b is difficult to translate. JPS translates the verse, "But Judah stands firms with God/And is faithful to the Holy One," contrary to Holt, *Prophesying the Past*, 30, who considers Judah to have been faithless. See *BDB*, 923, which suggests various emendations. Either way, the reference to Judah is most likely secondary to the pericope since Ephraim is the primary object of criticism.
9   Given the context, 'Judah.' was probably originally 'Israel' which was then modified to 'Judah' as an indictment of Judah during the exilic period. See the following bicolon which returns to reflect on the Jacob tradition of northern origin.

 וביד הנביאים אדמה

Sin 3 (Idolatry at Gilead and Gilgal; v. 12)

12) אם־גלעד און אך־שוא היו בגלגל שורים זבחו
גם מזבחותם כגלים על תלמי שדי

Past Jacob Tradition & Exodus (vv. 13-14)

13) ויברח יעקב שדה ארם
ויעבד ישראל באשה ובאשה שמר

14) ובנביא העלה יהוה את־ישראל ממצרים ובנביא נשמר

Provocation (v. 15a)

15) הכעיס אפרים תמרורים

Punishment (v. 15b)

ודמיו עליו יטוש וחרפתו ישיב לו אדניו

1) Ephraim has surrounded me with lies, the house of Israel, with treachery; Judah is also unfaithful with God, against the holy one.

2) Ephraim herds the wind and pursues the east wind all day; they multiply falsehood and lies; they make a covenant with Assyria and oil is carried to Egypt.

3) YHWH has a lawsuit against Judah and will visit Jacob according to his ways; according to his deeds will requite him.

4) In the womb, he grabbed his brother by the heel and in his manhood, strove with God.

5) He strove with the messenger and prevailed, he wept and sought his favor. He met God at Bethel, and there he spoke with him —

6) YHWH, the God of Hosts, YHWH, his fame.

7) You, to your God, return, keep mercy and justice and wait for your God always.

8) The merchant, in whose hands are treacherous balances, loves to oppress.

9) Ephraim says, "Ah, I am rich; I have gained wealth for myself." But all my gains bring me no guilt that would be sin.

10) I am YHWH, your God, from the land of Egypt. I will again make you dwell in tents like the days of the appointed feast.

11) I spoke to the prophets; I multiplied visions; through the prophets, I gave parables.

12) Is Gilead wicked? Surely they have become worthless. Do they sacrifice bulls in Gilgal? Also their altars will be like stone heaps over furrows of fields.

13) Jacob fled to the country of Aram and Israel served for a wife and for another he tended sheep.

14) With a prophet, YHWH brought out Israel from Egypt and with a prophet, he was preserved.

15) Ephraim bitterly provoked to anger, he will cast his blood upon him; his master will repay him his reproach.

Notwithstanding the lack of continuity between the subunits, the pericope (vv. 1-15) does have a general structure where vv. 1-14 function as the catalog of sins and v. 15 as the punishment. The first fourteen verses recount the treacheries of Ephraim, juxtaposing their past transgressions (vv. 4, 5, 13) with the present predicament (vv. 2, 8, 9, 12). The accusations are heightened with God's plea for their return (vv. 6-7, 10-11) only to be rebuffed with Ephraim's claim, "all my gains bring me no guilt that would be sin" (v. 9).[10] Such stubborn insistence on their treachery in the past and present leads to the provocation of God (v. 15a), setting the way for the punishment (v. 15b).

Based on alliteration and word links, v. 15 seems integrally connected to vv. 1-14. The word for "bitterly," המרורים, from the root, מרר, plays on the mem and resh sound of מרמה ("treachery") in vv. 1, 8.[11] It is as if the מרמה-treachery of the Israelites is המרורים-bitterly affecting God. Moreover, v. 15bβ, וחרפתו ישיב לו אדניו ("his master will repay him his reproach"), picks up on v. 3bβ where God declares his intent to "repay (Israel) according to his deeds" (לו ישיב[12] כמעלליו).[13] Yet these links do not necessarily demonstrate whether or not v. 15 was original to any of the units/level of redaction but most likely show how the final redactor made an ingenious effort to string the subunits together.[14]

As a result, v. 15 was inserted along with the latest additions to the 'loose' collection of subunits (vv. 1-14) to establish the pattern in which הכעיס (v. 15a) connected the list of sins (vv. 1-14) to the punishment (v. 15b):

Sins 1+2+3 (vv. 1-14) → Provocation (v. 15a) → Punishment (v. 15b)

---

10 As translated by Wolff, *Hosea*, 207. F. Andersen and D. N. Freedman, *Hosea*, 594, provide a freer translation, "None of my crimes will ever catch up with me, my iniquity which I have wrongfully committed," which seems to capture the essence of the verse.

11 As noted by Andersen and Freedman, *Hosea*, 595-596, and Wolff, *Hosea*, 207-208. It may also be playing with the words, אפרים ("Ephraim," vv. 1, 2, 9, 15) and מצרים ("Egypt," vv. 2, 10, 14), which has not been noted in either of the commentaries except for the observation by Andersen and Freedman that 'Ephraim' is a key term in the pericope.

12 For plays on the word, שוב ("to return"), see v. 7 ("you will return to God," ואתה באלהיך תשוב) and v. 10 ("until I return you to the tents," עד אושיבך באהלים).

13 It should be noted that v. 3a opens with the statement that "YHWH has a lawsuit against Judah" (וריב ליהוה עם־יהודה), reflecting the late Judean redaction of the passage. V. 3bα clarifies the original audience of the saying, ולפקד על־יעקב ("to visit Jacob").

14 After all, many of the sins listed in vv. 1-14 are not acts of idolatry which can provoke God to anger but treacherous practices. The people were primarily accused of "deceit" (כחש, v. 1; מרמה, v. 1; כזב, v. 2; שד, v. 2), alliances with foreign kings (v. 2), "conduct and deeds" (דרכים, מעללים, v. 3; this may include idolatry but not necessarily), "false balances" (מאזני, מרמה, v. 8), and inappropriate gain of riches (vv. 8, 9). Perhaps the only reference to idolatry may be in v. 12, where it alludes to "wickedness" (און) in Gilead and "emptiness" (שוא) in Gilgal. However, the verse is very corrupt and problematic. Andersen and Freedman, *Hosea*, 594, translate as "Gilead with idols, indeed, with false gods in Gilgal" while Wolff, *Hosea*, 207, reads as "if Gilead was wicked, then they truly have become useless." See the discussion above on the wording of the punishment for further elaboration on the secondary nature of v. 15.

Since הכעים functions as the pivot between the catalog of sins and judgment, God appears to act in response to the anger resulting from the sins. As a consequence, God's punishment seems justified in light of Ephraim's (and Judah's) sinful activities. In fact, God, the provoked deity, is the active agent who "will cast his [Ephraim's] blood upon him" (ודמיו עליו יטוש) and who "will repay him his reproach" (וחרפתו ישיב לו).

However, since the judgment is secondary to the unit, the description of the punishment does not specifically refer to nor correspond to any of the sins in vv. 1-14.[15] Nevertheless, in the very wording of the punishment, v. 15bα tries to correlate the punishment to the sin. In v. 15bα, God "casts (their) blood" upon Ephraim[16] (ודמיו עליו יטוש). The noun דם ("blood") does not usually occur with the verbal root נטש ("to cast"), but the expression דמיו עליו ("his blood upon him") is a legal formula for 'bloodguilt,' where a person is held accountable for their own or someone else's blood.[17] But Israel is never accused of spilling innocent blood in vv. 1-14; instead the bloodguilt is implied. Therefore, Israel will be punished according to the assumed sin.

Similarly, the following bicolon is worded to correlate the punishment to the sin. V. 15bβ alludes to the sin of reproach, not mentioned in vv. 1-14, as the basis for the consequent punishment. According to v. 15bβ, God "will repay him his reproach" (וחרפתו ישיב לו). In the succinct formulation of the punishment, חרפה ("reproach") signified both the sin and the punishment. Since God "returns" (שוב, hiphil) the 'reproach,' God is reciprocating what he had received from Ephraim so that the 'reproach'-sin[18] becomes the 'reproach'-punishment.[19] As a result, the correspondence between the

---

15 According to Wolff, *Hosea*, 2.5, who observes that the text "abruptly makes a summary statement of the guilt."

16 Contrary to Macintosh, *Hosea*, 513, who incorrectly translates, "His bloodguilt will be evident upon him," by understanding יטוש as intransitive with דמיו as the subject. Given the grammatical parallelism between v. 15bα and v. 15bβ, אדניו of v. 15bβ seems to function as the subject of both bicolons:

ודמיו עליו יטוש
וחרפתו ישיב לו אדניו

17 See Lev 17:4, 20:9, 11, 12, 13, 16, 27, Hos 1:4; also, see discussions in Wolff, *Hosea*, 217; Macintosh, *Hosea*, 514; and Kedar and Kopfstein, *TDOT* 3:241-244.

18 The people never expressed any 'reproach' against God in the catalog of sins (vv. 1-14). Perhaps their 'treacheries' can be considered as a 'reproach' against God but this is not explicitly laid out in the catalog.

19 The retributive sense of שוב also occurs in v. 3b where God will "requite him according to his deeds" (וכמעלליו ישיב לו), in parallel construction with לפקד על־יעקב כדרכיו ("to visit Jacob according to his ways"). This word for reproach is part of a common curse formula, applied to cities in ruins, usually with various combinations of קללה ("curse"),

punishment and the sin is derived secondarily only in the formulation of the punishment.

In sum, הכעיס functions as a pivot between the sins and punishment which does not correspond except within the very formulation of the judgment in v. 15b. This measure-for-measure formulation of the punishment is similar to those of DtrH2.

3.3. Ezekiel 8:1-18 (v.17)

Although הכעיס in Ezek 8:17 does not conform to the pattern derived in DtrH, the editor of the unit (8:1-18) appears to be aware of and actually plays off on the pivot-function of the word. In the chapter, הכעיס does not lead directly to the punishment but sums up the previous 'sins' while emphasizing the final abuse. The climatic function of הכעיס (v. 17) is ultimately connected to the punishment (v. 18) by reference to the "wrath" (חמה) which motivates God to destroy Judah:

Introduction (v. 1)

(1 ויהי בשנה הששית ... ותפל עלי שם יד אדני יהוה

Description of Figure (v. 2)

(2 ואראה והנה דמות כמראה אש ... כמראה־זהר כעין החשמלה

Sin 1 (Infuriating Image; vv. 3-6)

(3-6 וישלח תבנית יד... ותבא אתי ...
אל־פתח שער הפנימית הפונה צפונה
אשר־שם מושב סמל הקנאה ...
ועוד תשוב תראה תועבות גדלות

Sin 2 (Illustrations of Creatures and Fetishes; vv. 7-13)

(7-13 ויבא אתי אל־פתח החצר ...
והנה כל־תבנית רמש ובהמה שקץ וכל־גלולי בית ישראל ...
עוד תשוב תראה תועבות גדלות אשר־המה עשים

Sin 3 (Tammuz; vv. 14-15)

(14-15 ויבא אתי אל־פתח שער בית־יהוה אשר אל־הצפונה
והנה־שם הנשים ישבות מבכות את־התמוז...
עוד תשוב תראה תועבות גדלות מאלה

Sin 4 (Sun-Worship; vv. 16-17a)

(16-17a ויבא אתי אל־חצר בית־יהוה הפנימית ...

חרב/ה ("waste"), שמה ("waste"), שרקה ("hissing"), אלה ("oath"), and משל ("[object of a] proverb") (Jer 24:9, 29:18, 42:18, 44:8, 12, 49:13, and Ezek 5:14, 15; see Kutsch, *TDOT* 5:213-214). It is related to the utter shame that the defeated people experience among the nations.

והמה משתחויתם קדמה לשמש ...
הנקל לבית יהודה מעשׂות את־התועבות אשׁר־ עשׂו־פה

Sin 5 (Violence; v. 17b)

17bα) כי־מלאו את־הארץ חמס

Climatic הכעיס

וישׁבו להכעיסני

Sin 6 (Branch to the Nose. v. 17b)

17bβ) והנם שׁלחים את־הזמורה אל אפם

Punishment (v. 18)

18) גם־אני אעשׂה בחמה לא־תחוס עיני ולא־אחמל
וקראו באזני קול גדול ולא אשׁמע אותם

1)	In the sixth year ... the hand of my lord, YHWH, fell upon me there.
2)	I looked and here was a form like an appearance of a man[20] ... like the appearance of brightness like the gleaming bronze.
3-6)	He stretched out a form of a hand ... and brought me ... to the entrance of the gate to the inner court that faces the north where the image of jealousy stood ... But you will still see greater abominations.
7-13)	He brought me to the entrance of the court ... Here all the detestable forms of creeping things, and beasts and all the fetishes of the house of Israel ... But you will still see greater abominations which they are doing.
14-15)	He brought me to the entrance to the north gate to the house of YHWH ... Here the women were sitting, weeping for Tammuz ... But you will still see greater abominations than these.
16-17a)	He brought me to the inner court of the house of YHWH ... they were worshipping the sun to the east ... Is it too slight for the house of Judah to commit the abominations which they are committing here.
17ba)	that they should fill the land with violence and further provoke me to anger?
17bb)	Here they are stretching the branch to their nose.
18)	I also will deal in wrath; my eye will not spare and I will not have compassion. They will cry in my ears with a loud voice, but I will not listen to them.

---

20   With Greek rather than MT ("fire," אשׁ).

Chapter 8 narrates the beginning of Ezekiel's vision where he is transported to Jerusalem.[21] Once the "spirit" (רוח, v. 3) transports Ezekiel to the Temple precinct, God points out all the cultic abuses[22] (תועבות, "abominations," vv. 6 - twice, 9, 13, 15, 17), from the outer to the inner area of the Temple:[23] north of the outer gate, an "infuriating image" (סמל הקנאה, v. 6); entrance to the court, depictions of "detestable forms of creepings thing and beasts and all the fetishes of the House of Israel" (כל־תבנית רמש ובהמה שקץ וכל־גלולי בית ישראל, v. 10); in the gate of the Temple, "women sitting, weeping for Tammuz" (הנשים ישבות מבכות את־התמוז, 14); and in the innercourt of the Temple, sun-worship (והמה משתחויתם קדמה לשמש, "they were worshipping the sun to the east," v. 16). This catalog of cultic abuses in the Temple closes with the rhetorical question posed to Ezekiel: "Is it not enough for the House of Judah to practice the abominations that they have committed here?" (הנקל לבית יהודה מעשות את־התועבות אשר עשו־פה, v. 17). Such a statement would point to a list of additional sin(s):[24] "Is it not enough ... to practice the

---

21   According to Greenberg, *Ezekiel 1-20* (AB 22; Garden City: Doubleday, 1983), 192, chs. 8-11 is "organized into a single visionary experience whose complexity indicates a considerable literary effort." He outlines the chiastic framework of the chapters:

      (a) 8:1a   date, location, audience of exile elders

      (b) 8:1b   God's hand falls upon the prophet (start of vision)

      (c) 8:2-3   A luminous human figure seizes the prophet; a wind transports him to Jerusalem in vision

      (c′) 11:22-24a the Majesty is borne off eastward; the wind transports the prophet back to Chaldea in vision

      (b′) 11:24b   the vision "lifts off" the prophet (ends)

      (a′) 11:25   the prophet tells what he saw to the exiles

22   Note the rhetorical question God poses to Ezekiel, "Do you see what they are doing?," (הראה אתה מהם עשים, v. 6; and its various forms, vv. 12, 15, 17). This phrase closes up each description of idolatrous practices in the Temple precinct as a comment on the 'incredulous' nature of the acts. A similar phraseology occurs in Jer 7:17 which opens rather than closes a description of idolatry.

23   According to Meindert Dijkstra, "Goddess, Gods, Men and Women in Ezekiel 8," in *On Reading Prophetic Texts: Gender-Specific and Related Studies in Memory of Fokkelien van Dijk-Hemmes* (eds. Bob Becking and Meindert Dijkstra; Biblical Interpretation Series 18; Leiden: E.J. Brill, 1996), 83, the spirit leads Ezekiel "from the outer North-Gate (Benjamin Gate?) through the gates, which separate the outer and inner court of the temple from the city, to the temple proper."

24   A similar statement appears in 1 Kgs 16:31 in reference to Ahab. Based on the wording of the expression, Ahab does not just "follow in the footsteps of Jeroboam, son of Nebat" (נבט לכתו בחטאות ירבעם בן), but he also marries Jezebel and worships Ba'al. Moreover, he sets up an altar to Ba'al and makes the Asherah (v. 32). Greenberg, *Ezekiel 1-20*, 172-173, argues that it is a combination of two separate constructions: הנקל ... מעשות ("Is it too slight ... to commit") of 1 Kgs 16:31 and המעט ... כי ("Is it too trivial ... that") of Isa 7:13. This argument

abominations ... but they (also) have to (commit other sins)?" Yet what were these other 'sins'?

According to the text, they were "violent" (חמס v. 17). However, violence does not fit the list of idolatrous practices in vv. 5-16.[25] Because of the sudden shift in the nature of the sin, from descriptions of idolatry (human-divine offense) to a social wrongdoing (human-human offense), many commentators have considered the passage. כי מלאו את־הארץ חמס ("for they have filled the earth with violence"), to be secondary.[26] If the 'violence' passage in v. 17bαα is secondary, then הכעיס could only have resulted from the idolatries listed in vv. 5-16. However, if the phrase is original, then the following phrase, וישבו להכעיסני ("they continually provoke me to anger"), most likely an insertion,[27] would have referred to both the idolatries *and* violence:

Idolatries (Sin 1+2+3+4 vv. 5-16) + Violence (v. 17bα) → Provocation

---

would depend whether one considers the phrase, חמס כי מלאו את הארץ ("for they filled the land with violence"), a secondary insertion or not (see above for further discussion). Nevertheless, notice how הנקל ... במעשות construction also allows the author to include more offenses: "Is it not enough for you to ... *but you also* ... ?" For additional examples, see Gen 30:15, Num 16:9, 13, Ezek 16:20, 34:18 (both with just המעט).

25 The expression, "they filled the earth with violence" (מלא' את־הארץ חמס), refers to the prevalence of violent activity or wrong, not idolatry. For similar expression, see Ezek 7:23 where חמס is in parallel construction with משפט דמים ("bloody crimes"). See also 28:16 (מלו) in the MT; contra other Hebrew manuscripts and ancient versions) and other attestations of חמס in the book of Ezekiel (7:11, 12:19, 28:16, 45:9), where they do not refer to idolatry. The expression also occurs in the Priestly description of the whole earth before its destruction in the flood (Gen 6:11, 13). Here also, it does not refer to idolatry, in particular, but to the general human tendency toward corruption.

26 However, according to Nahum Sarna, "Ezekiel 8:17," HTR 57 (1964):348, "it is one of the outstanding characteristics of Ezekiel that he lays so much stress upon the ritual evils and that he constantly alternates sins of idolatry with violations of the socio-moral code." Greenberg, *Ezekiel 1-20*, 172-173, also has remarked on the juxtaposition of violence-sin with idolatry. Since 9:9, "The earth was filled with blood and the city filled with injustice" (ותמלא הארץ דמים והעיר מלאה מטה), refers to injustice, Greenberg argues that חמס in 8:17 could only be integral to the unit. However one could easily argue that the reference to חמס was added secondarily to link ch. 8 to ch. 9. Therefore, his observation is not unquestionable proof.

27 According to Walther Zimmerli, *Ezekiel* (Hermeneia; Philadelphia: Fortress Press, 1979), 221, as supported by the absence of the phrase in the Greek and Latin fragment Sangallensium. On the other hand, George Cooke, *A Critical and Exegetical Commentary on the Book of Ezekiel.* (ICC 21; New York: Charles Scribner's Sons, 1937), 100, has argued that the phrase is original since it is essential in the transition to the following passage. Yet this would only make sense if וישבו להכעיסני occurred before the pronouncement of the punishment in v. 18. That way, להכעיסני could function as the pivot between the description of the sins and the punishment, which is typical of the expression. However, it does not and therefore, the phrase, וישבו להכעיסני, was probably a secondary addition in an awkward place to emphasize the final act of abomination.

This would reflect a slightly different context in which הכעיס usually occurs; the sin of violence in addition to the already established grounds for provocation, namely idolatry, could potentially provoke God to anger.

Unfortunately, the following enigmatic offense, "thrusting the branch to their nose"[28] (והנם שלחים את־הזמורה אל־אפם, v. 17bβ) does not help in clarifying the problem. Despite the numerous attempts to explain the practice,[29] scholars have not come to any consensus, disagreeing even as to whether it was a cultic or social abuse.[30] If the 'branch to the nose' were a cultic abuse, then 'violence' would more likely be secondary than if the 'branch' was a social abuse, since 'violence' would be inconsistent with the surrounding cultic offenses. Given the lack of sufficient data, it would be difficult to ascertain what the Judahites were doing with the 'branch.' Therefore, v. 17bβ is not helpful in illuminating the status of the clause concerning 'violence' (v. 17bα). In such a case, without sufficient evidence, the clause should be considered original to the text. Even if it was secondary, it may have been added prior to the insertion of וישבו להכעיסני ("they continue to provoke me"). Therefore, both the idolatries and violence had repeatedly[31] provoked God to anger.

Then a question remains as to why the phrase, "they continue to provoke me to anger," was added between the 'violence' phrase and the final sin. Most likely, the phrase was inserted to emphasize the final sin ('branch-to-the-nose') by breaking up the pattern of sin-provocation-punishment:

---

28   It should read 'my nose' instead of 'their nose.' It was probably a euphemism (*tiqqun soperim*), to cover up the 'disrespectful' gesture towards God.

29   See Greenberg, *Ezekiel 1-20*, 172-173, Zimmerli, *Ezekiel*, 244-245, and Meindert Dijkstra, "Goddess, Gods, Men and Women in Ezekiel 8," 110-113, who have mainly argued for a cultic background of the offense while discussing many of the possible suggestions for the 'act.' Sarna, "Ezekiel 8:17," 350-352, considers the sin to be primarily socio-moral rather than cultic. He, 352, translates the passage as "and they provoke me still more, for see, they send out the strong men to execute their anger/to anger me."

30   There is a third possibility that the 'branch to the nose' generally refers to all the acts in vv. 3-16 as offensive to God. Thus 'the branch to the nose' is not a specific socio-moral or cultic act but a figure of speech summing up these activities as a nuisance before God. This may explain why a specific group of people, whether the seventy elders (v. 11), women wailing for Tammuz (v. 14), twenty-five men (v. 16), and House of Judah (v. 17), is not mentioned but a general reference to these people (הנה, "here they are") who are irritating God. Only with the addition of וישבו להכעיסני ("they continue to provoke me") does the 'branch to the nose' then become a description of a particular act. However, the third possibility is not completely evident and is therefore, not discussed above.

31   For this sense of שוב ("to turn back"), see *BDB*, 998, under definition 8.

EXPECTED PATTERN
Sins → Provocation → Punishment
INSTEAD
Sins → Provocation + Additional Sin → Punishment

With the mention of the provocation, one would expect an elaboration of the punishment; instead, the editor lists an additional sin, exacerbating the situation. After all those provocations, now they insist on thrusting a branch to their nose?![32] The final sin tips the scale, unleashing God's anger.

Since the people do not stop sinning even after provoking God to anger, the punishment is all the more inevitable and justified. Therefore, God responds in anger, which suppresses his compassion ("I will act in wrath," אעשה בחמה; "my eye will not spare," לא־תחוס עיני; and "I will not have compassion," לא אחמל; v. 18). As a result, God will not listen (לא אשמע, "I will not listen") to their cry.[33]

As the description of the punishment demonstrates, God is the primary agent of destruction:

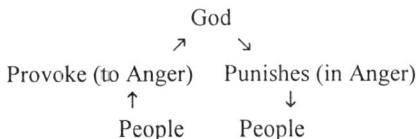

<pre>
                     God
                  ↗   ↘
    Provoke (to Anger)   Punishes (in Anger)
           ↑   ↓
        People   People
</pre>

There is no doubt as to who will punish the Judahites; the succession of first person verbs and pronominal suffixes (אשמע, באזני, אחמל, עיני, אני אעשה) all point to YHWH. Moreover, the punishment corresponds to the sins on two levels. On the one hand, God responds in "wrath" (חמה) since the people "provoked [him] to anger" with their idolatrous and wicked deeds. On another level, the correspondence occurs in the direction of the sin and the punishment. The people sin against God and it is God who punishes the people. The way in which this 'reverse-direction' is emphasized is by the phrase, וגם אני ("and

---

32   The description of the final sin opens with the presentative particle, הנה, with almost utter
     disbelief at the people's persistent sinning. The sins seem to be presented in "ascending order
     of gravity" (Sarna, "Ezekiel 8:17," 348). As v. 15 states, Ezekiel will see "greater
     abominations than these" (תועבות גדלות מאלה). But this is further emphasized by the
     addition of וישובו להכעיסני ("they continue to provoke me").

33   In poetic and late texts, קרא ("to call;" וקראו באזני קול גדול, "they will cry in my ears
     with a loud voice") also has the sense of "cry for help" (BDB,395). See also Isa 58:9, 65:24,
     Job 5:1, 9:16, Prov 21:13, Pss 42, 20:10, 147:9, etc. This part of the punishment is absent in
     the Greek and may be an addition.

also I").[34] The people may continually sin against God but he too will act against them.

In sum, the highlighting function of הכעיס built up the tension which found its release in a God who punishes with anger.

3.4. Ezekiel 16:23-30 (v. 26)

Through an allegory of an unfaithful wife, chapter 16:1-43[35] lays out the history of Judah. Within this tale, the pattern of sin-provocation-punishment is established in the immediate context of vv. 23-27 which is linked to the larger framework of the chapter (vv. 1-43) by the thematic root, כעס. Though God is portrayed as the primary agent of destruction, he also silently watches human instruments take their aggression out on his people.

Chapter 16:1-43 is a sexually violent diatribe against Jerusalem, who is depicted as the whore of the ancient Near East. The graphic and virulent tirade outlines the history of Jerusalem, the personified whore, in terms of a woman's physical development from her infancy to her sexual maturity. It traces Jerusalem from her ignoble birth to an Amorite father and Hittite mother to her womanhood during which she acquires beauty from her beneficent husband, YHWH. Rather than preserving her beauty for YHWH, she had exploited it to

---

34 As a means to counter the people's sins (Sarna, "Ezekiel 8:17," 349), the punishment is frequently introduced with the phrase (5:8, 11, 9:10, 16:43, 20:15, 23, 25, 21:22, 24:9). This is not an isolated expression to attribute the primary agency to God. Unlike the book of Jeremiah, where the agency of destruction shifts, in the book of Ezekiel, God is the main agent. Other expressions involving anger whereby God is the agent are: כלותי חמתי ("I brought my anger to pass") or variations thereof (5:13 [twice], 6:12, 7:8, 13:15, 20:8, 13, 21, 22:31, 43:8); הנחותי חמתי ("I let my anger subside") or variations thereof (5:13, 16:42, 21:22, 24:13); and שפכתי חמתי ("I poured out my wrath") or variations thereof (7:8, 9:8, 14:19, 20:8, 13, 21, 33, 34, 21:36, 22:22, 31, 30:15, 36:18). The need to assert God's agency over the punishment is consistent with the overall intent of the book, namely the need to assert God's supremacy (see Kutsko, *Between Heaven and Earth*). At the same time, the book of Ezekiel also describes the punishment in correspondence to the sin. In 9:10, God declares, "I requite their deeds upon their heads" (נתתי דרכם בראשם; also in 11:21, 22:31). In 36:19, it is phrased differently, where God states that he "judged them according to their conduct and deeds" (כדרכם וכעלילותם שפטתים).

35 This chapter has 63 verses which break up into three major sections (Greenberg, *Ezekiel 1-20*, 292; Zimmerli, *Ezekiel*, 333-334, and Julie Galambush, *Jerusalem in the Book of Ezekiel: The City as Yahweh's Wife* [SBLDS 130; Atlanta: Scholars Press, 1992], 91), the first of which comprises of vv. 1-43. Though the other two sections, vv. 44-58 (B) and vv. 59-63 (C), are integrally connected, they will not be included in the discussion since they do not have any bearing on the study of הכעיס.

fornicate[36] with "phallic images" (צלמי זכר, v. 17) and "every passerby" (לכל־עובר, v. 25), the Egyptians (v. 26), Assyrians (v. 28), and Chaldeans (v. 29). On account of her adulterous affairs, she is subject to her husband's anger. She will be publicly humiliated where her nakedness will be exposed to her lovers and then suffer violence in the hands of a "mob" (קהל, v. 40). In short, the story of Jerusalem's plight in vv. 1-43 can be outlined as follows:

vv. 1-2 Introduction - Legal Accusation[37]
vv. 3-5[38]   Jerusalem's Canaanite Origin and Abandonment[39]
vv. 6-14   Divine Claim, Covenantal Marriage, and Beneficent Gifts[40]
vv.15-19   Accusation of Idolatry
vv. 20-22   Accusation of Child Sacrifice
vv. 23-30[41]   Accusation of Inappropriate Foreign Alliances
vv. 30-34   Accusation of Bribery
vv. 35-43   Punishment

This basic structure of the chapter will provide the background for understanding הכעים in v. 26 which is in the subunit consisting of vv. 23-30:

Accusation of Harlotry (vv. 23-26a)

(23 ויהי אחרי כל־רעתך אוי אוי לך נאם אדני יהוה
(24 ותבני־לך גב ותעשי־לך רמה בכל־רחוב
(25 אל־כל־ראש דרך בנית רמתך ותתעבי את־יפיך ותפשקי
את־רגליך לכל־עובר ותרבי את־תזנתך
(26 ותזני אל־בני־מצרים שכניך גדלי בשר ותרבי את־תזנתך
Provocation (v. 26b)

---

36 The word for "harlotry" (זנה) pervades the chapter, vv. 15, 16, 17, 20, 22, 25, 26 - twice, 28, 29, 30, 31, 33 - twice, 34 - twice, 35, 36, 41.

37 This understanding of the introduction derives from the hiphil of ידע (הורדע), "to make known," in v. 2, which "carries a forensic sense, identifying what follows as a quasi-legal process," Daniel Block, *The Book of Ezekiel: Chapters 1-24* (NICOT; Grand Rapids: William B. Eerdmans, 1997), 471. Also see, Zimmerli, *Ezekiel*, 335-336.

38 Greenberg, *Ezekiel 1-20*, 292-306, divides the subunits into vv. 3-8 and 9-14, including the initial contact between Yahweh and the baby girl in the first subunit.

39 According to Galambush, *Jerusalem in the Book of Ezekiel*, 91, "the infant's physical expulsion simultaneously represents her legal abandonment." Also see, Meir Malul, "Adoption of Foundlings in the Bible and Mesopotamian Documents: A Study of Some Legal Metaphors in Ezekiel 16:1-7," *JSOT* 46 (1990):97-126.

40 Note the succession of first person converted imperfects (XXXא - vv. 1-12) with a shift in person to second feminine singular (תXXX) in vv. 13-26a, 28-29. Vv. 13-14 reflects the transition of Jerusalem from a child into a young woman who dressed herself.

41 Since v. 30 is a transition that closes up vv. 24-29 while connecting to vv. 31-34, it is included in both subunits.

להכעיסני

Punishment (v. 27)

27) והנה נטיתי ידי עליך ואגרע חקך
ואתנך בנפש שנאותיך בנות פלשתים הנכלמות מדרכך זמה

Further Description of Harlotry (vv. 28-29)

28) ותזני אל־בני אשור מבלתי שבעתך
ותזנים וגם לא שבעת

29) ותרבי את־תזנותך אל־ארץ כנען כשדימה
וגם־בזאת לא שבעת

Transitional Verse to Next Pericope (v. 30)

30) מה אמלה לבתך נאם אדני יהוה
בעשותך את־כל־אלה מעשה אשה־זונה שלטת

23)	After all your evil, 'Woe, woe to you,' says my lord, YHWH.
24)	You built for yourself a vaulted chamber and you made yourself a lofty place in every square.
25)	At the head of every street, you built your lofty place and you degraded your beauty and you spread out your legs to every passerby, multiplying your harlotry.
26)	You fornicated with the Egyptians, your well-endowed neighbors, multiplying your harlotry to provoke me to anger.
27)	Here, I have stretched out my hand against you and diminished your portion, and delivered you to the greed of your enemies, the daughters of the Philistines, who were ashamed of your lewd behavior.
28)	You fornicated with the Assyrians because you were insatiable; you harloted and again you were not satiated.
29)	You multiplied your harlotries with the land of merchants, the Chaldeans, but with this, you were not satiated.
30)	How weak is your heart, says my lord, YHWH, when you do all these deeds of a brazen prostitute?

The term, הכעיס, occurs in the immediate context of the accusation against Judah's fornication with foreign nations (vv. 23-29). The subunit moves from a general accusation of fornication to listing the particular lovers, the nations with which she had made alliances. In vv. 23-24, Jerusalem had set up a "rampart" (רמה) in every public thoroughfare, opening herself to everyone's advances. Then v. 26 focuses on the Egyptians, v. 28 on the Assyrians, and v. 29 on the Chaldeans.

In the elaboration of the alliances, הכעיס appears. Though the specific harlotry with the Egyptians (v. 26) forms the background for the expression, להכעיסני ("to provoke me to anger," v. 26b), the reference to the increased harlotries before it (ותרבי את־תזנתך, "you multiplied your harlotries"),[42] would include all the sins up to v. 26. Thus, the sins of idolatry (vv. 15-19), child sacrifice (vv. 20-22), and alliances (vv. 23-26) provoke God to anger, which inevitably leads to the punishment (v. 27).

The sudden description of the punishment in the middle of the elaboration of the foreign alliances (vv. 23-30) has baffled some commentators, leading some to conclude on its secondary nature.[43] However, v. 27 refers to a particular moment in Judahite history when they were subject to the Philistines, perhaps during Sennacherib's siege of Jerusalem.[44] This historical event is interpreted as God's means of judgment. At the same time, though, since Jerusalem's past is allegorized, the narration follows a literary pattern; the punishment is introduced in the pericope by הכעים:

Sins (vv. 15-26a) → Provocation (v. 26b) → Punishment (v. 27)

In the brief description of the punishment (v. 27), God is the primary executor. What rations God had bestowed to Jerusalem from her infancy, now God withdraws (אגרע חקך, "I withdrew your ration"). This withdrawal probably symbolized the lifting of God's protection over Jerusalem which then would enable God to deliver her to the enemy, the Philistines.

Despite the punishment, though, Jerusalem had failed to learn from her mistakes. Instead she continued her sinful activities, namely her harlotries with other nations, leading to yet another punishment:

Harlotries (vv. 15-26a) → Provocation (v. 26b) →
Punishment (v. 27) AND More Harlotries (vv. 28-34) → Punishment (vv. 35-43)

Jerusalem's nymphomania cannot be squelched. To punctuate this sexual appetite, the author inserts a refrain of Jerusalem's insatiable lust twice in v. 28 (מבלתי שבעתך, "not being satiated;" וגם לא שבעת, "again you were not satiated") and once in v. 29 (לא שבעת בזאת, "but even with this, you were

---

42 This expression occurs in vv. 25b, 29a. Also look at v. 51 where a variation refers to 'abominations' (ותרבי את־תועביתיך, you have multiplied your abominations").

43 Zimmerli, Ezekiel, 345, notes that v. 27 appear out of place, "a description of punishment which comes too soon." However, without any textual variants and the bizarre literary constructions within the chapter and book of Ezekiel, he seems hesitant to suggest a literary intrusion or outright misplacement.

44 Though Sennacherib was unsuccessful in capturing the royal city, he did manage to raze the surrounding area and partial out the Judean territory to the Philistines. See the brief but very good discussion of this in Greenberg, Ezekiel 1-20, 282-283, but also Zimmerli, Ezekiel, 345, Block, The Book of Ezekiel, 496, Galambush, Jerusalem in the Book of Ezekiel, 97-98.

not satiated"). Rather than repeating the refrain verbatim, the author intensifies by building up from the previous refrain:

(28 מבלתי... וגם לא ... (29 בזאת לא

28) not ... again not ... 29) but even with this, not

The dramatic build up closes with God's resigned declaration, "How weak is your heart?" (מה אמלה לבתך). The divine observation aptly depicts the weak-willed Jerusalem. Consequently, another punishment follows, playing off on the root of כעס.

Before elaborating on the punishment, vv. 31-34 describe the type of harlotries in which Jerusalem participates.[45] Unlike other whores, Jerusalem does not receive but rather gives gifts, i.e. bribes, to them. Therefore vv. 31-34, along with vv. 23-30, constitute the final episode. Then the judgment for the pericope is found in vv. 35-43.

Characteristic of judgment oracles, this section provides the reasons (יען, "on account of") for the punishment which fall under three categories: Inappropriate foreign alliances (מאהביך, "your lovers"), idolatry (כל־גלולי, חועבותיך, "all the fetishes of your abominations"), and child-sacrifice (וכדמי בניך, "and according to the blood of your children").[46] For these reasons, God (vv. 36-38, 41b-43) and then the foreign nations, to whom Jerusalem is delivered (vv. 39-41a), will mete out the punishment. In vv. 36-38, God, the primary actor, deals out the initial blows on Jerusalem:[47]

(37 הנני מקבץ ... וקבצתי ... וגליתי ... (38 ושפטתיך ... ונתתיך דם חמה וקנאה ...

---

45   Since v. 31 begins with a transition (בבנותיך גבך בראש כל־דרך ורמתך עשיתי בכל־ רחוב, "when you build your mound at the head of every street and made your lofty place in every public square;" see vv. 24-25 for similarities in the wording), that connects vv. 31-34 to the previous subunit (vv. 24-30), Zimmerli, *Ezekiel*, 345, has attributed vv. 31-34 to a second hand. Since it further develops the futility of vv. 24-29 rather than introduce new sins, this is highly likely and may explain the two-tier punishment in vv. 35-43.

46   Child sacrifice (כדמי בניך, "according to the blood of your children") is introduced by -כ ("according to") in the MT, which LXX, Targum, and Latin read as -ב ("because"). Since it is listing the reasons, -ב preposition would make more sense than -כ. However, Greenberg, *Ezekiel 1-20*, 286, actually prefers the MT, since he sees the punishment "in accord with that" blood, a measure-for-measure judgment. This is possible but Jerusalem is not killed, which would have accounted for the blood of the children. Rather she is razed to the ground and humiliated.

47   The centrality of Yahweh's agency is consistent with the description of a past punishment in v. 27 where there is also a succession of the deity's activity: "I had stretched out my hand" (נטיתי ידי), "I withdrew" (ואגרע), and "I delivered you" (ואתנך).

37)   I am about to gather ... I will gather ... I will uncover ...
38)   I will judge you ... I will make you into an bloody object of fury and
       jealousy ...

While YHWH is portrayed as a furious husband deliriously bashing his wife,[48] the lovers and those whom Jerusalem hate are mere spectators since they only "gaze"[49] (ראו את־כל־ערותך, "they looked at all your nakedness," v. 37b). However, this changes in vv. 39-41a, where God is the spectator while the lovers punish Jerusalem.

The following subunit opens with God delivering Jerusalem to the lovers (ונתתי אותך בידם, "I will deliver you into their hand"). From that moment onwards, God is absent and the lovers totally decimate and shame Jerusalem:

39) והרסו... ונתצו ... והפשיטו ... ולקחו ... וניחוך ...
40) והעלו ... קהל ... רגמו ... באבן ... ובתקוך בחרבותם ...
41) ושרפו ... ועשו בך שפטים לעיני נשים רבות

39)   They will demolish . . they will tear down ... they will strip ... they will
       take ...they will leave ...
40)   they will summon .. they will stone ... they will hack with swords ...
41)   they will burn ... they will inflict punishment before many women.

The succession of third masculine plural verbs stands in stark contrast with the series of first person singular verbs, referring to YHWH, in vv. 36-38. One could conclude that the executor of the punishment shifts from YHWH to the lovers after the husband removes his protection from Jerusalem.[50]

However, the two distinct formulations of the punishment, either with God or with the human instrument as the executor of the destruction, may possibly be attributed to two different authors/editiors. As Zimmerli noted, the shift in the agency of the punishment would indicate a work of a later redactor.[51] This is not so evident since the punishment as a totality corresponds well with the

---

48   In both depictions of the punishment, Jerusalem, who had been active in her harlotry, is
      altogether passive where God and the lovers act upon her.
49   The act of observing, according to Galambush, *Jerusalem in the Book of Ezekiel*, 104-105,
      creates "boundary between the subject and the 'other.'" As a result, the distance created
      between Jerusalem and her lovers ultimately objectifies Jerusalem; the intimacy between the
      lovers and Jerusalem has been severed so that they are then able to completely violate and
      expose her nakedness.
50   This appears to be Greenberg's, *Ezekiel 1-20*, 292-306, reading. He sees the pericope as a
      unity rather than with layers of redactions. See also Block, *The Book of Ezekiel*, 502-503,
      who argues that the lovers are "transformed into agents of divine wrath."
51   Zimmerli, *Ezekiel*, 347. He further attributes vv. 31-34 to this very redactor.

structure of the sins.[52] Both in terms of the agency and type of punishment, the judgment correlates to Jerusalem's sins. Jerusalem receives punishment from both her husband, whom she rejects, and her lovers, for whom she leaves God. Though God had bestowed favors upon Jerusalem, she had rejected YHWH, her husband, and fornicated with the idols and foreign nations. Therefore God punishes and then subjects her to the lovers' violence so that she is ultimately alone as she was before God had first passed her (v. 6). Her punishment befits her crime.

Only after God has spent his fury (והנחתי חמתי, "I will quiet my wrath," v. 42) will his passion subside (וסרה קנאתי, "my jealousy will turn aside"). Then he will be calm and not be provoked any more (עוד ושקטתי ולא אכעס, "I will be quiet and no longer be angry"). This final description is crucial since the provocation which incited God to initially punish Jerusalem (v. 27) is now spent so that the fuel firing his actions has been combusted.

3.5. Isaiah 65:1-7 (v. 3)

Here, in a late text, הכעיס introduces the catalog of sins which then becomes the premise for the consequent punishment. Though it is not the literary fulcrum, the term does signal the punishment in which God repays the people according to their deeds.

The final two chapters of the book of Isaiah (chs. 65-66) close Trito-Isaiah (chs. 56-66) and the entire book. These two chapters make cross-references and interpret passages in the first chapter and throughout the book.[53] Though

---

52 Galambush, *Jerusalem in the Book of Ezekiel*, 101-106, and Greenberg, *Ezekiel 1-20*, 292-306, mention the measure-for-measure punishment. Though the general description of the punishment is similar to her sins and her ultimate fate resembles her beginning, the exact structure of the punishment does not follow the sins. If the chiastic structure demonstrating the measure-for-measure punishment existed, then the lovers' demolition of Jerusalem would occur before God's execution of justice against her. Despite this, the general description does correspond.

53 So David Carr, "Reaching for Unity in Isaiah," *JSOT* 57 (1993):71-75. For some of these cross-references, see Marvin Sweeney, "Prophetic Exegesis in Isaiah 65-66," in *Writing and Reading the Scroll of Isaiah: Studies of an Interpretative Tradition* (vol. 2; eds. Craig Broyles and Craig Evans; VTSup 70; Leiden: Brill, 1997), 455-474. To a certain extent, Anthony Tomasino, "Isaiah 1.1-2.4 and 63-66, and the Composition of the Isaianic Corpus," *JSOT* 57 (1993):81-98, would agree with Carr and Sweeney. However, Tomasino sees structural parallelism between 1:2-2:4 and 63:7-66:24, minus ch. 65 which breaks up the parallelism. He conjectures that ch. 65 and 66:22-24 were later additions which drew upon other parts of Isaiah.

chs. 65-66 form a unit, they can be subdivided into three subunits reflecting the overall structure of the conclusion:[54]

65:1-7 — Problem in Refusing to Seek YHWH[55]
65:8-25 — Address to the Wicked
66:1-24 — Address to the Righteous

Despite the interdependence of the subunits to each other, they also form a distinct unit of their own. Since הכעיס occurs only in the first subunit, we will focus on this section:

God's Call (vv. 1-2)

נדרשתי ללוא שאלו נמצאתי ללא בקשני (1
אמרתי הנני הנני אל־גוי לא־קרא בשמי
פרשתי ידי כל־היום אל־עם סורר (2
ההלכים הדרך לא־טוב אחר מחשבתיהם

Description of the Idolatrous People (vv. 3-5) — Provocation

העם המכעיסים אותי על־פני[56] תמיד (3
זבחים בגנות ומקטרים על־הלבנים
הישבים בקברים ובנצורים ילינו (4
האכלים בשׂר החזיר ופרק פגלים כליהם
האמרים קרב אליך אל־תגש־בי כי קדשתיך (5
אלה עשן באפי אש יקדת כל־היום

Punishment (vv. 6-7)

הנה כתובה לפני (6
לא אחשה כי אם־שלמתי ושלמתי על־חיקם
עונתיכם ועונת אבותיכם יחדו אמר יהוה (7
אשר קטרו על־ההרים ועל־הגבעות חרפוני
ומדתי פעלתם ראשנה על־חיקם

1) I was to be sought by those who did not ask for me; I was to be found by those who did not seek me. I said, "Here am I, Here am I," to a nation that did not call upon my name.

2) All day, I spread out my hands to an obstinate people, those who walk in ways not good, after their schemes.

3) The people who continually provoke me to my face, sacrificing in gardens and burning incense upon bricks;[57]

---

54   According to Sweeney, "Prophetic Exegesis in Isaiah 65-66."

55   Carr, "Reaching for Unity in Isaiah," 74 actually breaks chs. 65-66 into ch. 65 (address to sinners) and ch. 66 (address to righteous). However, 65:1-7 is qualitatively different from vv. 8-25 and should thus be discussed as a subunit.

56   For similar attestations, see Exod 20:3, Deut 5:7. The exact sense is unclear but it clearly emphasizes how the offense was against God, not themselves or anyone else.

4) those who sit among the graves and spend their nights in secret places; those who eat pig-flesh and broth[58] of unclean meat in[59] their vessels;

5) those who say, "Keep to yourself,[60] don't draw near to me for I am set apart from you."[61] These are smoke in my nostils, fire kindling all day.

6) Here it is written before me: "I will not keep silent[62] but I will pay back; I will pay back on their bosom, your iniquities and the iniquities of your father together," says YHWH;

7) "because they burned incense on the mountains and on the hills, they reproached me, I will measure out their first deed upon their bosom."

This first subunit is a complete judgment oracle. In the first two verses, a frustrated God pleads with the stubborn people but to no avail. Therefore, vv. 3-5 lists God's indictment of the community in a series of participles describing the idolatrous bunch before announcing their punishment (vv. 6-7). It is at the beginning of the list of participles that הכעיס appears (v. 3), opening the catalog of sins with a general statement: "the people who provoke (God)" (העם המכעיסים אותי). Unlike the previous attestations, which function as climatic links or pivots between the indictment and the punishment, the term here introduces the various idolatrous practices of the people.[63] However, in the overall structure, הכעיס functions as the motivation for the punishment.

---

57 The reference to the practice of burning incense on "the bricks' (הלבנים), is quite enigmatic as noted by Claus Westermann, *Isaiah 40-66: A Commentary* (OTL; Philadelphia: Westminster Press, 1969), 401. The difficulty seems to have been present during its transmission since 1QJes^a provides a completely different reading וינקו ידים על האבנים ("they were cleaning [?] their hands over the stones"). Comparing the bricks to those used in rituals accompanying prayers in late Babylonia, Dietheim Conrad, "Mitteilungen zu Jes 65 3b," *ZAW* 80 (1968):232-234, suggests that the practice referred to worship of heavenly deities.

58 Though the MT Ketiv has פרק (?), the Qere has מרק ("broth"). The Qere reading is supported by 1 Q Is^a, LXX, Targum, and Vulgate.

59 1 Q Is^a, Targum, and Vulgate has ב-preposition before כליהם ("their vessels").

60 This meaning of קרב אליך is based upon context not the dictionary-definition. Usually אל קרב means "to draw near," not to "stay away."

61 According to the MT, קדשתיך ("I am set apart from you") is in the qal rather than the piel form. As a result, many commentators and even BHS have preferred emending the text. However, J.A. Emerton, "Notes on the Text and Translation of Isaiah XXII 8-11 and LXV 5," *VT* 30 (1980):446-450, argues that the qal should be retained and the suffix function like the ל-preposition.

62 According to the MT, it is אחשׂה (?). However, it is probably אחשׁה (root חשׁה, "to be silent") with other Hebrew editions.

63 Part of the reason may have been due to the form of the word. Previous examples of הכעיס were either a finite verb or infinitive complement to a verb (in Hos 12:15, it is conjugated in the perfect tense [הכעיס] while in Ezek 16:26, it is a infinitive construct) whereas the word

Before elaborating on the punishment, the pericope contrasts God's *presence* to the people's *absence*. The first two verses establishes God's everpresent willingness to be sought:

נדרשתי ... נמצאתי ... אמרתי הנני הנני ... 2) ... פרשתי ידי כל־היום (1

1) I was to be sought ... I was to be found ... I said, "Here am I, here am I" ... 2) I spread out my hands all day

This is contrary to the people who have failed to seek God:

ללוא שאלו ... ללא בקשני ... גוי לא־קרא בשמי (1

1) who did not ask for me ... who did not seek me ... a nation that did not call upon my name

Since the persistent God was constantly rejected, the description of the people was not too flattering. According to v. 2, they were a "stubborn people" (עם סורר). When one turns to vv. 3-5, a specific list of their erring ways is presented. Reference to the provocation (v. 3a) introduces the descriptive catalog of their particular idolatrous practices (vv. 3b-5). Though the list of sins is quite obscure, the activities seem to refer to non-Yahwistic practices. With their sins outlined, the stage is now set for God's punishment.

The indictment section closes with a summary observation of God's wrath (v. 5b). These very practices[64] supplied the fuel for the smoke which reaches the divine nose (עשן באפי, "smoke in my nostrils").[65] This idolatry-fed smoke is "perpetual blazing fire" (אש יקדת כל־היום), which is a referent to God's judgment. Therefore, v. 5b is the pivot to the consequent divine punishment:

---

here is a participle. However, other occurrences of the participial form (1 Kgs 14:15, 2 Kgs 21:15, Jer 7:19, 32:30) continue to function as a pivotal 'reason' for the punishment. Both the Kings passages explain the punishment "on account" (יען אשר) that they provoked God while the Jeremianic verses function as the link to the proclamation of the judgment.

64 Contrary to A.S. Herbert, *The Book of the Prophet Isaiah: Chapters 40-66* (CBC; vol.2; Cambridge: Cambridge University Press, 1975), 182, who translates אלה ("these") as "such *people* are a smouldering fire" (italics mine).

65 Smoke in relation to the 'nose' occurs in 2 Sam 22:9 (עלה עשן באפו, "smoke went up his nose"), which is duplicated in Ps 18:9. It is a description of YHWH as he marches out of his temple. The earth convulses "on account of his wrath" (כי חרה לו, v. 8). The accompanying image of YHWH in v. 9 resembles an active volcanoe: "Smoke" (עשן), "fire" (אש), and "live coals" (גחלים). The 'special effect' is a vehicle to describe an angry deity; it is not referring to anger itself.

Provocations (Catalog of Sins; vv. 3-5a) →
Pivot ('Smoke in Nose;' v. 5b) → Punishment (vv. 6-7)

Though הכעיס may not function as the pivot to the punishment, it does provide the active ingredient for God's anger, the fodder for the fire-judgment. Yet how is the punishment described?

The punishment (vv. 6-7) is described as a "recompense" (root שלם) for the community's sins. The section opens with a declaration, "Here it is inscribed before me" (הנה כתובה לפני), to document the permanence of their sin-record; it is written and it will not be erased. As a matter of fact, God will not remain inactive (לא אחשה, "I will not keep silent") but will finally punish the culprits: God will requite them (שלמתי, "I will pay back").[66]

Two distinct formulations seem to be at play in v. 7.[67] On the one hand, in v. 7a, God requites[68] "your iniquities and your fathers iniquities" (עונתיכם

---

66   The MT has repetition of שלמתי ("I will pay back;" שלמתי ושלמתי על־חיקם, "I will pay back and I will pay back on their bosom") whereas LXX, Syrohexaplarus, and Arabic versions represent a reading with just one. It is difficult to determine which reading is 'correct' or 'better' that may help explain whether there is an intentional addition or omission. The problem becomes more complicated with the repetition of (על־חיקם, "on their bosom"), which appears also in v. 7c. BHS considers it secondary although there are no ancient manuscripts that would support this suggestion. However, it is highly possible that ושלמתי על־חיקם ("I will pay back on their bosom") was added to perhaps provide a parallel structure to v. 7c, ומדתי פעלתם ראשנה על־חיקם ("I will measure out their first deed upon their bosom"): God requited their iniquities // God measured out their deeds. However, the parallelism is forced since v. 7a is most likely an addition.

67   The description of the punishment in vv. 6b-7 of the MT forms a chiastic structure, ABB'A':

A   Description of punishment - שלמתי על־חיקם ("I will pay back on their bosom")
B   Description of sin - עון ("iniquity")
B'   Description of sin - particular idolatrous practices
A'   Description of punishment - ומדתי פעלתם ... על חיקם ("I will measure out their deed ... on their bosom")

With this chiastic structure, the people's particular idolatrous practices are then placed in the same level as עון ("iniquity"). This 'iniquity' is the stain that blemishes the exilic community.

68   Though שלם can be translated as 'repay,' K. Koch, "Is There a Doctrine of Retribution in the Old Testament," 60-64, argues that the word is best translated as "complete" (see also, TDOT 10:556). If one follows his line of argument, then God is not necessary to carryout the punishment; the consequence is "built-in" the action. On the contrary, the agency of God is central to the depiction. The consequence may be in proportion to the action but God is the one who brings the punishment.

(וֹעֲוֹנֹת אֲבוֹתֵיכֶם).[69] The sudden shift from third person to second person in v. 7a and back again to third person in v. 7bc most likely hints at the secondary nature of v. 7a.[70] With this addition, the stubborn people are repaid for their and their ancestors' iniquities. Though not specific, in context, these iniquities were probably positioned to refer to those in vv. 1-5. If so, then they receive the consequence of their actions:

'Angry Deity'

↗   ↘

Sin (Implied עון)   Punishment (Requite עון)

↑   ↓

People (Past & Present)   People (Present)

Though the description of the punishment does not follow the sin word-for-word, it is nonetheless portrayed as measure-for-measure punishment; the 'stubborn' people are requited for the iniquities they had committed. After all, עון can denote both the misdeed as well as the punishment (for their misdeed).[71] It makes more explicit the relationship drawn between sin and the punishment in v. 7c.

On the other hand, if one excises the addition (v. 7a), then v. 7b provides the reason for the recompense[72] (אֲשֶׁר קִטְּרוּ עַל הֶהָרִים ... וְשִׁלַּמְתִּי "I will pay back ... *because* they burned incense on the mountains"), not the object of the requital as in v. 7a (שִׁלַּמְתִּי ... עֲוֹנֹתֵיכֶם, "I will pay back ... *your iniquities*"). Syntactically this nuanced difference is evident. In v. 7a, 'iniquities' is the direct object of the verb (שִׁלַּמְתִּי, "I will pay back") while in v. 7b, אֲשֶׁר

---

69   The LXX and Syriac has third masculine plural instead of second masculine plural. Though the ancient witnesses have the 'correct' reading, the MT may perhaps reflect an earlier form. The MT kept the redactor's addition while the LXX and Syriac may have tried to 'smooth-over' the discrepancies.

70   It may have been an effort to link vv. 1-7 with vv. 8-25, where the 'stubborn' people are referred to in the second person as opposed to the 'servants' who are in the third person. See vv. 11-15, אַתֶּם ("you"), אֶתְכֶם ("you"), כֻּלְּכֶם ("all of you"), תִּכְרָעוּ ("you will bend"), etc. At the same time, it may have been an addition by the editor who brought these pericopes together. Note how LXX and Syriac have tried to gloss over the difference. They have third masculine plural suffix rather than second person plural suffix.

71   According to *TDOT* 10:546, it is the "central term for human sin, guilt, and fate in prophetic and cultic writings." See also *HALOT* 2:800, and Jacob Milgrom, *Cult and Conscience: The Asham and the Priestly Doctrine of Repentance* (SJLA 18; Leiden: E.J. Brill, 1976), 4, who observes that עון ("iniquity") and other similar words "stand not only for evil, but for its inherent punishment."

72   If one follows LXX, Syrohexaplaris, or the Arabic versions, the second שִׁלַּמְתִּי is absent from v. 6b.

("because"), a demonstrative pronoun used as a conjunction, introduces the reason for the recompense:

Provocations (vv. 1-5a) → Angry Deity (v. 5b) →
Punishment (v. 6): Explicit Reason (Idolatry, v. 7b)

As can be seen from the foregoing diagram, v. 7b further bolsters or in some ways sums up[73] the reason for the 'recompense' rather than describe the punishment. It is only in v. 7c where the act of 'recompense' is specified. According to the bicolon, God will measure out their previous misdeeds (ומדתי[75] פעלתם ראשנה[74], "I will measure out their first deed"):

Sin (פעלה) → Punishment ('Measure Out' [according to] פעלה)

Similar to the addition of v. 7a, פעלה functions both as a reference to their past deeds and their punishment. Therefore, in both formulations (v. 7a and v. 7c), they are receiving their just dues though v. 7a, an addition, factors the ancestors into the equation. In the end, however, it is God, the ultimate agent, who pays (שלמתי ["I will pay back"], מדתי ["I will measure out"]) them back for their sins.

3.6. Psalm 78:56-64 (v. 58)

Though Psalm 78 is dated to a period earlier than DtrH1, הכעים in v. 58, like its attestations in DtrH, functions as a pivot between the sin and the

---

73   The description refers to the general sin of apostasy rather than refer specifically to those listed in vv. 1-5. God will requite them for offering incense upon the mountains (אשר קטרו על־ההרים, "because they offered incense on the mountains") and reproaching God upon the hills (ועל־הגבעות חרפוני, "they reproached me upon the hills"). These descriptions refer to the 'sins' of idolatry and rejection of God, the dual aspects of apostasy, not particular activities.

74   Though one would expect a ה-definite marker in front of ראשנה ("first") for the translation provided above, the definite marker does not always need to precede the adjective and the noun it modifies in late biblical poetry. At the same time, it could also be translated as 'their deeds at first (temporal reference).' However, it would be unclear to what this 'first' time referred. On account of the difficulty of this passage, BHS emends to בראשם ("upon their heads"). Then על־חיקם ("on their bosom") would become unnecessary.

75   This is the only attestation of מדד ("to measure") where it occurs in the "context of reprisal" (TDOT 8:133). It functions similarly to פקד ("to visit"), שלם ("to requite") and hiphil of שוב ("to return"). As TDOT 8:133 explains, "Yahweh will repay the apostates and 'measure' their deeds." For a similar concept see Jer 13:25.

punishment. As a pivot, it leads to an elaboration of the punishment where God is the executor with human instruments in the background.

On account of the difficulty in determining the historical events mentioned in the psalm, the dating of Psalm 78 has reached little consensus. Proposals for the dating of the psalm range from the tenth century to the late post-exilic period,[76] depending on whether one interprets the destruction of Shiloh (v. 60) as literal or as figurative, referring to the fall of Samaria. However, given the selection of collective memories of corporate Israel[77] rather than of the

---

76 The dating of this psalm has been quite problematic. Artur Weiser, *The Psalms* (OTL; London: SCM Press, 1962), 540, dates Psalm 78 to the pre-exilic date. Charles and Emilie Briggs, *A Critical and Exegetical Commentary on the Book of Psalms* (ICC 11; vol. 2; Edinburgh: T. & T. Clark, 1927), 181 also date Psalm 78 to the pre-exilic period. On account of its dependence on other literary traditions as well as late ideas, specifically that of the evil angels in v. 49, however, he attributes certain verses to glosses from the Greek or Maccabean period See also Antony Campbell, "Psalm 78: A Contribution to the Theology of Tenth Century Israel," *CBQ* 41 (1979):51-79, and Edward Greenstein, "Mixing Memory and Design: Reading Psalm 78," *Prooftexts* 10 (1990):197-218. In response to the early dating of the Psalm, Richard Clifford, "In Zion and David a New Beginning: An Interpretation of Psalm 78," in *Traditions in Transformation: Turning Points in Biblical Faith* (eds. Baruch Halpern and Jon D. Levenson; Winona Lake: Eisenbrauns, 1981), 121-141, dates the psalm to the period of Hezekiah, during whose reign, there was a movement toward centralization of the place of worship. For a similar dating, see Philip Stern, "The Eighth Century Dating of Psalm 78 Re-argued," *HUCA* 66 (1995):41-65. The main dissenter regarding the early dating is Hans-Joachim Kraus, *Psalms 50-150* (CC; trans. Hilton Oswald; Minneapolis: Augsburg, 1989), 123-124, who dates the psalm to the post-exilic period. According to Kraus, the close affinities with the Dtr school, which reached its peak during the exilic period, may point to the late dating.

77 Most likely, Ps 78 is not a historical credo (see Pss 105, 106, 135, and 136) but as Greenstein argues, a psalm which practices the memory, "not to recount the past, but to prompt the kind of remembrance that leads to change" ("Mixing Memory and Design: Reading Psalm 78," 197). If it was just a recital of the divine historical activities in the past, then the events would have a sequential order:
    I. Wonders in Egypt
    II. Parting of the sea
    III. Wanderings in the wilderness
    IV. Settlement in Canaan
Instead the order is somewhat haphazard:
    II. Parting of the sea (vv. 12-13)
    III. Wanderings in the wilderness (vv. 14-40)
    I. Wonders in Egypt (vv. 42-53)
    IV. Settlement in Canaan (vv. 54-55)

The psalmist stirs memory of God's extraordinary acts (תהלות יהוה ועזוזו ונפלאותיו, "the praiseworthy deeds of YHWH, his strength and his wondrous deeds," v. 4b) despite episodes of Israel's continual obstinacy (vv. 17-20, 29-30, 32, 36- 37, 40-42, 56-57) and periodic

northern kingdom,[78] Psalm 78 probably dates to the period of the United Monarchy when Jerusalem was established as the religio-political center.

Since the psalm comprises of distinct subunits integrated into a unit, this analysis will focus on the immediate context of the term, הכעים. The outline of the overall structure of the psalm is as follows:

vv. 1-8	Introduction
vv. 9-11	Present Ephraimite Sin Leading to Description of Past Sin[79]
vv. 12-55	Past Corporate Sin
vv. 56-64	Return to Present Sin and Punishment
vv. 65-72	Election of Jerusalem and David

The psalm calls upon the people to listen and bequeath to their children the stories of their ancestors' misdeeds (vv. 1-8), which is then listed (vv. 9-55). This recapitulation of the past sins then sets the stage for the present sin-provocation-punishment pattern in vv. 56-64:

Sin of Disobedience (vv. 56-58)

---

instances of God's angry outbursts (vv. 21-22, 31, 33-34) so that they are motivated to obey rather than disobey God.

78   Despite the ambiguity in the wording of the event, the list of collective memories in the psalm would seem to indicate an earlier rather than a later dating. The psalm focuses on the corporate history of Israel, only to distinguish between Ephraim and Judah at the end (vv. 65-72). If the psalm intended to emphasize the rejection of the North and election of the South *after* the collapse of Samaria, then it would not have listed the common national traditions but reflected on the apostasy of just the Northern kingdom. Thereupon, the rejection of Samaria would have been warranted. However, the psalm does not enumerate on any particular Ephraimite sin except the vague reference to their refusal to fight in battle (בני־ אפרים נושקי רומי־קשת הפכו ביום קרב, "the Ephraimites, those armed with bows, turned on the day of battle," v. 9) and their refusal to obey (vv. 10-11). Rather the psalm recollects corporate Israel's rebellion in the wilderness and in Canaan. In fact, the destruction of Shiloh was a punishment directed against all of corporate Israel, not just of the North. Thus, the rejection of Ephraim (v. 67) does not indicate a unilateral abandonment of the North, but of the northern cultic site situated in corporate Israel, which is to be replaced by Jerusalem, the new location of God's "sanctuary" (מקרש, v. 69). Such an interpretation would then place Psalm 78 in the period of the initial establishment of Jerusalem under King David. At the same time, though, the psalm would have probably acquired a heightened significance during the fall of Samaria (722 B.C.E.). Perhaps it was at this time in which reference to the captivity (v. 61) was added since Israel did not experience exile until the rise of the Neo-Assyrian empire.

79   Since there is explicit link between vv. 9 and vv. 56-57 (שמרו, "they keep," v. 10 and v. 56; הפכו, "they turned," v. 9 and נהפכו, "turned over/perverse," v. 57; and קשת, "bow," v. 9 and v. 57), the recollection in the intervening subunit seems to have been provided for the purpose of giving insight into the present predicament.

56) וינסו וימרו את־אלהים עליון ועדותיו לא שמרו
57) ויסגו ויבגדו כאבותם נהפכו כקשת רמיה

Provocation

58) ויכעיסוהו בבמותם ובפסיליהם יקניאוהו

Punishment (vv. 59-64)

59) שמע אלהים יתעבר וימאס מאד בישראל
60) ויטש משכן שלו אהל שכן באדם
61) ויתן לשבי עזו ותפארתו ביד־צר
62) ויסגר לחרב עמי ובנחלתו התעבר
63) בחוריו אכלה־אש ובתולתיו לא הוללו
64) כהניו בחרב נפלו ואלמנתיו לא תבכינה

56) However they tested and rebelled against God, Almighty; his statutes they did not keep.
57) They were faithless and treacherous like their fathers; perverted like a deceitful bow.
58) They provoked him to anger with their high places; with their idols they aroused his jealousy.
59) When God heard, he was angered. He surely rejected Israel.
60) He abandoned the tabernacle of Shiloh, the tent in which he dwelt among humanity.
61) He gave his might into captivity, his splendor to enemy hand.
62) He delivered his people to the sword, with his inheritance he was angered.
63) Fire consumed their young men, and their daughters remained unwed.
64) Their priests fell by the sword, but their widows did not weep.

Israel's collective memory ends with their settlement in Canaan (v. 55), lending itself to the present indictment that results in the destruction of Shiloh. Initially, the psalmist establishes the people's defiance (vv. 56-58). In a chiastic structure, the psalm develops the two-tier sin of apostasy:

Verbs-Direct Object:Direct Object-Verb
Verbs-Simile:Verb-Simile
Verb-Preposition:Preposition-Verb

וינסו וימרו *את־אלהים עליון ועדותיו* לא שמרו
ויסגו ויבגדו כאבותם נהפכו כקשת רמיה
ויכעיסוהו *בבמותם ובפסליהם* יקניאוהו

They tested and rebelled *against God, Almighty*; *his statutes* they did not keep.
They were faithless and treacherous like their fathers; they were perverted like a deceitful bow.
They provoked him to anger *with their high places*, *with their idols* they aroused his jealousy.

Israel rejects God and his statutes, the first part of apostasy, and then they replace God and his commands with "high places" and "idols," the second part of their apostasy. At the center of the chiastic structure is the essence of the whole psalm, specifically the evocation of their past sins. Like their ancestors, the Israelites were sinful. Even the first two verbs, "to test" (root נסה) and "to rebel" (root מרד), form the basis of Israel's sins in the past (vv. 17-18, 40-41). Therefore, the present apostasy is just another episode in the history of Israel's continual rebellion.

Nevertheless, this final act of deviance is qualitatively different from their previous misdeeds. Whereas the past sins involved lack of trust (לא בטחו, "they did not trust;" לא האמינו, "they did not believe") in God's power (vv. 19-20, 22, 32, 36-37), the present sin focuses on their apostasy. Despite the difference, the present situation will also result in a punishment and blessing as Israel's past sins were followed by an outburst of divine wrath and then beneficence.[80]

Given the catalog of their apostasy, capped with הכעים, punishment eventually follows. After a brief comment on God's anger (v. 59a), the preface to the judgment,[81] the full description of the punishment is outlined in vv. 59b-64. As a result, the pattern of sin-provocation-punishment is developed:

Sin (vv. 56-58) → Provocation (v. 58) →
Anger (ויתעבר, v. 59a) — Preface to Punishment (vv. 59b-64)

Here, הכעים functions as the pivot to the angry deity's punishment.

In the description of the punishment, God is ultimately the agent of the destruction. In the catalog of sins (vv. 56-58), Israel is the subject of the succession of verbs of disobedience (third masculine plural):

56) וינסו וימרו ... לא שמרו
57) ויסגו ויבגדו... נהפכו...
58) ויכעיסוהו ... יקניאוהו

56) They tested and rebelled ... they did not keep.
57) They were faithless and treacherous ... they were perverted ...
58) They provoked him to anger ... they aroused him to jealousy.

---

80   See note 77.
81   Note how this verse resembles v. 21 (לכן שמע יהוה ויתעבר, "therefore YHWH heard and became angry"), one of the past episodes of God's outburst.

Contrast this to vv. 59-61, in which God (third masculine singular) is the subject of the verbs of rejection and destruction:

59) שָׁמַע ... יִתְעַבֵּר וַיִּמְאַס ... 60) וַיִּטֹּשׁ... 61) וַיִּתֵּן ...62) וַיַּסְגֵּר ... הִתְעַבָּר

59) He heard ... he was angered. He rejected ...
60) He abandoned ...
61) He gave ...
62) He delivered .. he was angered.

They, Israel, sinned against God, so God will punish them. Even though a human instrument is mentioned (v. 61), it is altogether passive; the enemy only receives what God hands over to them (בְיַד־צָר, "into enemy hand").

Just as the outline of Israel's apostasy was developed in a chiastic structure, the description of God's punishment is also in a chiastic structure:

Verb:Verb-Object
Verb-Direct Object
Verb-Direct Object
Verb-Object:Object-Verb

יִתְעַבֵּר וַיִּמְאַס מְאֹד בְּיִשְׂרָאֵל
וַיִּטֹּשׁ מִשְׁכַּן שִׁלוֹ אֹהֶל שִׁכֵּן בָּאָדָם
וַיִּתֵּן לַשְּׁבִי עֻזּוֹ וְתִפְאַרְתּוֹ בְיַד־צָר
וַיַּסְגֵּר לַחֶרֶב עַמּוֹ וּבְנַחֲלָתוֹ הִתְעַבָּר

He was angered; he surely rejected Israel.
He abandoned the tabernacle of Shiloh, the tent in which he dwelt among humanity.
He gave his might into captivity, his splendor to enemy hand.
He delivered his people to the sword; with his inheritance he was angered.

The judgment begins and ends with God's wrath (וַיִּתְעַבֵּר, "he was angered," v. 59; הִתְעַבָּר, "he was angered," v. 62). As the structure moves inward, God rejects Israel and then abandons/delivers to the enemy. This parallels Israel's act of apostasy, in which they reject God and then adopt foreign deities. Therefore, in structure and in concept, the punishment is measure-for-measure.

Finally, vv. 63-64 provide a glimpse of a scene of the destruction.[82] After God punishes and leaves them to the enemy, the people are desolated:

---

82   There may perhaps be a link between the two sections: vv. 59-62, in which God rejects his people and vv. 63-64, in which the people suffer. In v. 61, God delivers first, "his strength" (עֻזּוֹ) and secondly, 'his splendor" (תִפְאַרְתּוֹ) to the enemy. One could argue that God's

בחוריו אכלה־אש
ובתולתיו לא הוללו
כהניו בחרב נפלו
ואלמנתיו לא תבכינה

> Their young men fire consumed.
> and their maidens remained unwed.
> Their priests fell by the sword,
> and their widows could not wed

Since the young men are dead, the young women are without husbands. Even when the religious leaders, the priests, die, their most intimate family members, the wives, will not mourn for them. It will be a dismal time.

Here, the executor of the punishment is the fire; everyone else reacts to what befalls them. Nevertheless, God initiated the punishment so that the surrounding disaster is only a description of the consequence of his activities (vv. 59-62). Thus, God is still the primary agent of the destruction. Despite the punishment, though, God bestows his favor upon Israel with the election of Jerusalem and David (vv. 65-72).

3.7. Psalm 106:28-31 (v. 29)

Compared to Ps 78, Ps 106 is a late text in which הכעים is a literary pivot with a minor role in the overall psalm. Rather than highlighting the final sin as in Ps 78, the term in Ps 106 occurs within the catalog of sins to illuminate a pattern in one particular episode. In this episode of Baʻal Peor, הכעים heralds a plague.

Unlike the multiple proposals for the dating of Ps 78, most commentaries would attribute Ps 106 to the post-exilic period.[83] Reference to the captors' "kindness" (רחמים, v. 46) would most likely point to Cyrus II's restoration of the exilic community in Babylon. It highlights God's final benevolent gesture toward the disobedient Israelites.

This historical psalm recounts the early rebellious years of Israel at the Sea of Reeds (vv. 7-12), Wilderness (vv.14-33), and Promised Land (vv. 34-46) in which they continuously fail to remember God's wonderful deeds in Egypt

---

"strength" refers to "his young men" (בחוריו, v. 63) and his "splendor" to "his priests" (כהניו, v. 64). Thus vv. 63-64 describe what God had enacted.

83   Briggs and Briggs, *The Book of Psalms*, 342, go as far as to date the psalm to the Greek period.

(נפלאותיך, "your wonderous deeds," vv. 6, 22; רב חסדיך, "your many kind acts," v. 6; גבורתו, "his might," v. 8; מעשׂיו, "his deeds," v. 13; גדלות, "great deeds," v. 21; נוראות, "awesome deeds," v. 22). In the narration of Israel's episodes of rebellion, a pattern develops. They forget God's deeds and sin against him which sometimes stirred his anger.[84] In response, God punishes the Israelites until someone ultimately intervenes:[85]

Sin → Anger → Punishment → Intervention → Stop Punishment

Although the succession of episodes do not progressively worsen, it does however seem to culminate into the final act. The final description of Israel's sins in the Promised Land exceeds the previous misdeeds and it is ultimately God (vv. 43-46), not a human intermediary,[86] who intervenes. However, הכעיס is not used in this final episode but the expression, ויחר אף ("he became angry," v. 40), which opens the description of that punishment (vv. 41-42). Instead הכעיס appears in the context of the Wilderness episode (vv. 14-33), in which the Israelites' misdeeds are listed. Among them is the incident of Ba'al Peor (vv. 28-31). Here, הכעיס occurs:

Sin (v. 28)

28) ויצמדו לבעל פעור ויאכלו זבחי מתים

Provocation (v. 29a) → Punishment (v. 29b)

29) ויכעיסו במעלליהם ותפרץ־בם מגפה

Intervention (v. 30)

30) ויעמד פינחס ויפלל ותעצר המגפה

Election of Phineas (v. 31)

31) ותחשב לו לצדקה לדר ודר עד־עולם

---

84   Variation of the pattern is repeated with different words for 'anger': להשׁיב חמתו ("to turn away his wrath," v. 23); ייכעיסו ("they provoked to anger," v. 29); ויקציפו ("they caused to be furious," v. 32); and ויחר אף יהוה ("YHWH became angry," v. 40). It should be noted, however, that the first few episodes (rebellion at the Sea of Reeds, תאוה ["desire"] in the wilderness, and envy of Moses/Aaron) are not accompanied by anger but just God's punishment. Anger becomes part of the pattern in the description of the Calf at Horeb (v. 19ff).

85   As with 'anger,' intervention also occurs in the later episodes. Intervention is absent in the incidents at the Sea of Reeds (vv 7-12), תאוה ("desire") in the wilderness (vv. 14-15), envy of Moses/Aaron (vv. 16-18), and possibly at the waters of Meribah (vv. 32-33).

86   Previously, Moses (v. 23) and Phinehas (v. 30) had intervened on their behalf. However, in vv. 44-45, God sees the people's distress and was reminded of his covenant. Therefore, "he relented" or perhaps better translated, "changed (his mind)" (וינחם).

28)   They yoked themselves to Ba'al-Peor and ate sacrifices offered to the dead.

29)   They provoked to anger[87] with their wicked deeds, and a plague broke out against them.

30)   Phinehas stood and intervened and the plague was stopped.

31)   This was credited to him as righteousness for generations forever.

Though הכעיס (v. 29) is not the pivotal term for the psalm, it still links a particular sin to its consequent punishment. The elaboration of the pattern is brief and simple. The people sin by worshipping Ba'al Peor,[88] which results in the provocation of God. As a consequence, punishment follows. Given the grammatical structure, i.e. the succession of converted imperfects, the plague stems directly from the idolatry:

Sin (ויאכלו ... ויצמדו, "they harnessed ... they ate") →

Provocation (ויכעיסו, "they provoked to anger") →

Punishment (ותפרץ, "it broke out")

They sinned so they will suffer from their provocation of God.

Yet the punishment does not correspond in the means of execution. The plague is the agent of the destruction, not God, the one who is provoked.[89] The "plague breaks out ... (and) ... the plague stops" (ותפרץ ... מגפה ...ותעצר המגפה); God is not the subject of these verbs. Nevertheless, God may be the implied manipulator of the plague since he is the main agent in other parts of the psalm.[90] In conclusion, הכעיס functions as a pivot that leads to the punishment consisting of a plague.

---

87   Similar to the construction in Hos 12:15, Ps 106:29 does not indicate the object of the verb but like in the book of Hosea, God appears to be the recipient. Few Hebrew manuscripts have והו-suffixed to the verb.

88   Compare with Num 25:1-13. Interestingly, Ps 106:28 adds a further offense by referring to sacrifices made to the dead.

89   The absence of the explicit mention of God's agency occurs in other parts of the psalm: The "earth opens, swallows ... and covers" (ותכס ... ותבלע תפתח־ארץ, v. 17) and "fire burns ... flame consumes" (להבה תלהט ... ותבער־אש, v. 18). The only time where the people's iniquities seem to be responsible for the punishment appears in v. 43. The phrase, וימכו בעונם ("they were brought low by their iniquity," according to the JPS translation), is problematic. If one follows the MT, then the people will be "humiliated" (Qal of מכך) while some other Hebrew manuscripts have וימקו ("pine away"; see Lev 36:39). The sense is similar in that the people will be punished. The interesting aspect of the phrase is the expression, "by their iniquity" (בעונם), where sin functions as the instrument of the punishment. Since it runs contrary to the overall grain of the psalm, BHS considers it a gloss.

90   He is the primary agent of punishment (וישלח, "he sent," v. 15; ידו וישא, "he lifted his hand," v. 26; ויתנם, "he delivered them," v. 41) and of deliverance (ויושיעם, "he saved

3.8. 2 Chronicles 28:22-25 (v. 25)

The only time הכעיס occurs in the book of Chronicles,[91] beside its parallels in the book of Kings, is in reference to Ahaz (2 Chr 28:25). Though the pattern of sin-provocation-punishment is developed in 2 Chr 28:25, the punishment is not as obvious as those laid out in previous passages. King Ahaz commits numerous sins, ultimately provoking God to anger. Yet no overt punishment is recorded; rather a note of his death, closing the account, follows the statement of the provocation. However, within the death formula, lies his punishment — the lack of a proper burial due to a king. No explicit agent is mentioned but the elusive "they" who bury him.

Although there are some similarities in the introduction and in the conclusion between the accounts of Ahaz in Kings (2 Kgs 16) and Chronicles (2 Chr 28), significant differences exist. The book of Chronicles takes the basic outline of Ahaz's career in the book of Kings and then embellishes and portrays a more cruel and idolatrous king.[92] According to the Chronicler, Ahaz had committed the greatest sacrilege — he had wilfully plundered the Temple in order to fund a bribe for the king of Assyria (v. 21). As a result, Ahaz suffered under the Edomites, Philistines, and Assyrians (vv. 17-20).

In the following section, the Chronicler describes additional sins (vv. 22-25), at the end of which Ahaz is depicted as having provoked God to anger:

Introduction to Catalog of Sins

---

them," vv. 8, 10; ויגער, "he rebuked," ויוליכם, "he led them," v. 9; ויגאלם, "he redeemed them," v. 10; וירא, "he saw," v. 44; ויזכר, "he remembered," וינחם, "he relented," v. 45; ויתן, "he gave," v. 46). The assertion, "God saved them time and again" (פעמים יצילם רבות, v. 43), seems to sum up his salvific deeds. Thus when the people cry for deliverance, they call upon God (v. 47).

91   Chronicles excludes the accounts of the northern kings, thus the occurrences attested in regards to the North is omitted. As for the attestations concerning Judah, Chronicles includes that of Manasseh (2 Kgs 21:6 // 2 Chr.33:6) and Josiah (2 Kgs 22:17 // 2 Chr 34:25). Interestingly, Chronicles does not have parallel accounts of 2 Kgs 21:15 (actually vv. 10b-16 is absent) and 2 Kgs 23:19 (against the North), 26. Beside the omitted attestations against the North, the other omissions are in judgments against Manasseh. Though Manasseh may have provoked God (2 Chr 33:6), the Chronicler does not hold him responsible for the destruction of Jerusalem.

92   What is presented in the book of Kings, namely that Ahaz had taken gold and silver from the Temple (2 Kgs 16:8) and made modifications on the Temple, moving the old altar and adding another altar (2 Kgs 16:10-16), had expanded and multiplied. He does not receive a favorable opinion in the books of Kings ("he does not do what is right," לא־עשה הישר, v. 2; "he follows the way of the kings of Israel," וילך בדרך מלכי ישראל, v. 3; etc.), nevertheless, he is not depicted as 'evil' par excellence.

22) ובעת הצר לו ויוסף למעול ביהוה הוא המלך אחז
Sin 1 (Sacrifice to Gods of Damascus)

23) ויזבח לאלהי דרמשׂק המכים בו
ויאמר כי אלהי מלכי־ארם הם
מעזרם אותם להם אזבח ויעזרוני והם היו־לו להכשילו ולכל־ישׂראל
Sin 2 (Destroy Temple Utensils)

24) ויאסף אחז את־כלי בית־האלהים ויקצץ את־כלי בית־האלהים
Sin 3 (Close Temple)

ויסגר את־דלתות בית־יהוה
Sin 4 (Build Altars Everywhere)

ויעשׂ לו מזבחות בכל־פנה בירושׂלם
Sin 5 (Build High Places Everywhere)

25) ובכל־עיר ועיר ליהודה עשׂה במות לקטר לאלהים אחרים
Provocation

ויכעס את יהוה אלהי אבתיו

22) In his time of distress, Ahaz, the same king, became more unfaithful against YHWH
23) He offered sacrifices to the gods of Damascus, who struck him. He thought, "Since the gods of the kings of Aram help them, to them I will offer sacrifices so that they may help me." They became the downfall for him and for all of Israel.
24) Ahaz gathered the vessels from the temple of God and cut up the vessels of the temple of God and closed up the doors of the house of YHWH. Then he made for himself altars in every corner of Jerusalem.
25) In every city in Judah, he made high places to burn incense to other gods and he provoked YHWH, the God of his fathers.

The catalog of sins — sacrifice to the gods of Damascus, destruction of the temple's utensils, closing of the temple, building of altars, and setting up high places to other gods — provoke God to anger.[93] Since the final list (vv. 22-25) is not followed by any overt punishment, הכעיס appears to function more as an assessment of Ahaz's deeds rather than a harbinger of the punishment. It sums up his sins as stirring God's wrath before closing his account with the death formula:[94]

---

93 Though listed in the sequence of sins, הכעיס is not one of the misdeeds but the consequence of the previous catalog of sins. One does not just provoke God to anger; one needs to have committed a sin to have caused the provocation. Moreover, the provocation is not only associated with the 'high places' dedicated to other deities, the last sin on the list, but with all of them.
94 With some variations, 1 Chr 29:29, 2 Chr 9:29, 12:15, 13:22, 16:11, 20:34, 25:26, 26:22, 27:7, 32:32, 33:18, 35:26, and 36:8.

26) ויתר דבריו כל־דרכיו הראשנים והאחרונים
הנם כתובים על־ספר מכלי־יהודה וישראל
27) וישכב אחז עם־אבתיו ויקברהו בעיר בירושלם
כי לא הביאהו לקברי מלכי ישראל וימלך יחזקיהו בנו תחתיו

26)   Now, rest of his deeds and all his ways, from first to last, they are written
        in the annals of the kings of Judah and Israel.
27)   Ahaz slept with his fathers and they buried him in the city, in Jerusalem,
        but they did not bring him to the tombs of the kings of Israel. Hezekiah,
        his son, ruled in his place.

However, within the death formula, the punishment is laid out so that the sin-
provocation-punishment pattern is ultimately established. Yet how could the
death formula function as the punishment? Do not the accounts of all the
kings, good and evil alike, record their deaths? Absolutely. Yet the Chronicler
provides a different twist at the end of formula, where according to v. 27, Ahaz
is brought into the city for burial but not into "the tombs of the kings of
Israel," contrary to 2 Kgs 16:20, in which he is buried with his fathers (דוד
ויקבר עם אבתיו בעיר, "he was buried with his fathers in the city of David").
The improper burial was the Chronicler's way of punishing the kings: The
'good' kings received proper burial in the kings' tomb while the 'evil' kings
were not.[95] Thus this historical note describes the punishment for Ahaz.[96]

---

95   The 'good' kings were buried in the tombs of the kings in the city of David: Solomon (2 Chr
     9:31), Rehoboam (2 Chr 12:16), Abijah (2 Chr 13:23), Jehoshaphat (2 Chr 21:1), Amaziah (2
     Chr 25:28), Jotham (2 Chr 27:9), Hezekiah (2 Chr 32:33 — in a more special place, במעלה
     קברי בני דוד, "in the ascent of the graves of the sons of David"), and Josiah (2 Chr 35:24).
     However, the 'evil' kings were not: Asa (2 Chr 16:14 — in his own plot, ויקברהו בקברתיו
     אשר כרה לו בעיר דוד, "they buried him in his tomb which he cut out for himself in the
     city of David"), Jehoram (2 Chr 21:20 — not in the kings' tombs, ויקברהו בעיר דוד ולא
     בקברות המלכים "they buried him in the city of David but not in the tombs of the kings"),
     Jehoash (2 Chr 24:25 — not in the kings' tombs, ויקברהו בעיר דוד ולא בקברות המלכים,
     "they buried him in the city of David but not in the tombs of kings"), and Manasseh (2 Chr
     33:20 — in the palace grounds, ביתו, "his house").
     The pattern is not always evident since there are unique situations and sometimes,
     absence of information on the kings' burial. Uzziah is a special case in that he was a leper;
     therefore he was buried in the royal burial field (ויקברו אתו עם אבתיו בשדה הקבורה
     אשר למלכים, "they buried him with his fathers in the field of the royal grave," 2 Chr 26:23).
     Moreover, it is unclear where Ahaziah, Athaliah, Amon, and Jehoiakim were buried. Ahaziah
     was given a burial (2 Chr 22:9, ויקברהו, "they buried him") since he was the son of
     Jehoshaphat but the text is silent as to the location. As for Athaliah (2 Chr 23:15), Amon (2
     Chr 33:24) and Jehoiakim (2 Chr 36:8), there is no mention of their burial whatsoever.
     The main differences between the books of Kings and Chronicles would seem to be in
     the accounts of Asa (1 Kgs 15:24), Jehoram (2 Kgs 8:24), Ahaziah (2 Kgs 9:28), Jehoash (2
     Kgs 12:22), and Jehoiakim (2 Kgs 24:6), who are buried with their fathers. Also, Hezekiah (2

Yet who executes this punishment? According to the wording of v. 27, it is the "they" who are usually responsible for the burial: "They buried him ... but they did not bring him" (ויקברהו ... כי לא הביאהו). The specific identity of the "they" is not essential, but rather the fact that humans carry out the execution.[97]

3.9. Conclusion

In non-Dtr pericopes containing הכעיס, the pivot-term usually forefronts God as the executor of the punishment, whether implicitly or explicitly. Despite the central role of God, there is a tendency to attribute more responsibility to the people whose punishments is in measured proportion to the sins. In passages dated to the exilic and post-exilic periods (Ezek 8:1-17, 16:23-30, Hos 12:15, and Isa 65:1-7), an effort is made to develop a measure-for-measure punishment, especially in editorial additions (Hos 12:15, Isa 65:6-7) which make the correspondence explicit by linking the punishment to the implied sin. However, there are exceptions to this tendency. In the earliest passage (Ps 78:56-64), God delivers Israel into enemy hands for their act of idolatry which corresponds in structure and concept to the punishment. While in late texts, Ps 106:28-31 and 2 Chr 28:22-25, God, behind the scenes, controls temporal instruments (whether natural calamities as in a plague or humans who bury the dead) to execute the punishment which are not in direct proportion to the sin.

Kgs 20:21) does not receive a preferential treatment while Manasseh (2 Kgs 21:18, בגן־ ביתו בגן־עזא, "in his palace garden, the garden of Uzza") and Amon (2 Kgs 21:26, בגן עזא, "in the garden of Uzza") do not fare well.

96   However, this punishment may not have sufficiently compensated the provocation since it is up to Hezekiah to avert God's anger (וישב ממנו חרון אפו, "so that his fierce anger will turn away from us," 2 Chr 29:10). This divine wrath could not have been kindled by any of the previous kings except Ahaz since Hezekiah's 'reforms' (2 Chr 29:3-7) undo what Ahaz had done.

97   According to Sara Japhet, *The Ideology of the Book of Chronicles and Its Place in Biblical Thought* (2nd rev. ed.; BEATAJ 9; trans. Anna Berber; Frankfurt am Main: Peter Lang, 1997), 135, the Chronicler espouses the notion of "only one cause: God." As a result, "God alone is responsible for whatever happens" (136) so that the Chronicler does not use the technique of dual causality (divine and natural) to explain historical events. However, here in 2 Chr 28:27, the principle of dual causality appears to direct the burial of king Ahaz.

Part IV: The Book of Jeremiah

4.1. Introduction

Here we come to the heart of the present study, the depictions of God's agency in meting out punishments as linked to the pivotal term, syukh, in the book of Jeremiah. As in DtrH and non-Dtr attestations, syukh usually functions as the pivot between the sin and the punishment in the book of Jeremiah (7:18, 19, 8:19, 11:17, 25:6, 7, 32:29, 30, 32, 44:3, 8). With the pivot-term, the authors of the book of Jeremiah provide elaborate explanations on the role of God in the events leading up to the fall of Jerusalem and, by analogy, to the consequent punishment of the fugitives in Egypt (44:8).

Since the term occurs in pericopes that are usually intricately redacted, several descriptions of the punishment are present in each pericope (see also chart D):

A. 7:16-20 (vv. 18, 19):
   v. 19 — self-destruction
   v. 20 — divine wrath
B. 8:18-23 (v. 19c):
   vv. 20-21 — natural instrument
C. 11:17 (v. 17)
   v. 17 — boomerang and partial self-destruction
D. 25:1-14 (vv. 6-7):
   v. 7 — partial self-destruction
   vv. 9-11 — God with human instrument
   vv. 12-14 — boomerang
E. 32:26-35 (vv. 29, 30, 32):
   vv. 28-29a — human as primary executor
   v. 31 — divine wrath and self-destruction
F. 44:1-14 (v. 3)
   vv. 2-3 — boomerang
   vv. 4-6 — divine wrath
   vv. 7-10 — self-destruction
   vv. 11-14 — God with natural instrument

For the purpose of accentuating the differences, the various formulations of the punishment in each pericope will be discussed.

As in DtrH, the authors of the book of Jeremiah depict God in mastery over temporal events involving human and natural catastrophes (8:20-21, 25:9-10, 32:28-29a, 44:11-14). Yet God is further removed from the destructive activities through other conceptualizations of his role in meting out punishments: 1) boomerang (11:17, 25:12-14, 44:2-3); 2) divine wrath (7:20, 32:31, 44:4-6); 3) self-destruction (7:19, 32:31, 44:7-10). This may have occurred not so much to divest God of mastery, but to shift the responsibility for the disaster to the people. Like DtrH2 and many of the non-Dtr attestations, the book of Jeremiah attempts to exonerate its God.

Any discussion involving the book of Jeremiah has to address, to a certain extent, the problematic issue of the history of its redaction. Since scholars have not come to any consensus and are still debating the relationship between the poetic oracles and the prose sermons, with little headway into levels of redaction within either one of these literary mediums, it is difficult, to say the least, first to distinguish the sources and second, to link the formulations. Nevertheless an attempt has been made throughout the discussion, though not always successfully, to analyze the levels of redaction and to demarcate the distinct formulations within these levels. Since the primary focus of the study is on the prose sermons, the present discussion will not include the redaction of the poetic material and historical prose which may have been redacted in a similar fashion.[1]

Based upon the analyses of the pericope containing the term, הכעים, five general levels/sources of redaction appear in the sermonic prose of the MT.[2] However, not all of these sources are evident in each pericope nor do they

---

1   This is most evident in the two vision reports in the opening chapter (1:11-14). These two visions, one of the almond tree branch (1:11-12) and the other of the boiling cauldron 'with its rims away from the north' (1:13-14), may (Berridge, *Prophet, People, and the Word of Yahweh*, 63-72) or may not (most commentaries) have been original to the call narrative. However, the interpretations of the second vision reflect the break-down of the various levels in the prose sermons. According to v. 14, the tilted cauldron represents the "evil" disaster (רעה) that is about to "break loose from the north" (מצפון תפתח). The first explanation (v. 15) describes the "evil" as "all the families of the kingdoms from the north" (כל־משפחות ממלכות צפונה), the human instrument which is set against Judah. In the second explanation (v. 16), most likely a later addition (Nicholson, *Jeremiah*, 113), God decrees their punishment because of their evil (ממלכות על כל־רעתם) ורדברתי משפטי אותם על כל־רעתם, "I have decreed my judgments against them on account of all their evil"), a boomerang-pattern (decree-editor; see discussion above). Thirdly in vv. 17-19, God calls upon Jeremiah, the prophet, to speak on his behalf, a prophetic editor (again see above for discussion). These three explanations correspond to the three major editorial levels in the prose sermons.

2   The levels/sources have been determined from the overall impression of 7:16-20, 8:19, 11:17, 25:1-14, 32:26-35, 44:1-14, and their surrounding passages. Some of the footnotes within the discussion of the passages lay out the various levels of the larger framework of the pericopes and even the parallel poetic formulations.

reflect other pericopes without the term, הכעים. On the first level are the 'original' prose sermons.[3] The second is the decree-additions with its emphasis on God as the 'decreer' (דבר) of the message. The third is the prophetic-tradition where the editor emphasizes the intermediary role of the prophets in Israelite's past. In both the second and third levels/sources, the central concern is with the obedience to the word/teaching of God. Fourth, are the various incipits of the pericopes. This may have actually included several redactions. Finally, in the fifth level, are the additions made to the earlier Hebrew Vorlage of the Greek, resulting in the MT.

Though most of the formulations of the punishments cannot be linked to the various levels/sources, the measure-for-measure judgments appear to be later. The boomerang, divine wrath, and self-destruction formulations of the punishment are usually secondary in relation to the formulations in which God acts with a human instrument. This is most evident in the boomerang-pattern, most likely the product of the decree-editor, where the punishment is formulated according to what God had previously decreed. In sum, with temporal distance to the fall of Jerusalem, the people are held more responsible for their own destruction.

---

3   'Original' here does not mean that Jeremiah himself composed the sermons. It is just a way to refer to the earliest level of the sermons.

Chart D: Pericopes with הרעה in the Book of Jeremiah

Passage	Source	Type of Sin	Form of הרעה	Pivot	Type of Punishment	Agency
7:16-20	Unit – Secondary	Queen of Heavens	See below			
V. 18	See above	See above	להכעסני	Yes	V. 20: Divine wrath	Divine wrath
V. 19	See above	See above	הם מכעסים	Yes	V. 19: Self-Destruction	People's sin
8:18-23 [19c]	Vv. 18-23: Poetry; V. 19c: Addition	V. 19c: Idolatry	הרעתי	Yes	Drought	God implied
11:17	Decree-editor	Evil	להרעת	Yes	Evil; Boomerang	God
25:1-14	Vv. 2-3: Disobedience / V. 4: Prophetic / Vv. 5-6: Core	Vv. 2-3: Disobedience / V. 4: Disobey Prophets / Vv. 5-6a: Do not follow other gods	See below			
V. 6b	Core ('original')	See above	הרעתי	Yes	Vv. 9-11: God deliver Judah to Nebuchadnezzar	God → Human
V. 7	Decree or prophetic editor / Unclear / Unclear	Disobedience	למען הכעסני	Yes	Vv. 13: (Decree-editor): Boomerang / V. 12: Punish Chaldeans: Boomerang / V. 14: Punish Chaldeans: Boomerang	God → Human / God → Implied Sin / God → Implied Sin
32:26-35						
V. 29b	Late	V. 29b: Idolatry	הכעסני למען	Yes; Reverse	Vv. 28-29a: Chaldean attack	God → Human
	Late	V. 30a: Evil from youth	NA	NA	Same as above	Same as above
V. 30b	Late	V. 30b: Idolatry	מכעסים	Yes; Reverse	Same as above	Same as above
V. 32	Late	Vv. 32-35: Political and religious leaders are evil (Idolatry)	להרעת	Yes; Reverse	V. 31: City set upon divine wrath; Self-destruction	Divine wrath

44:1-14						
V. 3	Late	V. 3: Evil (Idolatry)	להכעיסני	Yes; Reverse	V. 2: God brought evil; Boomerang	God
	Late	Vv. 4-5: Disobey prophets	NA	NA	V. 6: Divine wrath poured out	Divine wrath
V. 8	Late	Vv. 8-10: Idolatry and evil	להכעיסני	Yes	V. 7: People cut themselves; Self-destruction	People's sin
	Late	Vv. 2-10: Combination	NA	NA	Vv. 11-14: God with natural calamities	God → Natural instrument

4.2. Jeremiah 7:16-20 (vv. 18, 19)

In this pericope, we encounter two attestations of הכעים (vv. 18-19) which function as pivots to the punishment. While v. 18 establishes the expected development of the pattern where God is provoked by the sins of the people, v. 19 reverses the direction of the provocation so that the people provoke themselves. Consequently, their own sins lead to their punishment, the concretized result of their provocation, God's divine wrath.

Chapter 7:1-8:3, consisting of distinct prose sermons brought together under the rubric of cultic abuses, formed the larger framework of the tightly structured pericope, 7:16-20. The framework opens with the Temple Sermon (vv. 1-15),[4] which accuses the people of unwarranted trust in the concept of

---

4   A similar account of the Temple Sermon is present in ch. 26, which provides more of a 'historical' explanation of the events during and after the sermon and a different twist to the catalog of sins. The crux of the accusations in ch. 7 — the Temple Sermon — is formulated in imperatives; what they are suppose to do rather than what they had done wrong. Beside the negative injunction not to trust in the concept of the inviolability of the Temple, they are commanded to maintain justice and not to follow other deities. Then it shifts to demonstrate how they have abrogated these very commands.

When one turns to ch. 26, the focus of the sermon is on the failure of the people to follow the Teachings (תורתי, "my teachings," v. 4). This is unequivocally extended to include obedience to the words of the prophets (v. 5). Thus, while providing the 'historical' ramifications of Jeremiah's sermon, it modifies the sins which differs qualitatively from the earlier sermon. In many ways, it resembles the additional unit (7:21-28) linked to the Temple Sermon, in which the focus is on their evil hearts and refusal to listen to God. However, in 7:21-28, there are three distinct levels of redaction which would explain the repetition of the *Heilsgeschichte* (twice) and the people's refusal to obey (thrice):

Heilsgeschichte

ביום   הוציא אותם מארץ מצרים (v. 22)
למן־היום אשר יצאו אבותיכם מארץ מצרים עד היום הזה (v. 25)

On the day that he brought them out from the land of Egypt (v. 22).
From the day that your fathers came out from the land of Egypt until this day (v. 25).

Refusal to Obey

ולא שמעו ולא הטו את־אזנם
וילכו במעצות בשררות לבם הרע ויהיו לאחור ולא לפנים (v. 24)

ולוא שמעו אלי ולא הטו את־אזנם ויקשו את־ערפם הרעו מאבותם (v. 26)

זה הגוי אשר לוא־שמעו בקול יהוה אלהיו ולא לקחו מוסר (v. 28)

the inviolability of the temple (vv. 4, 10)[5] along with specific injunctions to maintain justice (vv. 5-6) and not to follow other deities (v. 6).[6] To enumerate additional sins, four distinct units of accusations (and their respective accounts of the punishment) were attached to the Temple Sermon: cult of the Queen of Heavens (7:16-20), ancestral disobedience (7:21-29), child sacrifice at Tophet (7:30-34), and astral worship (8:1-3).[7] These independent units may have been

---

They did not listen or turn their ear but followed the stubborn inclinations of their evil heart. They went backward, not forward (v. 24).

They did not listen to me or turn their ear but hardened their necks, doing more evil than their fathers (v. 26).

This is the nation which did not listen to the voice of YHWH, its God, or did it take correction (v. 28).

On one level, God directly commands the people to obey him (vv. 22-24). This is most likely linked to the decree-editor. Note the verbal (v. 22, דברתי, "I have decreed") and nominal (v. 23, הדבר הזה, "this decree") form of דבר ("decree") as well as the reference to God's command (צויתים, "I have commanded them," v. 22; צויתי, "I commanded," v. 23). At a later level of redaction, this message is relayed through the prophets (v. 25, עבדי הנביאים, "my servants, the prophets") and furthermore to Jeremiah (v. 27), in particular. It is evident that vv. 27-28, if not the whole unit (vv. 21-28), were an addition to the Temple Sermon. Whereas the people do not directly respond to God in v. 13, in v. 27, they do not respond to Jeremiah:

(v. 13, with God as the speaker) ולא שמעתם   ואקרא אתכם ולא עניתם
(v. 27, with you referring to Jeremiah) ולא ישמעו אליך וקראת אליהם ולא יענוכה

You did not listen. I called you but you did not answer (v. 13).
They will not listen to you. You called to them but they will not answer you (v. 27).

This reflects the enhanced status of Jeremiah while further distancing God from the people.

5   The sermon was not necessarily directed towards the temple cult itself but the lack of daily application of God's commands. See Else Kragelund Holt, "Jeremiah's Temple Sermon and the Deuteronomists: An Investigation of the Redactional Relationship Between Jeremiah 7 and 26," *JSOT* 36 (1986):73-87.

6   The Temple Sermon contains the accusation and threat of a punishment. Rather than maintaining "justice" (משפט, 7:5), the people rely upon "false words" (דברי שקר, 7:4, 8) and worship Ba'al and other gods (v. 9). Therefore, God will destroy Jerusalem just as he destroyed Shiloh, the former site of God's name (v. 14). Moreover, God will cast them (אתכם השלכתי, "I will cast you," v. 15) out of his sight as he had with Ephraim. In other words, God, the agent of destruction, is not hesitant to destroy the site of his name or to cast away the people of his covenant.

7   The demarcation of the units follow Charles Isbell and Michael Jackson, "Rhetorical Criticism and Jeremiah VII 1-VIII 3," *VT* 30 (1980):20-26, and Susan Ackerman, *Under Every Green Tree: Popular Religion in Sixth-Century Judah* (HSM 46; Atlanta: Scholars Press, 1992), 5-35, who provides different headings.

loosely organized to highlight the various sins.[8] Since 7:16-20 is a distinct unit, it will be examined independent of the surrounding units:

Introduction (v. 16)

16) ואתה אל־תתפלל בעד־העם הזה ואל־תשא בעדם רנה ותפלה
ואל־תפגע־בי כי־אינני שמע אתך

Accusation (vv. 17-18)

17) האינך ראה מה המה עשים בערי יהודה ובחצות ירושלם
18) הבנים מלקטים עצים והאבות מבערים את־האש
והנשים לשות בצק לעשות כונים למלכת השמים

Provocation

והסך נסכים לאלהים אחרים למען <u>הכעסני</u>

Inverted Provocation (v. 19)

19) האתי הם <u>מכעסים</u> נאם־יהוה הלוא אתם למען בשת פניהם

Punishment (v. 20)

20) לכן כה־אמר אדני יהוה הנה אפי וחמתי נתכת אל־המקום הזה
על־האדם ועל־הבהמה ועל־עץ השדה ועל־פרי האדמה ובערה ולא תכבה

16) "Do not pray for this people; do not lift up a cry or prayer on their behalf; and do not plead with me, for I will not listen to you.

17) Do you not see what they are doing in the cities of Judah and in the streets of Jerusalem?

18) The children gather wood, the fathers kindle the fire, and the women knead the dough, making cakes for the Queen of the Heavens, pouring out libations to other gods, <u>to provoke me to anger</u>.

19) Was it me they were bent on <u>provoking to anger</u>?," says YHWH. "Or was it not themselves, to the shame of their face?"

20) Therefore, thus says my lord, YHWH, "Here, my fiery wrath is being poured over this place, on man and beast, on the trees of the field and the fruit of the ground. It will burn and not be quenched."

---

8   The larger framework is not unified as the different addressee in the units demonstrate: The first addition is directed to Jeremiah, the prophet (vv. 16-17); second, to the "fathers" (אבות, vv. 22, 25); third, to "the children of Judah" (בני יהודה, v. 30); fourth, to everyone dwelling in Jerusalem, the kings, his officers, priests, prophets, and inhabitants of Jerusalem (8:1), the upper echelon of the kingdom. Sometimes the difference between "children of Judah" (בני יהודה) and "the inhabitants of Jerusalem" (ישבי ירושלם) is not apparent (Zeph 1:4). In the prose material of the book of Jeremiah, the children of Judah (32:30, 32, 50:4, 33) are differentiated from the inhabitants of Jerusalem (11:9, 12, 13:13, 17:20, 25, 18:11, 19:3, 25:2, 32:32, 35:13, 17, 36:31, 42:18). Even in the poetic material, the distinction is maintained (4:4, 11:2) where there is movement from the general to the specific (איש יהודה וישבי ירושלם, "the men of Judah and the inhabitants of Jerusalem"). It is most apparent in Jer 32:32, where the inhabitants of Judah and Israel are differentiated from the religious/political leaders ("her kings, her officers, her priests, her prophets, men of Judah, and inhabitants of Jerusalem, children of Israel, and children of Judah," מלכיה שריה כהניה נביאיה ואיש יהודה וישבי ירושלם בני ישראל ובני יהודה). Also, see 2 Kgs 23:2, 2 Chr 20:15, 18, 20, 21:11, 13, 32:33, 33:9, 34:30, 35:18, Ezra 4:6, Dan 9:7.

The first unit (vv. 16-20) of additional sins focuses on the family worship of the Queen of Heavens. Since the archaeological and biblical evidence is limited, it is difficult to determine whether the accusation was directed at the particular cult of the Queen of Heavens[9] or the cult as representative of the widespread non-Yahwistic practices in Judah. Though this is an important historical inquiry, for the purpose of the present study, what is more pertinent is the way in which the practice is portrayed — ultimately, as an abrogation of what the author considered to be an essential divine command, namely not to worship other deities, which had been mentioned in the Temple Sermon (vv. 6, 9). This outright disobedience is the reason for the incredulous God to first, deny the people of recourse to mediation and to second, justify the punishment of divine wrath.

To emphasize the gravity of the disobedience, God forbids Jeremiah to intercede on behalf of the people, whose punishment cannot and will not be averted. Beginning with v. 16, the pericope shifts from second person common plural in the previous address[10] to Jeremiah in the second person masculine singular. Without any formal introduction to indicate the shift in person and topic, v. 16 opens with a divine injunction to Jeremiah not to "intercede" (בעד התפלל) for the people.[11] Such a command is atypical since intercessions were expected of prophets, especially in DtrH. Both the people and kings sought

---

9   Driver, *Jeremiah*, 43; Nicholson, *Jeremiah*, 1:79; Holladay, *Jeremiah*, 1:254-255; McKane, *Jeremiah*, 1:171; Volz, *Jeremiah*, 100, think that the Queen of Heaven refers to the cult of Astarte whereas Bright, *Jeremiah*, Thiel, *Die deuteronomistische Redaktion*, and Hyatt, *Jeremiah*, argue for the cult of Ishtar. Susan Ackerman, "'And the Women Knead Dough': The Worship of the Queen of Heaven in Sixth-Century Judah," in *Gender and Difference in Ancient Israel* (ed. Peggy Day; Minneapolis: Fortress Press, 1989), 109-124 and *Under Every Green Tree*, 5-35, argues that the Queen of Heaven is a syncretistic goddess with the attributes of Astarte, a Semitic cult, and Ishtar. Whether the cult involves a Canaanite or a Mesopotamian goddess, it is unclear how prevalent and central the Queen of Heaven worship was in Judah. See Jer 44:17, 18, 19, 25, where the cult again appears in Egypt.

10   Contrary to 7:1, in which Jeremiah receives the message from YHWH. This incipit is probably a later editorial gloss as its absence, along with v. 2a+2b (עמד בשער בית ידוה וקראת שם את־הדבר הזה ואמרת, "stand at the gate of the house of YHWH and call out there this word, saying"), in the Greek would support. 7:2bβ, הבאים בשערים האלה ("those coming to these gates"), is also absent in the Greek but it sets the stage for the upcoming message directed to the people (כל יהודה, "all of Judah"). Note the second person common plural form of the verbs, personal suffixes, and object markers in vv. 3-15 (אתכם, "you;" מעלליכם, "your deeds;" דרכיכם, "your ways;" היטיב־, "make good;" etc.).

11   This is contrary to 29:12, where God appears more conciliatory. It asserts that when the people call upon God, he will listen to them (וקראתם אתי והלכתם והתפללתם אלי ושמעתי אליכם, "you will call me, come and pray, and I will listen to you"). The difference is largely on account of the reconciliatory tone of chs. 29-33.

intercession from the prophets and the prophets themselves considered intercession as part of their duties.[12]

Similarly, in the book of Jeremiah, the prophet, despite his battle with the
people, intercedes on their behalf. Even though God does not directly request
Jeremiah to pray for the people, Jeremiah himself laments[13] and prays for
either their benefit[14] or misfortune.[15] At the same time, political leaders, like
Zedekiah (21:2; 37:3) and Johanan with the army officers (42:2, 20), seek out
Jeremiah with requests for intercession. Moreover, God expects Jeremiah to
stand before him (לפני תעמד, "you will stand before me")[16] and to become his
'mouthpiece' (כפי תהיה, "you will become like my mouth," 15:19). Therefore, intercession is a function that Jeremiah, the people, and also God expect
from the prophet. As a result, God's command to Jeremiah not to pray for the

---

12 People ask Moses to intercede on their behalf (Num 21:7); Moses decides to intercede for
    Aaron (Deut 9:20); Samuel for the people (זעק ["to cry out"] – 1 Sam 7:5, 9; התפלל ["to
    pray"] – 1 Sam 12:19, 23); David for his child (בקש ["to seek"] – 2 Sam 12:16); Jeroboam
    requests of the man of God (1 Kgs 13:6); Hezekiah to Isaiah (נאש תפלה ["to lift up prayer"]
    – 2 Kgs 19:4 // Isa 37:4), Josiah to his officers (דרש ["to seek"] – 2 Kgs 22:13 // 2 Chr
    34:21); and a psalmist asks that the prayers be said for the king (Ps 72:15). For a discussion
    on prophetic intercession, see Yochanan Muffs, "Who Will Stand in the Breach?: A Study of
    Prophetic Intercession," in Love and Joy: Law, Language and Religion in Ancient Israel
    (New York: Jewish Theological Seminary, 1992), 9-48.
13 12:4, 14:7-9, 19-22, 17:18, 18:23. Though most of them are communal or individual laments,
    Jeremiah is attributed with them.
14 In 18:20, Jeremiah reminds God how he spoke up for the people to avert his wrath from them
    (זכר עמדי לפניך לדבר עליהם טובה להשיב את־חמתך מהם, "remember that I stood be-
    fore you to speak in their behalf good, to turn aside your wrath from them"). Jeremiah prays
    for himself by asking God to remember him (זכרני ופקדני והנקם לי מרדפי, "remember me
    and visit me; avenge me from my persecutors," 15:15). See also 17:14. According to 29:7,
    Jeremiah even asks the people to pray for the remnant in Jerusalem. He is said to have sent a
    letter to the exilic community in Babylon, imploring them to seek the benefit of the city and
    to pray for them.
15 In 11:20, Jeremiah wishes ill will toward his persecutors (אראה נקמתך מהם כי אליך גליתי
    את־ריבי, "let me see your vengeance upon them for to you I have committed my lawsuit").
    Also, see the two previous footnotes.
16 The expression, לעמד לפני ("to stand before"), related to the Akkadian, ina pani izuzzum (or
    its nominal form - manzaz/muzzaz/muzziz/mazziz/etc. mahri/pani, AHw, 1:409), could either
    refer to those who stand in royal court as officials (Gen 41:46, 1 Kgs 10:8, 12:8, Jer 52:12, 2
    Chr 9:7, 10:6, 8) or before God to serve him (Num 16:9, Deut 1:38, 10:8, 18:7, Judg 20:28,
    29:11, 1 Kgs 17:1, 18:15, 2 Kgs 3:14, 5:16, Ezek 44:11, 15, Dan 1:5, 19, 2 Chr 5:14) or to
    pray (Jer 15:1, 18:20, 2 Chr 20:9). Prophets and priests stand before God as officials before
    the king. Other definitions include, "to confront" (Exod 9:11), "to endure" (Judg 2:14, 1 Sam
    6:20), "to attend" (Jer 40:10), etc. For similar notion, see Jer 17:16.

people is somewhat unusual and more than anything, reflect the irreversible situation in which the Judahites had placed themselves.[17]

To provide the context and justification for the divine command, the unit then elaborates on the grave misdeed of the people. Yet the unit does not just begin listing or describing the offense; rather it calls upon Jeremiah and hence the listener/reader to witness the familial cult. [18] In 7:17, God asks Jeremiah, "Do you not see what they are doing in the cities of Judah and the streets of Jerusalem?" (האינך ראה מה המה עשׁים בערי יהודה ובחצות ירושׁלם). By posing this rhetorical question, it transports the reader/listener to the immediacy and veracity of the situation.[19] It has the effect of a courtroom drama in

---

17 Given the historical circumstances, the injunction becomes commonplace in the book of Jeremiah. Beside the present passage, God twice commands Jeremiah not to pray for the people (11:14, 14:11 — these verses do not follow 7:16 verbatim; however, the expression, אל תתפלל בעד ["do not intercede"] is in all of them). In fact, even if Moses and Samuel, two paradigmatic prophets, stood before him, he will not change his m nd (15:1). This resembles the book of Ezekiel where Noah, Daniel, and Job could not save anyone but themselves (Ezek 14:12-20). Interestingly, whereas Jeremiah uses exemplary prophets as examples of those who could intercede for the people, Ezekiel chooses to include men popularly known for their righteousness, who could 'exude' their righteousness over other people. Compare with Gen 18:1-32, where even 10 random righteous people could have saved Sodom and Gomorrah. According to Christopher Seitz, "The Prophet Moses and the Canonical Shape of Jeremiah," *ZAW* 101 (1989):3-27, the four commands not to pray for the people corresponds to Jeremiah's four-fold laments (11:18-12:6, 15:10-20, 18:18-23, 20:7-18).

18 In the Temple Sermon, God expresses how he had witnessed what was happening in the Temple, גם אנכי הנה ראיתי (7:11, "Here, also, I am watching"). *HALOT* 3:1158 discusses the difficulty in explaining this particular expression and provides several suggestions. Whatever the specific translation may be, the context appears to emphasize God's active seeing of the evil that is occurring in Jerusalem. The way in which the units — Temple Sermon and cult of the Queen of Heaven — are combined, it would appear that God's own observation (7:11) is not sufficient; he now needs Jeremiah to 'see' the appalling sights (7:17). However, the practices under scrutiny are qualitatively different; those listed in the Temple Sermon are more general and comprehensive while vv. 16-20 focus just on the cult of Queen of Heaven.

19 Similar rhetorical questions posed to Jeremiah to witness the sins of Israel/Judah to make Jeremiah/reader aware of the sins are also present in 3:6 and 33:23: הראית אשׁר עשׂתה משׁבה ישׂראל (3:6; "Have you seen what faithless Israel has done?") and הלוא ראית מה העם הזה דברו (33:24; "Have you seen what this people are saying?"). Both heighten the sins of Israel/Judah. The command or request to "see" (ראה) plays a significant role in the book of Jeremiah. The book opens with two vision reports which Jeremiah is asked to describe (מה־אתה ראה, "what do you see;" 1:11, 13). When Jeremiah observes and describes the 'visions,' he validates not only himself as a prophet of God, but also what he proclaims is the message of the 'visions.' See also the 'vision' of the good and bad figs, 24:3 מה־אתה ראה, "what do you see"). In essence, Jeremiah, the 'true' prophet, has "stood in God's council" (עמד בסוד יהוה) and "seen" (וירא) and "heard his word" (וישׁמע את דברו, 23:18). Whether it is God, Jeremiah, or the people, the importance of 'seeing' what is done in Judah is a prevalent rhetorical strategy to emphasize the utter sinful nature of the people (2:10, 19, 23, 3:2, 7, 8, 5:1, 7:11, 11:18, 13:26, 27, 23:13, 14). It is also a means to 'realize' the horror

which the prosecutor, God, points out the evidence to a bystander, Jeremiah, to validate his accusation of the gross cultic abuse in Judah.[20] God is not making up the accusations; it is actually occurring.[21] Now God has a witness who can also testify against the idolatrous people.

After having posed the question, anticipation mounts. What did the people do to incur God's silencing of Jeremiah's intercession? What could have been drastic enough for God to bar a prophet from his duty and to call him to witness their activities? The reason, though quite serious, is simple: the whole family participated in the cult of the Queen of Heavens — the children gather wood, the father makes the fire, and the women knead dough for cakes[22] dedicated to the goddess.[23] If worship of the Queen of Heavens was not sufficient, the unit lists an additional sin, that of "pouring out libations to other gods" (הסך נסכים לאלהים אחרים, 7:18).[24]

---

of the destruction (4:21, 23, 24, 25, 26, 7:12, 11:20, 20:4, 12, 18, 30:6, 32:24, 44:2, 17, 46:5), or not (5:12, 14:13, 42:14).

20 While the interrogative ה- before אינך expresses a rhetorical question, it also draws attention to the following verses, which explains the reason for God's adamant dismissal of all mediation. For this interpretation of a similar expression, הראה אתה ("do you see?"), in 2 Sam 15:27, see J. Hoftijzer, "A Peculiar Question: A Note on 2 Sam. XV 27," *VT* 21 (1971):606-609.

21 Since God describes the sin with a series of participles (מלקטים ["gather"], מבערים ["make fire"], לשות ["knead"]), the action seems to be happening right in front of Jeremiah

22 כונים ("cakes;" also in Jer 44:19) is probably a loan-word from the Akkadian word, *kamanu*, which is often associated with the cult of Ishtar and Dumuzi, see *CAD*, vol. K, 110-111. For a more detailed discussion on the cakes, see Walter Rast, "Cakes for the Queen of Heaven," in *Scripture in History and Theology: Essays in Honor of J. Coert Rylaarsdam* (eds. Arthur L. Merrill and Thomas W. Overholt; PTMS 17; Pittsburgh: Pickwick Press, 1977), 167-180, and Ackerman, "'And the Women Knead Dough,'" 109-124.

23 Given the gravity of the situation, one would expect their deeds to have been hidden from public scrutiny but instead their activities were public and pervasive. The people did not worship the Queen of Heavens or other deities in the privacy of their home but in the streets. Although the formulaic phrase, בערי יהודה ובחצות ירושלם "in the cities of Judah and in the streets of Jerusalem" (Jer 7:34, 11:6, 33:10, 44:6, 9, 17, 21), demonstrates the ubiquity of their deeds, covering the suburbs to the streets of the very capital city, it also attests to their public nature. One celebrates marriage (7:34, 33:10) and prophesies in public (11:6). In fact, 44:15 clarifies that men of various ranks knew what their wives were doing, namely worshipping other gods. Look at 44:20-21, where the passage specifies the audience in Jeremiah's address as all the people, men and women, the ancestors, kings and officials, and the people of the land. This is quite distinct from some of the description of the sins in the book of Ezekiel where God leads the prophet through "visions of God" (מראות אלהים, 8:3) in Jerusalem and shows him the vile deeds that the elders do in their chambers (חדרי משכיתו, "in the chamber of his shrine," 8:12). The same can be said for Isa 65:4, where people "sit in tombs" (הישבים בקברים) and "sleep in secret places" (ובנצורים ילינו).

24 V. 18bβ, והסך נסכים לאלהים אחרים ("pouring out libations to other gods"), could either be a clause modifying the cult of the Queen of Heaven or another sin. The particular expression for 'pouring libations to other gods' is found only in Jeremiah (19:13, 32:29, 44:17, 18, 19, 25). Though the phrase, הסיך נסכים ("to pour libations"), could occur in either legitimate or

As in DtrH, the worship of other deities forms the basis for the provocation of God (הכעסני [25]למען, v. 18bβ):

Sin (Worship of Queen of Heavens and Libations) → Provocation

Consistent with the pattern, then, one would expect the punishment in the following verse. However, rather than outline the punishment, the next verse (v. 19) tries to 'turn the table' and retroject the direction and consequences of the provocation to the people. Instead of provoking God, the people actually provoke themselves which inevitably results in their utter humiliation (בשׁת פניהם, "shame of their face," v. 19).

To understand how the author achieves this effect, one needs to look at the structure of the verse:

(A   האתי (direct object) הם (subject) מכעסים (verb) האם־יהוה
(B הלוא אתם (direct object)   למען בשׁת פניהם

A) Was it me   they were bent on provoking, says YHWH?
B) Or was it not them   to the shame of their face?

Given the structure of the contrastive poetic unit,[26] A is designed to parallel B so that the subject and verb of A (הם מכעסים) carries over into B, which does not have a verb. Thus one should read the passage as:

---

illegitimate contexts in the Hebrew Bible, it has come to signify syncretistic practice in the book of Jeremiah (*TDOT* 9:455-460). For examples of illegitimate cultic practices, see Exod 30:9, 2 Kgs 16:13, Ezek 20:28 Ps 16:4; and for those poured out to YHWH, see Gen 35:14, Num 28:7, 2 Sam 23:16 (the word occurs in the Piel conjugation in 1 Chr 11:18) — two occurrences in the hophal conjugation, Exod 25:29, 37:16, appear in legitimate contexts. These do not include attestations of the noun, נסך ("libation"), which also is used in both contexts: legitimate (Exod 29:40, 41, Lev 23:13, 15, 37, Num 4:7, 6:15, 17, 15:5, 7, 10, 24, 28:7, 8, 9, 10, 14, 15, 24, 31, 29:6, 11, 16, 18, 19, 21, 22, 24, 25, 27, 28, 30, 31, 33, 34, 37, 38, 39, Ezek 45:17, 1 Chr 29:21, 2 Chr 29:35) and illegitimate (2 Kgs 16:15, Isa 57:6). Though, the practice of pouring out libation in of itself does not have a pejorative connotation, in the prose material of the book of Jeremiah, the references appear only in non-Yahwistic contexts, usually in connection with other gods (Jer 19:13 and 32:29; without 'libation' in the book of Jeremiah, 1:16, 7:6, 9, 18, 11:10, 13:10, 16:11, 13, 19:4, 22:9, 25:6, 35:15, 44:3, 5, 8, 15) or the Queen of Heaven (Jer 44:17, 18, 19, 25). The very fact that the phrase is used with "other gods" here attests to the illegitimacy of the activity.

25 Like DtrH, למען here, has a sense of 'consequence' rather than 'intent' — the people serve other deities which result in provoking God to anger. The key to deriving this sense lies in the following verse (v. 19). The למען of v. 19 mirrors למען of v. 18 so that one would expect its function to be similar. It would be inconceivable for the people to *purposefully* bring about their own shame (פניהם בשׁת, "shame of their face"). Rather their 'provocations' would *result* in their 'shame.'

26 The verse opens with a direct object marker (את) with a interrogative-ה and a first person singular pronominal suffix referring to God and then proceeds to the pronoun and verb (האתי

A) Was it me they were bent on provoking? says YHWH.
B) Or was it not themselves that they were bent on provoking to the shame of
their face?

This contrastive parallel structure in which God (אֹתִי, "me") is set against the
emphatic "them" (אֹתָם),[27] intensified by the positive (הַאֹתִי, "me?") and then
the negative interrogative-ה (הֲלוֹא, "not?"), establishes a sharp antithesis[28] so
that the fault and, to a certain extent, the agency of the punishment fall upon
the people. In other words, the people thought they were 'provoking' *God* but
instead they were 'provoking' *themselves* to their shame.[29] Therefore, without
v. 19, the expected pattern would have been sin-provocation-punishment:

הַם מכעסים נֹאם יהוה, "was it me they were provoking, says YHWH;" see *GKC* §142 f, example d, note 1, 457.): "Was it God they were bent on provoking?" Here, the natural sequence in biblical Hebrew, verb-subject-direct object, is disrupted to emphasize the object of
הכעיס, God. Thereafter, a negative rhetorical question follows,"Or was it really not themselves [they were provoking] to the very shame of their face?" הלוא אתם למען בשת
פֿניהם; Lundbom, *Jeremiah*, 477, calls this a classical rhetorician's *correctio*, in which an
emphatic assertion is followed by a correction by the speaker himself; such a method of
speech adds more dramatic emphasis).

27   The nota accusativi, אוֹתָם, is rarely used to express the reflexive pronoun and when it does
occur, it is for the purpose of emphasis (*GKC* §135k.).

28   *GKC* §57, note 4, 154, and *Joüon* §146k note the antithetical nature of the אוֹתָם.

29   This concept whereby the people are causing their own punishment is not unfamiliar in other
parts of the book. In prose, the idea recurs in 44:7-10, which will be discussed below. In the
poetic units, the self-flagellation formulation of sin-punishment is also present in which the
people's ways and sins bring about their own disaster. In 4:18, a problematic verse demonstrates the idea. According to the MT, the first half of the verse reads, "on account of your
way and deeds, he did these to you" (דרכך ומעלליך עשו אלה לך):
People Sin (Way and Deeds) → God Punishes
The vocalization of עָשׂוֹ in the MT makes God the agent of "these" (אלה), referring to the
previous series of descriptions of destruction. Since a causal conjunction/preposition is absent, what is implied, though not explicit in the MT, is the understanding that God responded
with actions *'on account of'* the people's 'way and deeds.' Otherwise it would be unclear as
to the purpose of the phrase, דרכך ומעלליך ("your way and deeds"), in the verse. Such a
construction is awkward and may actually reflect the tendency of a later MT redactor, though
not always consistent, to locate the primary agency to God rather than the activities which
would make more grammatical sense. As the Targum and several Hebrew manuscripts reflect, the form of עשׂה was probably עָשׂוּ where the subject of the verb would have been the
'way and deeds' of the people ("your way and deeds did these to you"):
Sin (Way and Deeds) → Sin Punishes People
The very sins that the people commit become the ammunition for their very punishment; God
is absent from the configuration. Therefore, the 'original' version attributed the responsibility
and agency of the punishment to the culprits whereas the MT deliberately revocalized the
text to make God, not their activities, the agent of the punishments.
   A similar development is evident in 30:15 where the MT again has God as the subject,
"because of your great iniquities and many sins, *I did* these to you" (לך   על רב עונך עצמו
חטאתיך *עשׂיתי* אלה). In the Lucian and Origen recensions of Greek, עשׂיתי ("I did") is in
the third plural. It is unclear what the subject of the verb will be since חטאתיך ("your sins")

מלכת השמים ... ← למען הכעסני ... ← לכן ...

Queen of Heavens (v. 18) → To Provoke (God) to Anger (v. 18b) →
Therefore (Punishment, v. 20)

However, v. 19 shifts the agency to the people who were actually 'provoking'
themselves leading to the punishment:

מלכת השמים ... ← למען הכעסני ... ←
הלוא אתם למען בשת פניהם : לכן ...

Queen of Heaven (v. 18a) → To Provoke (God) to Anger (v. 18b) →
(Actually) Provoke Themselves (v. 19b) to their Shame: Therefore (Punishment,
v. 20)

The direction of the provocation from God to the people is clear — that is the
focus of the blame from God to the people. Yet how do the people become
agents of their own punishment? For that, it is essential to analyze the phrase,
בשת פניהם ("shame of their face").

The outcome of the 'vexation' is public humiliation (בשת פניהם, "shame
of their face"), an expression which is usually attested in the context of war.
Though the exact expression does not occur anywhere else in the book of Jeremiah,[30] it appears five times in late post-exilic texts (Ps 44:16, Dan 9:7, 8,

---

already has a corresponding verb (עמצו, "they multiplied"). Perhaps the noun carries over to
the following verb so that the sins of the people are causing the 'wound.' If that is the case,
then we have another instance where the MT corrects the reading whereby God, not the people's offense, bring about the punishment. Perhaps, the MT is trying to put v. 15 in line with
the previous verse, where God is the executor of the punishment. In v. 14b, God strikes
(הכיתיך, "I struck you") with the "blow of an enemy" (מכה אויב). See also 5:25 where the
people's iniquities (עונתיכם, 'your iniquities") and sins (חטותכם, "your sins") deflects
(מנעו, "they withheld;" הטו, "they turn aside") God's goodness (אלה, "these," referring to
the rains and harvest weeks in v. 24; הטוב, "the good").

Based on these examples, there seems to be a play on the word אלה ("these") in the
poetic units. It can refer to the sins of the people (2:34, 3:7, 5:9, 29) and the punishment
(4:18, 5:19, 13:22, 30:15). Yet among these attestations, a significant difference in the agency prevails: is it God or the sins that 'does' (עשה) the punishment? One needs to only examine the formulations of the question. In 5:19, the question asks why God brings 'these things'
while 13:22 wonders why 'these things' happen to the people.

30   A similar, though not the same, expression occurs in Jer 51:51, where "humiliation covered
our faces" (כסתה כלמה פנינו). See Ps 69:8 for the same expression. Whereas the full expression, בשת פניהם, does not occur again in the book of Jeremiah, the verb (בוש, "be
ashamed") seems to have a similar connotation. It may refer to shameful activity (in 6:15 and
8:12, people have acted shamefully for having committed תועבה but do not feel shame; other
examples of those who hoped in the wrong gods [48:13] or rejected the right God [17:13] and
have acted shamefully), feeling of shame from helplessness due to circumstances outside of
one's control (this may encompass a number of activities - the inability to do one's physical
labor due to external forces [12:13, 14:3, 14:4] or inability to fight [20:11]), and most commonly, shame in destitution (Judah [2:36, 15:9, 51:51], Ephraim [31:19], Moab [48:39], Ha-

Ezra 9:7, 2 Chr 32:21).[31] Based on the contexts of these texts, בשת פניהם is integrally connected to the communal shame experienced in the aftermath of a major military defeat.[32] It is not a mere grievous response to an embarrassing situation, but the excruciating humiliation in the face of annihilation.[33] There-

---

math and Arpad [49:23], Babylon [50:12, 51:47]; in some ways, this is an extension of the shame from helplessness — inability to protect their land from enemy encroachment). The noun (בשת, "shame") also occurs but with a general sense of 'shame.' It occurs in 3:25 where the word expresses the shame of the people who come to recognize their sins. Also, it is used as a metaphor of a thief's shame upon being caught (2:26) and as a reference to Jeremiah's miserable life in shame (20:18). The term used to express the object of public reproach has been used as a substitute for Baʻal (3:24; 11:13 [absent in Greek]) as if to demonstrate that the worship of Baʻal is to the shame of the people. The בשת substitute for בעל is considered to be late additions, *BDB*, 102.

Shame in the midst of destitution arises from having failed to protect the cities against enemy encroachment and becoming the object of the neighboring countries' "reproach" (חרפה, 51:51). Exposure to such reproach is one of the major parts of divine punishment. Beside the destruction of the city/temple and the exile, the people are subject to "reproach" (חרפה, which occurs in 6:10, 15:15, 20:8, 23:40, 31:19 but in context of other punishments, 24:9, 29:18, 42:18, 44:8, 12, and 51:51; it is also used against the Ammonites, 49:13), "horror" (שמה occurs in 5:30 and 8:21, but in a list, 25:9, 11, 18, 29:18, 42:18, 44:12, 22 and in a context of other nations: Ammonites [49:13], Edom [49:17], Babylon [51:37, 41]; it is difficult to differentiate from its other meaning, 'desolation' [2:15, 4:7, 18:16, 19:8, 25:38, 46:19, 48:9, 50:3, 51:29, 43]), and "derision" (שרקה, which occurs in 19:8, 25:9, 18, and 29:18, though a variation of the word is evident in 18:16: שריקת; it also appears in reference to the Babylonians [51:37]). Other similar words also occur in the book of Jeremiah: כלמה ("shame," 3:25, 20:11, 51:51); כלמות ("shame," 23:40); אלה ("curse," 23:10, 29:18, 42:18, 44:12); זועה ("terror," 15:4, 24:9, 29:18, 34:17); משל ("byword," 24:9); קללה ("curse," 24:9, 25:18, 26:6, 29:22, 42:18, 44:8, 12, 22, 49:13); יניד בראשו ("nodding of head," 18:16); חרבה ("desolation," 7:34, 22:5, 25:11, 18, 44:22, 49:13).

31   The books of Daniel (ca. 165 B.C.E.), Ezra (ca. 538-400 B.C.E.), and Chronicles (ca. 400 B.C.E.) are late books. Ps 44 is the only questionable text which can be dated to the exilic period or later (Briggs and Briggs, *Psalms I*, 374; though Kraus, *Psalms 60-150*, 446, refuses to date the psalm). A similar phraseology occurs in Isa 44:9 where it describes the futility of the idol-makers. Since the idols can do nothing, they (referring to the idol-makers) will be ashamed (למען יבשו).

32   One could possibly attribute this communal experience of shame to the initial exile in 597 B.C.E. (according to Seitz, *Theology in Conflict*, this event was a pivotal point in the redaction of the book of Jeremiah). Since the author/editor appears to have intentionally used the DtrH2 (2 Kgs 22:17) formulation of the punishment for the fall of Jerusalem in v. 20, the public humiliation (v. 19) may have been describing the scenario before the catastrophic event of 587 B.C.E. That is if the description of the punishment was trying to follow the sequence of the historical events but this is not clearly evident.

33   Ps 44, dated to (late?) exilic period, people experience military defeat (vv. 10-13) and thus public shame (vv. 14-17). They have become a "reproach" (חפרה), "derision" (לעג), "mockery" (קלס, v. 14), "byword" (משל), and "shaking of the head" (מנוד ראש, v.15) among the nations (שכנינו, "our neighbors;" סביבותנו, "those who surround us;" גוים, "nations;" אמים־ בל, "no people"). As a result, the prayer is a "disgrace" (כלמה; בשת usually occurs with כלמה, Jer 3:25, 51:51, Isa 30:3, 61:7, Pss 35:26, 69:8, 71:13, 109.29, Ezek 16:63, 39:26; Prov 18:13, Job 20:3) and a "shame" (בשת פניהם) from the "taunters" (מחרף), "revilers" (מגדף), "enemy" (אויב), and "avenger" (מתנקם). The shame is not merely personal nor emotional.

fore, within the compact expression, בשׁת פניהם, the people, it would seem, was being held responsible for their own destruction and humiliation.[34] However, in the end, it is the divine wrath which becomes the punishment but without an explicit agent.

In Jer 7:20, the provocation is concretized and subjectified into divine wrath, the ultimate punishment. God's fiery wrath,[35] materialized from and

---

It is a social humiliation in the face of major defeat and realization of their responsibility in their own downfall.

In 2 Chr 32:21, the narrative recounts the return of Sennacherib to Nineveh upon his failure to capture Jerusalem under Hezekiah (absent in 2 Kgs 19:35 // Isa 37:36). The Chronicler abbreviates the account in Kings but adds that Sennacherib returned, shame of face. Here, also, it expresses the foreign king's public humiliation before his people, Judah, and perhaps the surrounding nations in contrast to Hezekiah who was "exalted in the eyes of the nations" (וינשׂא לעיני כל הגוים", v. 23). This meaning is also evident in Ezra 9:7, where the prophet recounts the general history of the ancestors. On account of the great offense (אשׁמה גדלה, "great guilt," and עונתינו, "our iniquituies"), the people had been handed over to foreign rulers. According to Joseph Blenkinsopp, *Ezra-Nehemiah* (OTL; London: S.C.M. Press, 1988), 183, this one verse recapitulates the Chronicler's history — the idea that subjection to foreign rule is the result of religious infidelity. Similarly, in Dan 9:7, 8, shame is upon the banished people because they've committed treachery (v. 7) and sinned against God (v. 8). As seen from the examples, the specific phraseology is a late reference to the public humiliation experienced from military defeat.

34   The destruction of the city and the resulting shame undermines the name theology. The idea that the temple bears God's name is central to the book of Jeremiah and DtrH though they may use different phraseology. נקרא־שׁמי עליו ("he will be called by my name") occurs primarily in the book of Jeremiah (14:9, 15:16, 25:29, 32:34, 34:15), occurring few times in DtrH and other books (Deut 28:10, 2 Sam 6:2 // 1 Chr 13:6, 1 Kgs 8:43 // 2 Chr 6:33, 2 Chr 7:14, Amos 9:12, Isa 43:7, 63:19, Dan 9:18, 19) compared to שׁכן ("to dwell") or שׂים ("to place") which occurs very frequently (שׁכן also occurs in Jer 7:3 [which may refer to God letting the people dwell], 7 [which refers to God dwelling among the people], 12 [reference to God's name]; for a theological understanding of the ideas, see *TLOT* 3:1360-1362). Both expressions come to designate ownership and at the same time mark God's presence. The concept is especially essential in chapter 7 since the expression, נקרא־שׁם עליו, occurs in vv. 10, 11, 14, 30 and שׁכן in 3, 7, and 12. It is the sustaining power of the temple and for the people since they could and did ask God to act for the sake of his name (14:7, 21; for references outside of the book of Jeremiah, see Isa 48:9, 66:5, Ezek 20:9, 14, 22, 44, Pss 23:3, 25:11, 31:4, 79:9, 106:8, 109:21; 143:11; 2 Chr 6:32 in reference to name; without the name, 'for my/your sake,' see 2 Kgs 19:34, 20:6; Isa 37:35, 43:25, 48:11, Dan 9:19). However, the sins committed around the temple which bears God's name have led to its destruction. The name in of itself will not protect the people nor can the people call upon God in the temple. The protective shield has been lifted. See Holladay, *Jeremiah*, 1:245-6, for general information and bibliography. The expression is a play on the expression to "call upon the name of YHWH" (קרא בשׁם יהוה). The individual/community who calls/speaks in the name of the LORD is to be called by his name

35   The phrase for God's "fiery wrath " (אף וחמה) may be read as a hendiadys or as two separate words for differing aspects of God's anger. However the following verb seems to indicate that the phrase was intended to be read as a hendiadys; the verb is a feminine singular participle Niphal of נתך ("to pour out"). When the words are listed in a series of nouns, like Jer 21:5, 32:37, 33:5, and Deut 29:27, Ezek 5:13, 15, they should be understood as two separate

fueled by the provocation, is poured out (נתכה).[36] However, the agent, neither the people nor the usual suspect, God, is indicated.[37] Rather the divine wrath is

---

references to anger. However, the pair is also used in parallel structures, Pss 6:2, 90:7, and Isa 63:3, 6. The expression appears against the Israelites/Judahites - Deut 9:19, 29:22; Ezek 22:20; Dan 9:16; against foreign nations - Mic 5:14 (גוים who do not obey God) and Ezek 25:14 (Edom). In the book of Jeremiah, the expression occurs in 36:7, 42:18, and 44:6.

36 This formulation of the punishment (v. 20) resembles, though not completely, the doom oracle in 2 Kgs 22:17:

אפי וחמתי *נתכת* אל־המקום הזה ... ובערה ולא תכבה (v. 20)

ונצתה חמתי במקום הזה   ולא תכבה (2 Kgs 22:17)

My fiery wrath will *be poured out* on this place ... it will burn and not be quenched (v.20)

My wrath will *be ignited* against this place and it will not quenched (2 Kgs 22:17)

The significant difference lies in the choice of verbs. Whereas 2 Kgs 22:17 has the niphal of יצת ("to kindle a fire"), Jer 7:20 uses the niphal of נתך ("to pour out"). According to Sara Japhet, " חילופי שרשים בפועל בטקסטים המקבילים בספר דברי הימים," *Lešonenu* 31 (1966-67):261-279, the version in 2 Kgs 22:17 is original while Jer 7:20 and 2 Chr 34:25 with the substitution of נתך for יצת modifies the essence of the meaning (other verb that occurs with the expression is שוב, "to turn back;" ישב־נא אפך וחמתך מעירך ירושלם הר־ קדשך, "turn away your fiery wrath from your city, Jerusalem, your holy hill" [Dan 9:16]). The verb, יצת ("to kindle a fire"), is usually associated with fire imagery while נתך ("to pour out") is linked more with liquid or molten fire imagery. One may explain the difference in verbs as a reflection of the historical change in word usage where נתך replaces יצת. It would explain the parallel version of 2 Kgs 22:17 in 2 Chr 34:35 (also see Nah 1:6 which also uses נתך with divine anger [חמתי, "my wrath"]). However, יצת has not been completely replaced by נתך in the book of Jeremiah; it occurs in the qal (Jer 49:2, 51:58), niphal (Jer 2:15, 9:9 [both in the sense of waste]; 46:19 [fire]), and hiphil (11:16, 17:27, 21:14, 32:29, 43:12, 49:27, 50:30, 51:30). Therefore, the difference in the word selection could not have developed from historical change in the usage of the verb יצת; instead the choice of the verb, נתך, seems to reflect the shift in the imagery from fire to burning metallic liquid (see Ezek 22:20, Isa 54:16, and perhaps Job 41:12 where the fire is fanned for smelting). The same cannot be said for the books of Chronicles which do not have a single attestation of יצת; but this is expected since it occurs infrequently in the books of Samuel and Kings (2 Sam 14:30 [twice], 31, which do not have parallels in the books of Chronicles; 2 Kgs 22:13 where יצת is again replaced by נתך).

The fundamental meaning of נתך is to 'pour, gush forth,' (*TDOT* 10:85-89, *HALOT* 2:732-33) which has come to also mean, 'melt' and 'smelt' with its connection to metallurgy. The verb has been used in water imagery, in both literal and figurative contexts (Job 3:24, 10:10, Exod 9:33, 2 Sam 21:10) while in later texts, though, especially in the book of Ezekiel, the verb is associated with melting metal: God will gather the people as one gathers the metals to melt them in the crucible (Ezek 22:20, 22).

The two distinct meanings of the verb is combined in 7:20 to denote the 'pouring out' of the resulting hot metallic liquid, usually a metaphor for divine anger (Jer 42:18, 44:6, 2 Chr 12:7, 34:21, 25; Nah 1:6) or other general terms for punishment like "curse and oath" (האלה והשבעה, Dan 9:11) and "annihilation and strict decision" (כלה ונחרצה, Dan 9:27). This smoldering liquid does not trickle down but stream forth through self-propulsion like volcanic lava (*TDOT* 10:88, and *TDOT*:1, 358). This may correspond to יצא ("to go out")

the means by which the destruction is brought about. This divine wrath appears to be propelled by the force of the provocation:

← (v. 19b) למען הכעסני (v. 18b) ←אתם (הם מכעסים) למען בֹּשֶׁת פניהם

---

which can be used with fire, Num 21:28, Jer 48:45, Judg 9:15, 20, Lev 9:24, 10:2, Num 16:35, etc. See Exod 32:24, where the calf came out of the fire (though this part poses many difficulties). The basis of the imagery for the verb is crucial in understanding the reason for the choice of the verb נתך over יצ׳.

37　This image most likely alludes to the second vision of Jeremiah embedded in the call narrative (1:13):

ויהי דבר־יהוה אלי שנית לאמר מה אתה ראה
ואמר סיר נפוח אני ראה ופניו מפני צפונה

The word of YHWH came to me the second time, saying, "What do you see?" I said, "I see a fanned pot and its rim is tipped from the north."

In the vision, Jeremiah sees a "fanned pot" (סיר נפוח, 1:13) tipped over from the north. Unlike other oracle-vision reports which provide the premise for a proclamation, this vision along with 'almond-tree branch' (1:11-12) raise two major interrelated themes, establishing the framework of the book of Jeremiah (see Burke Long, "Reports of Visions Among the Prophets," *JBL* 95 [1976]:353-365). According to E.W. Nicholson, *Preaching to the Exiles*, 113-115, the first vision of an "almond tree branch" (שקד) summarizes the theme of "the vindication of Yahweh's Word of judgement and salvation upon his people," while the heated pot "crystallizes ... Yahweh's judgement upon Judah at the hands of the Babylonians" (114; see also Long, "Reports of Visions," 358). Though the vision does not mention Judah nor the Babylonians, Nicholson's, *Jeremiah*, 1:26, categorization of the vision as a judgment is correct. The vision is interpreted as "the evil" (הרעה) that is to "burst out from the north" (תפתח מצפון, v. 14) or "all the families of the kingdoms of the north" (ממלכות צפונה לכל־ משפחות, v.15). Though the vision itself does not indicate that סיר נפוח ("fanned pot") contained anything, the image of a tilted pot seems to hint at some fiery matter al that is about to be released. For the use of סיר ("pot") as a means of destruction, see Ezek. 11:3, 7, 11, 24:3, 6. In the book of Ezekiel, the people are the meat of the cauldron (the city) that is about to be cooked (ch. 11) and charred (ch. 24). Holladay objects to the 'boiling pot' translation since there is no mention of any water. According to Holladay, a pot does not need to contain water in order to be heated. See Ezek 24:11, where the empty pot is burned to purify it of its uncleanness. However, the passage needed to state explicitly that the pot was "empty" (רקה), hinting at its unusual practice. Otherwise, the pot usually contains liquid substance and/or foods (Exod 16:3, 2 Kgs 4:38-41, Ezek 11:3, 7, 11, 24:3, Mic 3:3, Zech 14:20, 21, Pss 60:10, 108:10, 2 Chr 35:13) or is used in the sanctuary to carry materials (Exod 27:3, 38:3, 1 Kgs 7:40, 45 // 2 Chr 4:11, 16, 2 Kgs 25:14 // Jer 52:18, 19).　Perhaps, though it is far from certain, the fiery wrath of 7:20 refers back to the inferred substance in the pot. Compare to Job 41:12 where smoke from Leviathan's nose comes out (מנחיריו יצא עשן, "from his nostrils, smoke comes out") "like the steaming, boiling cauldron" (כדוד נפוח ואגמן). If one looks at Ezek 22:21, it is not uncommon to find a pot being heated with the fire of divine wrath; God blows the fire of his fury (נפחתי עליכם באש) upon the crucible containing the House of Israel. If that is the case, then, the author/editor v. 20 adopted the DtrH2 formula of the destruction and adapted it for the book of Jeremiah, which would ultimately indicate that Jer 7:16-20 is later than DtrH2. This may be supported by the use of the expression, בשת פניהם, which occurs in late texts.

אפי וחמתי נתכת (v. 20)

Provoke God to Anger (v. 18b) →
They are Provoking Themselves to Their Shame (v. 19b) →
My Fiery Wrath is Poured Out (v. 20)

The 'provocation' did not necessarily provoke God which would have then motivated him to punish the people; rather the provocation directly impacts the people in that it fuels the fiery wrath which is about to be poured over the totality of creation.[38] Yet God is not completely absent from the scene of destruction; after all, it is his wrath. At the same time, though, it is only an aspect

---

38   The list of destroyed objects, "man" (האדם), "beast" (הבהמה), "tree of the field" (עץ השדה), and "fruit of the earth" (פרי האדמה), is unusual. In the book of Jeremiah, the catalog of objects susceptible to destruction usually includes 'man' and 'beast' (21:6, 32:43, 33:10, 12, 36:29, 51:63; even in recounting God's creative or restorative efforts, 'man' and 'beast' are listed [27:5, 31:27]). This range covers the whole spectrum of living creatures (Exod 9:25, 12:12, 13:15; and Gen 6:7, 7:23 which further classifies the "creeping things" [רמשׂ] and "birds of the air" [עוף השמים]) though other lists are more comprehensive and add on the "birds of the air" (עוף השמים, 4:25, 9:9). However, plant life is not generally enumerated in such lists in the book of Jeremiah. The most similar listing of plants is in 5:17 where an "ancient nation" devours vines (גפנך, "your vines") and fig trees (תאנתך, "your fig trees") with the harvest (קצירך, "your harvest"), food (לחמך, "your food"), sons (בניך, "your sons"), daughters (בנותיך, "your daughters"), flocks (צאנך, "your flocks"), and herds (בקרך, "your herds;" the same would apply to 8:10, where the wives and fields are given to others — see also 8:13). However, this catalog focuses on the 'domestic' realm — children, domesticated animals, and cultivated food and plants — not so much as to make an attempt to include all of plant life (perhaps one could look at the trees that are cut down for siegemounds [6:6]; however, it is ultimately the means by which to describe the destruction, not the object of destruction). Thus, the list in 7:20 is unique in its enumeration of the wide spectrum of plant life, the "tree of the field" (עץ השדה) and the "fruit of the ground" (פרי האדמה). The 'tree of the field' refers to plant life in uninhabited regions (Exod 9:25, Lev 26:4, Deut 20:19, Isa 55:12, Ezek 17:24, 31:4, 5, 15, 34:27, Joel 1:12, 19; though some of these passages are not too explicit, Deut 20:19 describes the 'tree of the field' as those outside of the city that can be either edible or not) while the 'fruit of the ground' alludes to the harvested crops (Gen 4:3, Deut 7:13, 26:2, 10, 28:4, 11, 18, 33, 42, 51, 30:9, Mal 3:11, Ps 105:35; it is a common Dtr expression for referring to the 'produce' of the soil, harvested plants). By incorporating all plant life along with all the living creatures, the judgment formula encompasses the totality of creation within the confines of "this place" (המקום הזה). This could refer to a variety of places in the Hebrew Bible. It indicates the location in which one is situated or has reached (Gen 20:11, 28:16, Deut 1:31, 9:7, 11:5, 26:9, 29:6, 1 Sam 12:8, 1 Kgs 13:8, 16, 2 Kgs 6:9, 18:25). At the same time, the expression can specifically refer to the Temple and/or the city of Jerusalem, especially in, though not limited to, the book of Jeremiah (1 Kgs 8:29, 30, 35, 2 Kgs 22:16, 17, 19, 20, Jer 7:3, 6, 7, 14:13, 16:2, 3, 9, 19:3, 4, 7, 12, 22:3, 11, 24:5, 27:22, 28:3, 4, 6, 29:10, 32:37, 33:10, 12, 40:2, 42:18, 44:29, 51:62, Zeph 1:4, Hag 2:9, 2 Chr 6:20, 21, 26, 40, 7:12, 15, 34:5, 24, 27, 28). Given the extensive list, 'this place' cannot refer only to the Temple area, as is the case in 2 Kgs 22:17, but extends beyond the holy site and encloses Jerusalem and its surrounding environ and perhaps even beyond.

of his divinity, activated and supplied by the provocation, that is passively set against the people.

Nothing is to escape God's fiery wrath which will "burn" (ובערה) and "not be extinguished" (ולא תכבה).[39] The fiery anger, once aroused by the people's idolatrous activities, will not die out. Instead it will be their punishment. In sum, 7:16-20 attempts to invert the responsibility of the execution from God to the people by describing the punishment, the fiery wrath, as the direct result of the provocation.

4.3. Jeremiah 8:18-23 (v. 19c)

Here, the clause containing הכעיס (v. 19c) is an ingenious addition to justify God's punishment of Judah in Jeremiah's lament (vv. 18-23). Originally, v. 19b expressed the people's doubt as to God's presence in Jerusalem but with the addition of v. 19c, their very misgivings is now interpreted as God's indictment of the people who failed to recognize his presence by provoking him to anger with their idolatry. Thus, the addition explains why there is a drought (v. 20), ultimately establishing the sin-provocation-punishment pattern.

In the poetic oracles (source A), הכעים is attested only once in 8:19c, which is embedded within the larger framework consisting of vv. 4-23.[40] Though vv. 4-23 is made up of several independent and somewhat miscellaneous units, there is a distinct plot. This plot as outlined below forms the context for the lament (vv. 18-23), the focus of this section:

vv. 4-7   God comments on the people's constant turning away[41]
vv. 8-12   God attacks the self-claimed religious leaders

---

39 Perhaps לא תכבה ("it will be not extinguished") should be לא מכבה ("no one will extinguish) based on 4:4, 21:12. However the other two attestations are in the poetic section and differ in phraseology. Since there are no variants in other textual witnesses, the reading is accepted as is. The minor difference is quite significant since the participle assumes that no external person/thing could extinguish the fire whereas the imperfect construction assumes that the fire itself will not wane. There is too much to burn.

40 According to Bright, *Jeremiah*, 60-63; Nicholson, *Jeremiah*, 1:88-91, and Holladay, *Jeremiah*, 1:287-288, demarcate the unit into vv. 14-23. Carroll, *Jeremiah*, 234-235; Driver, *Jeremiah*, 51-52; McKane, *Jeremiah*, 193; and Rudolph, *Jeremiah*, 55-57, consider the unit to be shorter, consisting of vv. 18-23, while Lundbom sees a poem only in vv. 18-21. I've included a larger framework to ascertain the flow of the surrounding pericopes. The particular unit is probably more in line with the suggestion of Carroll, Driver, McKane, and Rudolph, who delineate the unit to be vv. 18-23

41 Notice the concentration of שוב it occurs six times (vv. 4 [twice], 5 [thrice], 6). The unit closes with the indictment that the people do not know the judgment of God (v. 7).

v. 13	God in the image of a picker finds no fruits
vv. 14-16	People respond to the invading armies
v. 17	God promises to send snakes to bite the people
vv. 18-23	Jeremiah's lament

In short, God, the accuser, censures the people for being stubborn and the religious leaders for their shameful deeds. Since they are not divine-conscious, God was unable to harvest any fruit from the trees, thus providing the fodder for a foreign invasion. With the attack, the people respond in agitation, fully aware of their doom. To further torture the people, God sends serpents.

Thereupon Jeremiah is found lamenting for the people, voicing their exasperation, with the exception of the unusual clause (v. 19b+c) where Yahweh accuses the people of idolatry. On account of this interruption in the generally sympathetic lament, many scholars have considered v. 19b+c to be an addition to Jeremiah's lament (vv. 18-23).[42] Before analyzing the function of הכעיס, it is crucial to determine whether the clause is original to the lament or a gloss:

Beginning of Lament - Jeremiah Speaks (v. 18)

18) מבליגיתי עלי יגון עלי לבי דוי

Cry of People - Jeremiah Speaks (v.19a)

19a) הנה־קול שועת בת־עמי מארץ מרחקים

Interruption - Yahweh Speaks (v. 19b+c)

19b) היהוה אין בציון אם־מלכה אין בה

19c) מדוע הכעסוני בפסליהם בהבלי נכר

Cry of People - People Speak (v. 20)

20) עבר קציר כלה קיץ ואנחנו לוא נושענו

Lament Continued - Jeremiah Speaks (vv. 21-23)

21) על־שבר בת־עמי השברתי קדרתי שמה החזקתני

22) הצרי אין בגלעד אם־רפא אין שם

---

42 Beside Lundbom, *Jeremiah*, 528-534, and Holladay, *Jeremiah*, 1:288-290, most commentators attribute the verse to a Dtr editor (Nicholson, *Jeremiah*, 1:90; Carroll, *Jeremiah*, 234-237; Bright, *Jeremiah*, 64-66; McKane, *Jeremiah*, 1:193-194; Rudolph, *Jeremiah*, 55-57; and Thiel, *Die deuteronomistische Redaktion*, 1:135-136). Holladay admits to the complexities of the poem, yet argues for its unity based on the rhetorical effect — the complex succession of speakers where v. 19 provides God's rhetorical question as to why the misfortunes are occurring (in addition to his commentary, see William Holladay, "The So-Called 'Deuteronomic Gloss' in Jer. VIII 19b," *VT* 12 (1962):494-498). Lundbom concurs but bases his conclusion on the chiastic structure of the poem in vv. 18-21. Yet in his discussion and analysis of the structure, Lundbom excises שועת את־עמי מארץ מרחקים ("the cry of my people from distant land"), arguing that it reduces the length of the line (Jack Lundbom, *Jeremiah: A Study in Ancient Hebrew Rhetoric* [SBLDS 18; Missoula: Scholars Press, 1975], 84-86). The 'cutting up' of text to fit his version of structure is not a convincing method. However, most commentaries consider it secondary on account of one word, הכעיס, which appears primarily in the prose sections of the book of Jeremiah and in DtrH. This data, by in of itself, is also not a convincing argument but supported by additional evidence can be valid.

כי מדוע לא עלתה ארכת בת־עמי
(23 מ־־יהן ראשי מים ועיני מקור דמעה
ואבכה יומם ולילה את חללי בת־עמי

18) Without a cure,[43] grief comes up[44] against me, my heart is faint.
19a) Listen, the cry of my people from distant land.
19b) "Is YHWH not in Zion? Is her king not in her?
19c) Why have they provoked me with their images, with their foreign delusions?"
20) Harvest has passed, summer has ended; yet we are not saved.
21) Because of the wound of my people, I am crushed; I mourn and horror grips me.
22) Is there no balm in Gilead? Is there no physician there?
23) Why then is there no healing for my people?
24) Oh, that my head were waters, and my eyes a spring of tears,
25) I will weep day and night for the slain of my people.

Within the immediate context of הכעיס, Jeremiah is found lamenting for "the daughter of [his] people" (בת עמי, vv. 19, 21, 22, 23). The overall purpose and consequent effect of the lament is to evoke empathy for the people who are depicted in the image of a grief-stricken daughter.[45] Here, Jeremiah plays the paternal figure helplessly wailing over the desolation of his daughter who cries out.[46] However, unexpectedly, in v. 19b(?)+c,[47] God poses rhetorical

---

43   According to *BDB*, 114, מבליגית should mean "smiling, cheerfulness, source of brightening" based on the root, בלג ("gleam, smile"). However this meaning would not make sense in this context. As a result, the translation follows some of the ancient Hebrew manuscripts which have מבלי גיחי ("?") or מבלי גהת ("without healing").
44   With BHS notes which proposes עלה or יעלה for עלי ("comes up") and transposes the athnach under יגון to עלי ("against me").
45   בת עמי ("daughter of my people") is a personification of the people, commonly attested in the books of Jeremiah (4:11, 6:26, 8:11, 19, 21, 22, 23, 9:6, 14:17) and Lamentations (2:11, 3:48, 4:3, 6, 10); see also Isa 22:4. It is an expression common to poetry where the speaker, either God or representative of the people, usually expresses grief over the demise of Judah (exceptions to this depiction is Jer 4:11, 9:6, Lam 4:3, 6, 10). The feminine portrayal of Judah elicits more compassion from the masculine speaker; see Alan Mintz, "The Rhetoric of Lamentations and the Representation of Catastrophe," *Prooftexts* 2 (1982):1-17.
46   The noun, שועה ("cry"), is the anguished cry of an individual or group directed towards God. It is a cry for deliverance from the unpleasant circumstances (Exod 2:23, 1 Sam 5:12, 2 Sam 22:7 // Ps 18:7, Lam 3:56, Pss 34:16, 39:13, 40:2, 102:2, 145:19). For its variant form, שוע, see Job 30:24, 36:19. The verb of the word also has a similar function (Isa 38:13, 58:9, Jon 2:3, Hab 1:2, Lam 3:3, Pss 5:3, 18:7, 42, 22:25, 28:2, 31:23, 72:12, 88:2, 14, 119:147, Job 30:20, 36:13, 38:41). However, the verb is also used in general contexts, Job 19:7, 24:12, 29:12, 30:28, 35:9.
47   See below as to how v. 19b which was probably the speech of the people ultimately became part of the divine speech.

questions, first, to assert his divine presence in Jerusalem, and second, to ac-
cuse the people of provoking him with their idolatry. Without doubt, the divine
speech disrupts the flow of the lament and subverts the overall tone of the
lament which empathizes with the suffering of the people. Yet the issue is
whether or not the questions were original to the lament for the purpose of
justifying the dire condition of the people by pointing out the reason for their
punishment.[48] Since the ultimate intent of the lament is not to justify God's
actions but to procure divine help with its description of the people's desolate
situation, the questions were probably inserted.   Thus, God's questions (v.
19b+c) appear to be secondary.

However, only v. 19c[49] modifies the tone of the lament whereas v. 19b is
actually original to the passage that was meant to be voiced by the people. V.
19c is a strategically positioned addition. It is placed towards the beginning of
the lament where Jeremiah exclaims the "outcry" (שׁועה) of the people (v.
19a). Instead of voicing what would have been the *people's* complaint (v.
19b), the addition of v. 19c modifies the rhetorical question (v. 19b) concerning the divine presence into part of *God's* speech. Therefore God, not the people, exclaim:

היהוה אין ציון אם מלכה אין בה מדוע הכעסוני בפסליהם בהבלי נכר

Is not Yahweh in Zion? Is not her king in its midst? Why then did they anger me
with their images, with alien futilities?

If God is in Jerusalem, then why do the people insist upon provoking God?
What reasons do they have for turning to other gods who were impotent? V.
19b+c expresses God's frustrations with the people who bring upon the miserable circumstances with their idolatry. It is the people's fault, not God's.

---

48   As explained by Holladay, "The So-Called 'Deuteronomic Gloss'" (1962), 494-498.

49   Some of the terms in v. 19c are not characteristic of poetic units concerning Judah. First of
     all, פסל ("image"), in the plural construction, is used mostly in reference to Babylon and its
     images (Jer 50:38, 51:47). Even in the singular form, the word is used in the oracle against
     Babylon (51:17). The only other occurrence of the singular is attested in 10:14, which de-
     scribes an useless idol compared to the creator God. Many commentators consider the whole
     poem, 10:1-16, to be secondary, while a few, like Holladay would disagree and consider it
     authentic. Secondly, beside the present attestation, הכעים occurs only in the prose sermons of
     the book of Jeremiah. Thus v. 19c is probably secondary to the lament. At the same time,
     though, 19c does adopt words from the poetic oracles. The word for "why" (מדוע) appears to
     be a common expression (2:14, 31, 8:5, 19, 22, 12:1, 13:22, 14:19, 22:28, 26:9, 30:6, 32:3,
     36:29, 46:5, 15, 49:1), especially in the poetic parts. Moreover, הבל occurs in reference to the
     false, delusional deities (2:5, 10:3, 15, 14:22, 16:19, 51:18). The editor was quite aware of
     Jeremiah's original words and used them to re-interpret the events.

However, when one excises v. 19c, then the rhetorical question (v. 19b) becomes part of the people's speech which challenges God's presence: 'Is not YHWH in Zion? Is not her king within her?' If God is in the midst of the holy city, then why is there a famine with no reprieve (v. 20)? Where is this YHWH of Jerusalem in the center of this horrible situation? The people's question probing God's sphere of influence may have disturbed a later editor: How could Jeremiah have echoed the people's doubt over God's power? Thus the editor may have added v. 19c so that the verse becomes a series of rhetorical inquiries which God poses to the people rather than the people's expression of doubt. As a result, it is not God's absence but the people's rejection of God which had led to their own condition. Thus, v. 19c with the expression, 'to provoke,' placed the blame for the punishment on the people's idolatry ([50]נכר בהבלי, "with foreign illusions," בפסליהם, "with their images"). The table has been turned around and the people are depicted as receiving their due punishment.

Not only does the speaker of the verse change from the people (via Jeremiah) to God, but the perspective in the following verse also shifts from a general observation of the people's dismay to a description of a punishment. If the people had been the intended speaker of v. 19b, then v. 20 would have been a continuation of the people's questioning of God's power over fertility. The season of reaping, harvest and summer,[51] has passed (עבר קציר כלה קיץ, "harvest has passed, summer has ended"), yet the people have not been saved (אנחנו לוא נושענו, "we are not saved").[52] Therefore, v. 20 expresses the people's bewilderment as to how their God, the deity of Zion, could allow a famine to sweep over them.

---

50   This phrase only occurs here as opposed to אלהי הנכר ("the foreign gods"), Gen 35:2, 4, Deut 31:16, Josh 24:20, 23, Judg 10:16, 1 Sam 7:3, 2 Chr 33:15, Jer 5:19, or אלוה נכר ("foreign god"), Dan 11:39.

51   קציר ("harvest") is in parallel construction with קיץ ("summer," Prov 6:8, 10:5, 26:1) so that קיץ is the season for gathering the crops (Prov 30:25, Isa 28:4).

52   It does not clarify from what the people needed to be saved. From the context, though, it would appear to be some devastation during harvest since focus is on the season of gathering, perhaps a drought or some damage to the crops which have led to their despair. As a result, Rudolph, *Jeremiah*, 55-57, has conjectured that v. 20 was describing a famine. See 8:13 with its reference to the agricultural woes. It is quite uncertain but no better suggestions have been made. For instance, if the verse was primarily interested in the passing of time, then "summer" (קיץ) and "winter" (חרף) would have been indicated in v. 19c (see Gen 8:22, Zech 14:8, Ps 74:17, where both seasons are included), not just the harvest season. But the idea that v. 20 refers to a famine may not correlate well with v. 19 where the outcry of the people comes "from distant land" (מארץ מרחקים). One could infer that perhaps people were dispersed (i.e. in exile; see Zech 10:9,) and waiting to return. However, מרחק ("distant") seems to indicate "distant land" in its extent (*BDB*, 935; see Isa 13:5, 33:17, 46:11, Jer 4:16, 6:20, Prov 25:25), which may explain BHS reading, מרחבים ("bread") or מרוחים ("spacious").

However, with the insertion of v. 19c, their accusation of no-deliverance against God becomes a justified recompense for their idolatry. Since God points out the people's failure to worship him, the rightful king of Jerusalem, the people's observation of the fruitless season appears to be the expected punishment:

> People Cry out (v. 19a) → God Responds (v. 19b+c):
> Sin (Idolatry) → Provocation → Punishment (Drought, v. 20)

Since the people abandon God for vain idols and provoke him in the process, it should come as no surprise that they must now endure the drought. Their provocation could only have resulted in a punishment. Had the text been specific and attributed the people with seeking out idols/foreign gods with power over fertility, the punishment would have mostly fit the crime; but that is not the case. Thus, הכעים functions as a link between the punishment and the sin but not as an exact recompense.

As to the agency of the punishment, the passage is not explicit but seems to imply the presence of YHWH in both the original and secondary versions. If one follows the original reading (v. 19a+b and v. 20), then the people seem to attribute the drought to YHWH: If YHWH is supposedly in Zion, then why are we not saved from the drought? The people are undoubtedly blaming God for the natural catastrophe. However, if one adds v. 19c, then the punishment seems to stem from the people's provocation of YHWH, who responds accordingly: If I am here in Jerusalem, why are the people provoking me with their idolatry? Because of the provocation, God may have brought the drought. In both instances, though, God uses an instrument to punish the people. However, whereas the original does not hold the people responsible, the addition (v. 19c) holds the people accountable for the punishment.

In conclusion, with the addition of v. 19c, God indicts the people of provoking him to anger in order to justify the punishment of a drought.

4.4. Jeremiah 11:17

Through a linking verse (11:17), one of the later editors, namely the decree-redactor, provides the boomerang-formulation in which the people's punishment is in direct proportion to their sin:

Decree Evil (Punishment)

ויהוה צבאות הנוטע אותך דבר עליך רעה

Evil (Sin)

בגלל רעת בית־ישראל ובית יהודה אשר עשו להם

Provocation   לְהַכְעִסֵנִי לְקַטֵּר לַבַּעַל

YHWH of hosts, who planted you, has *decreed* evil against you
on account of the evil of the houses of Israel and Judah which they committed
against themselves, <u>provoking me to anger</u> by burning incense to Baʿal.

11:17 is secondary,[53] which has been inserted to link a prose sermon (vv. 1-
14)[54] and a corrupt poetic fragment (vv. 15-16) to the following laments (vv.

---

53 Carroll, *Jeremiah*, 272-274; McKane, *Jeremiah*, 1:252-253; Thiel, *Die deuteronomistische Redaktion*, 1:156; and Rudolph, *Jeremiah*, 69-70.

54 The prose sermon is not unified and betrays at least three levels of redaction. The separation of the sources will aid in understanding the level in which v. 17 may have been added. The earliest level of redaction seems to consist of vv. 4-5, 9-11; the second level of redaction adds vv. 2a, 3b, 6-8; and the third level of redaction adds vv. 1, 2b-3a. As for vv. 12-14, it is unclear to which level they belong or if they were additional layers in the sermon. Since it would be simpler to excise the additional levels before getting to the original message, we will analyze from the latest to the earliest level.

The unattributable additions at the end of the sermon, vv. 12-14, do not fit into the sin-punishment structure of the sermon. After the unit describes the punishment in v. 11, vv. 12-13 continues to list an additional sin which parallels an indictment in 2:28 (poetic unit), while v. 14 resembles God's command for Jeremiah not to intercede on behalf of the people (see discussion in section on Jeremiah 7:16-20). Why and when they were added is unclear.

In the third level of redaction, focus is on Jeremiah, the intermediary of God's word. V. 1, הַדָּבָר אֲשֶׁר הָיָה אֶל יִרְמְיָהוּ מֵאֵת יְהוָה לֵאמֹר ("the word which came to Jeremiah from YHWH, saying"), is the typical introductory incipit of the prose sermons (7:1, 18:1, 21:1, 25:1, 30:1, 32:1, 34:1, 8, 35:1, 40:1). This should be differentiated from other incipits which anthropomorphize God. Here, the word is described as deriving "from YHWH" (מֵאֵת יְהוָה). See Sa-Moon Kang, "The Authentic Sermon of Jeremiah in Jeremiah 7:1-20," in *Texts, Temples, and Traditions: A Tribute to Menahem Haran* (eds. Michael Fox, et al; Winona Lake: Eisenbrauns, 1996), 150, who argues that the introductory phrase "avoids the anthropomorphic expression of the words of God," and thus should be dated to the late post-exilic period, in contrast to the expression, "the word of YHWH came to me, saying" (וַיְהִי דְבַר יְהוָה אֵלַי לֵאמֹר, 1:4, 11, 13, 2:1, 13:3, 8, 16:1, 18:5, 24:4, and וַיְהִי דְבַר יְהוָה אֶל יִרְמְיָהוּ ("the word of YHWH came to Jeremiah"), 28:12, 29:30, 32:26, 33:1, 19, 23, 34:12, 35:12, 36:27, 42:7, 43:8). Moreover, it sets up Jeremiah in the third person rather than first person. The tendency to place Jeremiah as the intermediary is also evident in the additions, v. 2b (וְדִבַּרְתָּם, "you will speak to them;" see LXX which reflects וְדִבַּרְתֶּם, "you (plural) will speak") and v. 3a (וְאָמַרְתָּ אֲלֵיהֶם, "you will say to them"). This is distinct from vv. 6a, 9a (וַיֹּאמֶר יְהוָה אֵלַי, "YHWH said to me") which refers to Jeremiah in the first person.

The second level (vv. 6-8) repeats the *Heilsgeschichte* of vv. 4-5 but with a different twist. Part of v. 6, שִׁמְעוּ אֶת־דִּבְרֵי הַבְּרִית הַזֹּאת וַעֲשִׂיתֶם אוֹתָם ("listen to the stipulations of this covenant and do them"), is a *Wiederaufnahme* of v. 4aβ, שִׁמְעוּ בְקוֹלִי עֲשִׂיתֶם אוֹתָם ("listen to my voice and do them;" see also v. 2a, 3b) to link vv. 7-8 (vv. 7-8b is omitted in G which may indicate that perhaps vv. 7-8 is the latest addition but this is uncertain) to the earlier sermon. What is significant in the *Wiederaufnahme* is the replacement of בְקוֹלִי with דִּבְרֵי הַבְּרִית הַזֹּאת ("stipulations of this covenant," vv. 2a, 3b, 6; also see Exod 34:28, Deut 28:69, 29:8, 2 Kgs 23:3 // 2 Chr 34:31, Jer 34:18). Rather than directly receiving the impera-

18-20; 12:1-4) and God's respective responses (vv. 21-23; 12:5-6). As a link, v. 17 connects the various units by picking up and perhaps thereby accentuating the agricultural themes and the key word, רעה ("evil"), that pervades in the larger context. V. 17 develops the agricultural imagery of a "verdant olive tree" (זית רענן) and "fruit" (פרי) in v. 16 with a word common, though not limited, to the prose sermons of the book of Jeremiah, namely נטע ("to plant").[55] It is the very word which appears in 12:2 where the lament accuses

---

tive from God, it is through the means of the written covenant. Even the command to obey God's voice (שמעו בקולי, "listen to my voice") has been transmitted as a warning in the past. Since they disobey the 'stipulations of the covenant,' their punishment is formulated as the results of the 'stipulations of the covenant.' For further discussion, see below in the body of the paper.

Unlike v. 4 which uses the expression, ביום הוציאי אותם ("on the day I brought them out;" with some variations, Exod 3:10, 11, 12, 6:4, 13, 26, 27, 7:4, 12:17, 42, 51, 13:9, 14, 16, 14:11, 16:6, 32, 18:1, 20:2, 29:46, Lev 19:36, 22:33, 23:43, 25:38, 42, 55, 26:13, 45, Num 15:41, 23:22, 24:8, Deut 4:20, 5:6, 6:12, 7:8, 12, 8:14, 9:26, 29, 13:6, 11, 16:1, Judg 2:12, 1 Sam 12:8, 1 Kgs 8:21, 53, 9:9, Jer 7:22, 31:32, 32:21, 34:13, Ezek 20:6, 9, 10, 2 Chr 7:22, 29:24, Dan 9:15) to describe Israel's past, v. 7 uses the phrase, להעלות מארץ מצרים ("to bring up from the land of Egypt;" Exod 3:17, 17:3, 32:1, 4, 7, 8, 23, 33:1, Lev 11:45, Num 20:5, 21:5, Deut 20:1, Josh 24:17, 32, Judg 2:1, 6:8, 13, 1 Sam 8:8, 10:18, 12:6, 2 Sam 7:6, 1 Kgs 12:28, 2 Kgs 17:7, 36, Jer 2:6, 16:14, 23:7, Hos 12:14, Amos 2:10, 3:1, Mic 6:4, Ps 81:11, Neh 9:18). Though both expressions seem to occur side by side with no significant difference, clearly the editor of vv. 6-8 was trying to provide his own formulation of the past.

However, it is not in this phrase but what occurs in the heart of the addition that sheds light on the editor of vv. 6-8. According to v. 7a, God had perpetually warned their fathers (העד העדתי באבותיכם...ועד היום הזה השכם והעד, "I had continually warned your fathers over and over again"). This continual warning/teaching (למד...השכם ולמד, "continuously teaching;" 32:33)/speaking (...דבר השכם ודבר, "continuously speaking;" 7:13, 25:3, 35:14) is a distinct characteristic of the 'decree' editor. The reason for the emphasis on the 'perpetual' warning of the people is to leave no room for the people to make excuses since their disobedience is innate to their stubborn nature ("each person goes according to the firmness of their evil heart," וילכו איש בשרירות לבם הרע; 3:17, 7:24, 9:13, 13:10, 16:12, 18:12, 23:17; a variation of this expression occurs in Deut 29:18 and Ps 81:13). These people are incapable of obeying God. The concept of an evil heart is somewhat similar to the notion developed in Gen 6:5 where "every inclination of the thoughts of his heart was only evil all the time" (מחשבת לבו רק רע כל־היום). Whereas Gen. 6:5 refers to the "inclination," here in the book of Jeremiah, the very heart is evil. It does not so much reflect on the "intent" (כבנה) to do evil, but the perpetual state of their mind; they are unable to do anything but evil since their heart is evil.

In the first level, the message is clear. The fathers as well as the people have failed to obey the words of the covenant with their idolatry, thus have broken the covenant (vv. 3a-5, 9-10). As a result, God will bring the punishment (v. 11). This description of the punishment will also be discussed in the body of the paper below.

55   1:10, 2:21, 12:2, 18:9, 24:6, 29:5, 28, 31:4, 28, 32:41, 42:10, 45:4. It is used in three kinds of contexts: reference to God who planted the Judahites in their land (2:12, 45:4), the circumstances where God will uproot what has been planted, and more frequently, words promising restoration. Yet in all the attestations, the word is never used to indicate punishment unless it specifically mentions either the plant changing or God altering his mind (2:21, 18:9, 45:4). The anomaly of v. 17 is that it invokes a positive image of God for a destructive means which

God of planting (נטעתם, "you planted them") the wicked so that "they take root" (שרשו) and "bear fruit" (עשו פרי). Other agricultural images appear that make the link more explicit: "tree with its sap" (עץ לחמו)[56] in 11:19 and "grass of the whole field" (עשב כל־השׂ־ה) in 12:4.[57] At the same time, v. 17 plays with the word for "misfortune/evil" (רעה), which is concentrated in the larger framework, 11:8, 11, 12, 14, 15, 23, and 12:4. Also the phrase, לבעל לקטר ("to burn incense to Ba'al"),[58] in v. 17 is attested in 11:13. As a result, v. 17 connects the poetic units with the prose by playing with the agricultural imagery and key thematic words.

With the establishment of the link, the sermon (vv. 1-14) in which the sins are catalogued provides the justification for Jeremiah's laments (11:18-20; 12:1-4) against those who contrive plots to destroy him (11:19) and who worship God superficially (12:2). These laments are a "confession" expressing the inner turmoil of the prophet and his troubles. It beseeches God to vindicate him (אליך גליתי את ריבי, "to you I have committed my lawsuit," 11:20; אתה יהוה ידעתני תראני ובחנת לבי אתך,[59] "But you, YHWH, know me;

---

lends support to its secondary nature; see Saul Olyan, "'To Uproot and to Pull Down, To Build and to Plant': Jer. 1:10 and its Earliest Interpreters," in *Hesed ve-Emet: Studies in Honor of Ernest S. Frerichs* (eds. Jodi Magness and Seymour Gitin; BJS 320; Atlanta: Scholars Press, 1998), 63-72, who argues that the original focus on Jeremiah, the prophet, as Yahweh's agent, the planter, in 1:10 has been modified to make God the subject of the various building and destructive aspects of the initial calling. Given the hypothesis of the present study, it may be the other way around in which God as the subject of the planting has been altered with the image of Jeremiah as the planter.

56   *BDB*, 537, reads the text as בלחמו ("in its freshness"). It is unclear exactly what לחם was meant to indicate but in the lament the tree and its 'bread' refers to Jeremiah, the prophet, and some aspect of him

57   One should note further similarities between the two poetic pieces. 11:15 refers to "vile designs" (מזמה) while the lament mentions "conniving thoughts" (מחשבות, 11:19) of the conspirators against Jeremiah.

58   לקטר ("to burn incense") is generally not an offensive practice but to whom or to what one does the burning that determines whether it is illegitimate or not. However, in Jeremiah, the piel conjugation of the verb has a connotation of illegitimacy even when it is not specific to idolatrous nature (11:12, 44:21, 23). Otherwise it is made to other gods (1:16, 19:4, 44:3, 5, 8), Ba'al (7:9, 32:29), the host of the heavens (19:13), delusion (18:15), and the Queen of Heaven (44:17, 18, 25). When the verb is used in the hiphil, it indicates legitimate cult. God promises a Davidic to reign in the house of Israel and levitical priests to present burnt offerings, make meal offering smoke, and perform sacrifices (33:18). The hiphil form occurs again with reference to Moab (48:35), who make smoke to their god. The reference to the cultic practice was not intended to condemn but to describe the end of Moabites' regular life. They transgressed with their reliance upon their wealth (48:7), strength (48:14), and pride (48:29); they do not reject YHWH.

59   The verse picks up on 11:20a where YHWH is called a "just judge who tests the inner thoughts and mind" (שפט צדק בחן כליות ולב). Whereas the "inner thoughts" (כליותיהם, 12:2) of the wicked are distant from God, the mind of Jeremiah has been tested (ובחנת לבי אתך, "you have tested my heart about you," 12:3).

you see me and you test my heart about you," 12:3) and to destroy his oppo-
nents (11:20, 12:3). With God's previous accusations against the disobedient
Judahites, Jeremiah is justified in complaining and requesting their annihilation. Otherwise, Jeremiah's 'confession' may appear too severe; now, with
their sins listed, his demand for their death is somewhat warranted.

While v. 17 serves as a pivotal link between the units, it provides a distinct
formulation of the sin-punishment pattern, namely the measure-for-measure
punishment.[60] V. 17, the linking verse, reflects the characteristics of the 'decree' editor. In line with the 'decree' editor, God *decrees* (עליך דבר רעה, "he
spoke evil against you," 16:10, 18:8,[61] 19:15, 26:13, 19, 40:2)[62] rather than
brings evil against them. Moreover, the punishment is measure-for-measure.
God decrees this disaster (רעה, "evil") "on account" (בגלל) of their evil

---

60   The MT of 11:14bβ, בעד רעתם ("on behalf of their evil"), may perhaps reflect a develop-
      ment toward measure-for-measure punishment. One expects בעת רעתם ("in the time of their
      evil") as many of the Hebrew versions, LXX, Targum, Syriac, and Vulgate have (see 11:12
      and also 2:27, 28, 11:12, 15:11). Though it may be a scribal mistake, it could also possibly be
      an intentional play on the measure-for-measure punishment. God commands Jeremiah "nei-
      ther to pray nor lift up a cry or a prayer on behalf of this people" אל־תתפלל בעד־העם
      הזה ואל־תשא בעדם רנה ותפלה) since God will not listen "on behalf of their evil" (בעד
      רעתם). See Prov 6:26 where בעד can be used to mean 'for the sake of, on account of.'
61   אשר דברתי עליו ("which I spoke against it") is omitted in 18:8 in G and Syriac. See next
      footnote for comments.
62   It appears that the 'decree' of God extends beyond a description of 'evil.' God 'decrees'
      "judgments" (משפטים, 1:16, 4:12), against established nations for destruction and restoration
      (18:7, 9), "word/s" (דברים/דבר, 10:1, 19:2, 25:13, 30:2, 4, 34:5, 36:4, 46:13, 50:1), "death by
      sword, famine, and pestilence" (27:13, 32:24), "fiery wrath" (36:7), 'to not enter Egypt'
      (42:19), 'against inhabitants of Babylon' (51:12), 'destruction' (51:62), and others, 4:28,
      7:22, 18:20, 28:7, 31:20, 32:42. A variant include "what the mouth of YHWH has spoken"
      (ואשר דבר פי יהוה, 9:11).
            One cannot necessarily attribute all of these passages to the hand of the 'decree' editor
      without a careful analysis of the larger context. However, it is clear that the act of 'decreeing'
      is central in all these attestations. As a matter of fact, people are to ask, "'What has the
      LORD answered?' or 'What has the LORD decreed?'" מה־ענה יהוה ומה־דבר יהוה, 23:35,
      37). Also note 40:3 where God does "as he decreed" (ויעש יהוה כאשר דבר). Interestingly,
      כאשר דבר is not in the LXX, perhaps reflecting an earlier Hebrew manuscript before the
      editorial insertions. The same phenomenon is present in 18:8 and a similar redactorial activ-
      ity perhaps in 23:17 where the MT has למנאצי דבר יהוה ("to those who despise me,
      YHWH spoke"), a piel verb, as opposed to LXX which reads as the nominal form — 'word
      of God.' See also 7:27, where the whole verse is omitted in LXX, and 19:5, where ולא
      דברתי ("I did not speak") is absent. Again, the emphasis is on the having decreed the word,
      not the process of speaking the word of God. God has decreed; therefore, the people must lis-
      ten. This should be differentiated from what the prophets, Jeremiah and false prophets, have
      spoken (1:7, 17, 20:9, 22:1, 23:16, 28, 25:2, 26:2, 7, 8, 15, 16, 29:23, 38:4, 20, 43:1, 2, 44:16;
      attestations in which both God speaks but through the agency of a prophet, 37:2).

(רעת בית ישראל ובית יהודה, "evil of the houses of Israel and Judah") so
that 'evil' (punishment) occurs as a result of the 'evil' (sin).[63]

The structure of the verse epitomizes the talion-measure of the punishment:

יהוה ... דבר עליך רעה
בגלל
רעת ... אשר עשו להם להכעסני

YHWH ... decreed *evil* against you
because of
evil ... which they committed against themselves to provoke me to anger

If one reverses the order to reflect the development of the sin-punishment
pattern, there is a boomerang-effect behind the structure of the verse:[64]

---

63 This is quite distinct from another formulation for the destruction of Jerusalem with בגלל
("on account of") in the book of Jeremiah. In 15:4, Manasseh is attributed with the devastation of the land: "I will make them a horror ... on account of King Manasseh ... for what he
did in Jerusalem" (ונתתים לזועה ...בגלל מנשה ... על אשר עׂשה בירושלם), as opposed to
11:17, where the people's 'evil' are the reason for the punishment. See 2 Kgs 21:11, which
attributes "these abominations" (התעבות האלה) to Manasseh, and 23:26, where the king
provokes God with "all the provocations" (כל הכעסים). For other attestations of בגלל, see
Gen 12:13, 30:27, 39:5, Deut 1:37, 15:10, 18:12, 1 Kgs 14:16, Mic 3:12. Of these occurrences, the last three are significant in that בגלל indicates the reasons for the destruction of
Samaria/Judah: Deut 18:12 recounts the abominations, many of which appear in the account
of Manasseh; 1 Kgs 14:16, the sins of Jeroboam; Mic 3:12, the corrupt rulers, priests, and
prophets.
64 Given the poetic character of some of the prose sermons, one could assume that v. 17 was
merely a clever literary creation for a rhetorical effect, not an editor's intentional formulation
of the destruction of Jerusalem. This is unlikely since the boomerang pattern is not only present here but appears to have been inserted into the prose sermon (vv. 1-14) as well. Rather
than simply describing the punishment as 'evil' which does not remotely resemble the people's sins, v. 8b describes the punishment in terms of the sin:
   Command
                                    שמעו את דברי הברית הזאת ועשיחם אותם (6b
   Disobedience
                                    ולא שמעו ... (8a
   Punishment
            ואביא עליהם את־כל־דברי הברית־הזאת אשר צויתי לעשות ולא עשו (8b

   Listen to *the terms of this covenant* and keep them (v. 6b).
   They did not listen .. (v. 8a).
   I brought upon them all *the terms of this covenant* which I commanded (them) to fol-
   low but they did not (v. 8b).

God

↗   ↘

Evil → Provoke   Decree → Evil

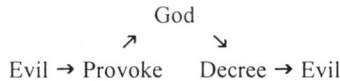

When the House of Judah and Israel 'commit evil,' this act inevitably affects God in that the deity is provoked to anger. As it has been argued above, in the הכעיס-theme, apostasy leads to the provocation of God, thus forming the outward thrust of the boomerang. Once the provocation reaches God, it motivates God to respond by decreeing the evil. Although, in a way, the people appear to be the agent of the 'thrust' since they provide the ammunition for their own destruction, nevertheless, the people do not shoot themselves; rather it is the provoked God who utilizes the ammunition, which the people had abundantly provided. After all, God is the one who decreed the evil, not the people. However, there is a hint of 'self-destruction' in 11:17 as there was in 7:19.[65]

Since the people have failed to obey the 'terms of the covenant,' (vv. 2a, 3b, 6), they have faced the consequences of these very terms (v. 8b). Here the 'boomerang' is more linguistic, rather than strictly contextual since the people suffer the curse inherent in the breach of the covenant, not the actual treaty, unlike 11:17, where the sin is the same as the punishment. What is interesting is the mood of the punishment. As opposed to v. 11 where God is "about to bring ... evil" (רעה ... מביא הנני), here the 'terms of the covenant' have been brought (ואב ואבי, "I brought," converted imperfect) against the people. This may be referring to a past event, perhaps the destruction of Samaria, but the accusation is directed to Judah (v. 6). No significant punishment seems to have resulted from the breach of the covenant in Judah except the fall of Jerusalem. This may then provide clues as to the date of the 'decree' editor who may have composed the addition in the post-exilic period in which the destruction of Jerusalem is constructed as a past event. It would be consistent with 11:7, where God "decreed" (דבר, piel perfect) the disaster against the people. Therefore, the simple formulation of the sin-punishment in v. 11 has been slightly modified in vv. 8b into a measure-for-measure punishment (sin=punishment) from which the new generations were expected to learn.

Various constructions of the boomerang-effect with רעה occurs throughout the book of Jeremiah in the poetic and prose sections: God will bring evil, that is "fruit of their schemes" (מחשבותם פרי, 6:19); he will "pour out their evil over them" (רעתם את עליהם שפכתי, 14:16); he will "repent" (נחמתי) of the evil if a nation turns away from its evil (18:8); he is "creating evil against you" (רעה עליכם יוצר) so that they turn evil (18:11); anyone who turns from evil, God will "repent" (נחמתי) the evil which he intended (26:3); he will bring evil which he spoke "on account that I spoke to them but they did not listen and I called them but they did not respond' (ענו ולא להם ואקרא שמעו ולא אליהם דברתי יען, omitted in LXX, 35:17); people will turn from their evil way (הרעה דרכו, "his evil way") if they hear that God intend to do evil (להם לעשות חשב אנכי אשר הרעה כל, "all the evil which I thought to do to them," 36:3). Others without רעה, i.e. he will visit (פקדתי, "I visited") upon them "their iniquity" (עונם את, omitted in LXX, 36:31). The same principle seems to work in the oracle against Babylon, 51:24, where God will requite (שלמתי, "I will pay back") Babylon and all the inhabitants of Chaldea for all their evil that they had committed in Zion before you.'

65   The 'self-destruction' also occurs in 2:19, 26:19, 44:7; without רעה, 4:18 where "your way and your deeds did these to you" (לך אלה עשו מעלליך דרכך).

Evidence for 'self-destruction' appears in the preposition-לְ with the third masculine plural pronominal suffix (לְהֶם) following עָשׂוּ ("they did"). It may have been a scribal mistake for אֱלֹהִים as the BHS note suggests since it would make more sense for the people to have done evil against God. However, the BHS emendation is without support from any of the ancient versions, therefore highly unlikely. As a result, the form in the MT (עָשׂוּ לְהֶם), the *lectio difi-cilior*, would appear to be the correct reading.[66] If that is the case, then one could read the לְ-preposition as either reflexive (*dativus commodi*) or denoting direction ('to act towards'). Since עָשׂה does not occur with the לְ-preposition as *dativus commodi*, which is frequently the case in the imperative of other verbs, it should be read as directional:[67] The people have done evil to themselves, not God. When they commit evil, this evil will only hurt them.

As distinctly developed in 11:17, the 'boomerang' plus a hint of 'self-destruction' lays out the manner in which the decree-editor tried to exonerate God from most of the responsibility in the execution of the punishment.

4.5. Jeremiah 25:1-14 (vv. 6, 7)

Chapter 25:1-14, a heavily edited pericope, lays out four different formulations of the punishment, two against Judah (vv. 8-11; v. 13) and the other two against Babylon (v. 12a ; v. 14). Whereas the earliest level (vv. 8-11) depicts God actively punishing as well as using human instruments, the other three formulations formulate the punishment according to the sin, thus reflecting a tendency to distance God from the destructive activities.

In the MT, chapter 25 concludes the first twenty-four chapters of poetic oracles, laments, and prose sermons and provides a transition to the miscellaneous oracles (chs. 26-36), biography of the prophet's life (chs. 37-45), the oracles against the nations (OAN; chs. 46-51), and the historical appendix (ch. 52).[68] Beside the series of editorial activity within the chapter, additional diffi-

---

66 Though it may be the correct reading, it does not necessarily follow that it was the original reading. Perhaps it is a later interpretive addition made to attribute the consequence of their action directly to the people.

67 The expression, עָשׂה רעה לְ- ("do evil to"), is attested in 1 Sam 6:9, 2 Kgs 8:12, Ezek 6:10, Ps 15:3, and Neh 6:2, all of which has the sense of 'acting towards (with hostile intent).'

68 Carroll, "Halfway Through a Dark Wood: Reflections on Jeremiah 25," in *Troubling Jeremiah* (eds. A.R. Pete Diamond, Kathleen O'Connor, and Louis Stulman; JSOTSup 260; Sheffield: Sheffield Academic Press, 1999), 74, describes the function of ch. 25 as the "Janus-like structure." See also Kathleen O'Connor, "Do Not Trim a Word," *CBQ* 52 (1989):617-630, and Hill, "The Construction of Time in Jeremiah 25 (MT)," in *Troubling Jeremiah*, 146-160.

Jeremiah, 146-160. An outline of the book of Jeremiah will help visualize the central position of ch. 25:

I. 1:1-1:18		Introduction - Call Narrative and Vision Reports
II. 2:1-4:4		Reasons for Judgment
    A. 2:1-3:5		Accusations
    B. 3:6-4:2		Call to Return
    C. 4:3-4		Closing Unit for 2:2-4:2
III. 4:5-10:25	Judgment Against Jerusalem and Israel
    A. 4:5-6:30		Foe and Lament Cycles
    B. 7:1-8:3		Temple Sermon and Additions
    C. 8:4-9:21		God and Lament Cycles
    D. 9:22-10:16	Yahweh, the Living God, as Opposed to Idols
    E. 10:17-24		Lament
    F. 10:25		Closing Verse
IV. 11:1-20:18 Jeremiah's Final Appeals and Rejection
    A. 11:1-12:17	First Confession and Other Material
    B. 13:1-15:21	Second Confession and Other Material
    C. 16:1 - 17:27	Third Confession and Other Material
    D. 18:1-20:18	Fourth Confession and Other Material
V. 21:1-24:10	Judgment Directed Against the Royal House and Prophets
    A. 21:1-23:8		Against the Royal House
    B. 21:9-40		Against the Prophets
    C. 24:1-10		Against the Royal House
VI. 25:1-38		Middle Chapter - Seventy Years under Babylon and Cup of Wrath
VII. 26:1-36:32 Royal and Religious Officials' Response
    A. 30:1-33:26	Words of Consolation
VIII. 37:1-45:5 Historical Retelling and Biographical Report
IX. 46:1-51:64 Oracles Against Nations
X. 52:1-34		Historical Conclusion

For another outline of the structure of the whole book, see T.R. Hobbs, "Some Remarks on the Composition and Structure of the Book of Jeremiah," *CBQ* 34 (1972):257-275. For partial outlines, see William Holladay, *The Architecture of Jeremiah 1-20* (Lewisburg: Bucknell University Press, 1976); Mark Smith, *The Laments of Jeremiah and Their Contexts: A Literary and Redactional Study of Jeremiah 11-20* (SBLMS 42; Atlanta: Scholars Press, 1990); Kathleen O'Connor, *The Confessions of Jeremiah: Their Interpretation and Role in Chapters 1-25* (SBLDS 94; Atlanta: Scholars Press, 1988); W.A.M. Beuken and H.W.M. van Grol, "Jeremiah 14,1-15,9: A Situation of Distress and Its Hermeneutics Unity and Diversity of Form — Dramatic Development," in *Le Livre de Jérémie: Le Prophete et son Milieu, les Oracles et leur Transmission* (ed. P.M. Bogaert; BETL 54; Leuven: Leuven University, 1981), 297-342; Martin Kessler and Else K. Holt, "The Potent Word of God: Remarks on the Composition of Jeremiah 37-44," in *Troubling Jeremiah*, 297-342; Martin Kessler, "Jeremiah Chapters 26-45 Reconsidered," *JNES* 27 (1968):81-88, and Kessler, "The Function of Chapters 25 and 50-51," in *Troubling Jeremiah*, 64-72.

culties arise from the differences between MT and G (the Greek).[69] First, G, which reflects the earlier version,[70] is shorter than the MT. It lacks all the explicit allusions to the name of the Babylonian king, Nebuchadnezzar, and attributes the 'decree' to God rather than to Jeremiah, the prophet.[71] Second, G inserts the OAN in ch. 25 (OAN in G: 25:14-20; chs. 26-32), whereas MT places them at the end of the book (chs. 46-51; 25:15-38). How do the editorial additions within MT and G and the differences between MT and G affect the various formulations of the punishment? On account of the complexity of the redaction of the pericope, an outline of the unit has been provided (italics = MT additions in relation to G[72]):

Incipit (v. 1)

1) הדבר אשר־היה על־ירמיהו על־כל־עם יהודה
בשנה הרבעית ליהויקים בן־יאשיהו מלך יהודה
היא השנה הראשנית לנבוכדראצר מלך בבל

Accusations (vv. 2-6a)

Decree (vv. 2-3)

2) אשר דבר ירמיהו *הנביא* על־כל־עם יהודה ואל כל־ישבי ירושלם לאמר

3) מן־שלש ועשרה שנה ליאשיהו בן־אמון מלך יהודה ועד היום הזה

---

69   The final redaction, as presented in the MT, was probably not done by a Dtr editor. As a matter of fact, the Hebrew behind the Greek has more affinity with the Dtr literature; see Louis Stulman, *The Prose Sermon of the Book of Jeremiah: A Redescription of the Correspondences with Deuteronomistic Literature in the Light of the Recent Text-Critical Research* (SBLDS 83; Atlanta: Scholars Press, 1986). Stulman argues further that the additions in the MT actually tend to sympathize more with the exiles in Babylon than those who remained in the land.

70   Tov, "The Literary History of the Book of Jeremiah," 211-237.

71   Though in both the LXX and MT, there is editorial activity to include the prophets (עבדיו הנבאים "his servants, the prophets" v. 4), MT tends to focus more attention on the figure of Jeremiah. In v. 2, the explicit mention of the subject, ירמיהו הנביא ("Jeremiah, the prophet"), which is absent in the Greek, makes Jeremiah the speaker of the oracle (vv. 3-14), aligning this verse with v. 1aα where the words comes to Jeremiah (הדבר אשר היה על [אל ירמיהו, with few Hebrew manuscripts], "the word which came to Jeremiah"). Without the incipit and addition of 'Jeremiah, the prophet' (v. 2), the speaker of the message could also possibly be identified with God. The tension is clearly laid out in v. 3. For 23 years, from (LXX has "in" [ἐν]) the 13th year of Josiah to this day, God has "persistently spoken to the people" (ודבר [or השכים with other Hebrew manuscripts] אדבר אליכם אשכים). However, the addition of היה דבר־יהוה אלי ("the word of YHWH came to me") in v. 3 again forefronts Jeremiah as the messenger of his words. A series of slight modifications in vv. 4-6 of the MT further emphasizes the role of Jeremiah by referring to God in the third person rather than first person. Jeremiah speaks about God; God does not speak for himself. Thus, in the MT, God sends "all his servants, the prophets" (כל עבדיו הנבאים) with the message for the people to dwell in the land which God had given them. Similarly, in v. 13, the addition of אשר־נבא ירמיהו על־כל־הגוים ("which Jeremiah prophesied against all the nations") makes Jeremiah the recipient of the 'word' which is prophesied against the nations.

72   The variations in some of the phraseology between MT and G will be noted in the body of the paper. The outline only italicizes the major omission in G.

זה שלש עשׂרים שנה היה דבר־יהוה אלי
ואדבר אליכם אשכים ודבר *ולא שמעתם*

Prophets (v. 4)

4) ושלח יהוה אליכם את־כל־עבדיו הנבאים השכם ושלח ולא שמעתם
ולא־הטיתם את־אזנכם לשמע

Core of Accusation (vv. 5-6a)

5) לאמר שׁובו־נא איש מדרכו הרעה ומרע מעלליכם
ושׁבו על־האדמה אשר נתן יהוה לכם ולאבוחיכם למן־עולם ועד־עולם

6) ואל־תלכו אחרי אלהים אחרים לעבדם ולהשתחות להם

Provocation (Core of Accusation)

ולא *תכעיסו* אותי במעשׂה ידיכם ולא ארע לכם

Provocation (Decree or Prophets)

7) ולא־שׁמעתם אלי *נאם־יהוה,*
למען *הכעסוני* במעשׂה ידיכם לרע לכם

Punishment Against Judah (vv. 8-11)

8) לכן כה אמר יהוה צבאות
יען אשר לא־שׁמעתם את־דברי

9) הנני שׁלח ולקחתי את־כל־משׁפחות צפון
נאם־יהוה ואל־נבוכדראצר מלך־בבל עבדי
והבאתים על־הארץ הזאת על־ישׁביה ועל כל־הגוים *האלה,* סביב
והחרמתים ושׂמתים לשׁמה ולשׁרקה ולחרבות עולם

10) והאבדתי מהם קול שׂשׂון וקול שׂמחה קול חתן וקול כלה
קול רחים ואור נר

11) והיתה כל־הארץ *הזאת לחרבה,* לשׁמה
ועבדו *הגוים האלה את־מלך בבל* שׁבעים שׁנה

Punishment Against Babylon (vv. 12-14)

12) והיה כמלאות שׁבעים שׁנה אפקד
על־מלך־בבל ועל־הגוי ההוא
נאם־יהוה את־עונם ועל־ארץ כשׂדים
ושׂמתי אתו לשׁממות עולם

13) והבאתי על־הארץ ההיא את־כל־דברי אשׁר־דברתי עליה
את כל־הכתוב בספר הזה *אשׁר־נבא ירמיהו על־כל־הגוים*

14) *כי* עבדו־בם גם־המה גוים רבים ומלכים גדולים
ושׁלמתי להם כפעלם וכמעשׂה ידיהם

1) The word that came to Jeremiah concerning all the people of Judah in the fourth year of Jehoiakim, son of Josiah, the king of Judah, *which was the first year of Nebuchadnezzar, the king of Babylon.*

2) What *Jeremiah, the prophet,* spoke concerning all the people of Judah and to all the inhabitants of Jerusalem, saying,

3) "For twenty-three years, from the thirteenth year of Josiah, son of Amon, the king of Judah, until this day, *the word of YHWH has been coming to me.* I have persistently spoken to you *but you did not listen.*

4) YHWH has been persistently sending all his servants, the prophets, to you but you did not listen and you did not turn you ears to listen,

5) saying, 'Turn, everyone of you, from his evil way and from the evil of your deeds. Dwell upon the land which YHWH had given to you and to your fathers for ever and ever.

6)   Do not go after other gods to serve them and to worship them. Do not <u>provoke</u> me with the work of your hands and I will not harm you.'"

7)   But you did not listen to me, *declares YHWH, <u>provoking me to anger</u> with the work of your hands to your evil.'*

8)   Therefore, thus says YHWH Almighty, "On account that you did not obey my word,

9)   I am about to send for and take all the families of the North, *declares YHWH, for Nebuchadnezzar, the king of Babylon, my servant,* and bring them against this land and all its inhabitatnts and all *these* surrounding nations. I will completely destroy them and make them an object of horror, hissing, and everlasting ruins.[73]

10)   I will banish from them, the sound of joy and gladness, the sound of bridegroom and bride, the sound of millstones, and a light of a lamp.

11)   All of *this* land will become *a ruin* and a desolation and *these nations* will serve *the king of Babylon* for seventy years.

12)   When the seventy years are fulfilled, I will visit *their iniquity upon the king of Babylon* and upon that nation *and upon the land of the Chaldeans, says YHWH.* I will make it desolate forever.

13)   I will bring upon that land all my words which I spoke against it, all that is written in this book *which Jeremiah prophesied concerning all the nations.*

14)   *For* they themselves will be enslaved by many nations and great kings; I will repay them according to their deed and according to the work of their hands.

Although it is quite difficult and sometimes impossible to distinguish the editorial modifications in the pericope (25:1-14), the unit appears to have undergone complex redactions prior to the final additions in the MT. For the purpose of this study, however, we will focus just on the editorial problems that would illuminate the sin-provocation-punishment pattern.

In the list of accusations (vv. 2-6a), three distinct levels are evident: the earliest core (vv. 5-6a), 'decree'-editor material (vv. 2-3), and prophetic-editor addition (v. 4). At the heart of the indictment, God implores the people to turn aside from their evil ways and not to commit idolatry (vv. 5-6a).[74] To this

---

73   MT has לחרבות ("ruin") in place of G Vorlage of לחרפה ("reproach").

74   The verses have expressions common in the book of Jeremiah: 1) variations on the command to turn away from their evil deeds (4:4, 18; 7:5; 17:10; 18:11; 21:12; 23:2, 22; 26:3, 32:19; 35:15; 36:3, 7; 44:22) and 2) not to follow other gods (2:5; 3:17; 7:9; 8:2; 9:13; 11:10; 13:10; 16:11, 12; 25:6; 35:15). Therefore it is not really clear whether the core accusation belonged primarily to the earliest level or one of the later redactors, i.e. the 'decree' and 'prophetic' editors. However, the presence of two formulations of the punishment, one in vv. 8-11 and another one hidden in v. 13, would seem to suggest that vv. 5-6 was the earliest core of the sermon. This separation is reflected in the pivotal verses with הכעיס (vv. 6b-7) where v. 6b continues and sets up vv. 5-6a for the punishment in vv. 8-11 while v. 7, linked to the prophet-editor, modifies the angle of the sin.

essential command, the 'decree'- editor adds vv. 2-3 to emphasize God's persistence in speaking directly to the people (ואדבר אליכם אשכים ודבר, "I
persistently spoke to you"), whereupon the 'prophetic'- editor then inserts v. 4
to attribute the message to the prophets (כל־עבדיו הנבאים, "all his servants,
the prophets"). Beside the differing aspects on the mediation of the divine
word, the core of the indictment is concerned mostly with the problem of
idolatry while the later additions stress the people's disobedience (שמעתם ולא,
"you did not listen," vv. 3, 4, and also 7). These accusations are then followed
by their successive formulations of the pivot-term, הכעיס, and the punishment.

Two attestations of הכעיס function as the pivot (vv. 6b-7) between the list
of accusations (vv. 2-6a) and the description of the punishment against Judah
(vv. 8-11). MT has what appears to be a doublet in vv. 6b-7 as opposed to G
which lacks v. 7b:[75]

6b)   ולא תכעיסו אותי במעשה ידיכם ולא ארע לכם
7)   ולא־שמעתם אלי נאם־יהוה למען הכעסוני במעשה ידיכם לרע לכם

  6b)   Do not provoke me with the works of your hands and I will not harm you.
    7)   But you did not listen to me, *declares YHWH, provoking me to anger with
        the work of your hands to your evil.*

Given the similar wording of the provocation, v. 7b in the MT may have been
a scribal mistake whereby the scribe duplicated the verse. However, significant
differences between the two verses actually prove otherwise. As positioned in
the MT, v. 6b resumes and completes the commands laid out in vv. 5-6a, the
core of the indictment: Turn from evil ways, dwell in the land, do not follow
other gods and do not provoke God to anger.[76] It is as if the sequence of verbs

---

75   According to J. Gerald Janzen, *Studies in the Text of Jeremiah* (HSM 6; Cambridge: Harvard
    University Press, 1973), 13, and BHS note, rather than Holladay, *Jeremiah*, 1:662. Holladay
    argues that ולא תכעיסו אותי במעשה ידיכם ולא ארע לכם ("do not provoke me with the
    work of your hands and I will not harm you," v. 6b) is absent in the G while v. 7b should be
    translated as "so that you do not offend me" (למען תכעסוני). The immense disparity be-
    tween his two suggestions emerges from the difference between a negative clause and a final
    resultative clause. Then he moves ולא־שמעתם אלי נאם־יהוה ("you did not listen to me,
    declares YHWH") to the end of the verse. The confusion as to which verse the G Vorlage
    may contain arise from the very similar phraseology of the two verses. Instead of moving
    clauses around, it would be better to just delete v. 7b in the MT and refine the meaning of the
    G.
76   If one heeds the suggested reading of the BHS notes and make it into ואל, the provocation of
    God becomes one more sin equal to following other gods: Do not follow other gods ... and do
    not provoke God. Unfortunately, there is no textual variant to support such a reading and
    therefore, should not be considered. Also, the Greek seems to reflect another reading. It has
    ὅπως μὴ παροργίζητε με which does not translate to ולא תכעיסו אותי but rather a pur-

leads to the final thought so if they keep these divine imperatives, they will not provoke God to anger. But if they fail to do so, they will provoke God to anger and thus receive their punishment.

However, in v. 7aβ-7bβ of the MT, נאם יהוה למען הכעסוני במעשה ידיכם לרע לכם ("declares YHWH, provoking me to anger with the work of your hands to your evil"), absent in G,[77] the provocation arises from their refusal to *obey* the divine command (לא שמעתם, "you did not listen" → provocation) not to follow other deities.[78] It presumes that the command had previously been relayed by God or his intermediary which would be consistent with either the 'decree' or 'prophetic' editor.[79] Therefore it would expand upon the emphases of either vv. 2-3 (decree-editor) or v. 4 (prophetic editor),[80] in which

---

      pose negative, probably representing the Hebrew Vorlage of G as למען לא תכעיסוני. This would be translated as 'Do not follow other gods ... in order that you do not provoke me.' Here, the people are discouraged from following other gods with the incentive of not provoking God, underlying perhaps a fear of punishment, whereas in the MT, provocation is the consequence of following other deities. If they follow other gods, then they will make God angry with jealousy. Whether it is originally intended to be resultative or purpose clause, the provocation is the final outcome.

77   Since the Ketiv is problematic, one should follow the Qere which reads, 'You did not listen to me, declares YHWH, offending me' (למען להכעסני). The Ketiv has למען הכעסוני whereas the Qere has למען הכעסני. The difference between the two forms lies in the conjugation of the verb הכעים. The Ketiv has a finite verb (third masculine plural with first person pronominal suffix) while the Qere has the infinitive construct with first person pronominal suffix. Since the person (third masculine plural) in the Ketiv does not agree with the second person masculine plural of the pericope, the Ketiv probably reflects a scribal mistake. If one follows the Ketiv, it would read: 'You did not obey me, declares YHWH, so that they offended me.' Their disobedience resulted in the provocation of God.

78   However, this distinction is not altogether evident since both forms of הכעים is followed by the expression, "work of their hands" (במעשה ידיכם). Even though it is the same expression, a different connotation seems to be indicated in the verses. V. 6a specifically refers to the act of following other deities. On the other hand, v. 7 refers to the disobedience to the command which includes idolatry as well as the wicked deeds (מעלליכם מדרכו הרעה ומרע, "from his evil way and from the evil of your deeds") of v. 5 since it refers to the people's failure to obey the whole message (vv. 5-6).

79   One could also attribute the addition to the Jeremiah-prophet redactor to emphasize the need to obey what has been mediated through Jeremiah. However, v. 7aβ-bβ (נאם יהוה למען הכעסוני במעשה ידיכם לרע לכם, "declares YHWH, provoking me to anger with the work of your hands to your evil") was probably added to the MT before this final Jeremiah-prophet redaction. Since it was so similar to v. 6b, G may have left it out when translating its Hebrew Vortext.

80   Another significant difference between v. 6b and v. 7 is to whom they attribute the source of the evil. In v. 6bβ, God declares that he will not harm the people (ולא ארע לכם, "I will not harm you") if they do not follow other gods whereas in v. 7bβ, the people will provoke God to their own evil (לרע לכם, "to your evil"). In limited examples, God is said to 'hurt' (hiphil of רעע) the people (25:29, 31:28). Based on this, it is difficult to ascertain whether ולא ארע לכם ("I will not harm you") is original or modified to fit a particular editor's formulation of the punishment. Since G seems to reflect and v. 7bβ actually has לרע לכם ("to your evil"), it

disobedience is the ultimate sin, not the act in of itself. In the final form, these two pivots then lead to the punishment as laid out in vv. 8-11. However, this elaboration of the punishment is probably linked to the core-indictment (vv. 5-6a) and provocation of v. 6b.

According to the description of the punishment (vv. 8-11), God with his temporal instrument, Nebuchadnezzar, sets out to punish Judah. God is at the center of the destructive activities: God fetches (הנני שלח ולקחתי, "I am about to send for and take") and brings (והבאתים, "I will bring them") the kingdoms from the north,[81] alluding to the opening vision in the call narrative (1:14); God destroys (והחרמתים, "I will completely destroy them")[82] and makes them (שמתים, "I will make them") into an object of desolation and public shame; and God banishes (והאבדתי, "I will banish") the sounds of everyday life.[83] Yet God does not act alone; he is depicted as manipulating the human instrument who is historically attributed with the actual destruction of Jerusalem, Nebuchadnezzar.

Nebuchadnezzar, the historical destroyer of Jerusalem, is an exalted leader who is simultaneously subordinated to the machinations of God in the MT.[84]

---

was probably original which then a later editor changed to make God the source of the punishment. As to why and when, that is unknown.

81   The G has a different reading, perhaps משפחה מצפון ("family from the north"). However, this is not the only instance where G has a different reading for משפחות ("families"), in reference to foreign nations, as compared to the MT. In 1:15, it is completely omitted while in 10:25, few Hebrew manuscripts, G (Marchalianus), Latin, and Targum appear to have ממלכות ("kingdoms"). משפחות ("families") may have been specific to the MT. Though the wording may be distinct, both the MT and G nonetheless are referring to a foreign nation(s). Given the plural third masculine suffix on the following verb (והבאתים, "I brought them [masculine plural]"), however, neither of the two noun forms seem to correspond to the gender, whether singular or plural.

82   It is an unusual verb of destruction against Judah in the book of Jeremiah. It is used primarily against Babylon to express utter annihilation (50:21, 26, 51:3). Perhaps the verb was later included when other nations were incorporated into the passage so that the complete destruction was intended for them rather than the Judahites.

83   It should be noted that 7:34 and 16:9 uses a different verb (hiphil of שבת, "to destroy") than the hiphil of אבד ("to banish"). The hiphil of אבד occurs in the book of Jeremiah as part of the words for destruction in the call narrative (1:10) and its various forms throughout the book (18:7, 31:28). It is also a word used against other nations (46:8, 49:38). Moreover, 25:10 lists more 'sounds.' Rather than just "the sound of joy and gladness, sound of bridegroom and bride", it includes the "sound of the millstone" (קול רחים, which G has ריח מור, "smell of myrrh") and "light of the lamp" (ואור נר). The tendency to fill out the list may perhaps hint at a later hand like v. 9b. See 33:11, where it includes קול אמרים הודו את יהוה צבאות ("voice of those who say, give thanks to YHWH Almighty").

84   In v. 1b, the cross-reference to the dating of the message as the first year of Nebuchadnezzar (היא השנה הראשנית לנבוכדראצר מלך בלל), "it was the first year of Nebuchadnezzar, the king of Babylon") is absent in the G. Since Nebuchadnezzar is now clearly identified with the evil from the north in the MT (according to Michael Fishbane, "Revelation and Tradition," *JBL* 99 [1980]:343-361, and also Holladay; this tendency is present in vv. 11, 12), the

God gathers all the families of the north under Nebuchadnezzar, the king of

---

synchronization of the Judahite king with Nebuchadnezzar becomes crucial. However, the correlation between the disaster and Babylonian onslaught had already been made in 20:4 without the explicit mention of Nebuchadnezzar and then in 21:2, with the actual naming of the king (the proper noun, נבוכדראצר, is absent in the G). Therefore v. 1b characterizes not the beginning but the trend toward identifying the enemy with the king of Babylon, and in particular to Nebuchadnezzar in the MT (this includes both spellings of Nebuchadnezzar [נבוכדנאצר and נבוכדראצר], 2 :2, 7, 22:25, 24:1, 25:9, 27:6, 8, 20, 28:3, 11, 14, 29:1, 3, 21, 32:1, 28, 34:1, 35:11, 37:1, 39 , 5, 11, 43:10, 44:30, 46:2, 13, 26, 49:28, 30, 50:17, 51:34, 52:4, 12, 28, 29, 30). Among these attestations, the name is omitted in LXX in the following passages, 21:2, 7, 22:25, 25:9, 27:8, 20, 28:3, 11, 14, 29:1, 3, 21, 32:28, 49:30, 50:17, 52:12, 28, 29, 30; though not the absolute rule, the name of Nebuchadnezzar appears in the LXX where the historical narrative occurs. As the book of Jeremiah's account of the history of Judah becomes more and more linked with the activities of Babylon, Babylon becomes a foreboding and ever-present presence. At the same time, the MT's insistence upon naming the actual king reflects a development toward attributing the destruction to a semi-independent human instrument.

The process of naming Nebuchadnezzar reflects the seed and perhaps the growth of the legendary status of this particular Babylonian ruler. A common noun, like the "king of Babylon" (מלך בבל; 20:4, 21:4, 10, 25:11, 12, 27:9, 11, 12, 13, 14, 17, 28:2, 4, 29:22, 32:2, 3, 4, 36, 34:2, 3, 7, 21, 36:29, 37:17, 19, 38:3, 23, 39:6, 40:5, 7, 9, 11, 41:2, 18, 42:11, 50:18, 43, 52:3, 10, 11, 15, 26, 27; these do not include occurrences that is in apposition with Nebuchadnezzar [see above]) or "Chaldeans" (כשדים; 21:4, 9, 22:25, 32:4, 5, 24, 25, 28, 29, 43, 33:5, 35:11, 37:5, 8, 9, 11, 13, 14, 10, 38:2, 18, 19, 23, 39:5, 8, 40:9, 10, 41:3, 18, 43:3, 52:8) does not imbue an entity with a personality capable of acting apart from the speaker whether it be the prophet or God. Thus, the generic titles, 'king of Babylon' and 'the Chaldeans' depict a mere puppet-instrument of God, without a will of its own. However, when the king is given a name, Nebuchadnezzar, he becomes a formidable character, an individual with a predilection to act independently. A clear example of this trend is evident in ch. 21:4-10, where Nebuchadnezzar replaces God in the account of Jerusalem's besiegement.

In 21:4-10, God initially appears to be the agent of destruction. God is the subject of the succession of verbs in vv. 4-7: He is about to turn the weapons of war (הנני מסב, "I am about to turn"); to gather them into the city (אספתי, "I will gather"); to fight against them (אני ונלחמתי, "I myself will fight"); to strike them (והכיתי, "I will strike"); and to hand over (נתן, "I will deliver") Zedekiah and company to Nebuchadnezzar (the explicit mention of Nebuchadnezzar, the king of Babylon, however, is present only in the MT). The Hebrew Vorlage of LXX appears to refer generically to only 'their enemies' (ביד איביהם, "into the hand of their enemies"), which is in apposition to 'those who seek their lives' (מבקשי נפשם; in the MT, the apposition is in parallel structure with two other clauses, 'in the hand of Nebuchadnezzar,' and 'in the hand of their enemies,' so that three 'predators' seem to be indicated). Beside the additional mention of Nebuchadnezzar, the MT provides a significant twist in the following string of verbs. Rather than attributing the agency to either the 'enemies' or God, the MT makes Nebuchadnezzar the merciless instrument of destruction. Instead of the 'enemies' striking the Judahites as the LXX reflects (και κατακόψουσιν αὐτούς), Nebuchadnezzar strikes them (הכם). Moreover, it is Nebuchadnezzar, not God (in the LXX, God is the subject of these three verbs), who fails to pity (לא יחוס, "he will not pity"), spare (לא יחמל, "he will not spare"), or have compassion (לא ירחם, "he will not have compassion") on Judah. Clearly, the MT editor of the modifications of 21:4-10 held Nebuchadnezzar more responsible for the utter decimation of Jerusalem. Thus, the depiction of Nebuchadnezzar in ch. 25 is quite distinct from the previous portrayal.

Babylon, his servant (עבדי, "my servant").[85] After gathering them to Nebuchadnezzar, God brings them against Judah and against "all these surrounding nations"(ועל כל־הגוים האלה סביב).[86] These nations are then to "serve" (ועבדו, v. 11b) the king of Babylon for seventy years.

Given the historical circumstances, it would make sense to elevate the Babylonian king in world politics. Yet it is unnecessary and quite unusual for a foreign ruler, especially, one who has earned his fame through the destruction of Jerusalem, to be designated the 'servant' of God (עבדי, "my servant"),[87] which is primarily reserved for the faithful Israel's servants of God.[88] Even Cyrus in the Bible is not called God's servant despite his favored status.[89] However, the title is more a means to subordinate rather than to elevate the ruler. Although the title is honorific for the people of God, it has the effect of taming the king to a mere puppet. He is the servant of God who moves and acts according to the will of God.[90] Therefore, despite the exalted portrayal of

---

85 This reading is different in the G, where God only takes 'a family from the north.'

86 Although both G and the MT includes other nations (v. 9) as recipients of the punishment, the verse probably originally referred to Judah and its inhabitants. The other nations were probably added with the expansion of vv. 15-38, where the cup of wrath passes from one nation to another.

87 See also 27:6 and 43:10, in all of which עבדי is absent in the LXX.

88 Many people are called God's servants but among them, select individuals are called 'my servant' (עבדי), Abraham (Gen 26:24), Caleb (Num 14:24), Moses (Num 12:7, 8, Josh 1:2, 7, 2 Kgs 21:8, Mal 3:22), David (2 Sam 3:18, 7:5, 8, 1 Kgs 11:13, 34, 36, 38, 14:8, 2 Kgs 19:34, 20:6, Isa 37:35, Jer 33:21, 22, 26, Ezek 34:23, 24, 37:24, 25, Ps 89:4, 21, 1 Chr 17:4, 7), Isaiah (Isa 20:3), Israel/Jacob (Isa 41:8, 9, 43:10, 44:1, 2, 21, 45:4, 49:3, Ezek 28:25, 37:25), Deutero-Isaiah's 'suffering servant' (Isa 42:1, 19, 52:13, 53:11), Zerubbabel (Hag 2:23), future Davidic king (Zech 3:8), and Job (Job 1:8, 2:3, 42:7, 8). Job is not an Israelite but notice how the expression appears only in the beginning and end of the book, which are secondary to the dialogues. Since the honorific title does not befit Nebuchadnezzar, Werner Lemke, "Nebuchadnezzar, My Servant," *CBQ* 28 (1966):45-50, argues that it is an "accidental error in the textual transmission of the book which bears the Prophet's name" (47). According to Lemke, Jer 27:6 provided the basis for a scribal error from לעבדו ("to serve him") to עבדי ("my servant"), which was then transferred to 25:9 and 43:10 (reflecting the positive view of the king in the book of Daniel). It is plausible but it does not account for its absence in other attestations of Nebuchadnezzar. More likely, the addition was intentional to accentuate Nebuchadnezzar's submissive role to God.

89 Isa 44:28, 45:1, Ezra 1:1, 2, 7, 8, 4:3, 5, Dan 1:21, 10:1, 2 Chr 36:22, 23. Cyrus is designated the LORD's shepherd (רעי, "my shepherd," Isa 44:28) and even "his anointed" (משיחו, 45:1) among other wonderful deeds attributed to him. On account of his part in the 'restoration' of the Judean cult, he would be more deserving of the titles and accolades. Yet Nebuchadnezzar does not receive similar laudable depictions in the book of Jeremiah (though he appears in a somewhat positive light in the book of Daniel). Therefore, the title, 'my servant,' is quite unusual.

90 He loses his autonomy and thus his power to act independently. Thus there is tension between the Nebuchadnezzar who usurps God's role as the agent of destruction which is evi-

Nebuchadnezzar in the formulation of the punishment, God is in control of the events. The people may have stirred him to action but he is without doubt the God who acts in history.

If vv. 8-11 is the early formulation of the punishment, do any of the later editors have their formulation of the punishment as well? As the accusation list has gone through some editorial work, the doom oracle also seems to have undergone some changes as well. The formulation of the punishment for the 'decree' editor (vv. 3b, 5-7) is not evident in vv. 8-11 but rather in v. 13,[91] where God brings (הבאתי, "I will bring")[92] against "that land" (הארץ ההיא) what he had decreed (כל דברי אשר דברתי, "all the words which I had spoken"). Though in the final form, the punishment is directed to Babylon, v. 13 was probably originally intended for Judah which a later editor responsible for the additions of the punishment against foreign nations (vv. 12, 14, 15-29) modified to indict Babylon. References to "land" (ארץ), in particular to "this land" (הארץ הזאת), allude to Judah[93] as outlined in v. 9 and v.11. The only other reference in which 'land' may be linked to Babylonia is evident in v. 12 where it refers to the "land of the Chaldeans" (ארץ כשדים).[94] Therefore "that land" (הארץ ההוא)[95] in v. 13 could possibly refer to the 'land of the Chaldeans' of v. 12 or the land of Judah. However, if 'land of the Chaldeans' was a later addition as confirmed by its absence in the G, then it could not have referred to the Chaldeans at all. Without the additions in the MT, the only reference to the enemy is "that nation" (הגוי ההוא, v. 12)[96] and 'that land' would have been unusual allusion to 'that nation.' As the BHS suggests, the phrase, הארץ ההיא ("that land"), probably was הארץ הזאת ("this land") which then would have referred to Judah. If the above reading is correct, the punishment may have been intended for Judah so that the boomerang pattern is established for the 'decree' editor:

---

dent in 21:4-10, and the Nebuchadnezzar, who is at the beck-and-call of God. Most likely, ch. 25 wanted to accentuate God as the primary agent of destruction in the judgment.

91 One could perhaps include v. 14 as part of the judgment formula of the 'decree'-editor. However, the wording of the punishment does not correspond to those of the 'decree' editor though reference to מעשה ידיהם ("work of their hands") would link v. 14 to vv. 6-7. Yet it is unclear as to whether the 'decree' editor is responsible for either attestations of הכעיס. As a result, v. 14 will be discussed separately above.

92 Following the Qere rather than the Ketiv (הבאיתי).

93 'This land' always refers to Judah; see 13:13, 14:15, 16:3, 6, 13, 22:12, 24:6, 8, 25:9, 11, 26:20, 32:15, 22, 41, 43, 36:29, 37:19, 42:10, 13.

94 24:5, 50:1, 8, 25, 45, 51:4, 54.

95 This phrase occurs one other time in the book of Jeremiah, 3:1, where it refers to a type of land where people remarry their spouses. Though it does refer to Judah, that expression does not necessarily allude to Judah.

96 This phrase could refer to any nation, 12:17 (Judah), 18:8 and 27:8 (any nation).

Accusation

היה דבר־יהוה אלי ואדבר אליכם אשכים דבר ולא שמעתם (v. 3a -3b)

Punishment

והבאיתי על־הארץ ההיא את־כל־דברי אשר־דברתי עליה (v. 13)

The *word* of YHWH came to me, I persistently *spoke* to you but you did not listen (v. 3a -3b).
I will bring upon that land all *my words* which *I spoke* against it (v. 13).

Since the people refuse to listen what God had persistently spoken to them (v. 3), God brings upon Judah the very words which he spoke (v. 13):[97]

Word - Disobedience (Sin) = Word (Punishment)

The people experience exactly according to what they had failed to do which is to obey God's word. Yet ultimately, it is God, the divine deliverer, who brings the consequences of their disobedience.[98]

Whereas the punishment for the decree-editor is evident in v. 13, no doom oracle seems to accompany the prophetic additions. Perhaps, though it is far from clear, the prophetic (or some other redactor) may have added v. 12 and v. 14[99] to include his interpretation of the punishment against the Chaldeans. Whoever is responsible for the additions, an effort is made to imitate the boomerang-punishment.

An examination of the insertion, v. 12aβ, demonstrates this tendency:

והיה כמלאות שבעים שנה אפקד על־מלך־בבל ועל־הגוי ההוא (12)
נאם־יהוה את־עונם ועל־ארץ כשדים ושמתי אתו לשממות עולם

When the seventy years are fulfilled, I will visit *their iniquity upon the king of Babylon* and upon that nation and *upon the land of the Chaldeans, says YHWH.* I will make it desolate forever.

---

97   The expression that is in apposition to the 'words,' כל הכתוב בספר הזה ("all that is written in this book"), would not help to determine whether v. 13 was originally intended for Judah or Babylon/enemy. The allusion to the 'book' could either allude to the 'oracles against Babylon' or those against Judah. For Judah, see 30:2, 36:2, 4, 8, 10, 11, 13, 18, 32, 45:1; for Babylon, see 51:60, 63.

98   When the brief oracle against the nations (vv. 15-29) was included, the doom-oracle against Judah was extended to include the Babylonians with the addition of v. 12 so that v. 13a was now seen as a punishment of the Babylonians. When v. 13a was moved to its current position, the MT made a further addition, אשר נבא ירמיהו על כל הגוים ('which Jeremiah prophesied against all the nations,' v. 13b) to establish an explicit relationship between the punishment and all the nations (vv. 14-29) while forefronting Jeremiah, the prophet.

99   This verse is absent in G. It may have been added to link to the following 'inebriation' of the nations.

Without the insertion, God punishes (אפקד על, "I will visit")[100] that nation, while with the addition, God visits their 'iniquity' (אפקוד ... את־עונם, "I will visit ... their iniquity):

Without v. 12a : God Punishes (אפקד על) Nation
With v. 12a : Sin (Implied עונם) → Punishment (God Visits עונם)

When the insertion is omitted, פקד denotes the punishment itself, whereas with the insertion, "their iniquity" (עונם) becomes the reason for and the very judgment itself. The very iniquity that may have caused the judgment is the punishment that will befall them. However, the Chaldeans' iniquity is never explicitly described in vv. 9-11; it is just assumed. After all, one cannot fault Nebuchadnezzar, God's servant, and his army for complying with God's commands. Therefore, v. 12aβ must have been added later first, to lay blame on the Babylonians for a misdeed, most likely their destruction of Jerusalem and second, to justify God's punishment of Babylon.[101] For this redactor, Babylon was not merely God's instrument; Nebuchadnezzar was his own agent responsible for the destruction of Jerusalem. Therefore, Nebuchadnezzar must be punished.

A similar construction of the punishment is also attested in v. 14:

כי עבדו־בם גם־המה גוים רבים ומלכים גדלים
ושלמתי להם כפעלם וכמעשה ידיהם

For they themselves will be enslaved by many nations and great kings; I will repay them according to their deed and according to the work of their hands.

---

100 The verbal root, פקד ("to visit"), is a common word for divine punishment in the book of Jeremiah, 5:9, 29, 6:6, 15, 9:8, 24, 11:22, 14:10, 15:3, 15, 21:14, 23:2, 34, 27:8, 29:32, 30:20, 32:5, 36:31, 44:13, 29, 46:25, 49:8, 19, 50:18, 31, 44, 51:25, 44, 47. Among them, 14:10 (ויפקד עליכם חטאחם, "he visited their sin" - lacking in G), 21:14 (ופקדתי עליכם כפרי מעלליכם נאם־יהוה, "I will visit you according to the fruit of your deeds, declares YHWH" - lacking in G), 23:2 (הנני פקד עליכם את רע מעלליכם, "I am about to visit you, the evil of your deeds"), and 36:31 ([omitted in G] פקדתי ... את עונם, "I will visit ... their iniquity"]) make explicit reference to their wrongdoing, patterned after the boomerang-effect. However, these wrongdoings are only assumed since these deeds are not fully described. This may have arisen on account of the secondary nature of most of these passages, except 23:2. This is distinct from the 'decree' editor who tends to use the very wording of the description of the sin to announce the punishment. There the boomerang-pattern is explicit whereas the פקד with reference to wrongdoing is a dim 'reflection' of the 'decree' editor.

101 Reference to 70 years appears in 29:10 where God promises to do good after that period of submission.

According to the first part of v. 14, 'many nations' and 'great kings,' perhaps referring to those listed in vv. 15-38, will enslave the 'unnamed' them (עבדו בם, גם־המה),[102] most likely the Chaldeans. This punishment is the means by which God requites (שלמתי, "I will repay")[103] them "according" (כ) to their misdeed and idolatry. Again, no mention has ever been made of Babylon's misdeeds in the previous section nor are they ever accused of idolatry.[104] Be that as it may, the redactor tries again to accord the recipient of the punishment the full responsibility for the punishment:

Sin (Implied — מעשׂה יד) (פעל + מעשׂה יד) → Punishment (מעשׂה יד + פעל — שׁלם)

The implied sin becomes the measuring rod for the 'amount' of punishment that God repays the Chaldeans. Though in both instances, the Chaldeans receive their due punishment, God is still the primary agent who measures the punishment against them.

In sum, within the four formulations, two distinct levels (vv. 9-11, v. 13) and two minor touch-ups (v. 12 and v. 14), there appears to be a movement towards conceptualizing the punishment more in terms of the people's sins. Like the tendency to formulate the sin-punishment pattern according to the boomerang-effect in later texts outside of the book of Jeremiah, the additions to the earlier description of the punishment seem to reflect this trend. In the earliest level (vv. 8-11), the people's sins provoke God to respond directly with the threat of foreign incursion which he orchestrates. Though the reaction is in response to the idolatry so that the people are held responsible, the punishment is not structured as a just recompense since it does not correspond at all to the sin. The later editors rectify this 'problem' by wording the punishment according to the misdeeds, even when the sins have not been described. First, the 'decree' editor formulates the punishment as the word (והבאיתי ... כל־דברי, "I will bring ... all my words," v. 13) which God had spoken against the people (v.3); second, the editor of the addition in v. 12, conceptualizes the punishment as visiting their iniquity (אפקוד ... את עונם , "I will visit their iniquity"); and third, the editor of v. 14 describes the punishment as 'recom-

---

102 עבד ב־ means to "work by means of another, use him as slave" (*BDB*, 713). See also Exod 1:14, Lev 25:39, 46, Jer 22:13, 34:9, 10.

103 Though this verb is used for requiting the Judahites (16:18, 32:18), it is primarily used against the Babylonians (50:29, 51:6, 24, 56). Look at 50:29 for similar wording, שלמו־לה כפעלה ככל אשׁר עשׂתה עשׂו־לה ("repay her according to her deeds; according to all that she did, do to her").

104 The phrase, מעשׂה ידיהם ("work of their hands"), may have been an effort to link this verse with the catalog of sins directed against Judah (vv. 6-7).

pense' (שלמתי, "I will repay"). However, God is not completely absent in any of these formulations; God is still the ultimate agent of the punishment.

4.6. Jeremiah 32:26-35 (vv. 29, 30, 32)

When we get to the second half of the book, there is a tendency to conglomerate several explanations for the destruction of Jerusalem within a pericope. Unfortunately determining the levels of redaction for the last two pericopes (32:26-35 and 44:1-14) has proven to be somewhat impossible. As a result, in the discussions of 32:26:35 and 44:1-14, I have tried to delineate the individual explanations more than elaborate upon the linear development of the various formulations of the sin-punishment.

In 32:26-35, two distinct descriptions of the punishment (vv. 28-29a and v. 31) are accompanied by several explanations (vv. 28-29a: v. 29b, v. 30a, v. 30b; v. 31: vv. 32-35). Though the explanations do not reveal any significant differences, the punishments reflect differing portrayals of the role of God in the destruction. While the first description of the punishment attributes the agency to God and his human instruments, the second lacks any reference to an executor. In fact, the people are the object of God's wrath, which functions neither as the agent nor the instrument. Although it is not evident within the wording of the punishments, the latter is probably chronologically later than the former based on parallel developments in other parts of the book and DtrH.

Before we analyze the pericope, the overall framework of the entire chapter needs to be outlined. The chapter opens with a brief historical background of Jeremiah's imprisonment for his unrelenting prophecies to king Zedekiah (vv. 3-5) during Nebuchadnezzar's siege of Jerusalem (vv. 1-2). The following section recounts the sign-act of restoration,[105] namely the purchase of the field in Anathoth (vv. 6-15). The perplexing act stirs Jeremiah to prayer (vv. 16-25), to which God responds by describing the people's sinful past that had led to the present predicament (vv. 26-35) and then expounds on their restoration and renewal of the covenant (vv. 36-44). It is in the context of narrating the past sins (vv. 26-35) that הכעים occurs three times:

Incipit (vv. 26-27)

26) ויהי דבר־יהוה אל־ירמיהו לאמר

---

105 Expression borrowed from Kelvin Friebel, *Jeremiah's and Ezekiel's Sign-Acts: Rhetorical Nonverbal Communication* (JSOTSup 283; Sheffield: Sheffield Academic Press, 1999). Friebel, 321, argues that Jeremiah's sign-act was the "metonymic expression for the resumption of normal economic, societal, familiar, and covenantal activities in the land."

(27) הנה אני יהוה אלהי כל־בשׂר הממני יפלא כל־דבר

Punishment A (vv. 28-29a)

(28) לכן כה אמר יהוה
הנני נתן את־העיר הזאת ביד הכשׂדים
וביד נבוכדראצר מלך־בבל ולכדה

(29) ובאו הכשׂדים הנלחמים על־העיר הזאת
הציתו את־העיר הזאת באשׁ ושׂרפוה

Accusation A1 (v. 29b)

את הבתים אשׁר קטרו על־גגותיהם לבעל

Provocation 1

והסכו נסכים לאלהים אחרים למען <u>הכעסני</u>

Accusation A2 (v. 30a)

(30) כי־היו בני־ישׂראל ובני יהודה אך עשׂים הרע בעיני מנעריהם

Accusation A3 (v. 30b) — Provocation 2

כי בני־ישׂראל אך <u>מכעסים</u> את במעשׂה ידיהם נאם־יהוה

Punishment B (v. 31)

(31) כי על־אפי ועל־חמתי היתה לי העיר הזאת
למן־היום אשׁר בנו אותה ועד היום הזה להסירה מעל פני

Accusation B (v. 32-36) — Provocation 3

(32) על כל־רעת בני־ישׂראל ובני יהודה אשׁר עשׂו <u>להכעסני</u>
המה מלכיהם שׂריהם כהניהם ונביאיהם אישׁ יהודה וישׁבי ירושׁלם

(33) ויפנו אלי ערף ולא פנים
ולמד אתם השׁכם ולמד אינם שׁמעים לקחת מוסר

(34) וישׂימו שׁקוציהם בבית אשׁר־נקרא־שׁמי עליו לטמאו

(35) ויבנו את־במות הבעל אשׁר בגיא בן־הנם
להעביר את־בניהם ואת־בנותיהם
למלך אשׁר לא־צויתים ולא עלחה על־לבי לעשׂות התועבה הזאת
למען החטי את־יהודה

26)   The word of YHWH came to Jeremiah, saying

27)   "Here, I am YHWH, God of all flesh. Is any deed too hard for me?"

28)   "Therefore," thus says YHWH, "I am about to give this city into the hand
       of the Chaldeans, into the hand of Nebuchadnezzar, the king of Babylon,
       and he will capture it.

29)   The Chaldeans, who are fighting against this city, will come and set this
       city on fire and they will burn it (as well as) the houses upon which they
       had burnt incense on their roofs to Ba'al and poured libation to other gods,
       provoking me to anger.

30)   For the children of Israel and the children of Judah have done nothing but
       evil in my eyes from their youth; for the children of Israel did nothing but
       provoke me to anger with the work of their hands," says YHWH.

31)   "For this city has been the object of my fiery wrath from the day they built
       it (i.e. the city) to this day so as to (be) removed from my presence,

32)   on account of all the evil of the children of Israel and the children of Judah
       which they committed to provoke me to anger, they, their kings, their offi-
       cers, their priests, their prophets, man of Judah, and the inhabitants of Je-
       rusalem.

33)   They turned their backs to me and not their faces; though I taught them
        persistently, they would not listen to take discipline.
34)   They set up their abominations in the house which is called by my name,
        defiling it.
35)   They built high places for Ba'al in the Valley of Hinnom to consign their
        sons, their daughters to Molech, which I did not command them nor did it
        enter my mind; doing this abomination in order to make Judah sin.

On account of the various explanations underlying the final composition, it is
quite difficult to first, find the structure of the sin-punishment and to second,
distinguish the sources/reflections on the destruction. Given the outline above,
the pericope appears to have two distinct descriptions of the punishment (vv.
28-29bαa and v. 31) which are then followed by their respective explanations.
Therefore two sin-punishment patterns are embedded within the unit. However, the first formulation of the punishment (vv. 28-29bα) is followed by a
series of explanations (vv. 29bβ, 30a, 30b) which do not appear to be related to
each other nor connected to any particular editor. These multiple explanations
are most probably a pastiche of 'sins' found in different parts of the book.[106]
At the same time, the second formulation of the punishment (v. 31) may perhaps be linked to the 'decree-editor' if v. 33, where God persistently teaches
the people (ולמד אתם השכם ולמד, "I taught them persistently"), is an integral explanation for the 'fiery wrath.'

Rather than begin with an explanation, the oracle opens with the description of the first punishment (v. 28). Since the city is already under siege (v. 2),
to a certain extent, the punishment is in progress. The dilemma, though, lies in
whether or not the city will be delivered into enemy hands. According to v. 28,
God will definitely deliver the city into the hands of the king of Babylon,
whom the MT further specifies as the Chaldeans and Nebuchadnezzar,[107] and
this human king "will conquer it" (ולכדה). Though Nebuchadnezzar is the
main instrument of conquest, his army, the attacking Chaldeans (v. 29a), are
the ones who "will come" (ובאו), "kindle the fire" (והציתו ... באש), and "burn
it" (ושרפוה), i.e. the city.[108]

---

106 It is unclear whether these explanations were compiled by one editor who is primarily re-
     sponsible for the final composition or were constantly modified by successive editors.
107 ביד הכשדים וביד נבוכדראצר, "in the hand of the Chaldeans and in the hand of
     Nebuchadnezzar," is absent in the G.
108 This description in which God delivers the city to either Nebuchadnezzar or the Chaldeans
     who then destroy the city is quite characteristic of historical prose (20:4, 5, 21:7, 10, 22:25,
     27:5, 6, 29:21, 32:3, 4, 24, 25, 28, 36, 43, 34:2, 3, 20, 21, 22, 37:17, 38:3, 18, 43:3, 46:26).
     This is distinct from 'summoning' (קרא) the enemy (1:15, 25:29 - 'sword'). What is unusual
     about the verse is how it attributes both active verbs, הצית ('to kindle') and שרף ('to burn'),
     to the Chaldeans whereas throughout the book, הצית is used primarily by God. All of the at-

After the description of the punishment (vv. 28-29a), a series of explanations for the destruction is outlined in vv. 29b-30.[109] These explanations probably reflect various levels of redaction, though it is not completely clear as to which level they should be attributed. Nevertheless they are all distinct.

In the first explanation (v. 29b), the punishment is explained as the result of the people's proclivity to idolatry which provoked God to anger. To integrate the explanation into the punishment (vv. 28-29a), v. 29b adds אֵת הבתים ("the houses") to the list of places burned. On initial reading of v. 29, the Chaldeans seem to burn down the city as well as the houses:

ובאו הכשדים הנלחמים על־העיר הזאת והציתו את־העיר הזאת באש
ושרפוה ואת הבתים אשר קטרו על־גגותיהם לבעל

> The Chaldeans, who are fighting against this city, will come and set this city on fire and they will burn it (as well as) the houses upon which they had burnt incense on their roofs to Ba'al and poured libation to other gods, provoking me to anger.

As underlined above, both the city and the houses are preceded by the definite direct object marker (את). However, on a closer reading, the object of the punishment is consistently "this city" (על־העיר הזאת, vv. 28-29a) which is delivered to Nebuchadnezzar and the Chaldeans who then come against (ובאו ... על־העיר הזאת ..., "they came ... against this city") and burn it (והציתו את־ העיר הזאת ... ושרפוה, "they set this city to fire and burned it"). Therefore, both verbs, הצית and שרף have 'this city' as the object, not "the houses" (את־הבתים) which the athnach, a major disjunctive accent mark, under ושרפוה ("they will burn it") would further support. The phrase, את־הבתים, is secondary, added to link v. 29a to v. 29b which elaborates on the reason for the punishment.

By connecting the punishment to the explanation in v. 29b, the Chaldean destruction of the city is constructed as the direct response to Baal worship and other idolatrous activities. If the two verbs הצית ("ignite") and שרף ("burn")

---

testations of יצת with fire imagery in the book of Jeremiah has God as the agent of the kindling, 11:16, 17:27, 21:14, 43:12 (LXX, Syriac, and Targum have third masculine singular, הצית), 49:27, 50:32; in the passive, 49:2, 51:30. On the other hand, the temporal instruments are usually attributed with 'burning' (שרף) the city in prose; see passages in which the king of Babylon/Chaldeans burns Jerusalem, 21:10, 34:2, 22, 39:8, 43:12, 13, 52:13. The failure to differentiate between the verbs may support the observation that vv. 26-35 is secondary to the extrapolation of the sign-act in vv. 36-44. Although the description of the punishment may be secondary, it is not completely a late redactor's creation; after all, the unit contains an eclectic collection of explanations for the destruction.

109 The series of explanations precede with a causal conjunction, either אשר (v. 29b) or כי (vv. 30a, 30b).

are constructed secondarily as governing the phrase, ‏ראה הבתים‏, then the Chaldeans burn down the *very* houses on which roofs the people commit idolatry. As a result, the location of idolatry becomes the object of the punishment:

Punishment (‏הצית‏ and ‏שרף‏ City and Houses, v. 29a) ←
Idolatry (‏קטר‏ and ‏הסיך‏ on Houses, v. 29b)

Though the punishment does not exactly correspond to the wording of the sin, the fire-image, whether of destruction (‏הצית‏, "to kindle fire," and ‏שרף‏, "to burn") or worship (‏קטר‏, "to burn incense"), seems to prevail.

Yet how does ‏הכעים‏ function? Here, in this explanation, the provocation stems from their idolatry, namely burning incense to Baal and pouring libation to other deities,[110] which triggered the punishment:

Punishment (vv. 28-29a) Because of Idolatry (v. 29bα) ← Provocation (v. 29bβ)

Thus in a reverse-pattern of sin-provocation-punishment, God destroys the places of idolatry through his human instruments.

In the second explanation (v. 30a), the punishment is attributed to the people's evil which they committed since their youth. However, here ‏הכעים‏ is altogether absent:

‏כי היו בני־ישראל ובני יהודה אך עשים הרע בעיני מנערתיהם‏

For the children of Israel and the children of Judah have done nothing but evil in my eyes from their youth.

It is not clear from the passage what the evil activities consisted of though one could perhaps connect the particular sins of v. 29b (i.e. worship of Baal and other deities) to the general statement of "committing evil in [God's] sight" (‏עשים הרע בעיני‏).[111] Whatever this evil may have been, it characterized

---

110 See 19:13b, which has similar in phraseology ("to all the houses where they burned incense on the roofs to all the starry hosts and poured out drink offerings to other gods," ‏לכל הבתים‏ ‏אשר קטרו על־גגותיהם לכל צבא השמים והסך נסכים לאלהים אחרים‏). Perhaps the editor of 32:28 coined or borrowed the description of the sin.

111 Though not limited to DtrH (Num 32:13, Isa 65:12, Mal 2:17), it is primarily attested in DtrH, in regards to kings (1 Sam 15:19, 1 Kgs 14:22, 15:26, 34, 16:25, 30, 22:53, 2 Kgs 3:2, 8:18, 13:2, 11, 14:24, 15:9, 18, 24, 28, 17:2, 21:2, 20, 23:32, 37, 24:9, 19, 2 Chr 21:6, 22:4, 33:2, 22, 36:5, 9, 12) and to the general population (Deut 4:25, Judg 6:1, 1 Sam 12:17). Here, the expression, atypical in the book of Jeremiah (see 7:30 and also 52:2, a chapter which was borrowed from the book of Kings [2 Kgs 24:18ff, in particular 24:19]; a byform of ‏רעה‏ + ‏עשה‏ also appears in 3:5 [‏ותעשי הרעות‏]), was a means to assess the general population, the Israelites and Judahites. This explanation seems to reflect on both destructions as similar

them "from their youth" (מנערתיהם)[112] so that they are unable to escape from their sins, and thus the punishment.

The third explanation (v. 30b) explains the punishment as the result of a provocation ensuing from idolatry. Interestingly, this verse is absent in G, which according to Janzen,[113] G had conflated with v. 30a. From his perspective, עשׂה הרע בעיני ("do evil in my eyes," v. 30a) and מכעסים ידיהם במעשׂה ("provoking to anger with the work of their hands," v. 30b) are similar enough to combine into one. However, the two expressions are quite distinct. While one focuses on the act of doing evil, the other is interested in the provocation of God. If one was to read the v. 30 as a whole, then v. 30b could be interpreted as a specification of v. 30a so that according to the MT, the act of doing evil is really provoking God with the works of their hands:

כי היו בני ישׂראל ובני יהודה אך עשׂים הרע בעיני
כי   בני ישׂראל[114]   אך מכעסים אתי במעשׂה ידיהם

> For the children of Israel and the children of Judah have done nothing but evil in my eyes from their youth; for the children of Israel did nothing but provoke me to anger with the work of their hands.

It is not just any evil that leads to the destruction but the evil of making God enraged with idolatry.[115] At the same time, though, there is no particular reason for reading the verse as one instead of two explanations for the Babylonian incursion. In fact, it may have been an insertion to first link the punishment to the sin with הכעיס and second to identify the sin with idolatry (מעשׂה ידיהם):

Punishment (Nebuchadnezzar, vv. 28-29a) Because of Sin (Idolatry, v. 30b) ←
Provocation (v. 30b)

---

manifestations of God's judgment. Both of them did evil so that both of them had been destroyed. Such development is also attested in the description of the Fall of Samaria (2 Kgs 17:7-23) which has been extended to model the sins listed against Manasseh.

112 The idea that the people sinned from their youth is present in the book of Jeremiah (3:24, 25, 22:21, 31:19).

113 Janzen, *Studies in the Text of Jeremiah*, 16; see also Holladay, *Jeremiah*, 2:205, who agrees with Janzen.

114 The reason why v. 30b does not include בני יהודה ("the children of Judah") may perhaps be due to the fact that בני ישׂראל ("the children of Israel") referred to both kingdoms. See Brettler, "Ideology, History and Theology," 268-282.

115 See 2 Kgs 21:15, where the Judahites 'commit evil in the eyes of God' and 'provoke God' from the day their fathers left Egypt until today. Given the similar wording and ideas, the hand that was responsible for this addition may also be involved in the redaction of the book of Jeremiah. Notice how the fathers leave Egypt rather than have God lead them out.

With the pivot expression, the punishment is more justified since their idola-trous activities have aroused God's anger. However, it is not God who directly reciprocates but his human instrument (vv. 28-29a). With this verse, the expla-nations for Nebuchadnezzar's invasion of Jerusalem end.

Beginning with v. 31, another formulation of the punishment and its ex-planation is outlined. Before discussing the structure and pattern of the sin-punishment, it is necessary to translate the difficult passage. Literally, the idiom is, "this city has been for me upon my fiery wrath"[116] (כי על־אפי על־ העיר הזאת חמתי דיתה לי), which has been translated in a similar fashion in the commentaries, without any explanation of its nuance.[117] However, *BDB* explains the function of על as "expressing (or implying) the direction of the mind," citing Isaiah 10:25: God's anger is "(directed) towards their destruc-tion," ואכי על־חבליתם.[118] Though the situations are just the opposite, where God's wrath is set toward destruction in Isa 10:25 while 'this city' is set to-

---

116 Holladay, *Jeremiah*, 2:219.
117 A similar expression occurs in Jer 52:3 (= 2 Kgs 24:20), which may aid in analyzing the passage:

כי על־אפי ועל־חמתי היתה לי העיר הזאת למן־היום אשר בנו אותה
ועד היום הזה להסירה מעל פני (32:31)

כי על־אף יהוה   היתה בירושלם ויהודה
עד־השליכו אותם מעל פניו (52:3)

For the wrath of YHWH was upon Jerusalem and Judah until he cast them from before his presence (52:3).

However, 52:3 does not have the awkward preposition with the first person pronominal suf-fix, לי ("to me"), and marks the recipient of the wrath with a preposition, ב־ (כי על־אף). ורה היתה בירושלם). Therefore, "the wrath of YHWH" (אף יהוה) is the subject of היתה: God's wrath was against Jerusalem. Despite the seeming similarities, though, a different con-struction appears to be at work in 32:31.

Also see 2 Kgs 24:3 where the MT has פי ('mouth, word') instead of אף in a similar construction, אך על־פי יהוה היתה ביהודה להסיר מעל פניו ("Surely, the mouth of YHWH was upon Judah, to remove from before his presence"). However, the Syriac, Tar-gum, and LXX has אף ("anger") for 'mouth'. The end-result of this verse is 'removal' whereas in 2 Kgs 24:20, God casts them from his presence (עד־השלכו אתם מעל פניו).

118 *BDB*, 757, section Cc. Also see Volz, *Jeremiah*, 304-5, who translates, "Diese Stadt ist mir, von dem Tag an, da man sie baute, bis auf diesen Tag, zum Zorn und Grimm gewesen, daß ich sie von meinem Angesicht verstoßen muß." On the other hand, *HALOT* (826, section 3) categorizes על under 'with regard to, concerning.' *HALOT* conjectures that it may imply 'reason for (anger)' with ל to strengthen the על. Some commentaries have translated this verse as if the subject was all the events that occurred in Jerusalem prior to and including Zedekiah. Thus, the fall and exile of Judah happened because of the anger of the LORD until he cast them aside. Tadmor and Cogan, *II Kings*, 315, and Gray, *I and II Kings*, 762, either translate in the plural as 'these things' or singular, 'this.'

ward divine wrath in Jer 32:31, the sense is similar. Both God's anger in Isa 10:25 and 'this city' in Jer 32:31 are directed "upon" (עַל) a particular goal. Thus, 'this city' is the subject of הָיְתָה and is set upon God's anger (punishment) from the beginning of their national identity.[119]

If the city is directed toward divine wrath, then no agent is implicated at all. The personified city itself is hurling toward its own destruction and causing its own removal. Neither God nor any human or natural instrument seems to be involved; the city was marching towards its doom from its inception. Yet what is the essence of the reason for this downward spiral?

In v. 32, an explanation is outlined for the punishment in v. 31. Instead of the causal conjunction (כִּי, "because") of the other explanations (vv. 30a, 30b), this verse opens with עַל ("on account of"). The punishment is attributed to "all the evil" (כָּל רָעַת) that the Israelites and the Judeans, the political (שָׂרֵיהֶם, "their officers," and מַלְכֵיהֶם, "their kings") and religious leaders (נְבִיאֵיהֶם, "their prophets," and כֹּהֲנֵיהֶם, "their priests")[120] and common people of Judah ([121]וְיֹשְׁבֵי יְרוּשָׁלִַם [122]אִישׁ יְהוּדָה, "men of Judah and the inhabitants of Jerusalem),[123] had committed to provoke God to anger. Then the following

---

119 Though this particular literary formulation is unparalleled, similar ideas are present in the book of Jeremiah. The people have either sinned or been warned from Israel's youth (3:25), from the day they came out from Egypt (7:25, 11:7), or from the period of Josiah's reign (25:3). Outside of the book of Jeremiah, the expression, מִן ... עַד הַיּוֹם הַזֶּה ("from ... until this day") in the context of sinning occurs in Judg 19:30 (cutting up of the concubine of the Levite), 2 Kgs 21:15 (Manasseh), and Ezra 9:7. In some ways, the verse resembles v. 30a, where the people do evil "from their youth" (מִנְּעֻרֹתֵיהֶם). However, the key difference between this verse and v. 30a as well as the previous examples is the angle of perception. Whereas v. 30a and other examples focus on the sin, v. 31 reflects on the consequence of the sin, the punishment. They were doomed from the beginning so that it warranted removal from God's presence (לַהֲסִירָהּ מֵעַל פָּנַי, "to remove her from my presence," perhaps the infinitive with -לְ present the immanent sense, usually about to happen, *IBHS* §36.2.g. The phrase, פְּנֵי לְהָסִיר מֵעַל, is used only in sermons explaining the downfall of both Israel (2 Kgs 17:18, 23) and Judah (2 Kgs 23:27, 24:3).

120 The list of people, kings, officers, priests, and prophets is attested in 2:26b. For a similar list but in construct with עַצְמוֹת ("bones"), see 8:1. Partial list is present in 13:13

121 It is attested in Josh 15:63, Ezek 11:15, 12:9, 15:6, Zech 12:5, 13:1, Zeph 1:4, 2 Chr 21:11, 22:1, 31:4, 34:32, and Neh 7:3. Also, see Jer 8:1, 13:13, and 42:18.

122 The expression, 'man of Judah' and 'inhabitants of Jerusalem,' comes up frequently in the book of Jeremiah. אִישׁ יְהוּדָה ("men of Judah") is common in DtrH to distinguish the tribe of Judah from Ephraim/Israel, Judg 15:10, 1 Sam 11:8, 2 Sam 19:17, 42, 43, 44, 20:2, 4, 24:9, and 2 Chr 13:15, 20:27. It is interesting to note that the Chronicler sometimes refers to Judah as Judah rather than man of Judah (see 2 Sam 24:9 // 1 Chr 21:5). Also, see Isa 5:7.

123 Jer 4:3, 4, 11:2, 9, 17:25, 18:11, 35:13, 36:32. For variations of the expression, see 11:12 (עָרֵי יְהוּדָה, "cities of Judah"), 19:3 (מַלְכֵי יְהוּדָה, "kings of Judah"), 25:2 (עַם יְהוּדָה, "people of Judah"), and just for Judah, 17:20, 35:17. The latter example occurs frequently in the book of Chronicles, 2 Chr 20:15, 18, 20, 21:13, 32:26, 33, 33:9, 34:32. The particular expression, אִישׁ יְהוּדָה וְיֹשְׁבֵי יְרוּשָׁלִַם only occurs in two other places outside of the book of

verses, vv. 33-35, seem to pile the list of 'evil,' most likely a pastiche of sins in
the prose sermons of the book of Jeremiah and DtrH.[124] On the one hand, the
people refuse to listen (v. 33) while on the other, they commit unspeakable
abominations (vv. 34-35).[125] Thus the overall structure of vv. 31-35 is as follows:

Punishment (Fiery Wrath, v. 31) ← Provocation (v. 32) ←
Sin (Evil-Catalog of Sins, vv. 33-35)

Nothing in the description of the punishment corresponds to the catalog of the
sins. Thus, the provocation caused by their lack of obedience and abominations is the reason for their doomed beginning.

In conclusion, the pericope presents two formulations of the punishment
with their successive explanations. First description of the punishment (vv. 28-
29a) attributes the execution of the destruction to God and his temporal instruments whereas the second one (v. 31) does not implicate anyone except the
people themselves. However, the explanations, though distinct, are ultimately
similar in pinpointing the blame on the people's idolatry and thus their provocation of God.

Jeremiah. It appears in Josiah's renewal of the covenant ceremony (2 Kgs 23:2 // 2 Chr
34:30) and Daniel's prayer (9:7). The attestation in the book of Daniel clearly draws upon the
language of Jeremiah since it says explicitly that Daniel was "pondering" (בִּין) the word of
Jeremiah (9:2). On the other hand, the relationship between the book of Kings and Jeremiah
is not so evident. Given the book of King's use of Jeremiah's expression, Josiah's account, in
particular the latest level of redaction, was probably influenced or dependent on the prophetic
book.

124 The various expressions are: 1) people "turned their backs to me rather than their faces" (פָּנִים
וַיִּפְנוּ אֵלַי עֹרֶף וְלֹא, 2:27, distinct from "to harden" [לְהַקְשׁוֹת] one's neck, 7:26, 17:23,
19:15; see also Deut 10:16, 31:27, 2 Kgs 17:14, Neh 9:16, 17, 29, 2 Chr 30:8, 36:13); 2) persistent action (see note); 3) not "taking correction" (לָקַחַת מוּסָר, 2:30, 5:3, 7:28, 17:23,
35:13; see also Zeph 3:7, Prov 1:3, 8:10, 24:32); 4) "to set their abominations" (לָשִׂים
שִׁקּוּצֵיהֶם, 7:30, without לָשִׂים, 4 1, 13:27, 16:18); 5) "house which is called by my name"
(בַּיִת אֲשֶׁר נִקְרָא שְׁמִי עָלָיו, 7:10, 11, 14, 30, 34:15; other things called by God's name,
14:9, 15:16, 25:29); 6) building of "high places of Ba'al" (בָּמוֹת הַבַּעַל, 19 5); 7) child sacrifice offered to "Molech" (מֹלֶךְ), which appears mainly in Leviticus (18:21; 20:2, 3, 4) and in
2 Kgs 23:10 (לְהַעֲבִיר בָּנִים וּבָנוֹת, "to consign sons and daughters" occurs only here while
לִשְׂרֹף ["to burn"] appears in 7:31, 19:5); 8) "I did not command them nor did it come up in
my mind" (לֹא צִוִּיתִים וְלֹא עָלְתָה עַל לִבִּי, 3:16, 7:31, 19:5). However, the expression,
הֶחֱטִי (Qere הֶחְטִיא, "cause to sin"), does not appear in the book of Jeremiah but is a distinct
DtrH phrase, 1 Kgs 14:16, 15:26, 30, 34, 16:2, 13, 19, 26, 21:22, 22:53, 2 Kgs 3:3, 10:29, 31,
13:2, 6, 11, 14:24, 15:9, 18, 24, 28, 17:21, 21:11, 16, 23:15.
125 In many ways, the catalog of sins resembles the accusations directed against the kingdom of
Israel (2 Kgs 17) and Manasseh (2 Kgs 21).

4.7. Jeremiah 44:1-14 [vv. 3, 8]

Like 32:28-35, 44:1-14 lays out several formulations of the sin-punishment pattern without clear indication of the chronological development. Yet all these formulations — boomerang (vv. 2-3), divine wrath (vv. 4-6), self-destruction (vv. 7-10), and God as the ultimate agent (vv. 11-14) — appear to be late since they explain events after the destruction of Jerusalem. In all but two of the explanations, הכעיס (v. 3 and v. 8) functions as the pivot.

Jeremiah 44:1-14,[126] a subunit of an appendix (43:4-44:30) concerning the Judahites in the land of Egypt, appears to be a pastiche of various formulations of the accusations and punishments attested in the book of Jeremiah. Though הכעיס occurs only in v. 3 and v. 8, the context of the passages, thus the overall structure, needs to be examined:

Incipit (v. 1)

1) הדבר אשר היה אל־ירמיהו אל כל־היהודים הישבים בארץ מצרים
היֹשבים במגדל ובתחפנחס ובנֹף ובארץ פתרוס לאמר

Past Punishment I - Judah (v. 2)

2) כה־אמר יהוה צבאות אלהי ישראל אתם ראיתם את כל־הרעה אשר
הבאתי על־ירושלם ועל כל־ערי יהודה
והנם חרבה היום הזה ואין בהם יושב

Past Accusation I - Judah (v. 3)

3) מפני רעתם אשר עשו

Provocation

<u>להכעסני</u> ללכת לקטר לעבד לאלהים אחרים
אשר לא ידעום המה אתם ואבתיכם

Past Accusation II - Judah (vv. 4-5)

4) ואשלח אליכם את־כל־עבדי הנביאים השכים ושלח לאמר
אל־נא תעשו את דבר־התעבה הזאת אשר שנאתי

5) ולא שמעו ולא־הטו את־אזנם לשוב מרעתם
לבלתי קטר לאלהים אחרים

Past Punishment II - Judah (v. 6)

6) ותתֹך חמתי ואפי ותבער בערי יהודה ובחצות ירושלם
ותהיינה לחרבה לשממה כיום הזה

Present Accusation - Judah (v. 7)

---

126 Though the subunit may have been a pastiche of formulations, רעה appears to be the thematic word which links them in the final form of the pericope. Within the subunit, the word appears ten times for references to both the sin and the punishment. The disaster, רעה (v. 2), came upon them because of the evil, רעה, they did (vv. 3, 7). Despite the warnings, they did not turn from their evil, רעה (v. 5), and they had even forgotten all the evils, רעת, of their predecessors and kin (v. 9 - 5 times). Therefore, God had set his face for disaster, רעה (v. 11). The impression one leaves from reading the unit is that the sins, רעה, of the people become the disaster, רעה, they must suffer. However, a careful analysis reveals distinct conceptualizations of the relationship between sin and punishment.

7) וְעַתָּה כֹּה־אָמַר יְהוָה אֱלֹהֵי צְבָאוֹת אֱלֹהֵי יִשְׂרָאֵל לָמָה אַתֶּם עֹשִׂים
רָעָה גְדוֹלָה אֶל־נַפְשֹׁתְכֶם לְהַכְרִית לָכֶם
אִישׁ־וְאִשָּׁה עוֹלֵל וְיוֹנֵק מִתּוֹךְ יְהוּדָה לְבִלְתִּי הוֹתִיר לָכֶם שְׁאֵרִית

Present Accusation - Egypt (vv. 8-9): Provocation

8) לְהַכְעִסֵנִי בְּמַעֲשֵׂי יְדֵיכֶם לְקַטֵּר לֵאלֹהִים אֲחֵרִים
בְּאֶרֶץ מִצְרַיִם אֲשֶׁר־אַתֶּם בָּאִים לָגוּר שָׁם לְמַעַן הַכְרִית לָכֶם
וּלְמַעַן הֱיוֹתְכֶם לִקְלָלָה וּלְחֶרְפָּה בְּכֹל גּוֹיֵי הָאָרֶץ

9) הַשְׁכַחְתֶּם אֶת־רָעוֹת אֲבוֹתֵיכֶם וְאֶת־רָעוֹת מַלְכֵי יְהוּדָה
וְאֵת רָעוֹת נָשָׁיו וְאֵת רָעֹתְכֶם
וְאֵת רָעֹת נְשֵׁיכֶם אֲשֶׁר עָשׂוּ בְּאֶרֶץ יְהוּדָה וּבְחֻצוֹת יְרוּשָׁלָ‍ִם

Present Accusation - Addition (v. 10)

10) לֹא דֻכְּאוּ עַד הַיּוֹם הַזֶּה וְלֹא יָרְאוּ וְלֹא־הָלְכוּ בְתוֹרָתִי וּבְחֻקֹּתַי
אֲשֶׁר־נָתַתִּי לִפְנֵיכֶם וְלִפְנֵי אֲבוֹתֵיכֶם

Present Punishment - Egypt (vv. 11-14)

11) לָכֵן כֹּה־אָמַר יְהוָה צְבָאוֹת אֱלֹהֵי יִשְׂרָאֵל
הִנְנִי שָׂם פָּנַי בָּכֶם לְרָעָה וּלְהַכְרִית אֶת־כָּל־יְהוּדָה

12) וְלָקַחְתִּי אֶת־שְׁאֵרִית יְהוּדָה אֲשֶׁר־שָׂמוּ פְנֵיהֶם לָבוֹא אֶרֶץ־מִצְרַיִם לָגוּר שָׁם
וְתַמּוּ כֹל בְּאֶרֶץ מִצְרַיִם יִפֹּלוּ בַּחֶרֶב בָּרָעָב יִתַּמּוּ מִקָּטֹן וְעַד־גָּדוֹל
בַּחֶרֶב וּבָרָעָב יָמֻתוּ וְהָיוּ לְאָלָה לְשַׁמָּה וְלִקְלָלָה וּלְחֶרְפָּה

13) וּפָקַדְתִּי עַל הַיּוֹשְׁבִים בְּאֶרֶץ מִצְרַיִם כַּאֲשֶׁר
פָּקַדְתִּי עַל־יְרוּשָׁלָ‍ִם בַּחֶרֶב בָּרָעָב וּבַדָּבֶר

14) וְלֹא יִהְיֶה פָּלִיט וְשָׂרִיד לִשְׁאֵרִית יְהוּדָה הַבָּאִים לָגוּר־שָׁם בְּאֶרֶץ מִצְרַיִם
וְלָשׁוּב אֶרֶץ יְהוּדָה אֲשֶׁר־הֵמָּה מְנַשְּׂאִים אֶת־נַפְשָׁם
לָשׁוּב לָשֶׁבֶת שָׁם כִּי לֹא־יָשׁוּבוּ כִּי אִם־פְּלֵטִים

1) The word that came to Jeremiah concerning all the Judahites who dwelt in the land of Egypt — in Migdol, Tahpanhes, Memphis, and the land of Patros, saying,

2) Thus says YHWH Almighty, God of Israel: You saw all the evil that I brought against Jerusalem, against all the cities of Judah. Today they are in ruins and no one dwells in them.

3) On account of their evil which they committed, <u>provoking me to anger </u>by going to burn incense and to serve other gods whom they, you and your fathers, did not know.

4) I have persistently send all my servants, the prophets, to you, saying, 'Do not do this detestable deed which I hate.'

5) But they did not listen or turn their ear, turning from their evil and not burning incense to other gods.

6) My fiery wrath was poured out and it burned the cities of Judah and the streets of Jerusalem. They became a waste, a desolation as they are today.

7) Now, thus says, YHWH, God of hosts, God of Israel: Why are you doing great evil to yourselves, cutting off for yourselves man and woman, infant and child, from the midst of Judah, not leaving for yourselves a remnant,

8) <u>provoking me</u> with the works of your hand, burning incense to other gods in the land of Egypt where you have come to dwell, cutting for yourselves and becoming an object of cursing and reproach among all the nations of the land?

9)   Have you forgotten the evil of your fathers, the evil of the kings of Judah, the evil of their wives,[127] your evil,[128] the evil of your wives[129] which they committed in the land of Judah and in the streets of Jerusalem?

10)   To this day, they are not humbled, nor have they feared, nor walked in my law and my statutes which I set before you and before your fathers.

11)   Therefore, thus says YHWH Almighty, God of Israel: I am about to set my face against you for evil, to cut off all of Judah.

12)   I will take the remnant of Judah who have set their face to enter the land of Egypt to dwell and all of them will be consumed in the land of Egypt. They will fall by the sword; they will be consumed by the famine. From the least to the greatest, they will die by the sword and by the famine. They will become an object of execration, horror, curse, and taunt.

13)   I will visit those who dwell in the land of Egypt as I visited Jerusalem with the sword, famine, and pestilence.

14)   There will be neither an escapee nor survivor among the remnant of Judah who have gone to dwell in the land of Egypt who will return to the land of Judah, where they long to return to dwell. They will to return except some fugitives.

Introduced as a message to the Judeans living in Migdol, Tahpanhes, Noph, and the land of Patros (v. 1), the pericope comprises of:

1) Two sin-punishment patterns against Judah:
   a)   The first is outlined in vv. 2-3 where the punishment precedes the accusation.
   b)   The second pattern is in vv. 4-6 which emphasizes the role of the prophets.
2) A complex list of accusations against the fugitives in Egypt (vv. 7-10), which is another formulation of the punishment.
3) A formulation of the punishment against the fugitives in Egypt (vv. 11-14).

Given the overall structure of the pericope, the past formulations of sin-punishment against Judah become the backdrop for the present accusation and warning against the newfound community in Egypt. Examples of Judah's demise function as a convincing witness to what could potentially occur to those settled in Egypt: Just as God destroyed Jerusalem, the site of his Temple,

---

127 This phrase is problematic since the MT has third masculine singular form when one should have a third masculine plural (perhaps attested in Syriac). Strangely the LXX seems to have 'your officers' (probably שׂריהם). Most likely, LXX has the original form which the MT revised to create the illusion of male-female pattern for the kings and the present individuals. Also, it may be a response to the prominence of women in vv. 15-30, who are the primary culprits in the worship of the Queen of Heavens, a goddess.

128 This is absent in LXX and Syriac versions.

129 This is absent in Syriac.

so will God punish the fugitives for similar sins. Despite the seeming coherence within the structure, there is lack of continuity between the sections within the pericope. In fact, the distinct sections appear to be a compilation of different formulations of the sin-punishment pattern. Therefore, some if not much editorial activitiy seems to have been at play but as to the exact nature of this process is beyond the scope of this study.[130] To clarify and distinguish the subunits, we will discuss them individually.

Since the geographical list of the address in v. 1 differs significantly from the context and content of the body of the pericope (vv. 2-14), it is most likely a later addition. The list of regions does not reflect the development of the story in the book of Jeremiah since, in the framework of the narrative, the Judahites in Egypt would have constituted an ad hoc group (43:4-7) running away from the Babylonians rather than a settled community in Egypt. However, the list of addressees in v. 1 includes Migdol (location in northern Egypt),[131] Tahpanhes (Daphnae), Noph (Memphis),[132] and the land of Pathros (Upper Egypt), which probably refers to the totality of settlements in the land of Egypt.[133] Thus v. 1 contextualizes a more widespread, settled community in Egypt rather than just a band of refugees running for their lives. As a consequence, v. 1 is most likely a late insertion to attribute the whole Egyptian community with the indictments in the book of Jeremiah.[134]

---

130 As with the analysis of ch. 32, the 'sermon' here is difficult to unravel. Though it is impossible to trace the exact development, the late editor(s) responsible for the 'sermons' in the historical prose section probably compiled the earlier sermons rather than have a succession of editors add to an 'original' sermon.

131 Holladay, *Jeremiah*, 2:303. See James Purvis, "Exile and Return: From the Babylonian Destruction to the Reconstruction of the Jewish State," in *Ancient Israel: From Abraham to the Roman Destruction of the Temple* (rev. and exp. ed.; Hershel Shanks; Washington D.C.: Biblical Archaeology Society, 1999), 213, who observes that Migdol was the "northeastern frontier" while Syene marked the southern border (see Ezek 29:10 and Isa 49:12).

132 Holladay, *Jeremiah*, 2:277, thinks it is an addition and omits with the Greek.

133 According to 43:8-13, Johanan ben Kareah led a band of Judahites to Tahpanhes, the background for the 'sermon' in 44:1-14. Therefore the list of locations would have referred to something other than the regions occupied by the refugees. After all, the complete list in 44:1 is not attested anywhere else; see 2:16 (Noph, Tahpanhes) and 46:14 (Migdol, Noph, Tahpanhes) where part of the list is present. It would appear that the list of locations represent the "catalogue of areas of Jewish residence" which "follows a line of defense systems established by the Egyptians, from the northeast border (Migdol) to Nubia (Pathros)" (Purvis, "Exile and Return," 214-215; see also Eliezer Oren, "Migdol: A New Fortress on the Edge of the Eastern Nile Delta," *BASOR* 256 [1984]:7-44). Although dated to a later period (495-399 B.C.E.), the Elephantine papyri may perhaps give a general idea of the life of Judahites in Egypt during the Babylonian period.

134 This incipit is similar to v. 15b where the address is widened to include those who dwell in the land of Patros (כל העם הישבים בארץ־מצרים בפתרוס, "all the people who dwell in the land of Egypt in Patros"). There appears to be an additional layer in the appendix (43:4-

Then the pericope introduces the first formulation of the destruction of Jerusalem, (vv. 2-3), in which the Judahites received their due punishment. Opening with a declaration of the divine origin of the message: "Thus says YHWH of Hosts, God of Israel" (כה אמר יהוה צבאות אלהי ישׂראל),[135] the oracle ensues with a theological assessment of the destruction of Jerusalem. The people have seen the 'evil' (אתם ראיתם את כל הרעה). The addressee is emphasized with the additional second person masculine plural independent pronoun (אתם ראיתם, "you, yourselves, have seen") to focus on the genera-tion that had witnessed the evil; they are the witnesses to the very fulfillment of God's judgment against the Judahites for their sins.

While the phrase, אתם ראיתם, focuses on the eyewitnesses of God's power, it simultaneously establishes the fall of Jerusalem as one of God's defining deeds. Beside the present passage, the exact expression, אתם ראיתם, occurs in three defining moments of Israel's past where God demonstrates his power: the exodus from Egypt (Exod 19:4, Deut 29:1), the theophany at Mt. Sinai (Exod 20:22), and the conquest of the promised land (Josh 23:3).[136] By placing the destruction of the Temple with these 'memorable' events, the au-thor/editor seems to define the destruction as a pivotal moment of God's inter-vention in Israel's history; yet not for their benefit but against them to punish

---

44:30) accompanying the incipit. Juxtaposed to the message against the "remnant of Judah who are about to enter the land of Egypt to dwell there" (יהודה אשר שמו פניהם לבוא ארץ מצרים לגור שם שארית; variations of phrase, 42:2, 15, 17, 19, 43:2, 5, 44:8, 12, 14, 28) is an address to 'those who are dwelling in the land of Egypt' (הישׁבים בארץ מצרים; variations of phrase, 44:1, 13, 15, 26)

135 7:3, 21, 9:14, 16:9, 19:3, 15, 25:27, 27:4, 21, 28:2, 14, 29:4, 8, 21, 25, 31, 32, 31:23, 32:14, 15, 35:13, 17, 18, 19, 38:17, 39:16, 42:15, 18, 43:10, 44:2, 11, 25, 48:1, 50:18, 51:33. With-out צבאות אלהי ישׂראל ("hosts, God of Israel"), 2:2, 5, 4:3, 27, 6:16, 21, 22, 8:4, 9:22, 10:2, 18, 11:11, 21, 12:14, 13:1, 9, 13, 14:10, 15, 15:2, 19, 16:3, 5, 17:5, 19, 21, 18:11, 13, 19:1, 20:4, 21:8, 12, 22:1, 3, 6, 11, 18, 30, 23:38, 24:8, 26:2, 4, 27:2, 16, 28:11, 13, 16, 29:10, 16, 30:5, 12, 18, 31:2, 7, 15, 16, 35, 37, 32:3, 28, 33:2, 10, 17, 25, 34:2, 4, 17, 36:29, 30, 37:9, 38:2, 3, 44:30, 45:4, 47:2, 48:40, 49:1, 12, 28, 51:1, 36; without אלהי ישׂראל ("God of Israel"), 6:6, 9, 9:6, 16, 11:22, 19:11, 23:15, 16, 25:8, 28, 32, 26:18, 27:19, 29:17, 33:12, 49:7, 35, 50:33, 51:58; without צבאות ("hosts"), 11:3, 12:12, 21:4, 23:2, 24:5, 25:15, 30:2, 32:36, 42, 33:4, 34:2, 13, 37:7, 42:9, 45:2; other variations, יהוה אלהי צבאות ("YHWH, God of hosts," 5:14), אדני יהוה ("Lord, YHWH," 7:20), אלהי ישׂראל יהוה אלהי צבאות ("YHWH, God of hosts, God of Israel," 44:7).

   There seems to be no set pattern whereby any one of these variations could appear in the prose and poetic sections. However, Alexander Rofé, "The Name YHWH SĔBĀ'ÔT and the Shorter Recension of Jeremiah," in *Prophetie und geschichtliche Wirklichkeit im alten Israel: Festschrift für Siegfried Herrmann* (eds. Rüdiger Liwak and Siegfried Wagner; Ber-lin: Verlag W. Kohlhammer, 1991), 307-316, 'surmises' that Jeremiah, the prophet, did not use צבאות. Moreover, he notes that there is a preponderance of צבאות ("hosts") in the prose sermons. His observations are not wrong but he himself notes that there are exceptions. Therefore, one cannot use the presence and/or absence of particular terms to date a saying.

136 The exact phraseology also occurs in Neh 2:17 in which Nehemiah tries to make the Judeans look at the ruins of Jerusalem to encourage them to build the walls of Jerusalem.

them for their wrongdoing. Therefore the people are without excuse for further disobedience since they have witnessed what God is capable of doing.

In terms of the locus of the activity, there is a clear distinction between the earlier 'founding' events and the destruction of Jerusalem. Whereas God brought the disaster (הבאתי אשר הרעה כל, "all the disaster which I brought," v. 2) in the book of Jeremiah,[137] God usually "did" (עשׂה) the saving deeds in the previous events, except the theophany where God decreed (דבר, Exod 20:22). The Israelites are called to remember what they have seen in terms of his deeds, 'what I/he did' (אשר עשׂיתי/עשׂה) to the Egyptians (Exod 19:4, Deut 29:1[138]) and "to all these nations before you" (לכל הגוים האלה מפניכם, Josh 23:3). However, in the book of Jeremiah, God only repays the disaster, which was created by the Judahites:

Punishment (v.2a)

כל הרעה אשר הבאתי ...

All the evil which I brought

Evil (v.3a) - Reason

מפני רעתם אשר עשׂו

on account of their evil which they committed,

---

137 In DtrH, the phrase, 'to bring evil' is usually curse formula against the 'founding' dynasties of Israel (for an exception, see 2 Sam 17:14 where God muddles Ahithophel's advice so that God could bring evil against Absalom), Jeroboam (1 Kgs 14:10) and Ahab (1 Kgs 21:21, 29), and the destruction of Jerusalem (1 Kgs 9:9 = 2 Chr 7:22; 2 Kgs 21:12, 22:16 = 2 Chr 34:24). Interestingly, the expression is not used in the explanation for the fall of Samaria (2 Kgs 17). The other reference occurs in Dan 9:12 which also describes the fall of Jerusalem as the "great disaster" (רעה גדלה). It goes on to elaborate that the disaster occurred "as it was written in the Teaching of Moses" (כאשר כתוב בחורת משׁה). It focuses on the תורה ("teaching") as the source of the punishment. One should further note the use of שׁקד ("YHWH had 'watched' the evil and brought it upon us," עלינו וישׁקד יהוה על הרעה ויביאה) since it echoes the first vision in Jer 1:11-12. This 'evil' that forebodes the cessation of a dynasty and a kingdom, is readily used in the book of Jeremiah to describe the punishment of Judah. The only exception is 49:37, which is set against Elam — on account of its formulaic nature. It was a primarily a literary creation for the purpose of completeness rather than an original 'oracle against nations'. Though the early poetic material seems to link the 'evil' to an invading army (4:6, 5:15), other references are not as clear (11:11, 19:3, 45:5). However, some strands of later traditions specify the 'evil' to divine wrath (חרון אף, "wrath," 49:37) or "fruit of their thoughts" (פרי מחשׁבותם, 6:19).

138 This passage is more elaborate, listing the individuals who were affected by God's deeds:

אתם ראיתם את כל־אשר עשׂה יהוה לעיניכם

בארץ מצרים לפרעה ולכל־עבדיו ולכל־ארצו

You have seen all that YHWH did before your eyes in the land of Egypt to Pharaoh, to all his servants, and to all his land.

Provocation (v.3a)

להכעיסני

underline: provoking me to anger

Specific Description of Evil (v.3a -b)

ללכת לקטר לעבד לאלהים אחרים

by going to burn incense and to serve other gods.

The 'evil' ("the evil," הרעה) that God had brought upon Jerusalem results as a consequence of the 'evil' ('their evil', רעתם) which they had committed.[139] Though the preposition, מפני ("on account") is the causal conjunction linking the punishment to the sin, the provocation is the motivation for the punishment. In other words, without the expression, להכעסני, the consequence of the 'evil'-sin is not clarified; however, with להכעסני, especially with the first person pronominal object suffix, God is clearly the one who is provoked by the 'evil' activities. Since God is provoked, God responds accordingly by bringing the same measure of 'evil' against the people responsible for the 'evil.'[140]

---

139 To understand the formulation better, it is critical to analyze 6:19. The poetic unit (6:16-21) containing a similar formulation (v. 19) is most likely a product of the prophetic tradition consistent with the prophet-additions in the prose material. Carroll, *Jeremiah*, 200-201, and Thiel, *Die deuteronomistische Redaktion*, 1:99-100, consider the unit to be a mosaic of Dtr elements. On the one hand, it emphasizes the role of the prophets in warning the people. The substantivized qal participle of צפה ("to watch," 6:17a) translated as 'watchman' can be a metaphor for a prophet (see Hos 9:8, Ezek 3:17, 33:2, 6, 7, Isa 56:10). On the other hand, it attributes the evil to the people's failure to obey God's word and rejection of his Teaching (v. 19). For this prophet-editor, the 'evil' is interpreted as the 'fruit of their thoughts' (LXX and Targum seem to reflect the Hebrew, משובתם ["their apostasy"]; משובות is a common word in the book of Jeremiah [2:19, 3:22, 5:6, 8:5, 14:7] and may be a variant reading):

    'Evil'-Punishment = 'Fruit of their Thoughts'

    הנה אכני מביא רעה אל־העם־הזה פרי מחשבות

    I am about to bring evil to these people, the fruit of their thoughts.

The sin is syntactically in apposition to the punishment so that they are one and the same. This differs from Jer 44:3 in that the 'evil'-punishment results *on account of* the people's evil (מפני רעתם, "on account of their evil"). The subtle difference is significant, in that 6:19aβ attributes the punishment more directly to the people's sin. The punishment (רעה) is unequivocably the sin (מחשבותם) while in 44:2-3, the 'evil' is explained as the *reason* for the punishment, not the punishment itself. Yet in both instances, it is God who brings the punishment.

140 This reverse-pattern and its very formulation resembles 11:17 where God speaks evil on account of the evil (... דבר עליך רעה בגל רעת, "he spoke evil against you because of the evil ... ") of the people. Here, their 'evil' seems to consist of provoking God (להכעסני) with the worship of other deities. It is a simple measure-for-measure punishment where הכעיס

Therefore, vv. 2-3 appears to be consistent with the boomerang explanation of the destruction in the book of Jeremiah.

With the addition of vv 4-6,[141] the 'evil' consisting of idolatry in v. 3 is formulated as the failure to obey the prophets' message concerning idolatry. V. 3 outlines the 'evil' as worshipping other deities: "going to burn" (ללכת לקטר) and "to serve" (לעבד)[142] other gods (לאלהים אחרים),[143] whom neither they nor their fathers knew.[144] Whereas idolatry is the reason for the provocation in v. 3, vv. 4-5 focuses on the disobedience of the command which the servants, the prophets (כל עבדי הנביאים, "all my servants, the prophets") mediate to the people. God had continuously sent the prophets (השכם ושלח ... ואשלח, "I persistently sent") with the message for them "not to do the matter of this abomination which [God] hates" (אל־נא תעשו את דבר־התעבה הזאת אשר שנאתי). In the immediate context, the 'abomination' appears to refer to the 'worship of other deities,' as it is elaborated in v. 5 (לבלתי קטר לאלהים אחרים, "not to burn incense to other gods").[145] However the crux of

---

141 It is unclear whether v. 6 was originally intended to be the punishment formulation of vv. 4-5 since there is no distinctive vocabulary which would link the verse to the prophet-editor. Nonetheless, it will be discussed as one addition.

functions as the pivot. Moreover, God is the agent, who just tips the scales of evil against the people.

142 לעבד is not in the Greek.

143 Other Dtr verbs of idolatrous worship that is not included in the list is השתחרה ("to worship"), Deut 4:19, 8:9, 19, 11:16, 17:3, 29:25, 30:17, Josh 23:7, 16, Judg 2:12, 17, 19, 1 Kgs 9:6, 9, 11:33, 16:31, 22:54, 2 Kgs 17:16, 35, 36, 21:3, 21, and ירא ("to revere"), 2 Kgs 17:7, 35, 37, 38, which does not appear in relation to worship of foreign deities in the book of Jeremiah. In the book of Jeremiah, השתחרה with foreign deities occurs in 1:16, 8:2, 13:10, 16:11, 22:9, 25:6; also in Exod 20:5, 23:24, 34:14, Num 25:2, Isa 2:8, Mic 5:12, Ps 81:10, etc. A verb that does occur in the book of Jeremiah but not in Dtr is אהב ("to love," 8:2). This particular verb, expressing covenantal love, is used mainly with Israel's relationship with God, William Moran, "The Ancient Near Eastern Background of the Love of God in Deuteronomy," 77-87. It is never used in relation to foreign deities which further demonstrates how the book of Jeremiah overturns popular expressions and concepts.

144 The MT seems to have a difficult reading which LXX rectifies by providing just the second person masculine plural of ידע ("to know"). The MT may have tried to incorporate both the third masculine plural (ידעום המה, "they knew them") and second person plural (אתם ואבתיכם, "you and your fathers") to reconcile the shift in persons from second person plural in v. 2 to third person in v. 3. Rather than resolve the 'tension,' it further accentuates the discrepancy. See 9:15 and 19:4, where 'they and their fathers' (המה אבותיהם/אבותם) did not know other gods. Also present in Deut 13:7, 28:36, 64.

145 The phrase, דבר תועבה ("matter of abomination"), is nowhere attested in the Hebrew Bible. The word, תועבה ("abomination"), could refer to a wide spectrum of activities that violate the boundaries which separates the Israelites from the other nations, whether they are issues of cultic purity, idolatry, or foreign practices. In the book of Jeremiah itself, the word is also associated with a variety of sins from ethical misconduct (6:15=8:12, 7:10) to idolatry (7:10, 44:22) and sacrifice of children (32:35). Similarly, references to God's hate (שנאתי, "I hate") alludes to a variety of sins in the Bible: abominations of foreign nations (Deut 12:31), sacred

the sin is not idolatry, but the act of disobedience, that is not "listening" (שמע)
and "turning the ear" (להטות אזן).[146]

In v. 6, the punishment for the accusation in vv. 4-5 is described as the
outpouring of God's fiery wrath. Similar to 7:20, this "fiery wrath" (ואפי
חמתי) is the molten liquid which is poured out and ends up burning the cities
of Judah and streets of Jerusalem (7:17; 44:6). However, the fuel for this wrath
is not extrapolated in 44:6 whereas 7:18-19 explains the provocation as the
trigger for the wrath.[147] Nevertheless, the wrath is the punishment and the
means by which the punishment is relayed. In some ways, v. 6 is the fulfillment of the prophesy in 7:16-20. What had been predicted in 7:20 (נתכת הנה
..., "about to be poured out," immediate future) is now completed in 44:6
(ותתך, "poured out," converted imperfect).

After the elaborations on the destruction of Jerusalem, the pericope then
shifts to the present audience of fugitives in Egypt (vv. 7-14). In the overall
structure of the pericope (vv. 1-14), vv. 7-10 function as the accusation against
the fugitives. Though it is far from clear, vv. 7-10 does not appear to be a continuation of either of the sin-punishment formulations in vv. 2-3 or vv. 4-6. In
fact, the repetitive accusation-section does not just list the sins but asks a series
of rhetorical questions, indicting the people of their wrongdoings, with the
exception of v. 10 which appears to be an distinct addition.[148] While the rhe-

---

posts and stone pillars (Deut 16:22), new moons and appointed festivals (Isa 1:14), Gilgal
(Hos 9:15), holidays (Amos 5:21), fortresses (Amos 6:8), evil and perjury (Zech 8:17), Esau
(Mal 1:13), divorce (Mal 2:16), evil-doers (Ps 5:6), and seven abominations (Prov 6:16).
Once, it refers to God's hate for the people (12:8). Here, the focus is not so much on the
'abomination' but the people's refusal to obey the prophets (ולא שמעו ולא הטו את אזנם,
"they did not listen nor turn their ear").

146 Both expressions are echoed throughout the book of Jeremiah and are not particular to the
prophetic tradition. The double expression for lack of obedience is present in non-prophetic
layer of the text (7:24, 11:8, 17:23, 25:3, 34:14) as well as the prophetic additions (7:26,
25:4, 35:15). Variations on not obeying the prophets also occur in 26:5 and 29:19 (לא
שמעתם, "you did not obey") so that all the occurrences of 'my servants, the prophets' are accompanied by the people's failure to obey. See also 2 Kgs 17:13, prophetic additions, where
the people "did not listen and hardened their necks like the necks of their fathers" (ולא
שמעו ויקשו את ערפם כערף אבותם) and 2 Chr 36:15 which substitutes מלאכים ("mes-
sengers") for נבאים ("prophets"). In 2 Chr 36:16, the people "make jest" (מלעבים) and "de-
spise" (בוזים) them. The only exceptions to the pattern are 2 Kgs 9:7, Ezek 38:17, and Zech
1:6, where expression, 'my servants, the prophets' is mentioned without reference to the disobedience. Outside of the book of Jeremiah, the expression, 'to turn the ear,' appears in 2
Kgs 19:16, Isa 37:17, 55:3, Pss 17:6, 31:3, 45:11, 49:5, 71:2, 78:1, 86:1, 88:3, 102:3, 116:2,
Prov 4:20, 5:1, 13, 22:17, Dan 9:18.

147 This difference may not exist if v. 6 is a continuation of vv. 2-3 rather than vv. 4-5. However,
vv. 2-3 provide a tight formulation of the boomerang pattern that v. 6 would seem secondary.

148 With its emphasis on "my teaching and my statutes" (בתורתי ובחקתי) and other odd expressions, v. 10 does not fit the general focus on evil in vv. 7-9. According to v. 10, the people
are "not crushed" (לא דכאו) and do "not revere" (לא יראו, v. 10). First, דכא is an unusual

torical questions catalog the accusations, they also provide a different formulation of the punishment whereby the people are held responsible for their own
harm.

Before a discussion on the content of the accusation, it is essential to analyze the syntactical relationship between v. 7 and v. 8. Given the syntax of vv.
7-8, the two verses constitute one main clause with a series of subordinate
clauses:

Main Clause (v. 7a)

7aα) למה אתם עשים רעה גדולה אל־נפשיכם

   Subordinate Clause (1a)

7aβ) *להכרית* לכם איש ואשה עולל ויונק מתוך יהודה

   Subordinate Clause (1b-apposition to 1a)

7b) לבלתי הותיר לכם שארית

   Subordinate Clause (2)

8a) *להכעסני* במעשי ידיכם

      Sub-subordinate Clause

לקטר לאלהים אחרים בארץ מצרים

        Sub-sub-subordinate Clause

אשר אתם באים לגור שם

   Subordinate Clause (3a)

8b) *למען הכרית* לכם
לקללה למדן היותכם

   Subordinate Clause (3b-conjoined to 3a)[149]

ולחרפה בכל גויי הארץ

If that is the case, then the final editor intended להכעיסני (v. 8a) to be in sequence with להכרית (v. 7aβ) and למען הכרית (v. 8b) so that the three subordinate clauses constitutes the consequences of the evil:[150]

---

word which seems to have caused some problems among ancient translations/versions. Second, the following statement, לא יראו, is somewhat awkward because of the absence of an
object. It is unclear as to who or what they had failed to 'revere' though the syntax could possibly point to the 'teaching and statutes'. However, one does not 'revere' the 'Teaching' but
God (5:22, 24, 10:7, 26:19, 32:39; also occurs in 'fear' of abandonment to trouble [1:8, 23:4,
30:10, 46:27, 28], prospect of disaster [3:8, 10:5, 51:46], and Babylonians [26:21, 40:9,
41:18, 42:11, 16]). LXX omits it altogether, which may reflect its secondary nature, perhaps
the tendency of the MT to extend the list in the pericope.

149 Although syntactically, למען היותכם ("becoming") and למען הכרית ("cutting off for yourselves"), joined by the conjunction -ו, constitute two separate subordinate clauses, the humiliation (לקללה ולחרפה, "an object of cursing and reproach") is probably the additional
consequence of the 'cutting off.' Therefore, the two subordinate clauses contain one punishment and should be considered as one subordinate clause.

150 See Holladay's, *Jeremiah*, 2:277 translation: "Why are you doing a great evil against yourselves, to cut off for yourselves man and woman, child and nursling from the midst of Judah,
so as to leave yourselves no remnant 8/ to offend me by the works of your hands, to make sa-

Sin (Evil, v. 7aα) → Punishment (Cut off [v.7aβ] + Provocation [v.8a] + Cut off [v.8b])

Therefore, the addressee would be destroying the remnant in Judah which is now in Egypt.

This rhetorical question leads to the next one in v. 9: "Have you forgotten (השכחתם)[151] the evils of your fathers (רעות אבותיכם),[152] evils of the kings of Judah (רעות מלכי יהודה), evils of their wives (רעות נשיו), your evils (רעתכם), evils of your wives (רעת נשכים) which they committed in the land of Judah and streets of Jerusalem?" If they knew what had happened to Jerusalem, then why would they continue to follow in their ancestors' footsteps? The parallel structure thus bolsters the accusation laid against the fugitives in

---

sacrifices ..." Contrast to those who consider להכרית (v. 7a) to be the result of the להכרית (v. 8a) so that the Judahite remnant is cut off on account of the provocation:

Sin (Evil; v. 7aα) = Punishment (Cut Off - הכרית; v. 7a) ← Provocation (להכעיס; v. 8a)

In other words, the provocation developing from the act of idolatry in Egypt provides the reason for the remnant in Judah to be destroyed. See Driver, *Jeremiah,* 260: "Why are ye doing a great evil ... to cut off from you ... in that ye vex me with the works of your hands; and Nicholson, *Jeremiah,* 2:153, - "Why bring destruction upon Judaeans ... This is what comes of your provoking me by all your idolatry." Also, see JPS, "Why are you doing such great harm... . For you vex me by your deeds." Another reading is placing להכעיסני (v. 8a) in parallel construction with אתם עשים so that the למה-interrogative carries over for both sentences:

7) למה אתם עשים רעה גדולה ... להכרית לכם ... בלתי הותיר לכם שארית

8) להכעסני במעשי ידיכם ... הכרית לכם ... היותכם לקללה ולחרפה

    7)   Why are you doing great evil ... cutting off for yourselves ... not leaving a remnant for yourself?

    8)   (Why are you) provoking me with the works of your hands ... cutting off for yourselves ... becoming an object of curse and reproach?

For this reading, see Carroll, *Jeremiah,* 728: "Why do you commit this great evil against yourselves ... Why do you provoke me to anger with the works of your hands ... Have you forgotten ...?"

151 When the Judahites are accused of forgetting something, it usually refers to God in the book of Jeremiah (2:32, 3:21, 13:25, 18:15, 23:27) so that the people are accused of having forgotten their God. However, here the accusation is for having failed to remember the 'evils' of their fathers, kings, and wives. If they had remembered their evil, they would not have repeated the same mistakes causing further punishment for themselves.

152 There appears to be two coexisting traditions concerning the fathers: 1) fathers did not know the gods that the present generation is worshipping; 2) fathers worshipped these gods and disobeyed God (2:5, 3:25, 7:18, 25-26, 9:13, 11:7, 10, 14:20, 16:11, 12, 19, 23:27, 34:14, 44:17). These 'fathers' are the ones with whom God made a covenant (11:10, 31:31, 34:13) and to whom he provided the land (3:18, 7:7, 11:5, 24:10, 30:3, 35:15). Here the fathers do not seem to be setting a good example.

Egypt. However, the rhetorical question in vv. 7-8 does not function only as accusations but also provides a distinct formulation of the punishment.

In v. 7, God inquires as to why the people are "doing great evil to (them)selves" (עשׂים רעה גדולה אל־נפשׁתכם),[153] "cutting off for (them)selves" (להכרית לכם) every adult and child so as "to leave no remnant for (them)selves" (לבלתי הותיר לכם שׁרית). The term, רעה גדולה,[154] could technically refer either to the 'evil'-sin or the 'evil'-punishment. Here, רעה refers simultaneously to both the sin and the punishment so that the evil which the people commit become the source of their disaster. Therefore, the people are ultimately responsible for their punishment. In fact, this 'evil'-punishment is further specified[155] as completely cutting off[156] everyone[157] off from Judah.

A similar construction of sin-punishment is apparent in v. 8. Just as the people's evil becomes their punishment in v. 7, the provocation resulting from idolatry ends directly in their extermination in v. 8. Though God may be the one who is provoked, as the first person pronominal object suffix (להכעסני, "provoking me") would indicate, he is not the executor of the punishment but rather the people who provoke God. The consequence of the provocation, לכם למען הכרית ("so as to cut off yourselves"), is parallel to להכעסני so that without a subject for the resultative clause, the agent of the provocation would then be the agent of the 'cutting off.' That would be the people. Therefore in the rhetorical question, the remnant of Judah in Egypt destroys itself.[158]

---

153 For similar phraseology, see Jer 26:19, where some of the elders opposed the killing of Jeremiah by recalling the incident of Micah. They would be doing a great harm to themselves if they kill Jeremiah and not turn aside from their sin. Instead of אל, it has על. Similar sentiment occurs in 7:19 where the people vex themselves to their own shame. See discussion above.

154 As opposed to just רעה, here it is רעה גדולה ("great evil," 16:10, 26:19, 32:42). No significance seems to be attached to the difference; see also Gen 39:9, 1 Sam 6:9, 2 Sam 13:16, Jonah 4:1, Neh 1:3, 2:10, 13:27, and Dan 9:12 where it refers to the fall of Jerusalem.

155 According to GKC §114o, the infinitive with ל is "very frequently used in a much looser connexion to state motives, attendant circumstances, or otherwise to define more exactly." Given the construction, להכרית appears to specify the method of harm that the people are committing against themselves.

156 The hiphil of כרת, concentrated in this pericope (vv. 8, 11), has a sense to 'completely destroy.' Beside these attestations, the word appears in 9:20, 47:4, 48:2, 51:62.

157 By means of merism, the totality of humans, both children (עולל יונק, "infant and child") and adults (אישׁ־ואשׁה, "man and woman"), are included in the punishment. עולל and יונק are distinct from men and woman and refer to the young. They commonly occur together to express totality of children (Lam. 2:11, 1 Sam 15:3, 1 Sam 22:19, Ps 8:3; עולל, with a different vocalization, is attested by itself in Jer 6:11, 9:20). For אישׁ־ואשׁה, see Exod 35:29, 36:6, Deut 22:22, Judg 9:49, 16:27, 1 Sam 27:9, 11, Jer 51:22, Esth 4:11.

158 Unlike v. 7 where הכרית is preceded by infinitive-ל, למען antecedes both הכרית and היותכם in v. 8. It is as if the הכעיס of God results not in God's provocation but in their own destruc-

This formulation of the 'destruction' (הכרית) is distinct from the development of הכרית in v. 11, the opening of the judgment oracle of the pericope.[159] V. 11 opens with לכן ("therefore") introducing the doom oracle whereby the punishment is carried out through the agency of God. God has decided to punish (הנני שם פני רעה, "I am about to set my face for evil") and destroy Judah (להכרית את־כל־יהודה, "to cut off all of Judah"). All the activities are centered on God: God takes (ולקחתי, "I will take," v. 12) the remnant of Judah about to enter Egypt and punishes them (ופקדתי, "I will punish," twice in v. 14). While God is clearly the agent of the punishment, vv. 11-14 also describes the people coming to their own end: They will be "consumed" (ותמו); "they will fall by the sword" (יפלו בחרב); "they will be consumed by famine" (ברעב יתמו); "they will die" (ימתו); "they will become" (והיו); and etc. In these instances, the executor of the punishment is not explicit though the passive instruments, sword, famine, and plague, are indicated. The 'evil' may have resulted from the people's sins but here, it is God who will punish; the people do not directly bring their own הכרית.

Though the pericope (vv. 1-14) has the appearance of a coherent structure, moving from the past formulation of the sin-punishment against Judah to the present one against the fugitives of Egypt, the distinct patterns in vv. 2-3, vv. 4-6, vv. 7-10, and vv. 11-14 would seem to suggest otherwise. The first formulation in vv. 2-3 follows the boomerang pattern whereby 'evil'-punishment occurs "on account of" (מפני) the 'evil'-sin. Secondly, the prophetic-formulation (vv. 4-6) which rephrases the 'evil'-sin as failure to obey God constructs the punishment as divine wrath. Third, vv. 7-10[160] attribute the people's 'evil'-punishment to their 'evil'-sin so that they destroy themselves. Finally, vv. 11-14 portrays God as the ultimate agent of the punishment with minor natural instruments. Since these distinct formulations appear to be compiled, it is difficult to determine the order of development based on this pericope.

---

tion and shame. An additional difference lies in the formulation of the destruction. While v. 7 intimidates no remnant (לבלתי הותיר לכם שארית, "not leaving a remnant for yourselves"), v. 8 expands upon the threat and includes public humiliation (לקללה ולחרפה, "[an object] of curse and reproach") among the nations (בכל גויי הארץ, "among all the nations of the earth;" common designation for all the nations, Gen 18:18, 22:18, 26:4, Deut 28:1, Jer 26:6, 33:9, Zech 12:3, Ezra 6:21, 2 Chr 32:13, 17).

159 Like the previous sections, vv. 11-14 do not appear to be linked with the any of the editorial levels in the pericope.

160 V. 10 is most likely an addition that may possibly linked to the prophetic-addition (see footnote above). However, since the final editor intended to make v. 10 as part of the accusation against the fugitives, it has been included in vv. 7-9.

4.8. Conclusion

In the book of Jeremiah, the pericopes containing the pivotal term, הכעיס,
reflect several distinct formulations of the punishment. Like DtrH1 and DtrH2,
God is portrayed working with the natural (8:19, 44:11-14) and historical instruments (25:8-10, 32:28-29a). At the same time, later editors of the book of
Jeremiah, more than DtrH2 and later non-Dtr attestations, try to attribute more
responsibility to the people. First, by focusing on his divine wrath (7:20,
32:31-32, 44:6), the people's provocation of God is depicted as directly leading to God's wrath which then function as the agent of the punishment. In
other words, the people provide fodder for the fire. Second, the punishment is
worded according to the people's sins so that God only carries whatever disaster they create (boomerang, linked to the decree-editor; 11:17, 25:12, 13, 14,
44:2-3). Thus, God is only the *Hermes* of the punishment. Third, the punishment is directly the result of the people's sins so that they punish themselves
(self-destruction; 7:19, 32:31-32, 44:7-10). Therefore, the people self-destruct.

Part V: Conclusion

The present study may perhaps reflect an ideational development from DtrH1 to DtrH2 and eventually to the book of Jeremiah.[1] To put it succinctly and schematically, DtrH1 seems to provide a conceptual framework in which temporal instruments, human and natural calamities, execute the divine punishment. DtrH2 (and later additions) and the editors of the book of Jeremiah continue to use this model but tend to add new features in which God is forefronted as the primary agent while simultaneously absolved of the responsibility for the destructive activities. Ultimately, the destruction is devised as the direct result of the people's sins, the catalyst for the divine ordained punishment.

We derived this tentative finding by examining pericopes containing a pivotal term, הכעיס. The root כעס, when used to refer to divine provocation, occurs primarily in the context of apostasy (see Charts A, 48-49; B, 77-78; C, 132; D, 176-177) in DtrH and the book of Jeremiah. Since apostasy severs the covenantal relationship between the people and YHWH, God, the offended party, responds with a punishment. Therefore, the punishment is depicted as a justified reaction to a wrong.

With the justification built into the term, DtrH used הכעיס to interpret Israel's history. For the editors of DtrH, history was not just a random series of events but a meaningful system of cause and effect in which sin against God would eventually lead to a potential or a real punishment. Thus, DtrH1 uses הכעיס to explain the demise of the first three dynasties of Israel. Through the prophets, God accuses the dynastic heads (Jeroboam, Baasha, Ahab [*de facto* ruler; also against Omri, another against Ahab, and Ahaziah]) of provoking God to anger in the pronouncements against each dynasty (1 Kgs 14:7-11, 16:2-4, 21:20b-26 [16:26, 16:30-33, and 22:53-54], respectively). Conse-

---

1   The present study of הכעיס in DtrH and the book of Jeremiah does not provide a sufficient data base on which to make a definitive conclusion. To further support the tentative finding, a thorough analysis of all the sin-punishment pericopes in DtrH1, DtrH2, and the book of Jeremiah should be made. Once one examines the various conceptual frameworks of the role of God in meting out punishments, the pattern derived from such a study, I think, will lend support to the present conclusion.

quently, God promises to completely annihilate the three dynasties. However in its fulfillment, the usurpers (Baasha, Zimri, and Jehu) carry out the punishment, which is again justified by the reason of provocation (1 Kgs 15:30, 16:13, absent in Omride dynasty). In accounts where the punishment is not explicit (16:30-33 and 22:53-54), DtrH1 arranges the narrative around the drought (1 Kgs 17:1) and attack of a temporal army (2 Kgs 1:1). Therefore, human and natural instruments execute the divine punishment set against the first three dynasties of Israel.

Then DtrH2 adopts the term used in dynastic curse formulae to explain the fall of Jerusalem. The explanation for the destruction of the religio-political center is built into the overall structure of DtrH. From the time of Moses, the people had been warned about the consequences of their provocation of God (Deut 4:25-28, 31:27-29, 32:15-25[2]). Also, the individual episode of the Golden Calf (Deut 9:18-20) and the pattern of sin-provocation-punishment-deliverance established in the book of Judges (Judg 2:11-16) function as warnings of what is to come. And even the brief oracle (1 Kgs 14:15-16a) and the actual account of the Assyrian conquest of Samaria (2 Kgs 17:7-23a) forebode the eventual demise of Jerusalem. To further build up a case for the destruction, DtrH2 indicts Manasseh for a catalog of sins which provoke God to anger (2 Kgs 21:2-15). As a result, the judgment against Manasseh and thus, Jerusalem, was sealed (2 Kgs 22:15-17; 23:26-27).

Contrary to DtrH1, in these descriptions of the punishment, God is usually portrayed as the primary agent of destruction. God is depicted as acting alone (Deut 4:25-28; 1 Kgs 14:15-16a, 16:7, 23:26-27). Even when he uses human instruments (Judg 2:14, 2 Kgs 17:19-20, 23:19-20), God's involvement is more explicit than the descriptions of the punishment linked by הכעיס in DtrH1, where human and natural instruments fulfill God's pronouncement against the dynasties. Here, in DtrH2, God punishes and then delivers the people into enemy hands, who are passive recipients. The only exception is 2 Kgs 23:19-20, where Josiah is the primary agent; however, here Josiah only corrects rather than punishes the culprits.

While God has mastery over the destructive activities, the people are increasingly culpable for their own destruction (see Chart E). First of all, the punishment corresponds more with the catalog of sins (Deut 4:28, Judg 2:15, 1 Kgs 14:15-16a, 16:7, 2 Kgs 17:19-20, 21:12-14, 22:16). Secondly, divine wrath, propelled by the people's provocation either motivates God (Deut 9:20,

---

2   Though the Song of Moses (Deut 32) is dated to the period of the Judges (ca. 1000 B.C.E.), given the surrounding literary context, it may have been inserted in DtrH to provide further warning for future apostasy. The outline of sin-provocation-punishment should have discouraged any would-be-offenders.

Judg 2:14, 2 Kgs 17:18, 21-22, 23:26-27), functions as an instrument (Deut 9:19), or acts as its own agent (2 Kgs 22:17). Third, the people destroy themselves directly with their sins (Deut 31:27-29).

Closely associated with DtrH2, the authors of the book of Jeremiah also use הכעיס to explain the destruction of Jerusalem. As demonstrated in the analysis of 2 Kgs 17:7-23a and 21:2-15, two additional sources were detected: decree and prophetic editors. Though the exact relationship between DtrH2 and the book of Jeremiah is not clear, similar sources are evident in the book of Jeremiah. In fact, the contributions of the decree and prophetic editors to the book of Jeremiah are more developed and extensive than in DtrH2, which may point to its later redaction.[3]

Consequently, the authors of the book of Jeremiah hold the people more responsible for the ruins of Jerusalem than DtrH2 (again see Chart E). As in DtrH1 and DtrH2, God is depicted as using human (25:8-11, 32:28-29a) and natural (8:20) instruments in response to the people's sins. How else would the authors of the book of Jeremiah explain the reality of the foreign troops marching into their land and the drought that plagued the people? Rather than shy away from reality, they lay claim to the divine mastery over such events. What a rare opportunity to bolster the veracity of their deity's power in the face of disaster! After all, didn't the Yahwistic prophets warn the people of the consequences of their apostasy earlier?

At the same time, this explanation in which God manipulates temporal events would have been inadequate for those, perhaps even including the authors of the book of Jeremiah, staring at the ruins of Jerusalem or sitting "by the rivers of Babylon" (Ps 137:1). Without the constant threat of (more) disaster, a person would have tried to understand God's role. How could our God let this happen? But more specifically, how could our God deliver us to the very enemies who treated our ancestors and us so cruelly? The editors of the book of Jeremiah respond: God was just a *Hermes* of the disaster which the people created by themselves (boomerang; 11:17, 25:12, 13, 14, 44:2-3); it was the divine wrath which the people fed with their provocations (divine wrath; 7:20, 32:31, 44:4-6); and finally, the people have created and brought about their own disaster (self-destruction; 7:19, 11:17, 32:31, 44:7-10). In the end, God is exonerated.

Yet, do other texts containing הכעיס (Hos 12:1-15, Ezek 8:1-17, 16:26-30, Isa 65:1-7, Pss 78:56-64, 106:28-31, 2 Chr 28:22-25)[4] reflect the development

---

3 This is clearly apparent in the selection of verb to describe the manner in which the fiery wrath was set against the people (נתך, "pour out,"Jer 7:20 and 44:6, versus יצת, "kindle," 2 Kgs 22:17). The use of נתך was probably later than that of יצת.

4 This list does not include Neh 3:37, which was not included in the body of the study.

within DtrH and the book of Jeremiah where people are held more culpable for their actions? This is difficult to say since הכעיס does not play a significant role in the overall structure of any of the books beside DtrH and the book of Jeremiah. Suffice it to say that the measure-for-measure pattern is present in a very early Psalm (78:58) and use of human/natural instruments is prominent in late texts (Ps 106:29 and 2 Chr 28:25). Even the early Song of Moses (Deut 32) lays out various formulations of the punishment: 1) measure-for-measure (v. 21); 2) divine wrath (v. 22); 3) God with his natural instrument (vv. 23-25). At the same time, though, the pericopes in the books of Hosea, Ezekiel, and Isaiah, all dated to the exilic and post-exilic period, reflect a tendency to describe the punishment more according to the sin. However, these examples are insufficient to generalize for the whole Bible or to fit into a historical-evolutionary framework.

What would have prompted DtrH2 and the authors of the book of Jeremiah to reconfigure the method in which DtrH1 explained the historical events? What necessitated the shift from depicting the temporal instruments carrying out the divine punishment to direct divine mastery over historical events while simultaneously attributing the responsibility for the punishment to the people? It could only have been the crisis arising from the destruction of Jerusalem in 587 B.C.E. and the deportations of its people to Babylon.

In a streamlined understanding of the monotheistic religious system, God is the active agent of both salvific and destructive acts. This would fit the prevalent theological notion that "Yahweh is the God of history and history is his foremost means of revelation."[5] However, this configuration would not be

---

5   Albrektson, *History and the Gods: An Essay on the Idea of Historical Events as Divine Manifestations in the Ancient Near East and in Israel* (ConBOT 1; Lund: CWK Gleerup, 1967), 11, quoting his translation of E. Jacob, *La tradition historique en Israël* (Montpellier: Études théologiques et religieuses, 1946), 12. God's activity in history is the basis of a number of studies, among which only a few will be listed here. Any number of books by G. Ernest Wright whose titles reflect the topic: *God Who Acts: Biblical Theology as Recital* (SBT 8; London: SCM Press, 1952), G. Ernest Wright and Reginald Fuller, *The Book of the Acts of God: Christian Scholarship Interprets the Bible* (Christian Faith Series; Garden City: Doubleday, 1957), and even a book dedicated to him, *Magnalia Dei, The Mighty Acts of God: Essays on the Bible and Archaeology in Memory of G. Ernest Wright* (eds. Frank Moore Cross, Werner Lemke and Patrick Miller, Jr.; Garden City: Doubleday, 1976). A similar but which includes a discussion of the ancient Near East is a pivotal book by Bertil Albrektson, *History and the Gods*. A recent discussion of God's power in history is Christoph Schroeder, *History, Justice, and the Agency of God: A Hermeneutical and Exegetical Investigation on Isaiah and Psalms* (BiblInt 52; Leiden: Brill, 2001). As Schroeder states, the purpose of the book is to "regain the universal dimension of the God of the Old Testament as the God who acts in the world perceived as history and creation" (29).

       One could argue, as a point of comparison, that unlike the Israelites, in the neighboring Mesopotamian polytheistic religious system the patron god/goddess supposedly leaves the

able to explain the theological dilemma: How can the God of Israel, who brought the people from under Pharaoh (the preeminent act of the *Heilsgeschichte*), punish the descendants under the same covenant, in 587 B.C.E.? The blunt answer, "because they abandoned the covenant of YHWH, their God, and worshipped other deities and served them" (Jer 22:9), would not have satisfied the audience of the book of Jeremiah. Would the people who had exclaimed, "I have not sinned" (Jer 2:35), and the *false* prophets who declared, "You will have peace" (Jer 23:17), readily accept the explanation that God used temporal and natural instruments to punish them?[6] So then how do the authors of the book of Jeremiah convince the audience skeptical of God's justice?

The authors of the book of Jeremiah tried to provide different conceptualizations of God's role in meting out punishment beside the theological model of "the God of history." Without divesting God of his

---

city, allowing the foreign army and their gods to enjoy the pillage. Here the patron god/goddess seems only to protect, not directly destroy his/her city. Look at the various commentaries on Sennacherib's destruction of Babylon, especially, Grant Frame, *Babylonia 689-627 B.C.: A Political History* (Uitgaven van het Netherlands Historisch-Archaeologisch Instituut te Istanbul 69; Te Istanbul: Nederlands Historisch-Archaeologisch Instituut, 1992), 52-63; Paul-Alain Beaulieu, *The Reign of Nabonidus: King of Babylon 556-539 B.C.* (Yale Near Eastern Researches 10; New Haven: Yale University Press, 1989), 104-115; and J.A. Brinkman, "Through a Glass Darkly: Esarhaddon's Retrospects on the Downfall of Babylon," *JAOS* 103 (1983):35-42. See also Peter Machinist, "The Epic of Tukulti-Ninurta I: A Study in Middle Assyrian Literature" (unpublished Ph.D. dissertation; Yale University, 1978), 149-170; comments scattered throughout Luigi Cagni, *The Poem of Erra* (Sources from the Ancient Near East, vol. 1, fasc. 3; Malibu: Undena Publications, 1977); various treatments of Sumerian lamentations, especially Jerrold S. Cooper, *The Curse of Agade* (JHNES; Baltimore: Johns Hopkins University Press, 1983), 20-23, 235-36; and W. G. Lambert, "Enmeduranki and Related Matters," *JCS* 21 (1967):126-138.

6   See Paul Volz, *Das Dämonische in Jahwe* (Sammlung gemeinverständlicher Vortrage und Schriften aus dem Gebiet der Theologie und Religionsgeschichte 110; Tübingen: Mohr, 1924), for an outdated and problematic discussion of a similar issue by pinpointing the 'evil' to the demonic in YHWH, and H.G.L. Peels, *The Vengeance of God: The Meaning of the Root NQM and the Function of the NQM-Texts in the Context of Divine Revelation in the Old Testament* (OtSt 31; Leiden: E.J. Brill, 1995), 4, 298-301, for a criticism of Volz's work.

The book of Job grapples with this very dilemma. Job cannot and will not accept the simple deterministic explanation (as shared by his so-called friends and other strands of the Bible, namely DtrH and the Chronicler), whereby his supposed sins form the basis for the punishment which he is experiencing from the hand of God. Since Job is undeterred in claiming his innocence, this forces him to question God's justice. However, the book never really extrapolates on God's justice but begs the question with an assertion of divine omnipotence — God is all-too-powerful for humanity to understand or even to question. Therefore, Job is to be content with the encounter with his judge and his accuser. He is ultimately left without a direct explanation or answer to his question, which the prelude and postlude of the book try to provide.

mastery over earth, the authors tried to hold the people directly responsible for their own disaster. In conclusion, the book of Jeremiah answers those grappling with the problem of theodicy arising from the destruction of Jerusalem: "Don't blame YHWH; you only have yourselves to blame."

Chart E: Passages Discussed in the Study (DtrH1, DtrH2, Non-Deuteronomic, and Book of Jeremiah)

Type of Punishment	Pre-exilic Period	Destruction and Exile	Post-exilic Period
Human/Natural Instrument Alone (I) or God Using Them (GI)	DtrH: Deut 32:23-25 (GI); 1 Kgs 15:29-30 (I); 16:11-13(I); 17:1(I); 22:37-38 (I); 2 Kgs 1:1 (I); 9:7, 25-26, 36-37, 10:9-11, 17 (I)		DtrH2: Judg 2:14 (GI); 1 Kgs 14:16a (hint of GI, but not developed); 2 Kgs 17:19-20 (GI); 2 Kgs 21:12-14 (GI); 2 Kgs 23:19-20 (I)
	Non-DtrH: Ps 78:59-64	Non-DtrH: Ezek 16:27 (GI); 16:39-41a (I)	Non-DtrH: Ps 106:29-30 (I); 2 Chr 28:27 (I)
		Jer: 8:20 (I; with the addition of v. 19c, God blames people), 25:8-11 (GI)	Jer: 32:28-29a (GI); 44:11-14 (GI)
God as only agent	DtrH1: 1 Kgs 14:7-11; 16:2-4; 21:20b-24; 2 Kgs 9:7-10 (tension with Greek which refers to human instrument); 2 Kgs 17:18, 21-22		DtrH2: Deut 4:25-28; 1 Kgs 14:15-16a; 1 Kgs 16:7; 2 Kgs 23:26-27
		Non-DtrH2: Hos 12:15; Ezek 8:18; 16:38, 41b-43	Non-DtrH: Isa 65:6-7
			Jer: 11:17, 25:12, 25:13, 25:14
Divine Wrath as Instrument (I) Motivation (M)/Agent (A)	Pre-DtrH1: Deut 32:21 (M), 22 (A)		DtrH2: Deut 9:19 (I); 9:20 (M); Judg 2:14 (M); 2 Kgs 17:18, 21-22 (M); 2 Kgs 17:18, 21-22 (M); 2 Kgs 23:26-27 (M)
	Non-DtrH: Ps 78:59-64 (M)	Non-DtrH: Ezek 8:18 (M); 16:38, 41b-43 (M)	
			Jer: 7:20 (A); 32:31 (A); 32:31 (AI); 44:4-6 (A)

Type of Punishment	Pre-exilic Period	Destruction and Exile	Post-exilic Period
Boomerang/Measure-for-Measure	DtrH1: Deut 32:21		DtrH2: Deut 4:25-28 (partial); Judg 2:15 (partial); 1 Kgs 16:7 (partial); 2 Kgs 17:19-20 (partial); 2 Kgs 21:12-14 (partial) 2 Kgs 22:16
	Non-DtrH: Ps 78:59-64	Non-DtrH: Hos 12:15; Ezek 16:38-43	Non-DtrH: Isa 65:6-7
			Jer: 11:17; 25:12; 25:13; 25:14; 44:2-3
Self-Destruction			DtrH: Deut 31:27-29
			Jer: 7:19 (hint); 11:17 (hint); 32:31; 44:7-10

Appendices

Appendix A: Descriptions of Punishment of Judah in Chs. 1-25 and Mowinckel's C Source in the Book of Jeremiah

This appendix lists descriptions of all the punishments in chs. 1-25 and C-source in the book of Jeremiah. It provides the various models of God's agency and type of punishment as a point of comparison to those observed in the prose sermons. Since the dating of the passages is difficult to ascertain, the redaction level is far from being conclusive. Therefore, one cannot derive definite conclusions from the chart below. Also, the appendix provides a list of linking conjunctions which can be compared to the pivotal term, הַמִּכֵּן.

Pericope	Type of Sin	Linking Conjunction	Type of Punishment	Redaction Level	Agency
1:13-14 (1:13-16)	None	None	Vision of a boiling cauldron, tilted from the north – interpreted as "evil" disaster	Poetry – Early	Not indicated
1:15 (1:13-16)	None	None	Calling of the northern kingdoms	Poetry – Early	God using human instruments
1:16 (1:13-16)	People's "evil" from their act of apostasy (rejection of God and following other deities)	עַל ("on account of")	God decrees his judgments (מִשְׁפָּטַי, "my judgments")	Poetry – Decree-editor	God – boomerang: "evil" for "evil"
2:14-19	Abandoning God (v. 17)	None	Lions (either Babylon or Egypt)[1] destroy its cities and people's wrongdoing punishes the people	Poetry – early with later additions (?)	Human instrument; however vv. 17-19 places the blame on the people's sin: הֲלוֹא־זֹאת תַּעֲשֶׂה־לָּךְ עָזְבֵךְ אֶת־יהוה ... תְּיַסְּרֵךְ רָעָתֵךְ וּמְשֻׁבוֹתַיִךְ תּוֹכִחֻךְ ("Did you not do this to yourselves, abandoning YHWH … your evil will chastise you, your apostasy will reprove you")[2]

2:27c-28 (2:20-28)	None	None	Time of their evil	Poetry – early	Rhetorical – God tells the people to have their gods save them
2:29-30 (subunit of 2:29-37)	"You rebelled" (פשׁעתם) against God	None	God struck the people	Poetry – early	God
2:33-37 (subunit of 2:29-37); see Appendix F	Refusal to accept guilt for innocent blood and pursuit of lovers	על ("because," v. 35)	God will pass judgment; Judah will be disappointed by their alliances	Poetry – early	God, with human instruments; implied divine wrath
3:1-5	Prostitution and evil (v. 2b)	None	Showers withheld	Poetry – early	Natural instrument
4:4 (4:3-4); see Appendix F	Failure to circumcise heart; and "the evil of your deeds" (רע מעלליכם)	מפני ("on account of")	Divine wrath sets out against the people	Poetry – early (?); but Thiel thinks it is Deuteronomistic	Divine wrath
4:8 (4:5-8); see Appendix F	None	None	Foe from north; conceptualized as "evil ... and great destruction" (רעה ... שׁבר גדול, v. 6b)	Poetry – early	God using human instrument conceptualized as divine wrath (v. 8)
4:13-17 (4:11-18)	Rebellion (v. 17)	כי ("because," v. 17)	Army comes to attack (vv. 13-17a)	Poetry – early	Human instrument
4:18 (4:11-18)	People's ways and deeds	None	Bitter punishment	Prose – after the destruction[3]	God (according to MT); but in other Hebrew manuscripts, the way and deeds (self-destruction): דרכך ומעלליך עשׂו אלה לך ("your way and your deeds did these to you")

Pericope	Type of Sin	Linking Conjunction	Type of Punishment	Redaction Level	Agency
4:19-21 but added v. 22 (reason)	People do not know God and know only evil (v. 22)	כִּי ("because," v. 22)	Battle	Poetry – early	Human instrument; later justification for war (because of sin, v. 22)
4:23-26; see Appendix F	None	None	Return to chaos	Poetry – late (?)[4]	God = divine wrath
4:27-28	None	None	Whole land will be desolated	Poetry – late (?)	God
4:29-31	None	None	Army attack	Poetry – early	Human instrument
5:1-6	People and leaders do not know God; their sins are great	כִּי ("for," v. 4, 6)	Lion/wolf/leopard (human army) will destroy them	Poetry – early	Human instrument
5:7-9	Adultery	הַעַל־אֵלֶּה ("on account of these?," v. 9)	Hypothetical question – should God not punish	Poetry – early	God
5:10-13	Prophets prophesy falsely	כִּי ("for," v. 11)	Command to cut off branches	Poetry – early	Human instrument
5:14 (5:14-19)	You spoke this word	יַעַן ("because," v. 14)	Fire consume	Poetry – early	God, with word = fire
5:15-17 (5:14-19)	None	None	Army attack	Poetry – early	Human instrument
5:18-19	Apostasy – reject God and serve other deities	תַּחַת מֶה ("why?")	Do these (destruction)	Prose – after destruction	God; measure-for-measure punishment: serve gods so serve foreigners
5:20-25	People are stubborn and not fear God	None	Deprived of good	Poetry – after destruction (?)[5]	People's sins (v. self-destruction): חַטֹּאותֵיכֶם מִנְעוּ הַטּוֹב מִכֶּם

					המאסתם מאס בעמם ("your iniquities turned these aside; your sins kept the good away from you")
5:26-29	Social abuse to get wealthy	הכל־אלה ("on account of these?", v. 29)	Hypothetical – should God not punish	Poetry – early	God
6:1-7 (6:1-8)	Evil, violence, and destruction (v. 7)	None	Army attack	Poetry – early	Human instrument; God (v. 8)
6:8 (6:1-8)	Positive command – accept rebuke	פן ("lest")	God will destroy land	Poetry – early	God
6:9-12	Not listen to God	None	Army attack (v. 9); pour God's wrath upon the people (v. 11)	Poetry early (?)	Human instrument, God, will divine wrath as instrument
6:13-15	Prophets and priests are deceitful	None	God punish them (בעת־פקדתים, "at the time I punish them; compare to Greek which has "at the time of their punishment")	Poetry – early (?)	God
6:16-21	People refuse to pay attention to God's word and teaching	כי ("because," v. 19)	God bring disaster and make them stumble	Poetry – prophetic editor (?) (v. 17)	God; measure-for-measure (v. 19): הנה אנכי נתן אל־העם הזה מכשלים ... ("here, I am about to bring evil ... the fruits of their thoughts")
6:22-26	None	None	Army attack	Poetry – early	Human instrument
6:27-30	Metal imagery – act corruptly	כי ("because")	God rejected them	Poetry – early	God

Pericope	Type of Sin	Linking Conjunction	Type of Punishment	Redaction Level	Agency
7:1-11	Command to maintain ethical standards, not to trust the Temple, and not to commit abominations (vv. 1-11a)	None	God is watching (v. 11b) – perhaps recalling the opening vision where God is watching to fulfill his word (1:12)	Prose – early	God
7:12-15	Evil (Shiloh) and disobedience of God's word (Judah)	מִפְּנֵי ("because," v. 12); יַעַן ("on account of," v. 13)	Shiloh is destroyed because of evil. Judah will be destroyed like Shiloh because of disobedience	Prose – decree-editor	God
7:16-20; see Part IV					
7:21-29; see Appendix F	Disobedience of God's command with v. 25 and vv. 27-28, adding disobedience of prophets	כִּי ("because," v. 22)	God has rejected and uprooted the generation of his wrath (v. 29)	Outline of sin (vv. 21-28): prose – decree and prophetic editors; v. 29 appears to be early poetry	God, motivated by divine wrath
7:30-34	Do evil and perform child-sacrifice which God did not command (vv. 30-31)	כִּי ("because," v. 30)	Turn the place of high places into a field of graves; cessation of daily life	Prose – decree-editor (?)	God; partial measure-for-measure; Valley of Ben-hinnom, where they burn children, will be Valley of Slaughter, their place of burial
8:1-3	Worshipped natural elements	None	Bones of religious and political leaders will be exposed to the natural elements	Prose – unclear	God, with natural instruments; measure-for-measure in that the leaders will be exposed to the very elements they worshipped

Passage	Sin	Connective	Description of Punishment	Date/Genre	Agent
8:8-9 (8:4-9)	8:4-7 (refusal to return to God) may function as the catalog of sins but v. 8 and v. 9b emphasize a different sin, lies of the 'wise men' and rejection of God's word	None	Wise put to shame, dismayed, and trapped	Poetry – early	Not indicated
8:10-12	Religious leaders spread false report	כִּי ("because," v. 10)	Two punishments: 1) give wives to other men (v. 10); 2) they will fall (v. 12)	Poetry – early	God (v. 10); unclear (v. 12)
8:13	None	None	Agricultural imagery where harvest is removed (?)	Poetry – early	God
8:14-17	Sinned against God (v. 14)	כִּי ("because," v. 14)	Enemy forces; God sends venomous snakes (v. 17)	Poetry – early	Human instrument; God with human instrument (v. 17)
8:18-23; see Part IV					
9:6-8	Deceit	עַל־אֵלֶּה ("on account of these," v. 8)	Hypothetical – God should punish them and be avenged	Poetry – early	God
9:9-10	None	None	Description of desolation in which God makes Jerusalem into a waste	Poetry – early (?; either initial attack of 597 or that of 587)	God
9:11-15	Disobedience of teaching and God	עַל ("because," v. 12)	Two punishments: 1) earth is desolated (v. 11); 2) God will make them experience difficulties and scatter them to enemies	Prose – decree or prophetic editor (?; emphasis on obedience)[6]	God, with minor role for human instrument
9:16-18	None	None	Desolation and shamed (lament)	Poetry – early	Not indicated
9:19-21	None	None	Death takes lives	Poetry – early	Death

Pericope	Type of Sin	Linking Conjunction	Type of Punishment	Redaction Level	Agency
9:24-25	None	None	God will punish all the uncircumcised	Prose – early (?)	God
10:17-18	None	None	God will fling away inhabitants	Poetry – early	God
10:19-21	Shepherds do not seek God	כי ("for," v. 21)	Scene of devastation	Poetry – early	Human instrument (?)
10:22	None	None	Army attack with north	Poetry – early	Human instrument
10:25	Nations destroyed Judah	כי ("for")	Pour out divine wrath over the nations	Poetry – after the destruction	God, with divine wrath as instrument
11:1-14	Disobey God	כי ("for," v. 13); secondary to accentuate number of gods	1) God brought the terms of the covenant (v. 8); 2) God will bring evil and will not listen (v. 11); 3) Jeremiah should not pray "on behalf of their evil" (v. 14)	Prose – decree-editor and additions to emphasize the role of Jeremiah	God; measure-for-measure punishment in which God brings the terms of the covenant (v. 8); God's refusal to listen because of their refusal to obey
11:15-16	Evil schemes	כי ("because")	God set fire	Poetry – early	God, with fire
11:17, see Part IV					
11:18-23	Persecutors plot to kill Jeremiah	None	God will punish them; men will die by sword and women by famine; evil will come	Vv. 18-20 – early poetry; Vv. 21-22 – early prose	God, with human and natural instruments
12:1-3 (12:1-6)	Wicked commit treachery	None	Jeremiah's request to slaughter them	Poetry – early	God
12:4 (12:1-6)	Evil of inhabitants	מ ("from")	Scene of drought	Poetry – early	Natural instrument
12:7-12 (12:7-13)	Roared against God (v. 8)	None	God abandons and delivers to enemy	Poetry – early	God, with human instrument

12:13 (12:7-13)	None	None	None	Lack of harvest	Poetry – early (?)	Divine wrath
12:14-17	None	Wicked neighbors who seize the inheritance of Israel	None	God will uproot them	Prose – unclear[7]	God
13:1-11	None	Symbolic act – ruined linen belt; people refused to listen and worshipped other gods	None	Ruin the pride of Judah (like the ruined loincloth)	Prose – decree or prophetic editor (?)	God
13:12-14	None	None	None	Make everyone, commoners and leaders, drunk and smash them	Prose – early	God: implied motivation from divine wrath (wine)
13:15-17	None	Failure to give glory and listen	None	Flock of YHWH taken captive	Poetry – early	Implied human instrument
13:18-20	None	None	כִּי ("because," v. 22)	Everyone carried into exile	Poetry – early	Human instrument
13:21-23	None	Iniquity	אֲשֶׁר ("because")	"These things" (the destruction)	Poetry – early (?)	Self-destruction
13:24-25	None	Apostasy; reject God and trust the deceit (false god)	None	God will scatter them	Prose – early	God
13:26-27	None	Adulteries → idolatry	None	God will expose them	Poetry – early	God
14:1-6	None	None	None	Drought	Poetry – early	Natural instrument
14:7-9	None	Iniquities; turn one's back to God	כִּי ("for," v. 7)	God does not save people	Poetry - unclear[8]	God
14:10 (14:10-16)	None	People love to wander	None	Not accept them, remember iniquity, and punish their sins	Poetry (?) – unclear	God, in measure-for-measure punishment: יִזְכֹּר עֲוֹנָם וְיִפְקֹד חַטֹּאתָם ("He will remember their iniquity *and punish their sin*" [italics not in Greek])
14:11-12 (14:10-16)	None	None	None	God will consume them with sword, famine, and plague	Prose – early (?)	God, with natural instrument

Pericope	Type of Sin	Linking Conjunction	Type of Punishment	Redaction Level	Agency
14:13-16 (14:10-16)	Prophets prophesy lies	None	Prophets will be killed by sword and famine; people will be killed by famine and sword; and God will pour out their evil	Vv. 13-14 – early prose (?); vv. 15-16 – early poetry (?)	God, with natural instrument, in a boomerang formulation: וְשָׁפַכְתִּי עֲלֵיהֶם אֶת־רָעָתָם ("I will pour out their evil [which function as both sin and punishment] over them")
14:17-19a	None	None	Scene of death and desolation	Poetry – early (?)	God, with natural instrument
14:19b-22	Wickedness, iniquity of ancestors (v. 20)	כִּי ("for," v. 20)	Terror	Poetry – unclear	God, with natural instrument
15:1-4	What Manasseh committed	בִּגְלַל ("because," v. 4)	God sends four kinds of destroyers: sword, dogs, birds, and beasts	Prose – early (?)	God, with natural instrument
15:5-9	Reject God and turn back	None	God destroys and brings destroyer	Poetry - early	God, with natural instrument
15:13-14; see Appendix F	Sins	כִּי ("because," v. 13)	God will deliver to enemies	Poetry - early	God, motivated by divine wrath, with minor role for instrument
16:1-9	None	None	Die of deadly diseases, sword, famine but no one will mourn or bury	Prose – early	God, with natural instruments
16:10-13	Apostasy: reject God and follow other deities	עַל אֲשֶׁר ("because," v. 11)	God decree great evil – cast people from land where they serve other gods	Prose – decree-editor	God, measure-for-measure punishment, see Introduction

16:16-18	People defile land with images and abominations	עַל ("because," v. 18)	God pay back double for their iniquity and sin	Prose – after the destruction (587)	God, measure-for-measure punishment (v. 18): וְשִׁלַּמְתִּי רִאשׁוֹנָה מִשְׁנֵה עֲוֹנָם וְחַטָּאתָם ("I will first repay double their iniquity and their sin")
17:1-4	Sins (altars and asherah poles)	כִּי ("because," v. 3)	Give to plunder and enslavement	Poetry - early	God, motivated by divine wrath with minor role for human instrument
17:19-27	Not obey the command not to work on the Sabbath	None	God ignite fire which burns the palaces of Jerusalem	Prose - late	God
18:7-12	People continue to follow evil hearts	None	God will create evil	Prose – decree-editor	God, measure-for-measure punishment; "evil" – punishment for "evil" - sin
18:13-17	Apostasy – reject God and follow other gods	כִּי ("for," v. 15)	God scatter them before enemy	Poetry - early	God, with human instrument
18:18-23	Persecutors' plot to ignore Jeremiah's word	כִּי ("for," v. 22)	Jeremiah pleads with God to deliver them to famine, sword, invaders	Poetry - early	God, with human and natural instruments; divine wrath
19:1-5 (19:1-9)	Apostasy – reject God and follow other gods; shed innocent blood and consign children to fire	יַעַן אֲשֶׁר ("on account of", v. 4)	God brings evil	Prose – decree-editor	God
19:6-9 (19:1-9)	Previous unit (?)	Previous unit (?)	God delivers them to the enemies	Prose – same as above (?)	God, with human instrument
19:10-13	Offerings made to other deities	None	Make city like Topheth	Prose – same as above (?)	God

Pericope	Type of Sin	Linking Conjunction	Type of Punishment	Redaction Level	Agency
19:14-15	Stiffen their neck, not obeying God's word	כִּי ("because," v. 15)	Bring evil	Prose – decree-editor	God; measure-for-measure (v. 15): הִנְנִי מֵבִיא (MT) אֶת־כָּל־הָרָעָה אֲשֶׁר דִּבַּרְתִּי עָלֶיהָ לְבִלְתִּי שְׁמוֹעַ אֶת־דְּבָרַי ("I am about to bring . . . all the evil which I spoke against it . . . [for] not obeying my word")
20:1-6	Pashhur beats Jeremiah	None	Deliver Judah to Babylon along with Pashhur and his household	Prose – early	God, with human instrument
21:1-10; see Appendix F	None	None	God will deliver them to Babylon, famine, plague, and sword; in/with divine wrath	Prose – early	God, with human and natural instrument, either motivated by or using divine wrath
21:11-12; see Appendix F	Evil of deeds	מִפְּנֵי ("because," v. 12)	Divine wrath will set out like fire	Poetry – early	Divine wrath
21:13-14	Implicit – deeds	None	God will punish and set fire to the forest	Poetry – unclear	God; measure-for-measure punishment (v. 14): וּפָקַדְתִּי עֲלֵיכֶם כִּפְרִי מַעַלְלֵיכֶם ("I will punish you according to your deeds," absent in Greek)
22:1-5	If kings fail to do what God prescribes – maintain justice	None	Palace will become a ruin	Prose – early	Implied God (who swears by himself)

22:6-7	None	None	God will make the place into a desert; send destroyer	Prose – early	God, with human instrument
22:8-9	Apostasy – rejection of God and follow other deities	על אשר ("on account of," v. 9)	Implicit – present devastation	Prose – after destruction (587)	God
22:10-12	None	None	Those who are exiled will not return	V. 10 – early poetry; vv.11-12 – early prose	Not indicated
22:13-19	Royal abuse of power	None	Improper burial	Poetry – early	Not indicated
22:20-23	People did not obey	כי ("because," v. 22)	Wind will graze shepherds, allies go into captivity, and people will be disgraced	Poetry – decree-editor	God; partial measure-for-measure punishment (play on רעה ["to pasture"] and רעה ["evil"])
22:24-27	None	None	Deliver king to the Chaldeans	Prose – early	God, with human instrument
22:28-30	None	None	Jehoiachin cast to unknown land; offspring will not become king	Poetry – early	Not indicated
23:1-4	Leaders who dispersed the flock	None	Punish their evil	Prose – after destruction (587)[9]	God; measure-for-measure punishment (v. הנני פקד עליכם את רע מעלליכם "I am about to visit the evil of your deeds upon you.")

Pericope	Type of Sin	Linking Conjunction	Type of Punishment	Redaction Level	Agency
23:9-12	Land filled with adulterers; religious leaders commit evil	כִּ ("for," vv. 10-11)	Land is dried up; God will bring evil	Poetry – early	God, with natural instrument; measure-for-measure punishment (evil path of people and evil of prophets and priests lead to evil punishment)
23:13-15	Prophets mislead and lead evil lives	כִּ ("for," v. 15)	God will make them suffer	Poetry – early	God
23:16-22	Prophets speak falsely	None	Divine wrath will set	Poetry – decree-editor	Divine wrath; partial measure-for-measure (play on רעה, "evil")
23:25-32	Prophets speak falsely	None	God is against them	Prose – unclear	God
23:33-40	Prophets speak falsely	יען ("on account of," v. 38)	God will uproot people and humiliate them	Prose – unclear	God
24:1-10	Bad figs = remnant in Judah and Egypt	None	God will make them an object of ridicule and send natural catastrophes against them	Prose – unclear	God, with natural instrument
25:1-14; see Part IV					
25:15-29	None	None	Make nations drink the wine of God's wrath	Prose – series of redactions	God, with divine wrath as instrument
25:30-32	None	None	God will deliver evil ones to the sword	Poetry – unclear	God, with natural instrument
25:33	None	None	Dead without proper burial	Prose – unclear	Not indicated
25:34-38	None	None	God destroy the pasture of shepherd	Poetry – unclear	God, divine wrath, and human instrument (?)

			Prose – early (?)	God, with human instrument
34:1-7	None	None	God will deliver city to king of Babylon	Prose – early (?)	God, with human instrument
34:8-22	Failure to declare freedom for slaves	None	Susceptible to sword, plague, and famine; deliver to enemies	Prose – early	God, with natural and human instruments; partial measure-for-measure (play on word, דרור, "freedom")
35:1-19	Disobedience	יען (v. 17)	God will bring evil	Prose – decree and prophetic editors (v. 15)	God; measure-for-measure punishment (v. : 1) evil sin lead to evil disaster; 2) הנני מביא אל ... את כל-הרעה אשר דברתי עליהם יען דברתי אליהם ולא שמעו ואקרא להם ולא ענו ("I am about to bring all the evil which I spoke to them on account that I spoke to them but they did not listen; I called out to them but they did not respond")

Appendix B: Attestations of הבמות Among Kings

This appendix lists all the attestations of הבמות in DtrH accounts of kings. It demonstrates how הבמות appears mainly in the accounts of the first three northern dynasties and justifications for the destructions of Samaria and Jerusalem.

Kings of United Monarchy

David

Solomon (וַיֶּאֱהַב - 1 Kgs 11:9)

Kings of Israel

Kings	Dynasty	הבמות
Jeroboam I (924-903)	Jeroboam	Yes
Nadab (903-902)	Jeroboam	Yes - Fulfillment
Baasha (902-886)	Baasha	Yes
Elah (886-885)	Baasha	Yes -Fulfillment
Omri (885-873)	Omride	Yes
Ahab (873-851)	Omride	Yes
Ahaziah (851-849)	Omride	Yes
Jehoram (849-843)	Omride	No - Removed pillars of Ba'al (2 Kgs 3:2)
Jehu (843-816)	Jehu	No - Removed Ba'al (2 Kgs 10:28)
Jehoahaz (816-800)	Jehu	No-אך הלך (2 Kgs 13:3)

Kings of Judah

Kings	Dynasty	הבמות
Rehoboam (924-907)	Davidic (Evil)	No-וַיִּבְנוּ (1 Kgs 14:22)
Abijam (907-906)	Davidic (Evil)	No
Asa (905-874)	Davidic (Right)	No
Jehoshaphat (874-850)	Davidic (Right)	No
Jehoram (850-843)	David – related to Ahab (?) (Evil)	No
Ahaziah (843)	David – related to Ahab(?) (Evil)	No
Athaliah (843-837)	Omride (NA)	No
Joash (837-?)	Davidic (Right-Partial)	No
Amaziah (?-?)	Davidic (Right-Partial)	No

Kings	Dynasty	הכעים	Kings	Dynasty	הכעים
Joash (800-785)	Jehu	No	Uzziah (Azariah) (?-?)	Davidic (Right)	No
Jeroboam II (785-745)	Jehu	No	Jotham(?-742)	Davidic (Right)	No
Zechariah (745)	Zechariah	No			
Shallum (745)	Shallum	No			
Menahem (745-736)	Menahem	No	Jehoahaz I (Ahaz) (742-727)	Davidic (Evil)	No
Pekah (735-732)	Menahem	No			
Hoshea (732-723)	Hoshea	No			
Diatribe → Israel (722)		Yes	Hezekiah (727-698)	Davidic (Right)	No
			Manasseh (722)	Davidic (Evil)	Yes
			Amon (642-640)	Davidic (Evil)	No
			Josiah (639-609)	Davidic (Right)	Yes – But against Manasseh
			Jehoahaz II (609)	Davidic (Evil)	No
			Jehoiakim (608-598)	Davidic (Evil)	No
			Jehoiachin (598-597)	Davidic (Evil)	No
			Zedekiah (597-586)	Davidic (Evil)	No – אך־יהוה (2 Kgs 24.20)
			Fall of Jerusalem		No

Appendix C: Attestations of Divine Wrath in DtrH1

This appendix lists other terms for divine wrath beside כַּעַס in DtrH: קָצַף/קֶצֶף, הִתְאַנַּף/אַף, אַף (without or without) חָרָה, אַף, חֵמָה, עֶבְרָה, זַעַם, קֶצֶף, חָרָה בְּ, אַף חָרָה, and אַף. It provides insight into the role of divine wrath in meting out punishments. Thus, the appendix demonstrates the pivotal functional of כַּעַס as opposed to others expressions for divine wrath which function primarily as motivation for punishment.

Passage-Pericope	Terminology – Category	Linking Conj./Pivot	Type of Sin	Type of Punishment	Agency
Deut 1:34 (1:19-45)	וַיִּקְצֹף ("God was angry") – prelude to punishment	Previous Phrase	Refusal to go up and fight	No one from this generation will enter the land except Caleb	Implicit – God, motivated by divine wrath
Deut 1:37 (1:19-45)	גַּם־בִּי הִתְאַנַּף יְהוָה בִּגְלַלְכֶם ("also YHWH became angry with me because of you") – prelude to punishment	Previous Phrase	Not outlined – God was angry with Moses	Moses will not enter the promised land, but Joshua	Implicit – God, motivated by divine wrath
Deut 3:26 (3:23-29)	וַיִּתְעַבֵּר יְהוָה בִּי לְמַעַנְכֶם ("YHWH became angry with me because of you") – description of punishment	None	Not outlined – Moses pleads with God to enter the promised land	Moses will not enter	Implicit – God, motivated by divine wrath
Deut 32:22 (32:1-43); see Part I	כִּי אֵשׁ קָדְחָה בְאַפִּי ("for fire was kindled in my nose") – punishment	עַם (v. 19)	Apostasy (vv. 15-18)	God brings devastation	Divine wrath. See Part I for other formulations
Josh 7:1 (7:1-26)	וַיִּחַר־אַף יְהוָה ("YHWH became angry") – prelude to punishment	Previous Phrase	Achan took from the "proscription" (חֵרֶם)	Men of Ai killed many Israelites; Joshua and community stoned Achan and family	Human Instrument
Josh 7:26 (7:1-26)	וַיָּשָׁב יְהוָה מֵחֲרוֹן אַף ("YHWH turned away from his fierce anger") – potential punishment	Same as above	Same as above	Same as above	Same as above; human activity prevented God from acting on his wrath

Josh 9:20 (9:3-27)	וְלֹא־יִהְיֶה עָלֵינוּ קֶצֶף עַל־הַשְּׁבֻעָה ("so that the wrath will not be over us on account of the oath") – punishment	NA	None	Divine wrath (since oath was sworn by YHWH) will be against them	Divine wrath develops from break in oath
Josh 22:18 (22:16-20, subunit of 22:7-34)	יִקְצֹף ("he will be angry") – punishment	None	Reubenites, Gadites, and half-tribe of Manasseh built an altar which is thought to be rebellious	God will be angry	God, motivated by anger
Josh 22:20 (22:16-20, subunit of 22:7-34)	וְעַל־כָּל־עֲדַת יִשְׂרָאֵל הָיָה קָצֶף ("wrath was upon the whole community of Israel") – punishment	None	Specific example – Achan violate the proscription	Anger came upon the people	Divine wrath
Judg 6:39 (6:1-8:32)	אַל־יִחַר אַפְּךָ בִּי ("do not be angry with me")	None	None	None – Gideon tests God and requests that God not be angry with him	God, motivated by divine anger
2 Sam 6:7 (6:1-19)	וַיִּחַר־אַף יְהוָה ("YHWH became angry") – prelude to punishment	Previous Phrase	Uzzah reached to hold the Ark from stumbling	God struck Uzzah and he died	God
2 Sam 22:8 (22:1-51)	כִּי חָרָה לוֹ ("because he was angry") – motivation	NA	None – psalm which praises God	None – psalm notes God's power	God, motivated by divine wrath (creation shakes)
2 Sam 22:9 (22:1-51)	עָלָה עָשָׁן בְּאַפּוֹ ("smoke went up in his nose) – description above of angry God	Same as above	Same as above	Same as above	Same as above

Passage-Pericope	Terminology – Category	Linking Conj./ Pivot	Type of Sin	Type of Punishment	Agency
2 Sam 24:1 (24:1-25)	וַיֹּסֶף אַף־יְהוָה לַחֲרוֹת בְּיִשְׂרָאֵל ("YHWH became angry with Isreal again") – prelude to punishment	Previous Phrase	None provided	God incites David to get a census which leads to a plague	God, motivated by divine wrath, with natural instrument
1 Kgs 11:9 (11:1-13)	וַיִּתְאַנַּף יְהוָה בִשְׁלֹמֹה ("YHWH became angry with Solomon") – prelude to punishment	Conjunction: כִּי ("because," v. 9); יַעַן אֲשֶׁר ("on account of," v.11); Pivot: previous phrase	Solomon married many foreign women and established foreign practices. However in the explicit formulation of the reason in v. 9 and v.11, it is for turning away from God and not keeping his command	Tear away the kingdom from his dynasty	God, with human instrument

Appendix D: Attestations of Divine Wrath in DtrH2 and later redactors

This appendix lists other terms for divine wrath beside הַכַּעַס in DtrH2: הַחֲרוֹן/חָרָה, הֶאֱנִיף/אַף, אַף (with or without) חָרָה, אַף, חֵמָה, עֶבְרָה, חֵמָה, זַעַם, קֶצֶף, אַף בָּאֵשׁ, and אֶרֶף/אַנְפֵי עַל בָּאֵשׁ עֲלֵי. It provides insight into the role of divine wrath in meting out punishments. Thus, the appendix demonstrates the pivotal functional of הַכַּעַס as opposed to other expressions for divine wrath which function primarily as motivation for punishment.

Passage-Pericope	Terminology-Category	Linking Conjunction/Pivot	Catalog of Sin	Description of Punishment	Agency
Deut 4:21 (4:21-24)	וַיהוָה הִתְאַנַּף בִּי עַל־דִּבְרֵיכֶם ("YHWH was angry with me on account of your deeds") – prelude to punishment	Previous phrase	None – Moses outlines his situation	Moses will not enter the promised land	Implied – God, who is described as "consuming fire, jealous God" (v. 24)
Deut 6:15 (6:10-19, addition to 6:4-9, 20-25)[10]	פֶּן יֶחֱרֶה אַף־יהוָה אֱלֹהֶיךָ בָּךְ ("lest YHWH, your God, become angry with you") – punishment	כִּי ("for," v. 15)	None – commands: do not follow other gods, do not test God, keep his commandments	God will become angry and destroy	God, motivated by divine wrath
Deut 7:4 (7:4-5, 7-16, 25-26, addition to 7:1-3, 6, 17-24)[11]	וְחָרָה אַף־יהוָה בָּכֶם ("YHWH become angry with you") – punishment	None	None – future scenario of what other nations will do: make them worship other gods	God will become angry and destroy	God, motivated by divine wrath
Deut 9:7 (9:7-24)	הִקְצַפְתָּ ("you stirred to wrath") – description of sin	None	Call to memory for molten image	Anger and potential extermination (v. 8)	God, motivated by divine wrath

Passage-Pericope	Terminology-Category	Linking Conjunction/Pivot	Catalog of Sin	Description of Punishment	Agency
Deut 9:8 (9:7-24)	הקצפתם ("you stirred to wrath") – description of sin	None	Same as above	Same as above	Same as above
Deut 9:8 (9:7-24)	ויתאנף ("he became angry") – prelude to punishment	Previous phrase	Same as above	Same as above	Same as above
Deut 9:19 (9:7-24)	אף החמה אשר החמה יהוה ("the fiery wrath which YHWH raged") – punishment	להכעיסו ("to provoke him to anger, v. 18); כי ("for," v. 19)	Made "molten image" (מסכה, vv. 12, 16)	Potential extermination (v. 19)	God, with divine wrath as instrument
Deut 9:20 (9:7-24)	התאנף ("he was angry") – prelude to punishment	Previous phrase	Same as above but includes Aaron specifically	Potential extermination of Aaron (v. 20)	God, motivated by divine wrath
Deut 9:22 (9:7-24)	מקצפים היו ("you were stirring to wrath") – description of sin	None	Stir God to wrath in wilderness (v. 22)	None	NA
Deut 11:17 (11:13-21, subunit of 10:12-11:32)	וחרה אף־יהוה בכם ("YHWH became angry with you") – prelude to punishment	Previous phrase	None – command to obey	God will become angry and prevent the rain from coming	God, motivated by divine wrath bring natural calamity
Deut 13:18 (addition to 12:29-13:18, which has additions throughout)[12]	ושב יהוה מחרון אפו ("YHWH will turn aside from his fierce anger") – punishment	None	None – future scenario in which scoundrels tell people to worship other gods	None – people should burn them and their town	Community needs to act before God's anger burn. God motivated by divine wrath

Reference	Hebrew phrase		Cause	Consequence	Agent
Deut 29:19 (29:15-20)	יֶעְשַׁן אַף־יהוה ("the anger of YHWH will blaze;" Samaritan Pentateuch has חרה, "he became angry") – prelude to punishment	Previous phrase; כִּ ("for," v. 19)	None – future temptation to worship images	God will become angry and bring upon the curses in the book and wipe out name from under heaven	God, motivated by divine wrath
Deut 29:22 (29:21-28)	בְּאַפּוֹ ("in his fiery wrath") – punishment	None within specific example	None – comparison to Sodom and Gomorrah	God overthrew Sodom and Gomorrah in his wrath	God, motivated by divine wrath
Deut 29:23 (29:21-28)	מֶה חֳרִי הָאַף הַגָּדוֹל הַזֶּה ("What [caused] this burning of great anger?") – punishment	See 29:26	See 29:26	God bring destruction to land	God and divine wrath
Deut 29:26 (29:21-28)	וַיִּחַר־אַף יהוה ("YHWH became angry") – punishment	עַל אֲשֶׁר ("because," v. 24)	Apostasy: People have abandoned the covenant of YHWH and followed other gods	God became angry and brought the curses within the book of the teaching. God uprooted them in anger	God, motivated by divine wrath (break the covenant, receive the consequences of the broken covenant)
Deut 29:27 (29:21-28)	בְּאַף וּבְחֵמָה וּבְקֶצֶף גָּדוֹל ("in anger, wrath, and great fury") – punishment	Same as above	Same as above	Same as above	Same as above
Deut 31:17 (31:16-22)	וְחָרָה אַפִּי בוֹ ("I will become angry with him") – prelude to punishment	Previous phrase for first formulation; כִּ ("because," v. 18)	Apostasy – follow other gods and reject God and commands	God will become angry and God will abandon them	God, motivated by divine wrath. Measure-for-measure punishment: they abandon God (v. 16) and God will abandon them (v. 17). Self-destruction: they do evil (v. 18) so evil will befall them (v. 17)

Passage-Pericope	Terminology-Category	Linking Conjunction/Pivot	Catalog of Sin	Description of Punishment	Agency
Josh 23:16 (23:14-16, subunit of 23:1-16)	וְחָרָה אַף־יְהוָה בָּכֶם ("YHWH will become angry with you") – prelude to punishment	Previous phrase	None – future sin in which people break the covenant and worship other gods	God will bring evil (v. 15); God will become angry and people will be destroyed	God, motivated by divine wrath
Judg 2:14 (2:11-19; see Part II)	וַיִּחַר־אַף יְהוָה ("YHWH became angry") – prelude to punishment	וַיַּכְעִסוּ ("they provoked to anger," v. 12)	Apostasy – reject God and worship other gods	Deliver Israel to enemy hands	God, motivated by divine wrath, and human instrument
Judg 2:20 (2:20-23)	וַיִּחַר־אַף יְהוָה ("YHWH became angry") – establish the context	יַעַן אֲשֶׁר ("because")	Broke covenant and did not obey	God will leave nations to test Israel	God, motivated by divine wrath, and human instrument
Judg 3:8 (3:7-11)	וַיִּחַר־אַף יְהוָה ("YHWH became angry") – prelude to punishment	Previous phrase	Apostasy – forgot their God and served Ba'alim and Asheroth	God sold to king Aram-naharaim	God, motivated by divine wrath, and divine instrument
Judg 10:7 (10:6-9, subunit of 10:6-16)	וַיִּחַר־אַף יְהוָה ("YHWH became angry") – prelude to punishment	Previous phrase	Apostasy – reject God and serve other deities	Sold into enemy hands	God, motivated by divine wrath, and human instrument
1 Sam 28:18 (28:1-25; level of redaction is unclear but not part of David's rise	כַּאֲשֶׁר לֹא־שָׁמַעְתָּ בְּקוֹל יְהוָה וְלֹא־עָשִׂיתָ חֲרוֹן־אַפּוֹ בַּעֲמָלֵק ("you did not execute his fierce anger against Amalek") – part of accusation	כַּאֲשֶׁר ("because," v. 18)	Saul did not obey God nor execute his wrath	Give kingdom to David and deliver Israel to the Philistines	God and human instruments; divine wrath = God's punishment of Amalek
1 Kgs 8:46[13] (8:44-53; subunit of 8:1-66)	וְאָנַפְתָּ בָם ("and you become angry with them") – prelude to punishment	Phrase with anger	People sin against God	Deliver them into the enemy and taken into captivity	God, motivated by divine wrath, with human instrument

		Previous phrase			
2 Kgs 13:3 (13:3–6a, addition to 13:1-2, 6b-9)	וַיִּחַר־אַף יְהוָה ("YHWH became angry") – prelude to punishment		V. 2 describes the sin of Jehoahaz which the addition builds up to establish the sin-anger-punishment-prayer-deliverance pattern established in the book of Judges	God gives Jehoahaz into the hands of Aram	God, motivated by divine wrath, with human instrument
2 Kgs 17:18 (17:7-23a); see Part II	וַיִּתְאַנַּף יְהוָה ("YHWH became angry") – prelude to punishment	לְהַכְעִיסוֹ ("to provoke him to anger," v. 18)	List of sins	God removed Israel	God, motivated by divine wrath. See Part II
2 Kgs 22:13 (22:11-13, subunit of 22:1-20)	כִּי־גְדוֹלָה חֲמַת יְהוָה ("for great is the wrath of YHWH ... [that is] kindled") – punishment	עַל אֲשֶׁר ("because," v. 13)	Ancestors did not obey the "terms of this book" (דִּבְרֵי הַסֵּפֶר, v. 13)	God's wrath is great	Divine wrath
2 Kgs 22:17 (22:14-20, subunit of 22:1-20); see Part II	חֲמָתִי ("my wrath is kindled") – punishment	תַּחַת אֲשֶׁר ("because"); Pivot: הִכְעִיסֻנִי ("provoking me to anger")	Apostasy – reject God and follow other deities	Divine wrath kindled	Divine wrath
2 Kgs 23:26 (23:26-27); see Part II	אַךְ לֹא־שָׁב יְהוָה מֵחֲרוֹן ("Yet YHWH did not turn aside from this fierce anger") – punishment	עַל ("on account of"); Pivot	Manasseh provoked God to anger	God removed and rejected Jerusalem	God, motivated by his divine wrath
2 Kgs 24:20 (24:18-20)	כִּי עַל־אַף יְהוָה הָיְתָה בִירוּשָׁלַ͏ִם ("because of YHWH's anger, [these things] happen to Jerusalem") – motivation	כִּי עַל־אַף יְהוָה ("because of YHWH's anger")	Zedekiah did evil	Assumed destruction of Jerusalem	God, motivated by divine wrath

Appendix E: Attestations of Divine Wrath in Pre-Exilic and Exilic Prophetic Books

This appendix lists other terms for divine wrath beside הַכֲעָסִים in the books of Isaiah, Ezekiel, Hosea, Micah, Nahum, Habakkuk, and Zephaniah: הַחֲרֹן/קֶצֶף, הַהֶאֱנָף/אַף, הִתְאַנַּף/אַף, אַף (with or without) יהוה, הֵמָה, חֲרִי, עֶבְרָה, זַעַם, קֶצֶף, אֵבֶל, מָשָׁא, קֶרֶב אֵשׁ, and בָּאֵשׁ/וַתָּאֵר אֵשׁ כָּעֲשֵׁן/אֵשׁ תֹּאכַל. It provides insight into the role of divine wrath in meting out punishments. Thus, the appendix demonstrates the pivotal functional of הַכֲעָסִים as opposed to other expressions for divine wrath which function as either motivation for, preface to, or actual description of the punishment in pre-exilic and exilic prophetic books.

Passage-Pericope	Terminology-Category	Linking Conjunction/Pivot	Type of Sin	Type of Punishment	Agency
Isa 5:25 (5:25-30)[14]	עַל־כֵּן חָרָה אַף־יהוה בְּעַמּוֹ ("therefore YHWH became angry with his people") – prelude to punishment	Previous phrase	Problem in the text – unclear what the original 'sin' may have been but in the final MT form, sin is for having rejected God's teaching (v. 24)	God became angry and struck people and calls a foreign nation to punish people	God, motivated by divine wrath, and his human instrument
Isa 5:25 (5:25-30)	בְּכָל־זֹאת לֹא־שָׁב אַפּוֹ ("in all this, his anger did not turn aside") - punishment	Same as above	Same as above	Same as above	Same as above
Isa 9:11, 16, 20, 10:4 (9:7-10:4)	בְּכָל־זֹאת לֹא־שָׁב אַפּוֹ ("in all this, his anger did not turn aside") - punishment	None	Interspersed – people and leaders not turn to God and ethical infractions	Several descriptions – foreign nations devour Israel (vv. 10-11); wickedness consume like fire (v. 17); neighbors devour each other (vv. 18-20)	Human instruments, described as motivated by divine wrath

			Same as above	Same as above	Same as above and divine wrath (agent)
Isa 9:18 (9:7-10:4)	בעברת יהוה ("by the fury of YHWH") – punishment	Same as above	Same as above	Same as above	Same as above and divine wrath (agent)
Isa 10:5 (10:5-19)	שבט ... אף ... עברתי ("rod of my anger ... my fury") – description of Assyria as God's instrument	None	Arrogance of Assyria	God sends wasting disease and set fire to Assyria (vv. 16-19); secondary to pericope – God will "visit the fruit of the arrogance of the king of Assyria" (אפקד על־פרי־גדל, v. 12)	God; secondarily worded in a measure-for-measure punishment (for Assyria's arrogance, God will bring the fruit of his arrogance)
Isa 10:6	עם עברתי ("people of my fury") - punishment	None	None – describing the people against whom Assyria was sent	God sends Assyria, his instrument against people	God and Assyria (conceived as the punisher of Judah) – human instrument
Isa 10:25 (10:24-26)	וכלה זעם ואפי על־תבליתם ("fury will be spend and my anger will be upon their destruction") – punishment	None	None	Anger initially set against Judah will now be directed to Assyria but v. 26 describes God acting	Divine wrath; God, with human instrument; and God alone
Isa 12:1 (12:1-6)	כי אנף בי ישב אפך ("when you were angry with me, your anger turned aside") – punishment	None	None – psalm in praise of God	None – instead of punishment, comfort	God; divine wrath = punishment
Isa 13:3 (13:2-3; subunit of 13:1-22; Babylonian period)	קראתי גבורי לאפי ("I have summon my warriors to [execute] my anger") – punishment	None	None – oracle against Babylon	Call of (heavenly or human) army against Babylon	God with (heavenly or human) army

Passage-Pericope	Terminology-Category	Linking Conjunction/Pivot	Type of Sin	Type of Punishment	Agency
Isa 13:5 (13:4-5; subunit of 13:1-22; Babylonian period)	זהו וכלי זעמו ("YHWH and weapons of his wrath") – punishment	None	Same as above	God as commander of army with his weapons of wrath to come to destroy earth	God with army and weapons of wrath
Isa 13:9 (13:9-16; subunit of 13:1-22; eschatological, and thus later)	אכזרי ועברה וחרון אף ("pitiless fury and fierce anger") – punishment	None	No explicit list of sins, but in the wording of the punishment, sin is provided. V. 11 lists the people's iniquity and arrogance	Day of YHWH – destroy earth, darkness, death, etc. Partial measure-for-measure in v. 11, requite world of evil; requite wicked of iniquity; humble the proud: ופקדתי על־תבל רעה ... ועל־רשעים עונם והשבתי גאון זדים ("I will visit evil upon the earth; over the wicked, I will visit their iniquity.... The haughtiness of tyrants, I will bring down.")	God and divine wrath
Isa 13:13 (13:9-16, subunit of 13:1-22; eschatological, thus later)	בעברת יהוה צבאות וביום חרון אפו ("at the fury of YHWH of hosts on the day of his fierce wrath") – punishment	None	Same as above	Same as above	God and divine wrath from which heavens (MT has ארגיז, "I will shake," while Greek has "they will shake") and earth shake

Reference	Wrath terminology		Context	Description	God and divine wrath
Isa 26:20 (26:20-21; subunit of 26:1-21; very late text)	עד יעבר זעם ("until wrath passes") - punishment	None	None – praise of God	God come to punish earth for its bloodshed; measure-for-measure punishment: לפקד ... עון ... ("to visit the iniquity .... upon it")	None
Isa 27:4 (27:2-6; eschatological, thus late)	חמה אין לי ("there is not anger in me") – punishment	None	None – future restoration	Whoever raises thorns in the vineyard, God will march against it	God, whose lack of wrath (motivation), makes him restore Jacob
Isa 30:27 (30:27-33; perhaps late – around 612)	בערה אפו ... שפתיו מלא זעם ("his anger/nose burning .... his lips full of wrath") – description of God as warrior	None	None	God, described as an angry warrior, fights against Assyria	God with his divine wrath
Isa 30:30 (30:27-33; perhaps late – around 612)	זעף אף ("in the raging of anger/nose")	Same as above	Same as above	Same as above	Same as above
Isa 34:2 (34:1-17; late)	כי קצף ליהוה על־כל־הגוים על־כל־צבאם ("for YHWH is angry against all the nations; wrath upon all their army") – punishment	None	None – oracle against Edom	God, with his sword, will destroy Edom completely	God, with his sword
Ezek 5:13 (5:11-17, subunit of 5:5-17)	כם אפי וחנחתי את־חמתי בם ("my anger will cease and I will rest my wrath against them .... I will stop my wrath") – punishment	יען ("on account of that," v. 11)	Sanctuary is defiled because of images	God will give a 1/3 to plague, 1/3 to famine, 1/3 to sword; conceptualized as spurred by wrath	God with natural and human instruments; motivated by anger

Passage-Pericope	Terminology-Category	Linking Conjunction/Pivot	Type of Sin	Type of Punishment	Agency
Ezek 5:15 (5:11-17, subunit of 5:5-17)	באף ובחמה ובתכחות חמה ("in fiery wrath and with rebukes of wrath") – punishment	Same as above	Same as above	God will shame Jerusalem, shoot arrows of famine, send wild beasts, etc.	God with natural and human instruments, motivated by anger
Ezek 6:12 (6:11-13a, subunit of 6:1-14)	וכליתי חמתי בם ("I will bring my wrath to pass against them") – punishment	אל ("on account of," v. 11)	Evil abominations	Fall by sword, famine, and plague	God with human and natural instruments
Ezek 7:3 (7:2-4, subunit of 7:1-27; late)	ושלחתי אפי ("I will send my anger") – punishment	None	No explicit list (description of the end) – within the description of punishment outlined: abominations and ways	God will judge Israel according to ways and set abominations ושפטתיך כדרכיך ונתתי עליך את כל תועבתיך ("I will judge you according to your ways; I will repay you all your abominations," v. 3b; see also v. 4b)	God with divine wrath as instrument; measure-for-measure punishment
Ezek 7:8 (7:5-9, subunit of 7:1-27; late)	אשפוך חמתי עליך וכליתי אפי בך ("I will pour out my wrath against you and I will bring my anger to pass against you") – punishment	None	Same as above	Same as above; see v. 8b and v. 9b	Same as above
Ezek 7:12 (7:10-12; subunit of 7:1-27)	כי חרון אל־כל־המונה ("for wrath is upon all its crowd") – punishment	None	None	Divine wrath upon everyone	Divine wrath

Reference	(wrath phrase)	כי ("because")	Because of his iniquity	Divine wrath upon everyone	Divine wrath
Ezek 7:14 (7:13-14; subunit of 7:1-27)	כי חרון אל־כל־המונה ("for my wrath is upon all its crowd") – punishment	כי ("because")	Because of his iniquity	Divine wrath upon everyone	God (who turns away from them, v. 22) with human and natural instrument
Ezek 7:19 (7:15-22; subunit of 7:1-27)	ביום עברת יהוה ("on the day of the fury of YHWH") – punishment	כי ("because," v. 16); כי ("because," v. 19b)	"Because of his iniquity" (חטאתו, v. 16); "because their iniquity was a stumbling block" (כי היה מכשול עונם v. 19b); maybe an addition	Sword, plague, delivery into enemy hands who desecrate the land	God, motivated by divine wrath
Ezek 8:18 (8:1-18)	אעשה בחמה ("I will deal in wrath") – punishment	None	Detestable forms of idolatry	God acts in wrath	God, with his divine wrath = human instrument killing idolaters
Ezek 9:8 (9:1-11)	בשפכך את־חמתך ("when you pour out your wrath") – punishment	None	"Exceedingly great iniquity," עון בית ישראל ויהודה ... מאד (v. 9), bloodshed, injustice	Command "men in charge" to kill the idolaters	God with natural instruments, motivated by anger. With imagery of whitewashed wall, develop measure-for-measure punishment
Ezek 13:13 (13:10-16, subunit of 13:1-23)	בחמתי ... באף ... in my anger ... with wrath ("in my wrath ... in my anger ... with wrath") – punishment	יען וביען ("because and by the cause that")	Prophets who lead people astray, coat with whitewash	God send storms, winds, hailstones; wall will fall	Same as above
Ezek 13:15 (13:10-16, subunit of 13:1-23)	וכליתי את חמתי ("I will stop my wrath") – punishment	Same as above	Same as above	Same as above	God with natural instruments
Ezek 14:19 (14:12-20, subunit of 14:12-23)	ושפכתי חמתי ("and I poured out my wrath") – punishment	None	Hypothetical – if a land was to sin and commit treachery	God sends famine, wild beasts, sword, plague, and poured out divine wrath (neither Noah, Daniel, nor Job can save them)	

Passage-Pericope	Terminology-Category	Linking Conjunction/Pivot	Type of Sin	Type of Punishment	Agency
Ezek 16:38 (16:36-42, subunit of 16:1-63); see part III	וּנְתַתִּיךְ דַּם חֵמָה וְקִנְאָה ("I will set blood, wrath, and zeal against you") – punishment	יַעַן ("on account of," v. 36)	Foreign alliances, idolatry, child sacrifice (v. 36)	God and lovers will degrade Jerusalem	God with divine wrath and human instruments; overall structure (measure-for-measure punishment)
Ezek 16:42 (16:36-42, subunit of 16:1-63); see Part III	וַהֲנִחֹתִי חֲמָתִי ("I have satisfied my wrath") – punishment	Same as above	Same as above	Same as above	Same as above; human instrument actions conceptualized as God acting in divine wrath
Ezek 19:12 (19:1-14)	וַתֻּתַּשׁ בְּחֵמָה ("it was uprooted in wrath") – punishment	None	None – lament depicting Jerusalem as a lioness	Nations come against it and finally uproot it from land and plant in desert	Human enemies; uprooting motivated by anger (here agent is not implied)
Ezek 20:8 (20:5-10, subunit of 20:1-44)	לִשְׁפֹּךְ חֲמָתִי . . . אֶל ("to pour out my wrath . . . to bring my anger to pass") – punishment	None	Israel rebelled against God in Egypt with their images	God was about to pour out wrath but did not	God, using divine wrath as instrument and motivated by divine wrath
Ezek 20:13 (20:11-17, subunit of 20:1-44)	לְכַלּוֹתָם . . . חֲמָתִי לִשְׁפֹּךְ ("to pour out my wrath . . . to annihilate them") – punishment	None	Israel rebelled against God in the wilderness (first generation) by not keeping his statutes and decrees, profaning the Sabbath	God was about to pour out wrath but did not	God, using divine wrath as instrument
Ezek 20:21 (20:18-22, subunit of 20:1-44)	לִשְׁפֹּךְ חֲמָתִי . . . אֶל ("to pour out my wrath . . . to bring my anger to pass") – punishment	None	Same as above	God was about to pour out his wrath but did not	God, using divine wrath as instrument and motivated by divine wrath

Ezek 20:33 (20:30-44, subunit of 20:1-44)	ביד חזקה ובזרוע נטויה ובחמה שפוכה ("with a mighty hand, outstretched arm, and poured wrath") – punishment	None	Previous rebellion and continuous idolatry, including child sacrifice; request to be like other nations	God will rule over them with a mighty hand, outstretched arm, and outpoured wrath	God with his instruments of salvific and destructive aspects
Ezek 20:34 (20:30-44, subunit of 20:1-44)	ביד חזקה ובזרוע נטויה ובחמה שפוכה ("with a mighty hand, outstretched arm, and outpoured wrath") – punishment	None	Same as above	God will gather the people with a mighty hand, outstretched arm, and outpoured wrath	Same as above
Ezek 21:22 (21:13-22, subunit of 21:1-37)	חמתי . . . ("I will satisfy my wrath") – punishment	None	None	Call upon sword, which will be placed in the hand of a slayer (v. 16), to decimate the people; God also strikes and satisfies fury	Sword and God, motivated by divine wrath
Ezek 21:36 (21:33-37, subunit of 21:1-37)	ושפכתי עליך זעמי באש עברתי אפיח עליך ("I will pour out my wrath and blow upon you the fire of my fury") – punishment	כי ("because," v. 34)	Ammonites prophesied and divined falsely	God pour wrath and deliver to enemies	God, using divine wrath and humans as instrument
Ezek 22:20 (22:17-22, subunit of 22:1-31)	באפי ובחמתי ("in my fiery wrath") – punishment	יען ("on account that," v. 19)	Israel = dross	God will gather in wrath and melt it	God with divine wrath as instrument
Ezek 22:21 (22:17-22, subunit of 22:1-31)	באש עברתי ("in the fire of my fury") – punishment	Same as above	Same as above	Same as above	Same as above

Passage-Pericope	Terminology-Category	Linking Conjunction/ Pivot	Type of Sin	Type of Punishment	Agency
Ezek 22:22 (22:17-22, subunit of 22:1-31)	שְׁפַכְתִּי חֲמָתִי ("I have poured out my wrath") – punishment	Same as above	Same as above	Punishment conceptualized as God pouring out his wrath	Same as above
Ezek 22:24 (22:23-31, subunit of 22:1-31)	בְּיוֹם זָעַם ("on the day of wrath") – description of day of punishment	See Ezek 22:31	See Ezek 22:31	See Ezek 22:31	See Ezek 22:31
Ezek 22:31 (22:23-31, subunit of 22:1-31)	וָאֶשְׁפֹּךְ עֲלֵיהֶם זַעְמִי בְּאֵשׁ עֶבְרָתִי ("I poured out my wrath over them; I consumed them with the fire of my fury") – punishment	None	Prophets violate teachings, officials abuse power, and people abuse poor	God pours out his wrath and set "their way upon their head" (דַּרְכָּם בְּרֹאשָׁם)	God with his divine wrath as instrument; worded to be measure-for-measure punishment
Ezek 23:25 (23:22-27, subunit of 23:1-49)	וְעָשׂוּ אוֹתָךְ בְּחֵמָה ("they will deal with you in wrath") – punishment	None	Jerusalem (Oholibah) prostituted herself to other lovers and Chaldeans (vv. 11-21)	God delivered Jerusalem to Chaldeans who punished her (vv. 22-27)	God but primarily human instruments who act in God's wrath; correspondence in that lovers are the destroyers
Ezek 24:8 (24:6-8, subunit of 24:1-14)	לְהַעֲלוֹת חֵמָה ("to bring up wrath") – punishment	כִּי ("because")	Blood shed on rock	God set her blood on bare rock	God, motivated by divine wrath – measure-for-measure punishment
Ezek 24:13 (24:9-14, subunit of 24:1-14)	עַד־הֲנִיחִי אֶת חֲמָתִי בָּךְ ("until I have satisfied my wrath against you") – punishment	כִּי ("because," v. 13)	Vile impurity (v. 13)	God will punish but "they will judge you according to your ways and deeds" (בִּדְרָכַיִךְ וְכַעֲלִילוֹתַיִךְ, v. 14; compare to other Hebrew	God – worded as measure-for-measure punishment but does not conceptually correspond

Reference	Wrath expression	"on account of" marker	Oracle / Cause		... which as "I will judge you," referring to God)	God description
Ezek 25:14 (25:12-14, subunit of 25:1-17)	בְּאַפִּי חֵמָה ("according to my fiery wrath") – punishment	כ׳ ("on account of")	Oracle against Edom = they took revenge on Israel		God destroys and takes revenge	God – according to wrath, try to establish measure-for-measure
Ezek 25:17 (25:15-17, subunit of 25:1-17)	בְּתוֹכְחוֹת חֵמָה ("with rebukes of wrath") – punishment	כ׳ ("on account of")	Oracle against Philistines – took revenge and tried to destroy Judah		God destroys and takes vengeance	God, with rebukes of wrath; measure-for-measure by playing on נקם ("to avenge")
Ezek 30:15 (30:13-19, subunit of 30:1-19)	וְשָׁפַכְתִּי חֲמָתִי ("I will pour out my wrath") – punishment	None	None – oracle against Egypt		God utterly destroys Egypt	God, with divine wrath
Ezek 36:6 (36:1-15)	בַּחֲמָתִי ("in my wrath") – punishment	יען ("on account that," vv. 2, 3, 6)	Enemies gloated over the defeat of Israel		God decreed in his wrath that the nations will be humiliated	God motivated by his wrath
Ezek 36:18 (36:16-21, subunit of 36:16-38)	וָאֶשְׁפֹּךְ חֲמָתִי עֲלֵיהֶם ... הַדָּם אֲשֶׁר-שָׁפְכוּ ("I poured out my wrath over them on account of the blood which they poured out") – punishment	על and ב ("on account of," v. 18)	Israel defiled the land with their ways and deeds, bloodshed, idolatry		God punishes them – pours out wrath, scatters them	God using divine wrath – worded as measure-for-measure punishment
Ezek 38:18 (38:14-23, subunit of 38:1-39:29)	תַּעֲלֶה חֲמָתִי בְּאַפִּי ("my wrath flared up in my nose") – punishment	None	None – future destruction of Israel (Gog and Magog)		God will bring Gog to Israel	God, motivated by divine wrath, with natural and human instrument
Ezek 38:19 (38:14-23, subunit of 38:1-39:29)	בְּאֵשׁ עֶבְרָתִי ("in the fire of my fury") – punishment	None	Same as above		God decreed that the created world will crumble	Same as above

Passage-Pericope	Terminology-Category	Linking Conjunction/Pivot	Type of Sin	Type of Punishment	Agency
Ezek 43:8 (43:1-12)	וָאֲכַל אֹתָם בְּאַפִּי ("I consumed them in my anger") – punishment	כִּי ("because," v. 8)	Past sin – kings put palace next to temple and committed abominations	God, motivated by divine wrath	God, motivated by divine wrath
Hos 5:10 (addition to 5:8-14)[15]	עֲלֵיהֶם אֶשְׁפּוֹךְ כַּמַּיִם עֶבְרָתִי ("over them I poured out my fury like water") - punishment	None	None – blow horn for battle	Destruction	God, with divine wrath as instrument
Hos 8:5 (8:4-6, fusion of Josianic [R1] and exilic [R2] editors)[16]	חָרָה אַפִּי בָּם ("I was angry with them," R1) – punishment	None	Calf in Samaria	Calf will turn into splinters	God, motivated by divine wrath
Hos 11:9 (11:8-9; R2)[17]	לֹא אֶעֱשֶׂה חֲרוֹן אַפִּי ("I will not act in my fierce anger") – punishment	None	None	God will not act in his wrath	God, motivated by divine wrath
Hos 13:11 (13:9-11; R2)[18]	אֶתֶּן ... בְּאַפִּי וְאֶקַּח בְּעֶבְרָתִי ("I give . . . in my anger and I take in my fury") – punishment	כִּי ("because," v. 9)	Rejection of God	God attack and destroy	God, motivated by divine wrath
Hos 14:5 (R2)[19]	כִּי שָׁב אַפִּי מִמֶּנּוּ ("for my anger has turned aside from him") – punishment	None	None – future return to God	God will heal for his wrath has turned aside	God, motivated by divine wrath
Mic 5:14 (5:9-14)	וְעָשִׂיתִי בְּאַף וּבְחֵמָה נָקָם ("I will take vengeance in my fiery wrath")	None	None	God will destroy army, city, idolatrous practices	God, motivated by divine wrath

Mic 7:9 (7:8-13)	זעף יהוה אשא ("I will bear the wrath of YHWH") – punishment	כי ("because," v. 9)	Larger context – none; immediate context – Israel sinned	Israel will bear God's wrath	Divine wrath
Mic 7:18 (7:18-20)	לא־החזיק לעד אפו ("who does not hold on to his anger forever") – punishment	None	None – hymn to God who forgives ("cast their sins")	None – God will have compassion	God, motivated by divine wrath
Nah 1:2 (1:2-8)	לפני זעמו מי יעמוד ומי יקום בחרון אפו חמתו נתכה כאש והצרים נתצו ממנו ("Before his wrath, who can stand? Who can stand his fierce anger? His wrath will be poured out like fire; rocks are shattered before him") – punishment	Same as above	Same as above	Same as above	Divine wrath
Hab 3:8 (3:8-15)	הבנהרים חרה יהוה אם בנהרים אפך אם בים עברתך ("Against the rivers, is YHWH angry? Is your anger against the rivers? Your fury against the sea?") – prelude to punishment	None	None – hymn exalting the power of God	God the warrior in battle	God, motivated by anger
Hab 3:12 (3:8-15)	בזעם תצעד ארץ באף תדוש גוים ("You tread the earth in wrath; you trample nations in anger") – punishment	None	Same as above	Same as above	God, motivated by anger

Passage-Pericope	Terminology-Category	Linking Conjunction/Pivot	Type of Sin	Type of Punishment	Agency
Zeph 1:15 (1:10-18)	יום עברה היום ההוא ("that day will be a day of wrath") – punishment	כי ("because," v. 17)	They sinned against YHWH	Day of punishment = day of God's anger	God and divine wrath
Zeph 1:18 (1:10-18)	ביום עברת יהוה ("on the day of the fury of YHWH") – punishment	Same as above	Same as above	Same as above	Same as above
Zeph 2:2 (2:1-4)	בטרם לא יבא עליכם חרון אף־יהוה בטרם לא יבא עליכם יום אף־יהוה ("Before the fierce anger of YHWH comes upon you; before the day of anger of YHWH comes upon you") – punishment	None	None	Day of punishment = day of God's wrath	God and divine wrath
Zeph 2:3 (2:1-4)	אולי תסתרו ביום אף־יהוה ("perhaps you will be hidden on the day of the anger of YHWH") – punishment	Same as above	Same as above	Same as above	Same as above
Zeph 3:8 (3:1-13)	לשפך עליהם זעמי כל חרון אפי ("to pour out my wrath over them, all my fierce anger") – punishment	None	Official abuse power, prophets are reckless, priests profane, people are corrupt	God will pour out wrath and bring future restoration	God with divine wrath as instrument

Appendix F: Attestations of Divine Wrath in the Book of Jeremiah

This appendix lists other terms for divine wrath beside חֵמָה in the book of Jeremiah: אַף/אַפּוֹ, חֲרוֹן/חֲרוֹן־אַף, אַף (with or without) חֵמָה, אַף, חֵמָה, עֶבְרָה, זַעַם, קֶצֶף, בְּאַף, אַף וְחֵמָה/בְאַף וּבְחֵמָה, and עֲבֵרָה שָׁפַךְ חֵמָה. It provides insight into the role of divine wrath in meting out punishments. Thus, the appendix demonstrates the pivotal functional of חֵמָה as opposed to other expressions for divine wrath which function as either motivation for, preface to, or actual description of the punishment.

Passage-Pericope	Terminology-Category	Linking Conjunction/Pivot	Type of Sin	Type of Punishment	Agency
2:35 (2:33-37)	אַךְ שָׁב אַפִּי מֶנִּי ("surely, his anger has turned from me") – punishment	עַל ("because," v. 35)	Refusal to acknowledge sin; immediate context – people *think* God's anger has turned aside	God is about to pass judgment (v. 35b)	God with human instruments; divine wrath
4:4 (4:3-4)	פֶּן־תֵּצֵא כָאֵשׁ חֲמָתִי ("lest my wrath go out like fire") – punishment	מִפְּנֵי ("on account of")	"Evil of your deeds" (רֹעַ מַעַלְלֵיכֶם); larger context – failure to circumcise heart	Divine wrath sets out	God using human instrument; divine wrath
4:8 (4:5-8)	כִּי לֹא־שָׁב חֲרוֹן אַף־יְהוָה ("the fierce anger of YHWH did not turn from us") – punishment	None	No list of sins – flight passage: series of imperatives to flee for safety	God brings disaster (v. 6) which is conceptualized as divine wrath (v. 8)	God =divine wrath
4:26 (4:23-26)	מִפְּנֵי יְהוָה מִפְּנֵי חֲרוֹן אַפּוֹ ("from before YHWH, from before his fierce anger") punishment	None	No list of sin – description of destruction	Return to chaos (inversion of creation)	God = divine wrath

Passage-Pericope	Terminology-Category	Linking Conjunction/Pivot	Type of Sin	Type of Punishment	Agency
6:11 (6:9-15, multiple levels, perhaps vv. 10-11 are addition)	חֲמַת יְהוָה מָלֵאתִי ("I am filled with the wrath of YHWH") – punishment	None	Disobedience (v. 10) (either decree or prophetic editor, depending on whether God or Jeremiah is the speaker of v. 10). Textual variant in v. 11 (חֲמַת יְהוָה ["wrath of YHWH" MT] compared to ["my wrath," Greek]); see discussion of ch. 25 where Jeremiah is forefronted in the MT	Pouring out of divine wrath (v. 11)	Imperative (שְׁפֹךְ, "pour") from Jeremiah to God so God is the agent; vv. 12-15 – God is the primary agent
7:20 (7:16-20); see Part IV	אַף וַחֲמָתִי ("my fiery wrath") – punishment	כִּמְעַבָּם (v. 19)	Worship of Queen of Heavens	Divine wrath poured out	Divine wrath
7:29 (7:29, added to 7:21-28)	דוֹר עֶבְרָתוֹ ("the generation of his wrath") – description of people under punishment	כִּי ("for")	None – call to lament	God rejected and abandoned the people	God, motivated by divine wrath
10:10 (10:1-16)	מִקִּצְפּוֹ תִּרְעַשׁ הָאָרֶץ וְלֹא־יָכִלוּ גוֹיִם זַעְמוֹ ("from his anger the earth shakes; the nations cannot endure his wrath") – punishment	None	None – praise of living God in contrast to inert images	None – God is powerful and incomparable	God and divine wrath
10:24 (10:23-25)	אַל־בְּאַפְּךָ ("not in your anger") – punishment	None	None – Jeremiah's plea to God for correction	None – plea not to punish in anger but justice	God, motivated by divine wrath

Reference	Hebrew phrase	Marker	Against foreign nations	Pour out wrath	God, to whom
10:25 (10:23-25)	שְׁפֹךְ חֲמָתְךָ ("pour out your wrath") – punishment	כִּי ("because," v. 25b)	Against foreign nations – destroyed Jacob	Pour out wrath	God, to whom imperative is directed, using divine wrath
12:13 (12:7-13)	מֵחֲרוֹן אַף־יְהוָה ("because of the fierce anger of YHWH") – punishment	None	Judah's arrogance (v. 8)	God delivers to enemy	God, with human instruments; divine wrath
15:14 (15:13-14)	כִּי־אֵשׁ קָדְחָה בְאַפִּי ("for fire is kindled in my nose") – motivation	v. 13: כִּי ("because"); v. 14: previous phrase	"because of all your sins" (בְּכָל־חַטֹּאותֶיךָ, v. 13b); parallel to v. 14b so that the fire is kindled because of the sins	Given to plunder and enslaved (according to other Hebrew manuscripts) by enemies	God, motivated by divine wrath, with minor role for human instrument
17:4 (17:1-4); doublet of 15:14	כִּי־אֵשׁ קְדַחְתֶּם בְאַפִּי ("for you have kindled fire in my nose") – motivation	v. 3: כִּי ("because"); v. 4: previous phrase	"because of all your sins" (בְּחַטֹּאות, v. 3b) which is elaborated in vv. 1-2 (idolatry)	Given to plunder and enslaved by enemies	God, motivated by divine wrath, with minor role for human instrument
18:20 (18:18-20)	לְהָשִׁיב אֶת־חֲמָתְךָ מֵהֶם ("to turn your wrath away from them") – punishment	None	None – plea to God to punish the persecutors, who plot to kill Jeremiah (v. 23)	None – recollect past intervention where Jeremiah asked God to turn from his wrath	God, with divine wrath as instrument
18:23 (18:18-23)	בְּעֵת אַפְּךָ ("in the time of your anger") – period of punishment	None	Same as above	Punish the persecutors in the time of God's wrath	God, to whom imperative is directed; but use of human instruments, famine, and divine wrath
21:5 (21:1-10)	וּבְאַף וּבְחֵמָה וּבְקֶצֶף גָּדוֹל ("in/with anger, wrath, great fury") – punishment	None	None – just description of punishment	God gather Chaldeans against Judah (vv. 4-10)	God and human instrument, either motivated by or using divine wrath

Passage-Pericope	Terminology-Category	Linking Conjunction/Pivot	Type of Sin	Type of Punishment	Agency
21:12 (11-12); doublet of 4:4b	פן־תצא כאש חמתי ("lest my wrath go out like fire") – punishment	מפני ("on account of")	"Evil of your deeds" (רע־מעלליכם); context – failure of royal house to administer justice	Divine wrath burns	Divine wrath. Compare to v. 14 (addition?) where God ignites the fire in a measure-for-measure punishment: והצתי יער / ופקדתי עליכם כפרי מעלליכם ("I will punish you according to the fruit of your deeds," absent in Greek)
23:19 (23:16-22)	הנה סערת יהוה חמה יצאה ("here, the whirlwind of YHWH, wrath, goes out") – punishment	None	Prophets who do not speak what God 'decrees' (vv. 16-18)	Whirlwind of YHWH, depicted as חמה ("wrath"), and divine wrath (vv. 19-20): decree-editor (?)	Divine wrath (אף יהוה, v. 20)
23:20 (23:16-22)	אף יהוה ("anger of YHWH") – punishment	None	Same as above	Same as above	Same as above; either divine wrath or God accomplishes its plan
25:15 (25:15-29)	כוס היין החמה ("cup [filled with] infuriating wine") – punishment	None	None listed – against the foreign nations	"Infuriating wine" and sword (vv. 16, 27, 29)	God, who brings the sword (vv. 16, 27, 29)
25:37 (25:30-38)	מפני חרון אף יהוה ("from the fierce anger of YHWH") – punishment	None	None listed – description of destruction of foreign nations	Utter destruction of all earth	God = divine wrath

25:38 (25:30-38)	מפני חרון היונה מפני חרון אפי ("from the wrath of the oppressor, from his fierce anger")	None	Same as above	Same as above	God = divine wrath, with the use of human instrument (?; depends on the identity of the 'oppressor')
30:23 (30:23-24); doublet of 23:19	הנה סערת יהוה חמה יצאה ("here, the whirlwind of YHWH, wrath, goes out") – punishment	None	Previous unit which condemns foreign oppressors (v. 20) – directed to enemy of Jacob	Whirlwind of YHWH, depicted as חמה, and divine wrath (vv. 23-24)	Divine wrath (v. 24)
30:24 (30:23-24); doubled 23:20	לא ישוב חרון אף יהוה ("the fierce anger of YHWH will turn away") – punishment	None	Same as above	Same as above	Same as above
32:31 (32:26-35); see Part IV	על־אפי ולחמתי ("upon my fiery wrath") – punishment	על ("because," v. 32); להכעסני ("to provoke me to anger," v. 32)	Catalog of sins (perhaps decree-editor)	City is the object of divine wrath	City; self-destruction
32:37	באפי ובחמתי ובקצף גדול ("in/with my fiery wrath and great anger") – punishment	None	None – future restoration	None – recollect past punishment; banished in/with anger	God, either motivated by or using divine wrath, and human/natural instrument
33:5 (33:1-13)	ובחמתי ("in/with my fiery wrath") – punishment	על ("because," v. 5)	Wickedness	God will strike in/with his wrath	God either motivated by or using divine wrath
36:7 (36:5-7)	האף והחמה ("the fiery wrath") – punishment	None	None – context: Jeremiah to Baruch. Message – turn from evil way	God spoke his wrath against city (decree-editor)	God, using divine wrath
42:18 (42:18-22)	אף ... חמתי ... my ("my fiery wrath ... my wrath") – punishment	None	None – command not to go to Egypt	Recollect past punishment – wrath poured out and will be poured out in Egypt	Divine wrath

Passage-Pericope	Terminology-Category	Linking Conjunction/ Pivot	Type of Sin	Type of Punishment	Agency
44:6 (44:1-14; see Part IV)	חמתי ואפי ("my fiery wrath") – punishment	None	Not obey the prophets (prophetic-editor)	Divine wrath poured out	Divine wrath
49:37 (34-39)	אפי חרון ("my fierce wrath") – punishment	None	Oracle against Elam	Scatter and shatter Elam	God, with divine wrath as instrument (in apposition to "evil")
50:13 (50:11-13)	מקצף יהוה ("from anger of YHWH") – punishment	כי ("because")	Oracle against Babylon – rejoiced in Jerusalem's fall	Because of God's wrath, Babylon will be desolated	Divine wrath
50:25 (50:24-25)	כלי זעמו ("weapons of war") – punishment	כי ("because")	Oracle against Babylon – opposed God (v. 24)	God brings weapons of wrath	God with his divine wrath
51:45 (51:45-53)	מחרון אף-יהוה ("from the fierce wrath of YHWH") – punishment	None	Oracle against Babylon – for Israel's slain (v. 49)	Run from fierce anger = God; ופקדתי ("I will visit," v. 47)	Divine wrath // God
52:3 (52:1-3)	כי על-אף יהוה ("for on account of the anger of YHWH") – reason	כי על ("for on account of")	God's anger as reason for the punishment – no explicit outline of the sin (though unrelated, v. 3 states that Zedekiah did evil)	'This' "happened" (היתה), namely the destruction of Jerusalem, until it was cast away	No agency is made explicit, though it is probably God

1   Lundbom, *Jeremiah*, 274.
2   Holladay, *Jeremiah*, 1:96, argues that "the expected point of view, that it is Yahweh who will punish the people, is constant through Jrm's oracles, but occasionally, as in v. 17 and here, Jrm suggests that it is most particularly the wrongdoing of the people that sets in motion, quite directly, the present miserable situation, and this idea is underlined by verbs whose subject one would expect to be God." This, to a certain extent, sums up the conclusion of the present study.
3   Lundbom, *Jeremiah*, 348.
4   McKane, *Jeremiah*, 106-108, considers the oracle to be apocalyptic.
5   Duhm, *Jeremiah*, xvi, dates to postexilic period; contrary to Lundbom, *Jeremiah*, 404-405, who would date it earlier than later.
6   According to Thiel, *Die deuteronomistische Redaktion*, 1:136-138, this is probably Deuteronomistic
7   See Lundbom, *Jeremiah*, 691-710; contrary to McKane, *Jeremiah*, 284, who dates it to the post-exilic community.
8   Contrary to Lundbom, *Jeremiah*, 691-710, who would date 14:1-6, 7-9, 10-16, to pre-597, McKane, *Jeremiah*, 324, would date 14:1-10 to the post-exilic period.
9   Contrary to Holladay, *Jeremiah*, 1:614.
10   According to A.D.H. Mayes, *Deuteronomy* (NCB; Greenwood: Attic Press, 1979), 175-176.
11   According to Mayes, *Deuteronomy*, 181-182.
12   According to Mayes, *Deuteronomy*, 230-231.
13   According to Brettler, "Interpretation and Prayer: Notes on the Composition of 1 Kings 8:15-53," in *Minhah le-Nahum: Biblical and Other Studies Presented to Nahum M. Sarna in Honor of his 70th Birthday* (eds. Marc Brettler and Michael Fishbane; JSOTSup 154; Sheffield: JSOT Press, 1993), 17-35. Contrary to M. Cogan, *I Kings* (AB 10; New York: Doubleday, 2000), 291-293.
14   According to Ronald Clements, *Isaiah 1-39* (NCB; Grand Rapids: W.B. Eerdsman Publishing Co., 1980), 5:25-30 should follow 9:11 where the phrase בכל־זאת לא־שׁב אפו ("in all this, his anger did not turn aside," 5:25, 9:11, 16, 20, 10:4) appears.
15   Contrary to Yee, *Composition and Tradition*, 272-275, who considers it Hosean.
16   According to Yee, *Composition and Tradition*, 189-193.
17   Yee, *Composition and Tradition*, 223-226.
18   Yee, *Composition and Tradition*, 255-257.
19   Yee, *Composition and Tradition*, 135-136.

Index of Biblical References

22:7	10	24:1	95 (n50), 195 (n84)
22:8-9	245 (App A)	24:3	165 (n19)
22:9	167 (n24), 217 (n143), 229	24:4	181 (n54)
22:10-12	245 (App A)	24:5	174 (n38), 197 (n94), 214 (n135)
22:11	174 (n38), 214 (n135)		
22:12	95 (n50), 197 (n93)	24:6	87 (n34), 182 (n55), 197 (n93)
22:13-19	245 (App A)		
22:13	200 (n102)	24:8	197 (n93), 214 (n135)
22:18	10, 214 (n135)	24:9	124 (19), 170 (n30)
22:19	10, 11	24:10	220 (n152)
22:20-23	10, 11, 245 (App A)	25	181-189
22:24-30	10, 11	25:1-14	3, 9, 155, 156 (n2), 158 (Chart D), 187-201, 246 (App A)
22:24-27	245 (App A)		
22:24	10, 55 (n94)		
22:25	195 (n84), 203 (n108)	25:1-11	10
22:28-30	245 (App A)	25:1	181 (n54)
22:28	10, 11, 178 (n49)	25:2	162 (n8), 184 (n62)
22:30	214 (n135)	25:3	182 (n54), 208 (n119), 218 (n146)
23:1-4	245 (App A)		
23:2	191 (n74), 199 (n100), 214 (n135)	25:4	108 (n89), 218 (n146)
		25:6	4 (n9), 44 (n68), 88 (n39), 155, 167 (n24), 191 (n74), 217 (n143)
23:4	219 (n148)		
23:5	10, 11		
23:7	55 (n94), 182 (n54)	25:7	4 (n9), 88 (n39), 155
23:8	55 (n94), 98 (n59)	25:8-11	227, 231 (Chart E)
23:9-12	10, 246 (App A)	25:8-10	223
23:9-15	10, 11	25:8	214 (n135)
23:10	170 (n30)	25:9-10	156
23:12	46 (n74), 109 (n92)	25:9	170 (n30), 195 (n84), 196 (n88), 197 (n93)
23:13-15	10, 246 (App A)		
23:13	165 (n19)	25:10	194 (n83)
23:14	165 (n19)	25:11	170 (n30), 195 (n84), 197 (n93)
23:15	214 (n135)		
23:16-22	246 (App A)	25:12-14	156
23:16-20	11	25:12	195 (n84), 223, 227, 232 (Chart E)
23:16	184 (n62), 214 (n135)		
23:17	182 (n54), 184 (n62), 229	25:13	6, 184 (n62), 223, 227, 232 (Chart E)
23:18	165 (n19)		
23:19	274 (App F)	25:14	223, 227, 232 (Chart E)
23:20	79 (n25), 274 (App F)	25:15-29	246 (App A)
23:21-24	11	25:15	11, 214 (n135), 274 (App F)
23:22	191 (n74)		
23:25-32	246 (App A)	25:18	170 (n30)
23:26	185 (n63)	25:27-38	11
23:27	220 (n151), 220 (n152)	25:27	214 (n135)
23:28	184 (n62)	25:28	214 (n135)
23:29	11	25:29	193 (n80), 171 (n34), 203 (n108), 209 (n124)
23:33-40	246 (App A)		
23:34	199 (n100)	25:30-32	246 (App A)
23:35	184 (n62)	25:32	214 (n135)
23:38	214 (n135)	25:33	246 (App A)
23:40	170 (n30)	25:34-38	246 (App A)
24:1-10	11, 246 (App A)	25:37	274 (App F)

Bibliography

Ackerman, Susan. "'And the Women Knead Dough': The Worship of the Queen of Heaven in Sixth-Century Judah." Pages 109-124 in *Gender and Difference in Ancient Israel.* Edited by Peggy Day. Minneapolis: Fortress Press, 1989.

Ackerman, Susan. *Under Every Green Tree: Popular Religion in Sixth Century Judah.* HSM 46. Atlanta: Scholars Press, 1992.

Albrektson, Bertil. *History and the Gods: An Essay on the Idea of Historical Events as Divine Manifestations in the Ancient Near East and in Israel.* ConBOT 1. Lund: CWK Gleerup, 1967.

Althann, Robert. *A Philological Analysis of Jeremiah 4-6 in the Light of Northwest Semitic.* Biblica Et Orientalia 38. Rome: Biblical Institute Press, 1983.

Amit, Yairah. "The Dual Causality Principle and Its Effects on Biblical Literature." *VT* 37 (1987):385-400.

Andersen, Francis, and D. Noel Freedman. *Hosea.* AB 24. Garden City: Doubleday, 180.

Bach, Robert. *Die Aufforderungen zur Flucht und zum Kampf im Alttestamentlichen Prophetenspruch.* WMANT 9. Neukirchen: Neukirchener Verlag, 1962.

Balentine, Samuel. *The Hidden God: The Hiding of the Face of God in the Old Testament.* Oxford Theological Monographs. Oxford: Oxford University Press, 1983.

Baloian, Bruce Edward. *Anger in the Old Testament.* American University Studies. New York: Peter Lang, 1992.

Beaulieu, Paul-Alain. *The Reign of Nabonidus: King of Babylon 556-539 B.C.* Yale Near Eastern Researches 10. New Haven: Yale University Press, 1989.

Becking, Bob. "A Josianic View on the Fall of Samaria." Pages 279-297 in *Deuteronomy and Deuteronomic Literature: Festschrift C.H.W. Brekelmans.* Edited by M. Vervenne and J. Lust. BETL 133. Leuven: Leuven University Press, 1997.

Begg, Christopher. "The Destruction of the Golden Calf Revisited (Exod 32,20/Deut 9, 21)." Pages 469-479 in *Deuteronomy and Deuteronomic Literature: Festschrift C.H.W. Brekelmans.* BETL 133. Edited by M. Vervenne and J. Lust. Leuven: Leuven University Press, 1997.

Berlin, Adele. *The Dynamics of Biblical Parallelism.* Bloomington: Indiana University Press, 1985.

Berridge, John. *Prophet, People, and the Word of Yahweh: An Examination of Form and Content in the Proclamation of the Prophet Jeremiah.* Basel Studies of Theology 4. Zürich: Evz-Verlag, 1970.

Beuken, W.A.M. and H.W.M. van Grol. "Jeremiah 14,1-15,9: A Situation of Distress and Its Hermeneutics Unity and Diversity of Form — Dramatic Development." Pages 297-342 in *Le Livre de Jérémie: Le Prophete et son Milieu, les Oracles et leur Transmission.* Edited by P. M. Bogaert. BETL 54. Leuven: Leuven University, 1981.

Blenkinsopp, Joseph. "God and the Moral Order." Pages 46-83 in *Wisdom and Law in the Old Testament: The Ordering of Life in Israel and Early Judaism.* Oxford Bible. Oxford: Oxford University Press, 1995.

Blenkinsopp, Joseph. *Ezra-Nehemiah.* OTL. London: S.C.M. Press, 1988.

Block, Daniel. *The Book of Ezekiel: Chapters 1-24.* NICOT. Grand Rapids: Eerdmans, 1997.

Boström, Lennart. *The God of the Sages: The Portrayal of God in the Book of Proverbs.* ConBOT 29. Stockholm: Almqvist & Wiksell International, 1990.

Botterweck, G. Johannes and H. Ringgren, eds. *Theological Dictionary of the Old Testament.* Rev. ed. Translated by J.T. Willis, G.W. Bromiley, and D.E. Green. 8 vols. Grand Rapids: Eerdmans, 1977-.

Brettler, Marc. "Ideology, History and Theology in 2 Kings XVII 7-23." *VT* 39 (1989):268-282.

Brettler, Marc. "Interpretation and Prayer: Notes on the Composition of 1 Kings 8.15-53." Pages 17-35 in *Minhah le-Nahum: Biblical and Other Studies Presented to Nahum M. Sarna in Honour of his 70th Birthday.* Edited by Marc Brettler and Michael Fishbane. JSOTSup 154. Sheffield: JSOT Press, 1993.

Briggs, Charles and Emilie Briggs. *A Critical and Exegetical Commentary on the Book of Psalms.* Vol. 2. ICC 11. Edinburgh: T. & T. Clark, 1927.

Bright, John. "The Date of the Prose Sermons of Jeremiah." *JBL* 70 (1951):15-35.

Bright, John. *Jeremiah: A New Translation with Introduction and Commentary.* AB 21. Garden City: Doubleday, 1965.

Brinkman, J.A. "Through a Glass Darkly: Esarhaddon's Retrospects on the Downfall of Babylon." *JAOS* 103 (1993):35-42.

Brongers, H.A. "Die Partikel למען in der biblisch-hebräischen Sprache." *OtSt* 18 (1973):84-96.

Brown, Francis, S.R. Driver, and Charles Briggs. *The New Brown-Driver-Briggs-Gesenius Hebrew and English Lexicon.* Peabody: Hendrickson, 1979.

Brueggemann, Walter. "Jeremiah: Intense Criticism/Thin Interpretation." *Interpretation* 42 (1988):268-280.

Burney, Charles. *The Book of Judges.* The Library of Biblical Studies. New York: Ktav Publishing House, 1970.

Buttrick, George Arthur, ed. *The Interpreter's Dictionary of the Bible*. 4 vols. New York: Abingdon Press, 1962.

Cagni, Luigi. *The Poem of Erra*. Sources from the Ancient Near East, vol. 1, fasc. 3. Malibu: Undena Publications, 1977.

Campbell, Antony and Mark O'Brien. *Unfolding the Deuteronomistic History: Origins, Upgrading, Present Text*. Minneapolis: Fortress Press, 2000.

Campbell, Antony. "Psalm 78: A Contribution to the Theology of Tenth Century Israel." *CBQ* 41 (1979):51-79.

Campbell, Antony. *Of Prophets and Kings: A Late Ninth-Century Document (1 Samuel 1 — 2 Kings 10)*. CBQMS 17. Washington D.C.: Catholic Biblical Association of America, 1986.

Carr, David. "Reaching for Unity in Isaiah." *JSOT* 57 (1993):61-80.

Carroll, Robert. "Halfway Through a Dark Wood: Reflections on Jeremiah 25." Pages 73-86 in *Troubling Jeremiah*. Edited by A.R. Pete Diamond, Kathleen O'Connor, and Louis Stulman. JSOTSup 260. Sheffield: Sheffield Academic Press, 1999.

Carroll, Robert. "Radical Clashes of Will and Style: Recent Commentary Writing on the Book of Jeremiah." *JSOT* 45 (1989):99-114.

Carroll, Robert. *Jeremiah: A Commentary*. OTL. London: SCM Press, 1986.

Childs, Brevard. *Exodus: A Commentary*. OTL. London: SCM Press, 1974.

Clements, Ronald. *Isaiah 1-39*. NCB. Grand Rapids: Eerdsman Publishing Co., 1980.

Clifford, Richard. "In Zion and David a New Beginning: An Interpretation of Psalm 78." Pages 121-141 in *Traditions in Transformation*. Edited by Baruch Halpern and Jon D. Levenson. Winona Lake: Eisenbrauns, 1981.

Cogan, M. and H. Tadmor. *II Kings: A New Translation with Introduction and Commentary*. AB 11. Garden City: Doubleday, 1988.

Conrad, Diethelm. "Mitteilungen zu Jes 65 3b." *ZAW* 80 (1968):232-234.

Conroy, Charles. "Hiel Between Ahab and Elijah-Elisha: 1 Kgs 16,34 in Its Immediate Literary Context." *Biblica* 77 (1996):210-218.

Cooke, George A. *A Critical and Exegetical Commentary on the Book of Ezekiel*. ICC 21. New York: Charles Scribner's Sons, 1937.

Cooper, Jerrold. *The Curse of Agade*. JHNES. Baltimore: Johns Hopkins University Press, 1983.

Cross, Frank Moore, Werner Lemke, and Patrick Miller, Jr., editors. *Magnalia Dei, The Mighty Acts of God: Essays on the Bible and Archaeology in Memory of G. Ernest Wright*. Garden City: Doubleday, 1976.

Cross, Frank Moore. *Canaanite Myth and Hebrew Epic: Essays in the History of the Religion of Israel*. Cambridge: Harvard University Press, 1973.

Daniels, Dwight. "Is There a 'Prophetic Lawsuit' Genre?" *ZAW* 99 (1987):339-360.

Diamond, A.R. Pete. "Introduction." Pages 15-32 in *Troubling Jeremiah*. Edited by A.R. Pete Diamond, Kathleen O'Connor, and Louis Stulman. JSOTSup 260. Sheffield: Sheffield Academic Press, 1999.

Dijkstra, Meindert. "Goddess, Gods, Men and Women in Ezekiel 8." Pages 83-114 in *On Reading Prophetic Texts: Gender-Specific and Related Studies in Memory of Fokkelien van Dijk-Hemmes*. Edited by Bob Becking and Meindert Dijkstra. Biblical Interpretation Series 18. Leiden: E.J. Brill, 1996.

Driver, S.R. *A Critical and Exegetical Commentary on Deuteronomy*. ICC 3. Edinburgh: T. & T. Clark, 1902.

Driver, S.R. *Notes on the Hebrew Text and the Topography of the Books of Samuel*. Oxford: Clarendon Press, 1913.

Driver, S.R. *The Book of the Prophet Jeremiah*. London: Hodder and Stoughton, 1906.

Duhm, Bernhard. *Das Buch Jeremiah, die poetischen und prophetischen Bücher des Alten Testaments*. KHC 11. Tübingen: Mohr, 1901.

Emerton, J.A. "Notes on the Text and Translation of Isaiah XXII 8-11 and LXV 5." *VT* 30 (1980):437-450.

Emerton, J.A. "The House of Ba'al in 1 Kings XVI 32." *VT* 42 (1997):293-300.

Evans, Carl. "Naram-Sin and Jeroboam: The Archetypal *Unheilsherrscher* in Mesopotamia and Biblical Historiography." Pages 97-125 in *Scripture in Context II: More Essays on the Comparative Method*. Edited by William Hallo, James Moyer, and Leo Perdue. Winona Lake: Eisenbrauns, 1983.

Eynikel, Erik. "Prophecy and Fulfillment in the Deuteronomistic History: 1 Kgs 13; 2 Kgs 23, 16-18." Pages 227-237 in *Pentateuchal and Deuteronomistic Studies*. BETL 94. Edited by C. Brekelmans and J. Lust. Leuven: Leuven University Press, 1990.

Eynikel, Erik. "The Portrait of Manasseh and the Deuteronomic History." Pages 233-261 in *Deuteronomy and Deuteronomic Literature*. BETL 133. Edited by M. Vervenne and J. Lust. Leuven: Leuven University Press, 1997.

Eynikel, Erik. *The Reform of King Josiah and the Composition of the Deuteronomistic History*. OtSt 33. Leiden: E.J. Brill, 1996.

Fishbane, Michael. "Revelation and Tradition." *JBL* 99 (1980):343-361.

Fishbane, Michael. *Biblical Interpretation in Ancient Israel*. Oxford: Oxford University Press, 1985.

Frame, Grant. *Babylonia 689-627 B.C.: A Political History*. Uitgaven van het Netherlands Historisch-Archaeologisch Instituut te Istanbul 69. Te Istanbul: Nederlands Historisch-Archaeologisch Instituut, 1992.

Freibel, Kelvin. *Jeremiah's and Ezekiel's Sign-Acts: Rhetorical Nonverbal Communication.* JSOTSup 283. Sheffield: Sheffield Academic Press, 1999.

Friedman, Richard Elliott. "The Biblical Expression: Mastîr Panîm." *HAR* 1 (1977):139-148.

Frymer-Kensky, Tikva. *In the Wake of the Goddesses: Women, Culture and the Biblical Transformation of Pagan Myth.* New York: Fawcett Columbine, 1992.

Galambush, Julie. *Jerusalem in the Book of Ezekiel: The City as Yahweh's Wife.* SBLDS 130. Atlanta: Scholars Press, 1992.

Gesenius, Wilhelm. *Gesenius' Hebrew Grammar.* Ed. and enl. by E. Kautzsch. Oxford: Clarendon Press, 1990.

Gray, John. *1 & 2 Kings: A Commentary.* OTL. London: SCM Press, 1970.

Greenberg, Moshe. *Ezekiel 1-20.* AB 22. Garden City: Doubleday, 1983.

Greenspahn, Frederick. "The Theology of the Framework of Judges." *VT* 36 (1986):385-396.

Greenstein, Edward. "Mixing Memory and Design: Reading Psalm 78." *Prooftexts* 10 (1990):197-218.

Halpern, Baruch and David Vanderhooft. "The Editions of Kings in the 7th-6th Centuries B.C.E." *HUCA* 62 (1991):179-244.

Hanson, Anthony. *Wrath of the Lamb.* London: S.P.C.K., 1957.

Herbert, A.S. *The Book of the Prophet Isaiah: Chapters 40-66.* Vol. 2. CBC. Cambridge: Cambridge University Press, 1975.

Hill, John. "The Construction of Time in Jeremiah 25 (MT)." Pages 146-160 in *Troubling Jeremiah.* Edited by A.R. Pete Diamond, Kathleen O'Connor, and Louis Stulman. JSOTSup 260. Sheffield: Sheffield Academic Press, 1999.

Hill, John. *Friend or Foe? The Figure of Babylon in the Book of Jeremiah MT.* BibInt 40. Leiden: Brill, 1999.

Hobbs, T.R. "Some Remarks on the Composition and Structure of the Book of Jeremiah." *CBQ* 334 (1972):257-275.

Hoffman, Yair. "The Conception of 'Other Gods' in Deuteronomistic Literature." *Israel Oriental Studies* 14 (1994):103-118.

Hoftijzer, J. "A Peculiar Question: A Note on 2 Sam. XV 27." *VT* 21 (1971):606-609.

Holder, John. "The Presuppositions, Accusations, and Threats of 1 K. 14:1-18." *JBL* 107 (1988):27-38.

Holladay, William. "A Fresh Look at 'Source B' and 'Source C' in Jeremiah." *VT* 25 (1975):394-412.

Holladay, William. "The So-Called 'Deuteronomic Gloss' in Jer. VIII 19b." *VT* 12 (1962):494-498.

Holladay, William. *Jeremiah 1: A Commentary on the Book of the Prophet Jeremiah, Chapters 1-25.* Hermeneia. Philadelphia: Fortress Press, 1986.

Holladay, William. *Jeremiah 2: A Commentary on the Book of the Prophet Jeremiah, Chapters 26-52.* Hermeneia. Minneapolis: Fortress Press, 1989.

Holladay, William. *The Architecture of Jeremiah 1-20.* Lewisburg: Bucknell University Press, 1976.

Holt, Else K. "The Potent Word of God: Remarks on the Composition of Jeremiah 37-44." Pages 37-44 in *Troubling Jeremiah.* Edited by A.R. Pete Diamond, Kathleen O'Connor, and Louis Stulman. JSOTSup 260. Sheffield: Sheffield Academic Press, 1999.

Holt, Else K. "Jeremiah's Temple Sermon and the Deuteronomists: An Investigation of the Redactional Relationship Between Jeremiah 7 and 26." *JSOT* 36 (1986):73-87.

Holt, Else K. *Prophesying the Past: The Use of Israel's History in the Book of Hosea.* JSOTSup 194. Sheffield: Sheffield Academic Press, 1995.

Huffmon, Herbert. "The Covenant Lawsuit in the Prophets." *JBL* 78 (1959):285-295.

Hyatt, J.P. "The Deuteronomic Edition of Jeremiah." Pages 247-267 in *A Prophet to the Nations: Essays in Jeremiah Studies.* Edited by L. Perdue and B.W. Kovacs. Winona Lake: Eisenbrauns, 1984. Repr. from pages 71-95 in *Vanderbilt Studies in the Humanities.* Edited by R. Beatty, et al. Nashville: Vanderbilt University Press, 1951.

Hyatt, J. P. "The Book of Jeremiah." *IB* 5:777-1142.

Isbell, Charles, and Michael Jackson. "Rhetorical Criticism and Jeremiah VII 1-VIII 3." *VT* 30 (1980):20-26.

Janzen, J. Gerald. *Studies in the Text of Jeremiah.* HSM 6. Cambridge: Harvard University Press, 1973.

Japhet, Sara. "חילופי שרשים בפועל בטקסטים המקבילים בספר דברי הימים." *Lešonenu* 31 (1966-67):261-279.

Japhet, Sara. *The Ideology of the Book of Chronicles and Its Place in Biblical Thought.* Translated by Anna Berber. Frankfurt am Main: Peter Lang, 1997.

Jastrow, Marcus. *A Dictionary of the Targumim, the Talmud Babli and Yerushalmi, and the Midrashic Literature.* New York: Title Publishing Co., 1943.

Joüon, Paul. *A Grammar of Biblical Hebrew.* Subsidia Biblica 14/1-14/2. Roma: Editrice Pontificio Istituto Biblio, 1991.

Kang, Sa-Moon. "The Authentic Sermon of Jeremiah in Jeremiah 7:1-20." Pages 147-162 in *Texts, Temples, and Traditions: A Tribute to Mena-*

hem Haran. Edited by Michael Fox, et al. Winona Lake: Eisenbrauns, 1996.

Kessler, Martin. "Jeremiah 25:1-29: Text and Context. A Synchronic Study." *ZAW* 109 (1997):44-70.

Kessler, Martin. "Jeremiah Chapters 26-45 Reconsidered." *JNES* 27 (1968):81-88.

Kessler, Martin. "The Function of Chapters 25 and 50-51 in the Book of Jeremiah." Pages 64-72 in *Troubling Jeremiah*. Edited by A.R. Pete Diamond, Kathleen O'Connor, and Louis Stulman. JSOTSup 260. Sheffield: Sheffield Academic Press, 1999.

Kessler, Martin. "The Function of Chapters 25 and 50-51." Pages 64-72 in *Troubling Jeremiah*. Edited by A.R. Pete Diamond, Kathleen O'Connor, and Louis Stulman. JSOTSup 260. Sheffield: Sheffield Academic Press, 1999.

Keulen, Percy. *Manasseh Through the Eyes of the Deuteronomists: The Manasseh Account (2 Kings 21:1-18) and the Final Chapters of the Deuteronomistic History*. OtSt 38. Leiden: E.J. Brill, 1996.

Klein, Ernest. *A Comprehensive Etymological Dictionary of the Hebrew Language for Readers of English*. Jerusalem: Carta, 1987.

Knoppers, Gary and J. Gordon McConville, editors. *Reconsidering Israel and Judah: Recent Studies on the Deuteronomistic History*. Sources for Biblical and Theological Study 8. Winona Lake: Eisenbrauns, 2000.

Knoppers, Gary. "Aaron's Calf and Jeroboam's Calves." Pages 92-104 in *Fortunate the Eyes That See: Essays in Honor of David Noel Freedman in Celebration of His Seventieth Birthday*. Edited by Astrid Beck, et al. Grand Rapids: Eerdmans, 1995.

Knoppers, Gary. *Two Nations Under God: The Deuteronomistic History of Solomon and the Dual Monarchies*. HSM 52-53. Atlanta: Scholars Press, 1993-1994.

Koch, Klaus. "Gibt es ein Vergeltungsdogma im Alten Testament?" *ZTK* 52 (1955):1-42. Repr. pages 57-87 in *Theodicy in the Old Testament*. Edited by James Crenshaw. Translated by Thomas Trapp. Philadelphia: Fortress Press, 1983.

Koehler, Ludwig, Walter Baumgartner, and Johann Stamm. *The Hebrew and Aramaic Lexicon of the Old Testament*. Rev. and enl. ed. Leiden: Brill, 1995.

Kraus, Hans-Joachim. *Psalms 60-150*. Translated by Hilton Oswald. Minneapolis: Augsburg, 1969.

Kutsko, John. *Between Heaven and Earth: Divine Presence and Absence in the Book of Ezekiel*. Biblical and Judaic Studies 7. Winona Lake: Eisenbrauns, 2000.

Lambert, W.G. "Enmeduranki and Related Matters." *JCS* 21 (1967):126-138.

Lasine, S. "Manasseh as Villain and Scapegoat." Pages 163-183 in *The New Literary Criticism and the Hebrew Bible*. JSOTSup 143. Edited by J. C. Exum and D. Clines. Sheffield: JSOT Press, 1993.

Latvus, Kari. *God, Anger and Ideology: The Anger of God in Joshua and Judges in Relation to Deuteronomy and Priestly Writings*. JSOTSup 279. Sheffield: Sheffield Academic Press, 1998.

Lemke, Werner. "Nebuchadnezzar, My Servant." *CBQ* 28 (1966):45-50.

Levenson, Jon. "Who Inserted the Book of the Torah?" *HTR* 68 (1975):203-233.

Levenson, Jon. *Creation and Persistence of Evil: The Jewish Drama of Divine Omnipotence*. San Francisco: Harper and Row, 1988.

Lindars, Barnabas. *Judges 1-5: A New Translation and Commentary*. Edinburgh: T. & T. Clark, 1995.

Lindenberger, James. *The Aramic Proverbs of Ahiqar*. JHNES. Baltimore: Johns Hopkins University Press, 1983.

Long, Burke O. *1 Kings with an Introduction to Historical Literature*. FOTL 9. Grand Rapids: Eerdmans, 1984.

Long, Burke O. "Framing Repetitions in Biblical Historiography." *JBL* 106 (1987):385-399.

Long, Burke. "Reports of Visions Among the Prophets." *JBL* 95 (1976):353-365.

Lundbom, Jack. *Jeremiah 1-20: A New Translation with Introduction and Commentary*. AB 21a. New York: Doubleday, 1999.

Lundbom, Jack. *Jeremiah: A Study in Ancient Hebrew Rhetoric*. Second edition. SBLDS 18. Winona Lake: Eisenbrauns, 1975.

Machinist, Peter. "The Epic of Tukulti-Ninurta I: A Study in Middle Assyrian Literature." Ph.D. diss. New Haven: Yale University, 1978.

Macintosh, A.A. *Hosea*. ICC 17a. Edinburgh: T. & T. Clark, 1997.

Malul, Meir. "Adoption of Foundlings in the Bible and Mesopotamian Documents: A Study of Some Legal Metaphors in Ezekiel 16:1-7." *JSOT* 46 (1990):96-126.

Mayes, A.D.H. *Deuteronomy*. NCB. London: Oliphants, 1979.

Mayes, A.D.H. *Judges*. OTG. Sheffield: JSOT Press, 1985.

Mays, James. *Hosea: A Commentary*. OTL. Philadelphia: Westminster Press, 1969.

McCarter, P.K. *1 Samuel*. AB 8. New York: Doubleday, 1980.

McCarthy, Dennis. "The Wrath of Yahweh and the Structural Unity of the Deuteronomistic History." Pages 97-110 in *Essays in Old Testament Ethics*. Edited by James Crenshaw and John Willis. New York: Ktav Publishing House, 1974.

McKane, William. "Relations Between Poetry and Prose in the Book of Jeremiah with Special Reference to Jeremiah iii 6-11 and xii 14-17." Pages 269-284 in *A Prophet to the Nations*. Edited by L. Perdue and B. Kovacs. Winona Lake: Eisenbrauns, 1984. Repr. from VTSup 32 (1980):220-237.

McKane, William. *A Critical and Exegetical Commentary on Jeremiah.* ICC 19. Edinburgh: T. & T. Clark, 1986.

McKenzie, Steven. "The Prophetic History and the Redaction of Kings." *HAR* 9 (1985):203-220.

Mendenhall, George. "Samuel's 'Broken Rîb': Deuteronomy 32." Pages 63-74 in *A Song of Power and the Power of Song: Essays on the Book of Deuteronomy.* Edited by Duane Christensen. Sources for Biblical and Theological Study 3. Winona Lake: Eisenbrauns, 1993.

Milgrom, Jacob. "Profane Slaughter and a Formulaic Key to the Composition of Deuteronomy." *HUCA* 47 (1976):4-17.

Milgrom, Jacob. *Cult and Conscience: The Asham and the Priestly Doctrine of Repentance.* SJLA 18. Leiden: E. J. Brill, 1976.

Milgrom, Jacob. *Numbers: The Traditional Hebrew Text with the New JPS Translation.* The JPS Torah Commentary. Philadelphia: The Jewish Publication Society, 1990.

Miller, J. Maxwell and John Hayes. *A History of Ancient Israel and Judah.* Philadelphia: Westminster Press, 1986.

Miller, Patrick. *Sin and Judgment in the Prophets: A Stylistic and Theological Analysis.* SBLMS 27. Chico: Scholars Press, 1982.

Miller, Robert D. II. "Review of God, Anger and Ideology: The Anger of God in Joshua and Judges in Relation to Deuteronomy and the Priestly Writings." No pages. 2000. Online: http://www.bookreviews.org/Print/1850759227-P.html.

Mintz, Alan. "The Rhetoric of Lamentations and the Representation of Catastrophe." *Prooftexts* 2 (1982):1-17.

Montgomery, James. *A Critical and Exegetical Commentary on the Books of Kings.* ICC 6. Edinburgh: T. & T. Clark, 1951.

Moore, George. *A Critical and Exegetical Commentary on the Book Judges.* ICC 4. New York: Charles Scribner's Sons, 1895.

Moran, William. "The Ancient Near Eastern Background of the Love of God in Deuteronomy." Pages 103-115 in *Essential Papers on Israel and the Ancient Near East.* Edited by Frederick Greenspahn. Essential Papers on Jewish Studies. New York: New York University Press, 1991.

Mowinckel, Sigmund. *Zur Komposition des Buches Jeremia.* Videnskapsselskapets skrifter II. Hist.-filos.klasse; 1913; no. 5. Kristiania: Dybwad, 1914.

Muffs, Yochanan. "Who Will Stand in the Breach?: A Study of Prophetic Intercession." Pages 9-48 in *Love and Joy: Law, Language and Religion in Ancient Israel.* New York: Jewish Theological Seminary, 1992.

Mullen, E. Theodore. "The Sins of Jeroboam: A Redactional Assessment." *CBQ* 49 (1987):212-232.

Na'aman, Nadav. "Prophetic Stories as Sources for the Histories of Jehoshaphat and Omrides." *Biblica* 78 (1997):153-173.

Nelson, Richard. *The Double Redaction of the Deuteronomistic History.* JSOTSup 18. Sheffield: JSOT Press, 1981.

Nicholson, Ernest. *Preaching to the Exiles: A Study of the Prose Tradition in the Book of Jeremiah.* New York: Schocken Books, 1970.

Nicholson, Ernest. *The Book of the Prophet Jeremiah, Chapters 1-25.* CBC. New York: Cambridge University Press, 1973.

Nicholson, Ernest. *The Book of the Prophet Jeremiah, Chapters 26-52.* CBC. New York: Cambridge University Press, 1975.

Niditch, Susan. *Chaos to Cosmos: Studies in Biblical Patterns of Creation.* Scholars Press Studies in the Humanities 6. Chico: Scholars Press, 1985.

Noth, Martin. *Exodus: A Commentary.* OTL. London: SCM Press, 1962.

O'Brien, Mark. *The Deuteronomistic History Hypothesis: A Reassessment.* OBO. Freiburg, Schweiz: Universitätsverlag; Göttingen: Vandenhoeck u. Ruprecht, 1989.

O'Connell, Robert H. "Deuteronomy IX 7 — X 7, 10-11: Panelled Structure, Double Rehearsal and the Rhetoric of Covenant Rebuke." *VT* 42 (1992):492-509.

O'Connor, Kathleen. "Do Not Trim a Word." *CBQ* (1989):617-630.

O'Connor, Kathleen. *The Confessions of Jeremiah: Their Interpretation and Role in Chapters 1-25.* SBLDS 94. Atlanta: Scholars Press, 1988.

Olyan, Saul. "'To Uproot and to Pull Down, To Build and To Plant': Jer. 1:10 and its Earliest Interpreters." Pages 63-72 in *Hesed ve-Emet: Studies in Honor of Ernest S. Frerichs.* BJS 320. Edited by Jodi Magness and Seymour Gitin. Atlanta: Scholars Press, 1998.

Olyan, Saul. *Asherah and the Cult of Yahweh in Israel.* SBLMS 34. Atlanta: Scholar's Press, 1986.

Oren, Eliezer. "Migdol: A New Fortress on the Edge of the Eastern Nile Delta." *BASOR* 256 (1984):7-44.

Peels, H.G.L. *The Vengeance of God: The Meaning of the root NQM and the Function of the NQM-Texts in the Context of Divine Revelation in the Old Testament.* OtSt 31. Leiden: E. J. Brill, 1995.

Person, Raymond. "II Kings 24, 18-25, 30 and Jeremiah 52: A Text-Critical Case Study in the Redaction History of the Deuteronomistic History." *ZAW* 105 (1993):174-205.

Polk, Timothy. *The Prophetic Persona: Jeremiah and the Language of the Self.* JSOTSup 32. Sheffield: JSOT Press, 1984.

Provan, Iain. *Hezekiah and the Books of Kings: A Contribution to the Debate about the Composition of Deuteronomistic History.* BZAW 172. Berlin: Walter de Gruyter, 1988.

Purvis, James. "Exile and Return: From the Babylonian Destruction to the Reconstruction of the Jewish State." Pages 151-175 in *Ancient Israel: From Abraham to the Roman Destruction of the Temple.* Edited by

Hershel Shanks. Washington D.C.: Biblical Archaeology Society, 1999.

Rad, Gerhard Von. *Deuteronomy: A Commentary*. OTL. Philadelphia: Westminster Press, 1966.

Raitt, Thomas. *A Theology of Exile: Judgement/Deliverance in Jeremiah and Ezekiel*. Philadelphia: Fortress Press, 1977.

Rast, Walter. "Cakes for the Queen of Heaven." Pages 109-124 in *Scripture in History and Theology: Essays in Honor of J. Coert Rylaarsdam*. Edited by Arthur L. Merrill and Thomas Overholt. PTMS 17. Pittsburgh: Pickwick Press, 1977.

Roche, Michael De. "Yahweh's *rîb* Against Israel: A Reassessment of the So-Called 'Prophetic Lawsuit' in the Preexilic Prophets." *JBL* 102.

Rofé, Alexander. "The Name YHWH SĔBĀ'ÔT and the Shorter Recension of Jeremiah." Pages 307-316 in *Prophetie und geschichtliche Wirklichkeit im alten Israel: Festschrift für Siegfried Herrmann*. Edited by Rüdiger Liwak and Siegfried Wagner. Berlin: Verlag W. Kohlhammer, 1991.

Rosenberg, Joel. "Jeremiah and Ezekiel." Pages 184-194 in *The Literary Guide to the Bible*. Edited by Robert Alter and Frank Kermode. Cambridge: Belknap Press of Harvard University Press, 1987.

Rudolph, Wilhelm. *Jeremia*. HAT 1/12. Tübingen: J.C.B. Mohr, 1958.

Ruiten, J.T.A.G.M. Van. "The Use of Deuteronomy 32:39 in Monotheistic Controversies in Rabbinic Literature." Pages 223-241 in *Studies in Deuteronomy: In Honour of C.J. Labuschagne on the Occasion of his 65th Birthday*. Edited by F. Garcia, et al. VTSup 53. Leiden: E.J. Brill, 1994.

Sanders, Paul. *The Provenance of Deuteronomy 32*. OtSt 37. Leiden: E.J. Brill, 1996.

Sarna, Nahum. "Ezekiel 8.17." *HTR* 57 (1964):347-352.

Schmidt, W.H. *Die Schöpfungsgeschichte der Priesterschrift*. WMANT 17. Neukirchen-Vluyn: Neukirchener Verlag, 1973.

Schniedewind, William. "History and Interpretation: The Religion of Ahab and Manasseh in the Book of Kings." *CBQ* 55 (1993):649-661.

Schroeder, Christoph. *History, Justice, and the Agency of God: A Hermeneutical and Exegetical Investigation on Isaiah and Psalms*. BibInt 52. Leiden: Brill, 2001.

Seitz, Christopher. "The Prophet Moses and the Canonical Shape of Jeremiah." *ZAW* 101 (1989):3-27.

Seitz, Christopher. *Theology in Conflict: Reactions to the Exile in the Book of Jeremiah*. BZAW 176. Berlin: de Gruyter, 1989.

Seters, John Van. *The Life of Moses: The Yahwist as Historian in Exodus-Numbers*. Kampen, Netherlands: Kok Pharos Publishing House, 1994.

Simpson, William. "Divine Wrath in the Eighth Century Prophets." Ph.D. diss., Boston University, 1968.

Skehan, Patrick. "The Structure of the Song of Moses in Deuteronomy (32:1-43)." Pages 153-163 in *A Song of Power and the Power of Song: Essays on the Book of Deuteronomy*. Edited by Duane Christensen. Sources for Biblical and Theological Study 3. Winona Lake: Eisenbrauns, 1993.

Smith, Mark. *The Laments of Jeremiah and Their Contexts: A Literary and Redactional Study of Jeremiah 11-20*. SBLMS 42. Atlanta: Scholars Press, 1990.

Soggin, Alberto. *Judges*. OTL. London: S.C.M. Press, 1987.

Soisalon-Soininen, Ilmari. "Der Infinitivus Constructus mit ל im Hebräischen." *VT* 22 (1972):82-90.

Stern, Philip. "The Eighth Century Dating of Psalm 78 Re-argued." *HUCA* 66 (1995):41-65.

Stulman, Louis. "The Prose Sermons as Hermeneutical Guide to Jeremiah 1-25: the Deconstruction of Judah's Symbolic World." Pages 34-63 in *Troubling Jeremiah*. Edited by A.R. Pete Diamond, Kathleen O'Connor, and Louis Stulman. JSOTSup 260. Sheffield: Sheffield Academic Press, 1999.

Stulman, Louis. *The Prose Sermons of the Book of Jeremiah: A Redescription of the Correspondences with Deuteronomistic Literature in the Light of Recent Text-Critical Research*. SBLDS 83. Atlanta: Scholars Press, 1986.

Sweeney, Marvin. "Prophetic Exegesis in Isaiah 65-66." Pages 455-474 in *Writing and Reading the Scroll of Isaiah: Studies of an Interpretative Tradition*. Vol. 2. Edited by Craig Broyles and Craig Evans. VTSup 70. Leiden: E.J. Brill, 1997.

Talmon, Shemaryahu. "Polemics and Apology in Biblical Historiography — 2 Kings 17:24-41." Pages 57-68 in *The Creation of Sacred Literature: Composition and Redaction of the Biblical Text*. Edited by Richard Elliott Friedman. University of California Publications, Near Eastern Studies 22. Berkeley: University of California Press, 1981.

Tasker, R.V.G. *The Biblical Doctrine of the Wrath of God*. Tyndale Biblical Theology Lecture. London: Tyndale Press, 1951.

Thiel, Winfried. *Die deuteronomistische Redaktion von Jeremia 1-25*. WMANT 41. Neukirchen-Vluyn: Neukirchenen Verlag, 1973.

Thiel, Winfried. *Die deuteronomistische Redaktion von Jeremia 26-45*. WMANT 52. Neukirchen-Vluyn: Neukirchenen Verlag, 1981.

Tigay, Jeffrey. *Deuteronomy: The Traditional Hebrew Text with the New JPS Translation*. JPS Torah Commentary. Philadelphia: Jewish Publication Society, 1996.

Tomasino, Anthony. "Isaiah 1.1-2.4 and 63-66, and the Composition of the Isaianic Corpus." *JSOT* 57 (1993):81-98.

Toorn, Karel van, Bob Becking, and Pieter w. van der Horst, eds. *Dictionary of Deities and Demons in the Bible*. Leiden: Brill, 1999.

Tov, Emanuel. "The Literary History of the Book of Jeremiah in the Light of its Textual History." Pages 211-237 in *Empirical Models for Biblical Criticism*. Edited by Jeffrey Tigay. Philadelphia: University of Pennsylvania, 1985.

Tucker, Gene M. "Sin and 'Judgment' in the Prophets." Pages 373-388 in *Problems in Biblical Theology: Essays in Honor of Rolf Knierim*. Edited by Henry Sun and Keith Eades. Grand Rapids: William B. Eerdmans Publishing Company, 1997.

Unterman, Jeremiah. *From Repentance to Redemption: Jeremiah's Thought in Transition.* JSOTSup 54. Sheffield: JSOT Press, 1987.

Viviano, Pauline. "2 Kings 17: A Rhetorical and Form-Critical Analysis." *CBQ* 49 (1987):548-559.

Volz, Paul. *Der Prophet Jeremia*. KAT 10. Leipzig: Deichertsche Verlagsbuchhandlung Scholl, 1928.

Volz, Paul. *Das Dämonische in Jahwe*. Sammlung gemeinverstandlicher Vortrage und Schriften aus dem Gebiet der Theologie und Religionsgeschichte 110. Tübingen: Mohr 1924.

Wallace, H.N. "The Oracles Against the Israelite Dynasties in 1 and 2 Kings." *Biblica* 67 (1986):21-40.

Waltke, Bruce, and M. O'Connor. *An Introduction to Biblical Hebrew Syntax*. Winona Lake: Eisenbrauns, 1990.

Weinfeld, Moshe. *Deuteronomy 1-11: A New Translation with Introduction and Commentary*. AB 5. New York: Doubleday, 1991.

Weinfeld, Moshe. *Deuteronomy and the Deuteronomic School*. Oxford: Oxford University Press, 1972.

Weippert, Helga. *Die Prosareden des Jeremiabuches*. BZAW 132. Berlin: de Gruyter, 1973.

Weiser, Artur. *The Psalms*. OTL. London: S.C.M. Press, 1962.

Weitzman, Steven. "Lessons from the Dying: The Roles of Deuteronomy 32 in its Narrative Setting." *HTR* 87 (1994):377-393.

Westermann, Claus. *Basic Forms of Prophetic Speech*. Translated by H. White. Philadelphia: Westminster, 1967.

Westermann, Claus. *Genesis 1-11, A Commentary*. BKAT 1. Translated by John Scullion. Minneapolis: Augsburg Publishing House, 1984.

Westermann, Claus. *Isaiah 40-66: A Commentary*. OTL. Philadelphia: Westminster Press, 1969.

White, Marsha. "Naboth's Vineyard and Jehu's Coup: The Legitimation of a Dynasty Extermination." *VT* 44 (1994):66-76.

Williams, Michael. "An Investigation of the Legitimacy of Source Distinctions for the Prose Material in Jeremiah." *JBL* 112 (1993):193-210.

Wilson, Robert. "Poetry and Prose in the Book of Jeremiah." Pages 413-427 in *Ki Baruch Hu*. Edited by Robert Chazan, et al. Winona Lake: Eisenbrauns, 1999.

Winkle, D.W. "1 Kings XII 25-XIII 34: Jeroboam's Cultic Innovations and the Man of God from Judah." *VT* 46 (1996):101-114.

Wolff, Hans W. "Die Begrundung der prophetischen Heils und Unheilsspruche," *ZAW* 52 (1934):1-22. Repr. from pages 9-35 in *Gesammelte Studien zum Alten Testament*. Munchen: Kaiser, 1973.

Wolff, Hans. *Hosea*. Hermeneia. Philadelphia: Fortress Press, 1974.

Wright, G. Ernest "The Lawsuit of God: A Form-Critical Study of Deuteronomy 32." Pages 26-67 in *Israel's Prophetic Heritage*. Edited by Bernhard Anderson and Walter Harrelson. New York: Harper and Brothers, 1962.

Wright, G. Ernest, and Reginald Fuller. *The Book of the Acts of God: Christian Scholarship Interprets the Bible*. Christian Faith Series. Garden City: Doubleday, 1957.

Wright, G. Ernest. *God Who Acts: Biblical Theology as Recital*. SBT 8. London: SCM Press, 1952.

Yee, Gale. *Composition and Tradition in the Book of Hosea: A Redaction Critical Investigation*. SBLDS 102. Atlanta: Georgia, 1987.

Zimmerli, Walther. *Ezekiel*. Hermeneia. Philadelphia: Fortress Press, 1979.

Zipor, Moshe. "The Deuteronomic Account of the Golden Calf and Its Reverberation in Other Parts of the Book of Deuteronomy." *ZAW* 108 (1996):20-33.

Zvi, Ehud. "The Account of the Reign of Manasseh in II Reg 21,1-18 and the Redactional History of the Book of Kings." *ZAW* 103 (1991):355-374.